Yvonne Nolan

with Colette Burgess and Colin Shaw

HEALTH & SOCIAL CARE

3rd edition

www.pearsonschoolsandfe.co.uk

✓ Free online support
✓ Useful weblinks
✓ 24 hour online ordering

0845 630 44 44

Heinemann

Part of Pearson

Heinemann is an imprint of Pearson Education Limited, Edinburgh Gate, Harlow, Essex, CM20 2JE.

www.pearsonschoolsandfecolleges.co.uk

Heinemann is a registered trademark of Pearson Education Limited

Text copyright © Yvonne Nolan 2011 for Units SHC 21, SHC 22, SHC 23, SHC 24, HSC 024, HSC 025, HSC 026, HSC 027, HSC 028, HSC 2003, HSC 2014, HSC 2002 and HSC 2013
Text copyright © Colette Burgess and Colin Shaw 2011 for Units IC 01, HSC 2007, HSC 2012, HSC 2015 and HSC 2028
Text copyright © Julia Barrand, Royal National Institute of Blind People (RNIB) 2011 for Unit SS MU 2.1
Typeset by Saxon Graphics Ltd, Derby
Original illustrations © Pearson Education Ltd 2011
Illustrated by Andrew Cameron Karate/Grafika
Cover design by Wooden Ark
Picture research by Emma Whyte
Cover photo © moodboard

First published 2011

14 13 12
10 9 8 7 6 5 4 3

British Library Cataloguing in Publication Data
A catalogue record for this book is available from the British Library

ISBN 978 0 435 03194 7

Printed in Spain by Grafos, S.A. Barcelona.

Websites
Pearson Education Limited is not responsible for the content of any external internet sites. It is essential for tutors to preview each website before using it in class so as to ensure that the URL is still accurate, relevant and appropriate. We suggest that tutors bookmark useful websites and consider enabling students to access them through the school/college intranet.

Contents

Acknowledgements

The publisher would like to thank Jane Kellas for providing the further reading features for each unit.

The publisher would like to thank the following for their kind permission to reproduce their photographs:

(Key: b-bottom; c-centre; l-left; r-right; t-top)

Alamy Images: ACE STOCK LIMITED 66bl, Adam James 266, Amana Images CD-1/4, Caro 345, Catchlight Visual Services 49, Christina Kennedy CD-1/17, Cultura 57, Paul Doyle CD-3/16, 241, Paul Doyle CD-3/16, 241, John Fryer 146, ICP-UK 172, Niall McDiarmid 316, Dean Mitchell CD/6, Photofusion Picture Library 66l, PhotosIndia.com LLC 43, Science Photo Library 273, Ian Shaw 103, Robert Stainforth 154, Jack Sullivan 167, Tetra 84, Travel Lib History 158, Kathy de Witt 195; **Corbis:** Kirk Aeder / Icon SM 294, Helen King 6b; **Fotolia.com:** Svetoslav Radkov 151, Sutra 239, Matka Wariatka 351; **Getty Images:** Biggie Productions 2, DAJ 153, John Howard 27, Realistic Reflections CD/3, Sports Illustrated 63; **iStockphoto:** William Britten 66bc, Mike Darling 292, Digitalskillet 135, Tom Fullum 66br, Joshua Hodge Photography 66c, Rich Legg 119, Sean Locke 39, Michael Svoboda 94; **Pearson Education Ltd:** David Sanderson 225, Jules Selmes CD-3/8, CD-3/17, CD-3/19, 139, 213, 214, 335, 337, 354t, 354b, 366, Lord & Leverett 16, 243, CD/9, CD/23, MindStudio CD-2/18, CD-3/23, CD-3/24, 220, 363, Richard Smith CD-2/10, 280, Stuart Cox CD-3/13; **Science Photo Library Ltd:** DR. KEN GREER / VISUALS UNLIMITED 293, Klaus Guldbrandsen 275, Mark Thomas 264; **Shutterstock.com:** Valentin Agapov 81, Avava 136, Bendao 214, Andre Blais 175, Phil Date 6, dream designs CD-2/1, GeoM 212, Colman Lerner Gerardo CD-2/17, Imageman 311, Amy Johansson CD-4/1, Kasza 1, Sebastian Kaulitzki 185, 257, Sebastian Kaulitzki 185, 257, Zastol`skiy Victor Leonidovich CD-1/1, Svetlana Lukienko 327, Johnny Lye 291, marikond 33, Merkushev Vasiliy CD-3/1, Monkey Business Images 61, NikkyTok 93, Guner Pipel CD/1, SSGuyy 131, Stocklite 44, 66r, StockLite 44, 66r

Every effort has been made to trace the copyright holders and we apologise in advance for any unintentional omissions. We would be pleased to insert the appropriate acknowledgement in any subsequent edition of this publication.

Introduction

Welcome to the Level 2 book to accompany the Diploma in Health and Social Care. Your studies for the qualification will give you the chance to learn about the major changes in the way social care and support services are delivered. The transformation of services and the personalisation agenda has put people in control of their own care and support planning and budgets, and given people real choice in how money is spent on their services. People are at the centre of all your work, and services are now designed to fit around people's lifestyles, abilities and existing informal support networks.

All this means that this is a very exciting time to be working in social care. You will be able to play your part in making real changes in people's lives and giving them opportunities to make decisions and choices for themselves that they may never have experienced. Working in social care is always challenging but is always a privilege.

The book is designed to give you knowledge linked to the learning outcomes in the Diploma, so it is easy to follow and should support you throughout your studies. You should also find it a useful reference even after you have gained your qualification.

I am delighted that you have chosen to work in this most challenging, but also most rewarding, career and I wish you every success.

Yvonne Nolan

How to use this book

Look out for the following special features as you work through the book.

Case study
Real-life scenarios that explore key issues and broaden your understanding

Activity
A pencil and paper icon marks opportunities for you to consolidate and/or extend learning, allowing you to apply the theoretical knowledge that you have learned to health and social care situations

Doing it well
Information around the skills needed to perform practical aspects of the job. These are often in the form of checklists that you can tick off point by point to confirm that you are doing things correctly

Reflect
Reflect features have thought bubbles, to remind you that they are opportunities for you to reflect on your practice

Key term
Look out for the keyhole symbol that highlights these key terms – clear definitions of words and phrases you need to know

Functional skills
The building blocks icon indicates where you can demonstrate your English, mathematics or ICT skills while carrying out an activity or answering a case study

Getting ready for assessment
Information to help you prepare for assessment, linked to the learning outcomes for the unit

Getting ready for assessment

Legislation
Summarises all the laws referred to in a unit

Legislation

Further reading and research
Useful for continuing professional development, including references to websites, books and agencies

Further reading and research

Unit SHC 21

Introduction to communication in health, social care or children's and young people's settings

Working in health and social care is about communication and relationships. It is simply not possible to provide support and care services without developing relationships with those you support, and good communication is an essential part of relationship building. Communication is much more than talking. It can include touch, facial expression, body movements, dress and position.

You will also need to think about the different ways in which people communicate and the barriers which some face. You will need to be able to respond to a range of different approaches to communication.

Developing and keeping the trust of the people you work with is an essential part of providing effective support; maintaining confidentiality is a key part of trust. You will need to understand what information must remain confidential, how to ensure that it is and the rare occasions when it is necessary to break confidentiality.

In this unit you will learn about:

1. **why communication is important in the work setting**
2. **how to meet the communication and language needs, wishes and preferences of individuals**
3. **how to overcome barriers to communication**
4. **how to respect equality and diversity when communicating**
5. **how to apply principles and practices relating to confidentiality at work.**

1. Understand why communication is important in the work setting

1.1 The different reasons people communicate

In general, human beings like to live with other human beings. Most of us are sociable creatures who want to reach out to other people around us. Very few humans lead completely solitary lives.

People also communicate for specific reasons; in order to express emotions such as:

- fear
- anger
- pain
- joy
- love.

People want to get views, wishes and information across to others for all kinds of reasons. Sometimes this can be essential — even life saving in the case of a warning. It can be vital to make a person's quality of life better if they are communicating that they are in pain or it can be to make emotional contact with others to express feelings.

People live and communicate within a range of different groups and communities, including:

- families
- neighbourhoods
- workplaces
- schools and colleges
- interest/activity groups
- commercial settings
- users of professional services.

How do you think intimate communications can be identified?

The nature of communication is very different dependent on the circumstances. Some communications are personal and very intimate; these are usually with people to whom we are very close.

Other communications are for a wider audience and are aimed at groups of people. Communication can be formal, such as in a courtroom setting, or informal, such as friends chatting.

Can you see how this is different from intimate communication — for a much wider audience?

Reflect

You are the most important tool you have for doing your job. Care and support workers do not have carefully engineered machinery or complex technology – your own ability to relate to others and to understand them is the key you need.

Activity 1

Recording communication

Over a period of just one day, keep a record of the people you communicate with. Next to each record, write down the type of communication. You may find that most of your communication is informal, or mostly formal, or like most of us, it will be a mix of the two.

1.2 How effective communication affects all aspects of the learner's work

In your job you need to communicate with people all the time. First and foremost is the person you are supporting, but there are also their family and friends, who are likely to be involved in the support plan. You will also have to communicate with colleagues and with other professionals.

The way in which you communicate will be different depending on the person with whom you are communicating and the purpose of the communication. As the case study opposite shows, different approaches to communicate the same information are appropriate for different people.

Functional skills

English: Writing

Report writing requires you to use a suitable format that is fit for purpose and contains set information. You must pay careful attention to the layout of the document using appropriate headings. This report is going to be used to give information to other professionals in your place of work and should be written in a factual way. Careful attention needs to be given to spelling, punctuation, grammar and sentence construction to ensure that it is accurate. You will need to proofread your work to check for errors before submitting a final copy to your tutor.

Activity 2

Producing a report

Your task in this activity is to produce a report just as you would when working in a care setting. You should work individually on your report, but share and discuss your results in a group if you are able. If not, look at your own results and see what you can learn.

1. Read the following scenario carefully.

> You are working in Jasmine House, a 38-bed residential facility for older people. You worked on the late shift: you came into work at 2pm and left at 9.30pm. Mrs Jerrold, an older person, had been very agitated throughout your shift. She kept asking to go home and had tried to leave several times. She had gone out through the front door on one occasion and you had managed to persuade her to come in from the garden. Mrs Jerrold is quite mobile with the aid of a walking frame and her eyesight is poor; otherwise she is well and, until this latest episode, had seemed settled and happy.
>
> She has a daughter who comes in to visit her several times each week.

2. Write this record up as if you were at work and include everything you normally would if this was your report for the records to hand over to the next shift.
3. Write a report about Mrs Jerrold for a review meeting that your supervisor has arranged in order to discuss this episode and concerns about her current condition.
4. Write a note for Mrs Jerrold's daughter when she comes in the next day, to let her know about what has happened with her mother.
5. Compare the differences in records written for different purposes and see what you can learn from each other. Give and receive feedback between everyone in the group about their records.

Case study

Communicating the same information to different people

Mrs Henson was a long-term resident in a residential care home. She had been unwell for some time, and had been treated for a bad dose of flu. Her heart was failing and it was known that her death was a possibility. One morning, the staff went in to find that she had died in her sleep. The information was passed on by phone to various people involved in the following ways.

To the GP: 'Hello, this is Redcroft. A patient of Dr Williams', Mrs Henson, has just died. Could we have someone out to certify, please? Dr Williams saw her only yesterday. He was expecting this.'

To the funeral director: 'Hello, this is Redcroft. One of our residents, Sarah Henson, died this morning. Dr Williams from the health centre will be out to do the certificates. Can you call later this morning? Thank you.'

To the social worker: 'Hello, Gill, this is Sue from Redcroft. Just to let you know that Sarah Henson died this morning. I know you were fond of her, so I wanted to let you know straight away. We went in to see her just before handover, and she had died. As you know from yesterday, it wasn't unexpected – I just wish one of us had been with her.'

To her niece: 'Hello, Mrs Johnson? This is Sue from Redcroft. I'm afraid I have some sad news about your aunt. She passed away a short while ago. It was very peaceful, she just slipped away in her sleep – she didn't suffer at all. I know you were expecting it, but it's still upsetting isn't it? As you asked, we've put all the arrangements in hand. You don't have to worry about anything, but there will be papers for you to sign later on if you feel up to calling in.'

1. What is it about each of these calls that makes them appropriate to the person receiving the call?
2. Which call do you think the care home would have had to consider most carefully first?

1.3 Why it is important to observe an individual's reactions when communicating with them

All communication has an effect on the person you are communicating with. It is a two-way process called an interaction, and it is important that you watch the effects so that any problems can be identified and dealt with.

Any relationship comes about through communication. In order to be effective in providing care and support, you must learn to be a good communicator. But communication is about much more than talking to people. People communicate through:

- speaking
- facial expression
- body language
- position
- dress
- gestures.

You will have to know how to recognise what is being communicated to you, and be able to communicate with others without always having to use words.

Activity 3

Communicating emotions

Do this with a friend or colleague.

1. Write the names of several emotions (such as anger, joy, sadness, disappointment, fear) on pieces of paper.
2. One of you should pick up a piece of paper. Your task is to communicate the emotion written on the paper to your partner, without saying anything.
3. Your partner then has to decide what the emotion is and say why.
4. Change places and repeat the exercise. Take it in turns, until all the pieces of paper have been used. Make sure that you list all the things that made you aware of the emotion being expressed.
5. Discuss with your partner what you have discovered about communication as a result of this exercise.

When you carried out the previous activity, you will have found out that there are many factors that told you what your partner was trying to communicate. It is not only the expression on people's faces that tells you about how they feel, but also the way they use the rest of their bodies. This area of human behaviour is known as **non-verbal communication**. It is very important for developing the ability to understand what people are feeling. If you understand the importance of non-verbal communication, you will be able to use it to improve your own skills when you communicate with someone.

Key term

Non-verbal communication – body language, the most important way in which people communicate

Can you see the different message from each of these photos?

Recognising the signals

Look at a person's facial expression. Much of what you will see will be in the eyes, but the eyebrows and mouth also contribute.

Notice whether someone is looking at you, or at the floor or at a point over your shoulder. Lack of eye contact should give a first indication that all may not be well. It may be that they are not feeling confident. They may be unhappy, or feel uneasy about talking to you. You will need to follow this up.

Look at how a person sits. Are they relaxed and comfortable, sitting well back in the chair, or tense and perched on the edge of the seat? Are they slumped in the chair with their head down? Posture can indicate a great deal about how somebody is feeling. People who are feeling well and cheerful tend to hold their heads up, and sit in a relaxed and comfortable way. Someone who is tense and nervous, who feels unsure and worried, is likely to reflect this in the way they sit or stand.

Observe hands and gestures carefully. Someone twisting their hands, or playing with hair or clothes, is displaying tension and worry. Frequent little shrugs of the shoulders or spreading of the hands may indicate a feeling of helplessness or hopelessness.

Case study

Identifying body language

Mrs Morrison is very confused. She has little recognition of time or place and only knows her daughter, who has cared for her over many years. As Mrs Morrison became increasingly frail and began to fall regularly, she finally stopped eating and drinking, and her daughter had to arrange for her admission to hospital for assessment. Mrs Morrison is in a large psycho-geriatric ward. Many of the patients are aggressive and disinhibited in their behaviour. She is quiet, gentle and confused, and has no idea where she is. She does not know anyone, and she keeps asking to go home.

1. What would you expect Mrs Morrison's body language to be?
2. What would you look for in her facial expression?
3. As her support worker, how do you think you might make her feel better?
4. How would you communicate with her?
5. How might you help her daughter?

Reflect

Research shows that people pay far more attention to facial expressions and tone of voice than they do to spoken words. For example, in one study, words contributed only 7 per cent towards the impression of whether or not someone was liked, tone of voice contributed 38 per cent and facial expression 55 per cent. The study also found that if there was a contradiction between facial expression and words, people believed the facial expression.

Giving out the signals

Being aware of your own body language and what you are communicating is just as important as understanding the person you are talking to.

Doing it well

Communicating with people

- Maintain eye contact with the person you are talking to, although you should avoid staring at them. Looking away occasionally is normal, but if you find yourself looking around the room, or watching others, then you are failing to give people the attention they deserve.
- Be aware of what you are doing and try to think why you are losing attention.
- Sit where you can be easily seen.
- Sit a comfortable distance away – not so far that any sense of closeness is lost, but not so close that you invade their personal space.
- Show by your gestures that you are listening and interested in what they are saying.
- Use touch to communicate your caring and concern if appropriate. Many people find it comforting to have their hand held or stroked, or to have an arm around their shoulders.
- Be aware of a person's body language, which should tell you if they find touch acceptable or not.
- Always err on the side of caution if you are unsure about what is acceptable in another culture and do not use touch as a means of communication until you are sure that it will be acceptable.
- Think about age and gender in relation to touch. An older woman may be happy to have her hand held by a female carer, but may be uncomfortable with such a response from a man.
- Ensure that you are touching someone because you think it will be a comfort, and not because you feel helpless and cannot think of anything to say.

2. Be able to meet the communication and language needs, wishes and preferences of individuals

2.1 Finding out an individual's communication and language needs and preferences

Not everyone communicates in the same way and it is important that you make sure that you are able to communicate with the people you support in the best way for them. People have a wide range of communication needs that involve the consideration of many different factors such as:

- sensory ability
- cultural background
- language
- self-confidence
- level of learning ability
- physical ability.

As a professional, it is your responsibility to make sure that your communication skills meet the needs of the people you support. You should not expect people to adjust their communication to fit in with you.

The best way to find out about what people want and need, of course, is to ask! The person concerned is always your first and best source of information about their needs and the best way to meet them. But asking is not always possible. You can discover some information about communication needs, wishes and preferences by observing someone or by talking with other colleagues who have worked with the person previously, and often by talking to family or friends. They are likely to have a great deal of information about the communication needs of that person. They will have developed ways of dealing with communication, possibly over a long period of time, and are likely to be a very useful source of advice and help.

Passing on information

There would be little point in finding out about effective means of communication with someone and then not making an accurate record so that other people can also communicate with that person.

You should find out your employer's policy on where such information is to be recorded – it is likely to be in the person's case notes. Be sure that you record:

- the nature of the communication needs, wishes and preferences
- how they show themselves
- ways that you have found to be effective in meeting their needs.

Information recorded in notes may look like this.

> Mr Perkins has communication difficulties following his stroke. He is aphasic, with left-side haemaplaegia. Speech is slurred but possible to understand with care. Most effective approaches are:
>
> a) allow maximum time for communication responses
>
> b) modify delivery if necessary in order to allow understanding
>
> c) speak slowly, with short sentences
>
> d) give only one piece of information at a time
>
> e) offer physical reassurance (holding and stroking hand) as this seems to help while waiting for a response
>
> f) use flashcards on bad days (ensure they are placed on the right-hand side)
>
> g) check Mr Perkins has understood the conversation.

This is important in order to ensure all that colleagues do not continually have to go through a process of establishing the communication needs of each person.

Doing it well

Identifying communication needs
- Check what each person's communication needs, wishes and preferences are.
- Remember they can be dictated by cultural as well as physical factors.
- Examine the effects of the communication for each person.
- Use all possible sources to obtain information.
- Make sure you have all the skills necessary to communicate, or look for extra support where necessary.

Communication needs people have

Language

When someone speaks a different language from those who are providing support, it can be an isolating and frustrating experience. The person may become distressed and frightened, as it is very difficult to establish exactly what is happening, and they are not in a position to ask or to have any questions answered. The person will feel excluded from anything happening in the care setting and will find making relationships with support staff extremely difficult. There is a strong possibility of confusion and misunderstanding.

Hearing loss

A loss or reduction of ability to hear clearly can cause major differences in the ability to communicate.

Communication is a two-way process, and it is very difficult for somebody who does not hear sounds at all or hears them in a blurred and indistinct way to be able to respond and to join in. The result can be that people may feel very isolated and excluded from others around them. This can lead to frustration and anger that may cause people to present behaviour that provides you with some challenges.

Profound deafness is not as common as partial hearing loss. People are most likely to suffer from loss of hearing of certain sounds at certain volumes or at certain pitches, such as high sounds or low sounds. It is also very common for people to find it difficult to hear if there is background noise – many sounds may jumble together, making it very hard to pick out the voice of one person. Hearing loss can also have an effect on speech, particularly for those who are profoundly deaf and are unable to hear their own voices as they speak. This can make communication doubly difficult.

Visual impairment

Visual impairment causes many communication difficulties. Not only is a person unable to pick up the visual signals that are being given out by someone who is speaking, but also, because they are unaware of these signals, the person may fail to give appropriate signals in communication. This lack of non-verbal communication and lack of ability to receive and interpret non-verbal communication can lead to misunderstandings about somebody's attitudes and behaviour. It means that a person's communications can easily be misinterpreted; they may seem to be behaving in a way that is not appropriate.

Physical disability

Depending on the disability, this can have various effects. People who have had strokes, for example, may have communication difficulties, not only in forming words and speaking, but also possibly from **aphasia** (or **dysphasia**). People can lose the ability to find the right words for something they want to say, or to understand the meanings of words said to them. This condition is very distressing for the person and for those who are trying to communicate. Often this is coupled with a loss of movement and a difficulty in using facial muscles to form words.

In some cases, the communication need is a symptom of a condition. For example, many people with cerebral palsy and motor neurone disease have difficulty in controlling the muscles that affect voice production, and so clear speech becomes very difficult. Other conditions may have no effect at all upon voice production or the thought processes that produce spoken words, but the lack of other body movements may mean that non-verbal communication is difficult or not what you would expect.

Learning disability

Dependent upon severity, a learning disability may cause differences in communication in terms of the level of understanding of the person and their ability to respond appropriately to any form of communication. This will vary depending on the degree of learning disability of the person, but broadly the effect of learning disabilities is to limit the ability of someone to understand and process information given to them. It is also possible that some people will have a short attention span, so this may mean that communications have to be repeated several times in an appropriate form.

Dementia/confusion

This difficult and distressing condition is most prevalent in older people and people who live with Alzheimer's disease. The confusion can result ultimately in the loss of the ability to communicate, but in the early stages it involves short-term memory loss to the extent of being unable to remember the essential parts of a conversation or a recent exchange. It can mean the constant repetition of any form of communication. This can be frustrating for you as you try to communicate, but is equally frustrating for the person. You will need to make sure your frustration is under control and that you do not allow it to influence how you relate to the person.

Communication disorder

Someone with a communication disorder, such as people who are on the **autistic spectrum**, may have difficulty in communication, social interaction, and may show some repetitive and obsessive behaviours. As each person who has a communication disorder will behave differently, you will need to find out about the person you are supporting and the particular aspects of communication and social interaction that are affected.

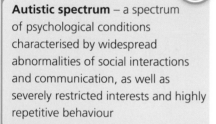

Key term

Autistic spectrum – a spectrum of psychological conditions characterised by widespread abnormalities of social interactions and communication, as well as severely restricted interests and highly repetitive behaviour

2.2 Communication methods that meet an individual's needs

Overcoming language differences in communication

Where you are supporting someone who speaks a different language from you, it is clear that you will need the services of an interpreter for any serious discussions or communication.

- Your work setting is likely to have a contact list of interpreters.
- Social services departments and the police have lists of interpreters.
- The embassy or consulate for the appropriate country will also have a list of qualified interpreters.

You should always use professional interpreters wherever possible. It may be very tempting to use other members of the family — very often children have excellent language skills — but it is inappropriate in most situations. This is because:

- the family member's English and their ability to interpret may not be at the same standard as a professional interpreter's, and misunderstandings can easily occur
- the person may not want members of their family involved in very personal discussions about health or care issues.

It is unlikely that you would be able to have a full-time interpreter available throughout somebody's period of care, so it is necessary to consider alternatives for encouraging everyday communication.

Can you see how you could use these cards?

Be prepared to learn words in the person's language. You could try to give the person some words in your language if they are willing and able to learn them.

There are other simple techniques that you may wish to try which can help basic levels of communication. For example, you could use flashcards and signals, similar to those you would use for a person who has suffered a stroke. The person can show a flashcard to indicate their needs. You can also use these cards to find out what kind of assistance the person may need.

The suggestions shown on the previous page are not exhaustive and you will come up with others that are appropriate for the person and the particular setting. They are a helpful way of assisting with simple communication and allowing people to express their immediate physical needs.

The most effective communication with a person who speaks a different language is non-verbal communication. A smile and a friendly face are understood in all languages, as are a concerned facial expression and a warm and welcoming body position.

However, be careful about the use of gestures – gestures that are acceptable in one culture may not be acceptable in another. For example, an extended thumb in some cultures would mean 'great, that's fine, OK', but in many cultures it is an extremely offensive gesture. If you are unsure which gestures are acceptable in another culture, make sure you check before using them.

Meeting communication needs for someone with a hearing impairment

Ensure that any means of improving hearing (for example, a hearing aid) which the person uses is:

- working properly
- fitted correctly
- installed with fresh, working batteries
- clean
- doing its job properly in terms of improving the person's hearing.

Ensure that you are sitting in a good light, not too far away and that you speak clearly, but do not shout. Shouting simply distorts your face and makes it more difficult for a person with hearing loss to be able to read what you are saying.

Some people will lip read, while others will use a form of sign language for understanding. This may be BSL (British Sign Language) or Makaton, which uses signs and symbols. The person may rely on a combination of lip reading and gestures.

If you are able to learn even simple signing or the basic rules of straightforward spoken communication with people who have hearing loss, you will significantly improve the way in which they are able to relate to their care environment.

Telecommunication services such as minicom or typetalk are very useful for people with hearing loss. These allow a spoken conversation to be translated in written form using a form of typewriter, and the responses can be passed in the same way by an operator who will relay them to the hearing person. These services have provided a major advance in enabling people who are hard of hearing or profoundly deaf to use telephone equipment. For people who are less severely affected by hearing impairment, there are facilities such as telephone handsets with adjustable volume. Texting using a mobile phone has proved to be a very useful means of communication for people with a hearing impairment, and its use is by no means confined to young people. All age groups are making full use of technology to improve communication.

Meeting communication needs for someone with a visual impairment

One of the most common ways of assisting people who have visual impairment is to provide them with glasses or contact lenses. You need to be sure that these are clean and that they are the correct prescription. You must make sure that people know they should have their eyes tested every two years and regularly update their glasses or lenses. A person whose eyesight and requirements for glasses have changed will obviously have difficulty in picking up many of the non-verbal signals that are part of communication.

Doing it well

Meeting the needs of people with visual impairments

- Let them know that you are there by touching and saying hello, rather than suddenly beginning to speak to someone.
- Make sure that you introduce yourself when you come in to a room. It is easy to forget that someone cannot see. A simple 'hello John, it's Sue' is all that is needed so that you do not 'arrive' unexpectedly.
- You may need to use touch more than you would when speaking to a sighted person, because the concerns you will be expressing through your face and your general body movements will not be seen. So, if you are expressing concern or sympathy, it may

be appropriate to touch someone's hand or arm, at the same time as saying you are concerned and sympathetic.

- Ask the person what system of communication they require – do not impose your idea of appropriate systems on the person. Most people who are visually impaired know very well what they can and cannot do, and if you ask they will tell you exactly what they need you to do.
- Do not decide that you know the best way to help. Never take the arm of somebody who is visually impaired to help them to move around. Allow the person to take your arm or shoulder, to ask for guidance and tell you where they want to go.

Meeting communication needs of people with a physical disability

Physical disability or illness has to be dealt with according to the nature of the disability or the illness. For example, if you were communicating with somebody who had a stroke, you might have to work out ways of coping with dysphasia. This is best dealt with by:

- using very simple, short sentences, speaking slowly, and then being prepared to wait while the person processes what you have said and composes a reply
- using gestures – they make it easier for people to understand the idea you are trying to get across
- using very simple, closed questions which only need a 'yes' or 'no' answer. Avoid long, complicated sentences with interrelated ideas (for example, do not say, 'It's getting near tea time now, isn't it? How about some tea? Have you thought about what you would like?' Instead say, 'Are you hungry? Would you like fish? Would you like chicken?' and so on, until you have established what sort of meal the person wants)
- drawing or writing or using flash cards to help understanding.

Other illnesses, such as motor neurone disease or cerebral palsy, can also lead to difficulties in speech, although not in comprehension. The person will understand perfectly what you are saying but the difficulty may be in communicating with you. There is no need for you to speak slowly, although you will have to be prepared to allow time for a response, owing to the difficulties the person may have in producing words.

You will also have to become familiar with the sound of the person's voice and the way in which they communicate. It can be hard to understand people who have illnesses that affect their facial, throat or larynx muscles. The person may have been provided with assistive technology that will enable them to communicate through producing an electronic 'voice'.

Meeting the communication needs of people with a learning disability

Where people have a learning disability, you will need to adjust your methods of communicating to take account of the level of disability that they experience. You should have gathered sufficient information about someone to know the level of understanding they have – and how simply and how often you need to explain things and the sorts of communication which are likely to be the most effective.

Some people with a learning disability respond well to physical contact and are able to relate and communicate on a physical level more easily than on a verbal level. This will vary between people and you must find out the preferred means of communication for the person you are supporting.

Sometimes touch can be helpful.

Communication through actions

For many people, it is easier to communicate by actions than by words. You will need to make sure that you respond in an appropriate way by recognising the significance of a touch or a sudden movement from somebody who is ill and confined to bed, or a gesture from somebody who speaks a different language. A gesture can indicate needs and what sort of response the person is looking for from you. You may be faced with a person with challenging behaviour who throws something at you – this is a means of communication. It may not be a very pleasant one, but nonetheless it expresses much of the person's hurt, anger and distress. It is important that you recognise this for what it is and respond in the same way you would if that person had been able to express their feelings in words.

2.3 How and when to seek advice about communication

Do not assume that you can do everything yourself without any help. You should always be ready to ask for advice and support when you are unsure or when situations are highly complex. The best people to ask for advice are, of course, the person themselves and their family and friends. However, sometimes you may need to talk to your line manager to get specialist advice. Your manager will be able to advise you about how to contact specialist organisations who will have information about communication with people with particular conditions such as a stroke or Alzheimer's disease, or organisations with specific knowledge about communication with people with sensory loss. There is plenty of expert information available, so make sure that you find out about it and never guess what to do or think that you will be able to manage. Your professional duty is to find whatever expert advice you may need in order to provide the best possible service.

3. Be able to overcome barriers to communication

3.1 Identifying barriers to effective communication

Not all communication is straightforward — on many occasions there are barriers to overcome before any effective interaction can take place. Barriers can exist for all sorts of reasons, some to do with the physical environment, some to do with the background and circumstances of the person, and some to do with your approach.

The first barriers to check out are those that you could be creating. You may think that you are doing everything possible to assist communication, but be sure that you are not making it difficult for people to understand what you say.

As professional care workers, you will use all kinds of shortcuts to speak with colleagues. Using initials (acronyms) to refer to things is one of the most common ways in which professionals shortcut when talking to each other. Some acronyms are commonplace and others are particular to that work setting. Often, particular forms or documents are referred to by initials — this is obviously useful in one workplace, but not in any others! Referring to medical conditions, types of medication or therapies, or activities by initials or professional jargon can make it difficult for someone to understand because this is terminology they do not use everyday. Many of us would have difficulty following the explanation of a mechanic as to what is wrong with a car — similarly people and their families may have difficulty following communication littered with jargon and technical terms.

It is not that unusual to hear something on the lines of: 'Right — we've checked your BP — that's fine; your Hb came back OK so that means we can do an RF down to Gill our OT. She'll come and see you then fill out a 370 — that'll go to social services who'll send a CCM out to do an UA and formulate a support plan — OK?'

It may have been more useful to say: 'Your blood pressure's fine, the blood test showed that you're not anaemic, so that means you're well enough for us to contact Gill, the occupational therapist. She will see you and assess what you can do and what help you may need. After that she'll contact social services, and one of the community care managers will visit you to talk about the sort of help and support you would like to have.' It takes a little longer, but it saves time and confusion in the long run.

Some barriers to communication can be caused by failing to follow some of the steps towards good communication, such as those shown on the diagram on the next page.

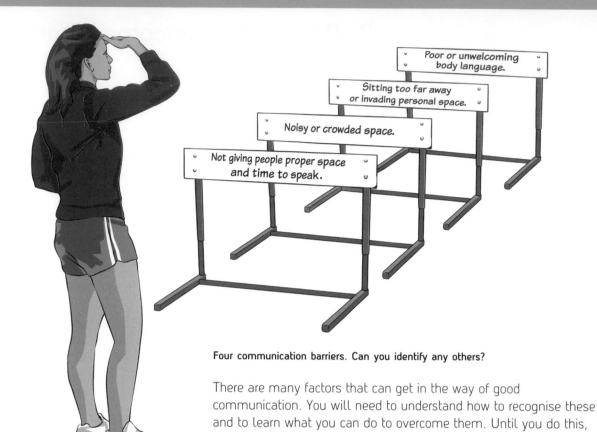

Four communication barriers. Can you identify any others?

There are many factors that can get in the way of good communication. You will need to understand how to recognise these and to learn what you can do to overcome them. Until you do this, your communication will always be less effective than it could be. It is easy to assume that everyone can communicate, and that any failure to respond to you is because of someone's unwillingness rather than an inability. There are as many reasons why people find communication a challenge as there are ways to make it easier.

Thinking about the obstacles

Never assume that you can be heard and understood, and that you can be responded to, without first thinking about the person and their situation. Check to ensure you are giving the communication the best possible chance of success by dealing with as many barriers as possible. Do not just go in and decide that you will deal with obstacles as they arise; some forward planning and thinking about how you will deal with barriers will result in far better outcomes.

3.2 Ways to overcome barriers to effective communication

Encouraging communication

The best way to ensure that somebody is able to communicate to the best of their ability is to make the person feel as comfortable and as relaxed as possible. There are several factors to consider when thinking about how to make people feel confident enough to communicate. Table 1 (see next page) summarises these.

Reflect

Choose two different ways in which you communicate with people, for example, talking, writing, telephone, email – you can probably think of others. Consider the most important element in each one. For example, for talking it could be language, for telephone it could be hearing, and so on. Now think about how you would manage that communication without that important element. List the problems you would have and the ways you could try to overcome them. Do you begin to see how difficult it can sometimes be for people to communicate?

Communication difference	Encouraging actions
Different language	<ul><li>Smile and maintain a friendly facial expression.</li><li>Use gestures and pictures.</li><li>Be warm and encouraging — repeat the person's words with a smile to check understanding.</li></ul>
Hearing impairment	<ul><li>Speak clearly, listen carefully, respond to what is said to you.</li><li>Remove any distractions and other noises.</li><li>Make sure any aids to hearing are working.</li><li>Use written communication where appropriate.</li><li>Use signing where appropriate and understood.</li><li>Use properly trained interpreter if high level of skill is required.</li></ul>
Visual impairment	<ul><li>Use touch to communicate concern, sympathy and interest.</li><li>Use tone of voice rather than facial expressions to communicate mood and response.</li><li>Do not rely on non-verbal communication such as facial expression or nodding your head.</li><li>Ensure that all visual communication is transferred into something which can be heard, either a tape or somebody reading.</li></ul>
Confusion or dementia	<ul><li>Repeat information as often as necessary.</li><li>Keep re-orientating the conversation if you need to.</li><li>Remain patient.</li><li>Be very clear and keep the conversation short and simple.</li><li>Use simple written communication or pictures where they seem to help.</li></ul>
Physical disability	<ul><li>Ensure that surroundings are appropriate and **accessible**.</li><li>Allow for difficulties with voice production if necessary.</li><li>Do not patronise.</li><li>Remember that some body language may not be appropriate.</li></ul>
Learning disability	<ul><li>Judge appropriate level of understanding.</li><li>Make sure that you respond at the right level.</li><li>Repeat things as often as necessary.</li><li>Remain patient and be prepared to keep covering the same ground.</li></ul>

Table 1: Ways of encouraging communication.

Key term

Accessible – able to be obtained, used or experienced without difficulty

3.3 Ways to ensure that communication has been understood

Although it is unacceptable to talk down to people, it is pointless trying to communicate with them by using so much jargon and medical terminology that they do not understand anything you have said. You must be sure that your communication is being understood. The most straightforward way to do this is to ask someone to recap on what you have discussed.

You could say something like, 'Can we just go over this so that we are both sure about what is happening? You tell me what is happening tomorrow', or you can rephrase what you have just said and check with the person that they have understood. For example:

'The bus is coming earlier than usual tomorrow because of the trip. It will be here at eight o'clock instead of nine — is that OK?'

'Yes.'

'So, you're sure that you can be up and ready by eight o'clock to go on the trip?'

Listen effectively

As already mentioned, communication is a two-way process. This may sound obvious, but a great deal of communication is wasted because only one of the parties is communicating. Think about setting up communication between two radios — when communication is established, the question is asked: 'Are you receiving me?' The answer comes back: 'Receiving you loud and clear.' Unfortunately, human beings do not do this exercise before they talk to each other!

You can communicate as much information as you like, but if no one is listening and receiving the information, you are wasting your time. Learning how to listen is a key task for working as a professional support worker.

You may think that you know how to listen and that it is something you do constantly, that you are listening to all sorts of noises all day long — but simply hearing sounds is not the same thing as actively listening.

For most people, feeling that someone is really listening to them makes a huge difference to how confident they feel about talking and thus improves the chances of them being clearly understood. You will need to learn about ways in which you can show people that you are listening to what they are saying.

Using body language

You have already looked at non-verbal communication earlier in this unit. It is an essential part of ensuring that communication is understood. Although you may think that you do most of your communicating by speaking, in fact over 90 per cent of what you communicate to others is done without speaking a word. Body language, or non-verbal communication, is the way in which we pick up most of messages people are trying to convey — and some that they are not!

The way in which you use your body can convey messages about your:

- feelings
- attitudes
- intentions

- interest
- concern
- attention.

Reflect

Think about a time you have talked to someone you felt was really interested in what you were saying and listening carefully to you. Try to note down what it was that made you so sure they were really listening. Did the fact you thought they were really listening to you make it easier to talk?

Can you see how the actions and words do not match?

The messages are made clear by such things as facial expression, maintaining eye contact, sitting forward when you are listening or having an open and relaxed posture.

Remember: body language backs up the words you use — or can make a liar of you!

Your body language will let people know that you are really listening to what they are saying and are understanding what they trying to communicate. Practise your listening skills in just the same way you would practise any other skill — you can learn to listen well.

Doing it well

Practising your listening skills

- Look at the person who is talking to you.
- Maintain eye contact with them, but without staring.
- Nod your head to encourage them to talk and show that you understand.
- Use 'aha', 'mm' and similar expressions which indicate that you are still listening.
- Lean slightly towards the person who is speaking, as this indicates interest and concern.
- Have an open and interested facial expression, which should reflect the tone of the conversation — happy, serious and so on.

Using verbal communication

Body language is the key to effective listening, but what you say is also important. You can back up the message that you are interested and listening by checking that you have understood what has been said to you. Using 'So...' to check that you have got it right can be helpful. 'So... it's only since you had the fall that you are feeling worried about being here alone.' 'So... you were happy with the service before the hours were changed.' You can also use phrases such as 'So what you mean is...' or 'So what you are saying is...'

You can use short, encouraging phrases while people are talking to show concern, understanding or sympathy. Phrases such as 'I see', 'Oh dear', 'Yes' and 'Go on' all give the speaker a clear indication that you are listening and want them to continue.

Using questions

Sometimes questions can be helpful to prompt someone when they are talking, or to try to move a conversation forward. Asking the right questions can help you to understand what is being communicated.

A **closed question** can be answered with 'yes' or 'no' — for example, 'Would you like to go out today?'

An **open question** needs more than 'yes' or 'no' to answer it — for example, 'What is your favourite kind of outing?' Open questions usually begin with:

- what
- how
- why
- when
- where.

Depending on the conversation and the circumstances, either type of question may be appropriate. For example, if you are encouraging someone to talk because they have always been reluctant, but have suddenly begun to open up, you are more likely to use open questions to encourage them to carry on talking. On the other hand, if you need factual information or you just want to confirm that you have understood what has been said to you, then you may be better off asking closed questions.

Activity 4

Open and closed questions

What type of question is each of the following?

1. 'Are you feeling worried?'
2. 'What sorts of things worry you?'
3. 'What have you got planned for when your daughter comes to visit?'
4. 'Is your daughter coming to visit?'
5. 'Why were you cross with Marge this morning?'
6. 'Were you cross with Marge this morning?'
7. 'Do you want to join in the games tonight?'
8. 'Do you live here alone?'
9. 'How do you feel about living alone?'

Reflect

Think about two particular occasions when you have been involved in communicating with people you were supporting. Write a brief description of the circumstances, and then write notes on how you showed that you were listening to them. If you have not yet had enough experience of working with people to be able to think of two occasions, think about times when you have listened effectively to a friend or relative and write notes about that instead.

One of the main points to remember is that whatever you say, there should not be too much of it! You are supposed to be listening in order to understand, not speaking. Some 'do nots' for good listening are as follows.

- Do not interrupt – always let people finish what they are saying; wait for a gap in the conversation.
- Do not give advice – even if asked. You are not the person concerned, so cannot respond to a question beginning, 'If you were me...' Your job is to encourage people to take responsibility for their own decisions, not to tell them what to do.
- Do not tell people about your own experiences. These are relevant to you because they teach you about how they have made you the person you are, but your role is to listen to others, not talk about yourself.
- Do not ever dismiss fears, worries or concerns by saying, 'That's silly' or 'You shouldn't worry about that.' People's fears are real and should not be made to sound trivial.

3.4 Sources of information and support or services to enable more effective communication

Sometimes, you will need to find specialist advice because a person's communication needs are too complex for you to deal with alone. Someone who has an illness that affects their ability to produce sounds or control their neck and facial muscles may need to speak using a piece of assistive technology. For these sorts of complex issues, you will need the advice of a speech and language therapist who is an expert and can advise on any kind of specialised communication needs.

Where there are language issues, you may need to use the services of an interpreter. You should be able to find details of how to contact one from your line manager. Social services and the police will also have a list of language interpreters and, if necessary, the embassy or consulate of the relevant country will also have a list.

There is the NRCPD (National Registers of Communication Professionals working with Deaf and Deafblind People). This includes sign language interpreters, lip speakers, deaf-blind communicators and note takers. The register can be accessed on www.nrcpd.org.uk

There are condition-specific organisations such as the Alzheimer's Society (www.alzheimers.org) and the Stroke Association (www.stroke.org.uk) that can help with expert advice on communication with people with specific issues related to their conditions. Specialist organisations exist for most conditions and can provide much useful advice and information.

4. Be able to respect equality and diversity when communicating

4.1 How people from different backgrounds may use and/or interpret communication methods in different ways

Communication is about much more than words being exchanged between two people — it is influenced by a great many factors. People's background, what they believe in and the culture in which they live has a significant effect on communication.

Culture is about more than language — it is about the way that people live, think and relate to each other.

It is also important that you always communicate at a language level that people are likely to understand, but do not find patronising. Everyone has the right to be spoken to as an adult and not be talked down to.

Talking to carers over someone's head is infuriating and insulting to the person — commonly known as the 'Does he take sugar?' attitude.

Can you imagine how angry this would make you?

What words mean

Be aware that the words you use can mean different things to different people and generations — for example, words like 'cool', 'chip', 'wicked' or 'gay'. Be aware of particular local words that are used in your part of the country, which may not mean the same to someone from another area.

Think carefully about the subject under discussion. Some people from particular cultures, or people of particular generations, may find some subjects very sensitive and difficult to discuss. These days, it is not unusual among a younger age group to discuss how much people earn. However, people of older generations may consider such information to be highly personal.

4.2 Communication that respects equality and diversity

You will need to be aware of cultural differences between you and the person you are talking to. For example, using first names, or touching someone to whom you are not related or a very close friend with, can be viewed as disrespectful in some cultures. Talking in a familiar way to someone of a different gender or age group can be unacceptable in some cultures. For example, some young Muslim women do not talk at all with men to whom they are not related.

Many older men and women consider it disrespectful to address people by their first names. You will often find older people with neighbours they have known for 50 years, who still call each other 'Mrs Baker' or 'Mrs Wood'.

In some cultures, for example, children are not allowed to speak in the presence of certain adults. Beliefs in some cultures do not allow women to speak to men they do not know.

Some people may have been brought up in a background or in a period of time when challenging authority by asking questions was not acceptable. Such people may find it very hard to ask questions of doctors or other health professionals and are unlikely to feel able to raise any queries about how their care or treatment should be carried out.

Activity 5

Checking cultural preferences

Find out the policy in your workplace for checking on people's cultural preferences. Ask who establishes the information about the cultural background of people who use your service, and what the policies are to ensure their needs are met.

5. Be able to apply principles and practices relating to confidentiality at work

5.1 Explaining the term confidentiality

Confidentiality means not sharing information about someone without their knowledge and agreement and ensuring that written and electronic information cannot be accessed or read by people who have no reason to see it. Confidentiality is important because:

- people may not trust a support worker who does not keep information confidential
- people may not feel valued or able to keep their **self-esteem** if their private details are shared with others
- people's safety may be put at risk if details of their property and habits are shared publicly.

A professional service that maintains respect for people must keep private information confidential. There are legal requirements under the Data Protection Act 1998 to keep personal records confidential (see page 240). There are also professional requirements laid down by the regulators that make it the duty of professionals to keep information confidential.

5.2 Confidentiality in day-to-day communication

The basic rule is that all information someone gives, or that is given on their behalf, to an organisation is confidential and cannot be disclosed to anyone without the consent of that person.

There are, however, circumstances in which it may be necessary to pass on information.

In many cases, the passing on of information is routine and related to someone's care. For example, medical information may.be passed to a hospital, to a residential home or to a private agency. It must be made clear to the person that this information will be passed on in order to ensure they receive the best possible care.

The key is that only information that is required for the purpose is passed on. For example, it is not necessary to tell the hearing aid clinic that Mr Smith's son is currently serving a prison sentence. However, if he became seriously ill and the hospital wanted to contact his next of kin, that information would need to be passed on.

Key term

Self-esteem – how people value themselves; how much self-respect and confidence they have

Each organisation should have a policy which states clearly the circumstances in which information can be disclosed. According to government guidelines (Confidentiality of Personal Information 1988) the policy should state:

- who the members of senior management designated to deal with decisions about disclosing information are
- what to do when urgent action is required
- what safeguards are in place to make sure that the information will be used only for the purpose for which it is required
- arrangements for obtaining manual records and computer records
- arrangements for reviewing the procedure.

The most common way in which workers breach confidentiality is by chatting about work with friends or family. It is very tempting to discuss the day's events with your family or friends over a drink or a meal. It is often therapeutic to discuss a stressful day, and helps get things into perspective. But you must make sure that you talk about issues at work in a way that keeps people's details confidential and anonymous.

For example, you can talk about how an encounter made you feel without giving any details of the other people involved. You can say, 'Today this person accused me of stealing all their money – at first I was so angry I didn't know what to say! What would you have done?' You can discuss the issue without making reference to gender, ethnicity, age, physical description, location or any other personal information that might even remotely identify the person concerned. The issue is how you felt and what you should do, and you are always free to discuss yourself.

Do you discuss your day with friends?

Reflect

Think of a time when you have told someone something in confidence and later discovered that they had told other people. Try to recall how you felt about it. You may have felt angry or betrayed. Perhaps you were embarrassed and did not want to face anyone. Note down a few of the ways you felt.

1. Have you ever betrayed someone's confidence – even accidentally?
2. Are you honestly always as careful as you should be about what you say and to whom you say it?

It might be considered a breach of your professional code of conduct to discuss a person's details with people who do not have a need to know. The essential issue is trust; even if no one can identify the name of the person involved, others might perceive you as displaying a lack of respect if you talk in public places about the personal characteristics of the people you work with.

Imagine you were in a restaurant and you overheard staff from a local clinic saying: 'You wouldn't believe how ugly some of the patients are! The other day we had this 40-year-old, dark-haired woman — lives in Meadow Close — she had a face like the back of a bus. Well, the operation went wrong — but I mean, what's she got to live for anyway?' Now imagine that you were about to attend that clinic. Would you want those staff to look after you? The principle of confidentiality is about trust and confidence in professional workers, not only about protecting the identity of someone.

You also need to be sure you do not discuss one person you support with another whom you also support. You may not think you ever would, but it is so easy to do, even if you do not mean to.

Imagine the scene. A woman says, 'Ethel doesn't look too good today', and your well-meant response is, 'No, she doesn't. She's had a bit of an upset with her son. She'd probably be really glad of some company later, if you've got the time.' This response could cause great distress and, above all, distrust. If the woman later says to Ethel, 'Sue said you were a bit down because of the upset with your son', Ethel is not going to know how much you have said. As far as she is aware, you could have given her whole life history to the woman who enquired. The most damaging consequence of this breach of confidentiality is the loss of trust. This can have damaging effects on someone's self-esteem, confidence and general well-being.

In this case, the best way to respond to the woman's comment would have been, 'Don't you think so? Well, perhaps she might be glad of some company later if you've got the time.'

Functional skills

English: Speaking and listening

Have a discussion with the team you are working with about the importance of maintaining confidentiality for people in your place of work. This discussion could include when/if confidentiality needs to be broken. You will need to take an active role in this discussion to show that you can both present information and pick up on points made by others, and that all your contributions are presented clearly using appropriate language.

Case study

Security and confidentiality

Orchard Way Care Home is a 14-bed residential unit for older people with moderate care needs. Mrs Reynolds has been there for five years. Her daughter visits most days and she has regular visits from former neighbours, so has been able to stay in touch with her local community.

One day, her daughter arrives and is extremely angry. She said that one of the neighbours was discussing how awful it was that her mother's money had now almost gone on the residential fees. She explained that the woman's niece worked in the home and the subject was being discussed in general at a family occasion. Her niece had given examples of some of the people at the home who had had money in the bank when they first arrived, but now it had all been spent on fees. Mrs Reynolds' daughter was furious and demanded that the member of staff be sacked immediately.

1. What are the confidentiality issues in this situation?
2. What action should be taken over the member of staff?
3. What actions could be taken to improve understanding of confidentiality at Orchard Way?

Policies of the organisation

Every organisation will have a policy on confidentiality and the disclosure of information. You must be sure that you know what both policies are in your workplace.

The basic rule is that all information someone gives, or that is given on their behalf, to an organisation is confidential and cannot be disclosed to anyone without the consent of that person. You will need to support people in contributing to and understanding records and reports concerning them, and ensure they understand how the rules of confidentiality affect them.

5.3 Situations where normally confidential information might need to be passed on

There are several reasons why decisions about disclosing information without consent may need to be made, and you should inform the person about what has been disclosed at the earliest possible opportunity. Information may be required by a tribunal, a court or by the ombudsman. Ideally this should be done with the person's consent, but it will have to be provided regardless of whether the consent is given.

You may have to consider the protection of the community, if there is a matter of public health at stake. You may be aware that someone has an infectious illness, or is a carrier of such an illness and is putting people at risk. For example, if someone was infected with salmonella, but still insisted on going to work in a restaurant kitchen, you would have a duty to inform the appropriate authorities. There are other situations where you may need to give information to the police. If a serious crime is being investigated, the police can ask for information to be given. Not only can information only be requested in respect of a serious offence, it has to be asked for by a senior-ranking officer of at least the rank of superintendent. This means that if the local constable asks if you know whether Mr Jenkins has a history of mental health problems, this is not information you are free to discuss.

There may also be times when it is helpful to give information to the media. For example, an elderly confused man, who wanders regularly, may have gone missing for far longer than usual. A description given out on the local radio and in the local paper may help to locate him before he comes to any serious harm.

If you have been given information by a child concerning abuse, you have to pass on the information to your line manager, or whoever is named in the alerting procedures. This is not a matter of choice; even if the child refuses to agree, you have a duty to override their wishes. There are no circumstances in which disclosures of abuse of children must be kept confidential.

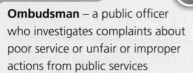

Key term

Ombudsman – a public officer who investigates complaints about poor service or unfair or improper actions from public services

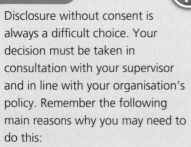

Reflect

Disclosure without consent is always a difficult choice. Your decision must be taken in consultation with your supervisor and in line with your organisation's policy. Remember the following main reasons why you may need to do this:

- if it is in the person's interest
- if there is a serious risk to the community
- if there has been a serious crime, or if the risk of one exists
- in the case of an official/legal investigation.

The situation with an adult, perhaps an older person, who is being abused is different. You can only try to persuade them to allow you to pass on the information.

You may be faced with information which indicates that someone intends to harm themselves. In that situation, you would be justified in breaking a confidence to prevent harm.

If someone is threatening to harm someone else, you should pass on the information immediately to your line manager, who will inform the police. It is not appropriate to contact the threatened person directly.

People who need to know

It can be difficult when people claim to have a right or an interest in seeing someone's records. Of course, there are always some people who do need to know, either because they are directly involved in supporting the person or because they are involved in some other support role. However, not everyone needs to know everything, so it is important that information is given on a 'need to know' basis. In other words, people are told what they need to know in order to carry out their role.

Relatives will often claim that they have a right to know. The most famous example of this was Victoria Gillick, who went to court in order to try to gain access to her daughter's medical records. She claimed that she had the right to know if her daughter had been given the contraceptive pill. Her GP had refused to tell her and she took the case all the way to the House of Lords, but the ruling was not changed and she was not given access to her daughter's records. The rules remain the same. Even for close relatives, the information is not available unless the person agrees.

It is difficult, however, if you are faced with angry or distressed relatives who believe that you have information they are entitled to. One situation you could encounter is where a daughter, for example, believes that she has the right to be told about medical information in respect of her parent. Another example is where someone is trying to find out a person's whereabouts. The best response is to be clear and assertive, but to demonstrate that you understand that it is difficult for them. Do not try to shift responsibility and give people the idea that they can find out from someone else. There is nothing more frustrating than being passed from one person to another without anyone being prepared to tell you anything. It is important to be clear and say something like, 'I'm sorry. I know you must be worried, but I can't discuss any information unless your mother agrees' or 'I'm sorry, I can't give out any information about where Jennie is living now. But if you would like to leave me a name and contact details, I will pass on the message and she can contact you.'

Proof of identity

You should always check that people are who they claim to be. It is not unknown for newspaper reporters, unwanted visitors or even a nosy neighbour to claim that they are relatives or professionals from another agency. If basic precautions are not taken to confirm their identity, then they may be able to find out a great deal of confidential information.

5.4 How and when to seek advice about confidentiality

If you are in a situation where you are unsure about how or if to maintain confidentiality, then you must discuss it with your manager. Every organisation will have policies on information sharing and confidentiality and you will be able to access advice to ensure that you are working within policy guidelines. Maintaining trust and relationships with people while taking care of their best interests or risks to others involves decisions you should not make alone. You always need to discuss and think about these carefully, but these situations are rare. The general rule is always that people's information is not shared with others without a very good reason.

Doing it well

Passing on confidential information safely

In person: if you do not know the person who is claiming to have a right to be given information, you should:

- find out whether they are known to any of your colleagues
- ask for proof of identity – if they claim to be from another agency involved in providing care, they will have an official ID (identity card); otherwise, ask for a driving licence, bank cards and so on.

On the telephone: unless you recognise the voice of the person, you should:

- offer to take their telephone number and call them back after you have checked
- arrange a password if various family or friends are likely to be telephoning about a particular person
- generally only give the information with consent
- only give people the information they need to know to do their job
- ensure the information is relevant to the purpose for which it is required
- check the identity of the person to whom you give information
- make sure you do not give information carelessly.

Case study

Giving out information

Mr Roberts is 59 years old. He is a resident in a nursing home, and he is now very ill. He has Huntington's disease, which is a disease causing dementia, loss of mobility and loss of speech. It is incurable and untreatable, and it is hereditary. Mr Roberts was divorced many years ago when his children were very young and he has had no contact with his family for over 30 years. A young man who says he is Mr Roberts' son comes to the nursing home in great distress. He is aware, through his mother, that his paternal grandfather died 'insane' and he has now heard about his father being in a nursing home. He is terrified that his father has a hereditary disease and that he may also have it. He has young children and is desperate to know if they are at risk too.

1. What can you tell Mr Roberts' son?
2. Does he have a right to know?
3. What do you think should happen?
4. Whose rights are your concern?

Getting ready for assessment

LO1

This requires you to show that you understand why communication is important. Other parts of this unit are about demonstrating skills, but for this outcome you will need to show that you understand the theories behind communication. You may be asked to prepare an assignment or a presentation, but you will need to be able to show your assessor that you know why people communicate, how people communicate and what can get in the way of good communication.

LO2–4

These outcomes are about demonstrating your skills. It is likely that you assessor will observe your communication skills while observing other skills.

Communication is so fundamental to being an effective care and support worker, that it is essential in all the work you do. Assessors will be looking to see that you treat people with respect and that you recognise and value diversity. You will need to show that you use a method of communication that the person chooses and not use a 'one size fits all' approach. You will need to show that you are able to overcome barriers to communication and that you can use techniques and approaches to make it possible for people to communicate. You can do this by asking people, and by using other sources of information to find out the best way to communicate. Your assessor will be looking to see what approaches you are using and is likely to ask you about the reasons for using particular methods.

Functional skills

English: Reading

Use the websites here to extend your knowledge on the types of illnesses/disabilities that people you support may have. Ensure that you understand the terminology within the texts and make notes on new information to help you with your work. By reading a range of texts, you will develop your vocabulary and see different writing styles.

Legislation

- Confidentiality of Personal Information 1988
- Data Protection Act 1998

Further reading and research

- www.alzheimers.org (the Alzheimer's Society)
- www.nrcpd.org.uk (National Registers of Communication Professionals working with Deaf and Deafblind People)
- www.stroke.org.uk (the Stroke Association)

Unit SHC 22

Introduction to personal development in health, social care or children's and young people's settings

The care sector is constantly benefiting from new research, new developments, policies and guidelines. You need to make sure that you are up to date in work practices and knowledge, and aware of current thinking. As a social care worker, you have a responsibility to review and improve your practice constantly. It is the right of people to expect the best possible quality of support and care from those who provide it.

The knowledge and skills addressed in this unit are key to working effectively in all aspects of your practice. It is essential to know how to start to evaluate your work, how you can improve on what you do, and understand the factors that have influenced your attitudes and beliefs. The information in this unit will help you to identify the best ways to develop and update your own knowledge and skills.

In this unit you will learn about:

1. what is required for competence in own work role
2. how to reflect on own work activities
3. how to agree a personal development plan
4. how to develop knowledge, skills and understanding.

1. Understand what is required for competence in own work role

1.1 Duties and responsibilities of your role

The specific duties and responsibilities of your job will vary depending on your role and the employer you work for. If you work for a large employer, whether in the public, private or voluntary sectors, you will probably have had a period of **induction**, where you will have learned about:

- the policies and procedures of the organisation
- how the structures work
- the people who are your managers and supervisors.

If you work for a large organisation in the private, voluntary or independent sector, such as a large charity or a private company with many establishments across the country, you will also be likely to have had a similar induction experience.

Working for smaller private or voluntary organisations, or working as a personal assistant directly employed by the person you are supporting, may mean that your initial induction was less formal and you learned more 'on the job'.

Regardless of how it happened, you will have been given an idea of the duties and responsibilities of your job and what your employer expects of you, and what you can expect in return.

However, the duties and responsibilities required by your employer are not the only requirements of working in social care. The regulator in the UK country in which you work will require that you follow the Code of Practice that lays out the duties and expectations for everyone who works in the sector.

Having Codes of Practice is important; in social care you work with some of the most vulnerable people in society, who have a right to expect a certain standard of work and a certain standard of moral and ethical behaviour.

In order to work in social work anywhere in the UK and in social care in some parts (soon to be all) of the UK, there is a requirement to be registered. This means having, or working towards, a minimum level of qualification and agreeing to work within the Code of Practice that sets out the behaviour required. Employers have to ensure that everyone who works for them is registered and eligible to work in social work or social care. Currently, only social care practitioners in Scotland and Wales are registered, but England and Northern Ireland will be following in the near future. In any event, abiding by the Codes of Practice is a good way of making sure that your practice is following ethical and professional guidelines.

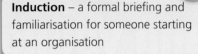

Key term

Induction – a formal briefing and familiarisation for someone starting at an organisation

Case study

Dealing with theft

Joanne works as a personal assistant to Esme, who lives in Cardiff and has cerebral palsy. Esme is a regional organiser and fund-raiser for a large charity; she has a very busy and active life. She needs support workers to accompany her during all her business time in order to support her personal needs and to take notes at meetings. Esme has recruited a team of support workers and they work in shifts. Several months after Joanne started working for her, Esme noticed that items were going missing from her house. Initially this was just small things like CDs, then larger items, and money also started going missing from her purse. It always seemed to link in to when Joanne had been working. Esme confronted Joanne, who initially denied any

involvement. Eventually Joanne broke down and admitted that she had been stealing the items because her boyfriend had a drug habit and he kept demanding more and more money.

Esme dismissed Joanne from her post and reported the matter to the police. She reported Joanne to the Care Council for Wales, where she was interviewed by a disciplinary panel and was banned from working in social care for three years.

1. Do you think that Esme took the right actions?
2. What else could she have done?
3. What would have been the consequences of these other courses of action?

1.2 Standards that influence the way your role is carried out

Your job may have come with a job description, but while that tells you *what* you need to do, it does not usually tell you *how* you need to do it. To find that out, you need to look at the Standards that apply to your work.

Standards and Codes of Practice will vary depending on the UK country in which you work. Each UK country has National Minimum Standards that are used by inspectors to ensure that services are being delivered at an acceptable level. The National Minimum Standards apply to all organisations that deliver social care, so your employer will have to make sure that the services are up to the necessary standards. The inspections are carried out by different bodies for each of the UK countries, but they cover similar areas. The examples in Table 1 are from the Care Quality Commission, which inspects provision in England for all nursing homes, residential care homes and domiciliary services. Their work is carried out under the Health and Social Care Act 2008.

Finally, and most importantly, in terms of how you carry out your work are the **National Occupational Standards**. These apply across the whole of the UK, and explain what you need to be able to do, and what you need to know in order to work effectively in social care.

Key term

National Occupational Standards – UK standards of performance that people are expected to achieve in their work, and the knowledge and skills they need to perform effectively

Area	Required outcome
Care and welfare of people who use services	People experience effective, safe and appropriate care, treatment and support that meets their needs and protects their rights.
Assessing and monitoring the quality of service provision	People benefit from safe, quality care because effective decisions are made and because of the management of risks to people's health, welfare and safety.
Safeguarding people who use services from abuse	People are safeguarded from abuse, or the risk of abuse, and their human rights are respected and upheld.
Cleanliness and infection control	People experience care in a clean environment, and are protected from acquiring infections.
Management of medicines	People have their medicines when they need them, and in a safe way. People are given information about their medicines.
Meeting nutritional needs	People are encouraged and supported to have sufficient food and drink that is nutritional and balanced, and a choice of food and drink to meet their different needs.
Safety and suitability of premises	People receive care in, work in or visit safe surroundings that promote their well-being.
Safety, availability and suitability of equipment	Where equipment is used, it is safe, available, comfortable and suitable for people's needs.
Respecting and involving people who use services	People understand the care and treatment choices available to them. They can express their views and are involved in making decisions about their care. They have their privacy, dignity and independence respected, and have their views and experiences taken into account in the way in which the service is delivered.
Consent to care and treatment	People give consent to their care and treatment, and understand and know how to change decisions about things that have been agreed previously.
Complaints	People and those acting on their behalf have their comments and complaints listened to and acted on effectively, and know that they will not be discriminated against for making a complaint.
Records	People's personal records are accurate, fit for purpose, held securely and remain confidential. The same applies to other records that are needed to protect their safety and well-being.
Requirements relating to workers	People are kept safe, and their health and welfare needs are met, by staff who are fit for the job and have the right qualifications, skills and experience.
Staffing	People are kept safe, and their health and welfare needs are met, because there are sufficient numbers of the right staff.
Supporting workers	People are kept safe, and their health and welfare needs are met, because staff are competent to carry out their work and are properly trained, supervised and appraised.
Cooperating with other providers	People receive safe and coordinated care when they move between providers or receive care from more than one provider.

Table 1: Examples of standards in areas of social care.

The National Occupational Standards form the basis for all the qualifications in the social care sector. They are divided into units of competence — some of these are mandatory, and everyone should be able to demonstrate competence in these areas. Other units are optional and you should be able to demonstrate competence in those units relevant to your job role.

Functional skills

English: Reading

Use the websites listed in Activity 1 to gather information that shows you have met the requirements for your area of expertise. From your reading, make notes to show the links between the work you are doing and the skills you have developed from working in the care sector.

Activity 1

Linking your work to the National Occupational Standards

Each of the units of assessment in the Level 2 Diploma is based on units of competence from the National Occupational Standards. Choose any of the units of assessment from your Diploma qualification and find the matching unit of competence. Can you see the links to the work you are doing for your qualifications? You will be able to find the Standards from your relevant Sector Skills Council as follows.

- England: Skills for Care (www.skillsforcare.org.uk)
- Wales: Care Council for Wales (www.ccwales.org.uk)
- Scotland: Scottish Social Services Council (www.sssc.uk.com)
- Northern Ireland: Northern Ireland Social Care Council (www.niscc.info)

How can you show that you have met the requirements set out in the National Occupational Standards?

All of the standards and people who support good practice.

Competence

In general terms, **competence** means that you are able to do something well, but when it applies to performing your job role, it has a quite specific meaning. Competence means that you have been able to provide evidence that you can demonstrate the skills and the underpinning knowledge contained in the National Occupational Standards. It is important to understand that competence is not only about doing the job, it is also about understanding why you do what you do and the theories that underpin the work.

1.3 How to ensure that your attitudes or beliefs do not obstruct your work

Everyone has their own values, beliefs and preferences. They are an essential part of who you are. What you believe in, what you see as important and what you see as acceptable or desirable are as much a part of your personality as whether you are shy, outgoing, funny, serious, friendly or reserved.

People who work supporting others need to be more aware than most of how their work can be affected by their own beliefs. If you are working in a factory producing electronic chips, the production line will continue to operate regardless of whether you view your job as interesting or boring; it will still continue if you shout abuse at it – your opinion will have no effect on the end result of the work. As long as you continue to play your part in the process, the chips will be turned out and the job will be completed satisfactorily.

If you work in a library, people will still continue to borrow and read books that you consider boring, poorly written or distasteful. With the exception of a small number of those who might ask your advice, most of the people for whom you provide a service will remain unaware of your beliefs, interests or values. However, if you work supporting others and your work involves you making relationships with vulnerable people and carrying out tasks which affect their health and well-being, then your own attitudes, values and beliefs are very important.

The way in which you respond to people is linked to what you believe in, what you consider important and the things that interest you. You are likely to find that you respond warmly to people who share your values and less warmly to people who have different views. When you develop friendships it is natural to spend time with people who share your interests and values, those who are 'on your wavelength'. If you are a person who enjoys a night out where there is plenty of lively activity, modern music and dancing, you are not likely to choose to spend time with someone whose perfect evening is to stay in with a bottle of wine and listen to opera. Everyone is different and while you can recognise and respect the enjoyment that someone may achieve from an evening with Mozart, you may not choose to share it or feel that you have much in common.

Have you noticed how you have friendships with people who reflect your own values, interests and beliefs?

However, the professional relationships you develop with people you support are another matter. As a professional social care worker, you are required to provide the same quality of care for all, not just for those who share your views and beliefs. This may seem obvious, but knowing what you need to do and doing it well are not the same things.

Case study

Dealing with differing views

Frank is providing support for a young man, Greg, who has a degree of autism and a learning disability, but he is very capable and functions well. Greg's parents, however, believe that he needs to be looked after and that he will never be able to do anything for himself or have any degree of independence. Frank believes very strongly that everyone should be able to live life to the full and to make their own decisions about their future.

1. How would this affect Frank's relationship with the parents?

Ellie believes that a healthy lifestyle is very important and that everyone has a responsibility to themselves, their families and to society to eat well and to stay as fit as possible. She is supporting Kate, a wife and mother, whose family smoke, drink, eat fast food every day and spend their time either watching TV or playing computer games. They are all obese and have difficulty getting around; as a result, none of the family is able to do much to support Kate, who has personal care needs.

2. How would Ellie be able to work with this family?

You may believe that you treat everyone in the same way, but there can often be differences in approach or attitude of which you may be unaware. For example, you may spend more time with someone who is asking your advice about a course of action which you think is sensible than you would with someone who wanted to do something you considered inadvisable. There are many ways in which your beliefs, interests and values can affect how you relate to people. A useful first step is to identify and understand your own views and values.

Belief, value or interest	Situation	Possible effect
People have a responsibility to look after their health.	Someone being supported has heart disease but continues to smoke and eats a diet high in fried foods and cream cakes.	You find it difficult to be sympathetic when they complain about their condition and make limited responses.
War and violence are wrong and people who fight should not be glorified as heroes.	An older man being supported constantly recalls tales of his days as a soldier and wants his bravery and that of his comrades to be admired.	You try to avoid spending time chatting with him and limit your contact to providing physical care.
You like modern chart and disco music.	One person being supported constantly plays country and western music very loudly.	You find it hard not to ask them to turn it down or off. You hurry through your work and your irritation shows in your body language.

Table 2: Example beliefs, values or interests and their potential effects.

There are many other situations in which you may find that you are behaving differently towards different people. There is nothing wrong, or unusual in this. However, it is important that you are aware of it, because it potentially makes a difference to the quality of your work. Being aware of the factors that have influenced the development of your personality is not as easy as it sounds. You may feel that you know yourself very well, but knowing *who* you are is not the same as knowing *how* you got to be you.

Activity 2

Exploring your values

1. Take a range of items from a newspaper, about six or seven. Make a note of your views on each of them: say what your feelings are on each one – does it shock or disgust you, make you sad, or angry, or grateful that it has not happened to you?
2. Try to think about why you reacted in the way you did to each of the items in the newspaper. Think about what may have influenced you to feel that way. The answers are likely to lie in a complex range of factors, including your upbringing and background, experiences you had as a child and as an adult, and relationships you have shared with others.

Thinking about these influences is never easy, and you are not being asked to carry out an in-depth analysis of yourself — simply to begin to realise how your development has been influenced by a series of factors. Everyone's values and beliefs are affected to different degrees by the same range of factors.

Functional skills

English: Speaking and listening

Have a discussion with your peers about the major factors that have affected the way you work and relate to people you support. Use the headings listed in the bullet points as a guide to help you prepare for and focus the discussion. Present your ideas clearly, using appropriate language, and allow others to give their opinions and feedback. Show that you are listening to others in the group by giving them feedback on their points.

These include:

- life stage
- housing
- lifestyle
- recreational opportunities
- health
- income
- the effects of relationships
- social class
- employment
- education
- cultural background
- religious beliefs and values.

Thinking about the major factors that have influenced your development will help you to look at how they affect the way you work and how you get along with colleagues and the people you support. This way you can constantly be aware of the risk that the quality of your work is being affected by your personal views and take action to deal with it.

2. Be able to reflect on own work activities

2.1 Why reflecting on practice is an important way to develop knowledge, skills and practice

and

2.3 Reflect on work activities

In order to be an effective practitioner and to provide the best possible service for those you support, you need to be able to reflect on what you do and the way you work, and to identify your strengths and your weaknesses. It is important that you learn to use reflection on your own practice in a constructive way. Reflection should not be used to undermine your confidence in your own work – rather you should use it in a constructive way to identify areas which require improvement.

Being able to recognise areas of your work that need improvement is not an indication of poor practice, it is an indication of excellent practice. Any worker in social care who believes that they have no need to improve their practice or to develop and add to their skills and understanding is not demonstrating good and competent practice, but rather an arrogant and potentially dangerous lack of understanding of the nature of work in the social care sector.

Becoming a reflective practitioner is not about torturing yourself with self-doubts and examining your weaknesses until you reach the point where your self-confidence is at zero! But it is important that you examine the work that you have done and identify areas where you know you need to carry out additional development. A useful tool in learning to become a reflective practitioner is to develop a checklist which you can use either after you have dealt with a difficult situation or at the end of each shift or day's work which will allow you to:

- look at the way you approached the situation or your work
- consider the effect your approach appeared to have on those you were working with – you should include both clients and colleagues in this reflection
- make an honest assessment of the quality of the work that you have produced that day, or in the situation. This will need to be an honest reflection or it is of little value, but you also need to allow for the fact that nobody produces first-class work every day – everyone has days when they are less effective than they would like to be, so be careful that you are not too hard on yourself when reflecting on this area.

Checklist to evaluate practice

1. How did I approach my work?

2. Was my approach positive?

3. How did the way I worked affect the people I support?

4. How did the way I worked affect my colleagues?

5. Did I give my work 100 per cent?

6. Which was the best aspect of the work I did?

7. Which was the worst aspect of the work I did?

8. Was this work the best I could do?

9. Are there any areas in which I could improve?

10. What are they, and how will I tackle them?

Taking time out to think and reflect is important.

The purpose of reflective practice is to improve and develop your practice, skills and knowledge by thinking about what you are doing. Reflection involves thinking things over, a bit like reflecting ideas inside the mind like light bouncing between mirrors. Reflection helps us to realise new ideas and make new sense of practice issues.

Sometimes it can be as simple as remembering a detail that suddenly makes a situation become clear. Other times reflection can involve much more complex thinking, such as thinking about how someone may have been feeling, or how you were feeling and why that might have been. It can also involve thinking about wider issues; perhaps realising that there are areas where you need to learn more and new skills that you have not yet developed.

Reflection means thinking about situations and learning from what you have discovered.

2.2 How well your knowledge, skills and understanding meet standards

There is a range of ways in which you can ensure that you keep up to date with new developments in the field of care, and particularly those which affect your own specialist area of work. However, you should not assume that your workplace will automatically inform you about new developments, changes and updates which affect your work – you must be prepared to actively maintain your own knowledge base and to ensure that your practice is in line with current thinking and emerging theories.

Fortunately the area of health and care is topical and relatively easy to find out information about in respect of new studies and research. You will need to be aware when watching television programmes or listening to radio news bulletins of new developments, legislation, guidelines and reports which are being reported in relation to health and care clients and workers. These items regularly occur in news and current affairs television and radio programmes, and you are also likely to find a wide range of documentary programmes about relevant issues on television.

Newspaper articles and articles in professional journals are also excellent sources of information. Where they are reporting on a recently completed study, they will always give a reference at the end of the article that will enable you to obtain a copy of the study or report. Professional journals are also places where you will find

Activity 3

News references to health and social care

For one week, keep a record of every item which relates to health and care services which you hear on a news bulletin, in a television programme, or in a newspaper or magazine article. You may be surprised at the very large number of references that you find. This is not to suggest that you should be able to watch or listen to every programme that you are able to identify in the programme listings, but it will give you a good idea of the amount of information that is regularly available.

Have you thought about how many TV programmes are relevant to social care?

advertisements for conferences and training opportunities; in addition, you may find that information about such opportunities is circulated at your workplace. There is often a cost involved with attending these sorts of events and so it may not always be possible within the training budget of your workplace. However, it is valuable to pass on information about conferences or seminars which appear to be of interest, as it may be possible for one person to attend and to pass on (or cascade) the information to others, or it may be possible to obtain conference papers and handouts.

The Internet provides a vast resource for information, views and research. However, you will need to be wary of the information that you obtain in this way and unless it is from an accredited source such as a government department, a reputable university or college, or an established research establishment, you should make every effort to check out the validity of what you are reading. Anyone can publish information on the Internet; there is no requirement for it to be checked or approved through any central agency. This can mean that people are able to produce their own views and opinions which may not have any basis in fact. These views and opinions from a wide range of people are valuable and interesting in themselves, but be careful not to assume anything to be factually correct unless it is from a very reliable source.

Never overlook the obvious and one of the sources of information which may be most useful to you could also be one of those which is closest at hand — your own workplace supervisor and colleagues may have many years of experience and knowledge which they will be happy to share with you. They may also be updating their own practice and ideas, and may have information that they would be willing to share.

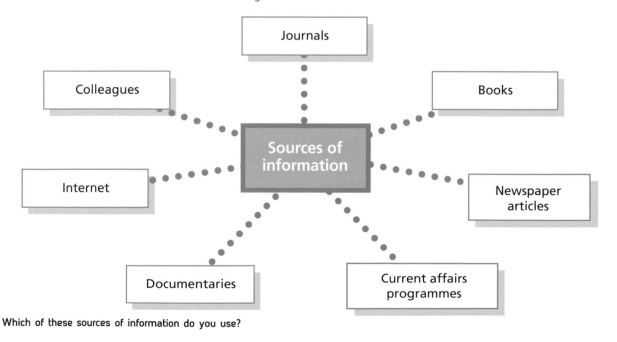

Which of these sources of information do you use?

Reflecting is closely connected with learning; you do something, then you reflect on it and learn from it, so that the next time you are involved in the same situation you will be able to deal with it better and more effectively. It is difficult to separate reflection and learning as they are closely linked.

English: Writing

Keep a reflective diary for a week by writing down notes on issues that concern or irritate you during your working day. Use the appropriate level of detail to cover the requirements of the task set by your tutor and ensure that all your information is written clearly and coherently. Present your information in a logical way, choosing a suitable format and language fit for your level of NVQ. Proofread your work for accuracy of spelling, punctuation and grammar.

Reflect

Keep a reflective diary for a week. At the end of each working day, spend half an hour writing down one or two key issues that concerned you or irritated you – or even that you did well. How did you respond to these issues? How could you learn from this experience to take your own practice forward?

Examples might include an incident such as noticing a wastepaper basket placed where someone could trip over it, failing to move it because you were in a hurry, then returning with a jug of water and tripping over the basket yourself. The result might be that you had to spend much more time cleaning up your water spill than it would have taken to move the basket in the first place. Or perhaps there was a difficult interaction with someone with whom you do not get along very easily – perhaps nothing significant, but a niggling feeling that you could have done better.

3. Be able to agree a personal development plan

3.1 Sources of support for your learning and development

Support for your learning and development can come from a wide range of sources, including:

- formal support networks
- informal support networks
- supervision
- appraisal
- in-house and external training and development.

Many of you will be connected to a computer network at work; all of our public transport is usually described as a network — a network of railway lines, or a network of roads; most of us communicate through a mobile telephone network and so on. Essentially networks are about the routes by which things link together. Social networks are about how people link together.

Formal support networks

Your employer is likely to set up formal networks, or they may be part of the service offered by a professional organisation. They may include your immediate supervisor and possibly other more senior members of staff on occasion, or they may be made up of other colleagues doing similar work to you. Network meetings could be at differing intervals depending on the system in your particular workplace; some networks operate online for people who find it difficult to make time for meetings.

Action learning sets are a type of formal network where people share issues and there is a general discussion around problem solving and how to deal with issues. Often you can discover that problems are shared and others are experiencing the same concerns and issues.

Formal networks will usually have a set meeting time, and someone who coordinates and sends out agendas and notices of meetings. Minutes may be taken and usually the same group of people meet regularly.

Informal support networks

Informal support networks are likely to consist of your work colleagues. These can be major sources of support and assistance. Part of the effectiveness of many workplace teams is their ability to provide useful ideas for improving practice, and support when things go badly.

Some staff teams provide a completely informal and ad hoc support system, where people give you advice, guidance and support as and when necessary. Always be sure to make the most of these

Feedback from colleagues can help put things in perspective.

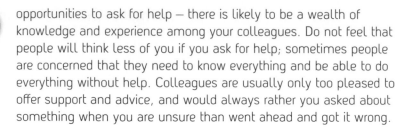

Formal and informal support networks

Identify the formal and informal support networks in your workplace. Note down the ways in which you use the different types of network and how they support your development. If you identify any gaps or areas where you feel unsupported, discuss this with your supervisor or manager.

Activity 5

Your workplace's supervision policy

Ask your supervisor for a copy of the relevant policy or plan at work on the supervision of staff.

Read the plan and note down what it covers, for example, how you will be supervised, how often you can expect to be formally supervised and what kinds of things your supervisor will be able to help you with in your work role and career.

If the plan is not clear, make a list of the things on which you would like your supervisor's support and agree a time and place to discuss these.

opportunities to ask for help — there is likely to be a wealth of knowledge and experience among your colleagues. Do not feel that people will think less of you if you ask for help; sometimes people are concerned that they need to know everything and be able to do everything without help. Colleagues are usually only too pleased to offer support and advice, and would always rather you asked about something when you are unsure than went ahead and got it wrong.

There can also be informal networks for support among candidates for a qualification, so if you are working for your Diploma with a group of other people, there will be plenty of opportunities for informal networking and sharing newly acquired knowledge.

Supervision

Your supervisor's role is to support and advise you in your work and to make sure that you know and understand:

- your rights and responsibilities as an employee
- what your job involves and the procedures your employer has in place to help you carry out your job properly
- the beliefs, values and attitudes of your organisation about how social care is delivered and how people are supported
- your career development needs — the education and training requirements for the job roles you may progress into, as well as for your current job.

Supervision is extremely useful in giving you the opportunity to benefit from feedback from your supervisor, who will be fully aware of the work you have been doing, and able to identify areas of practice that you may need to improve and areas in which you have demonstrated strength.

You should have the opportunity to meet on a regular basis with your supervisor to discuss the individual people you support and any general issues relating to your practice, including any training and development needs. The frequency will vary between employers but is usually every six weeks or so.

Make sure that you are well prepared for sessions with your supervisor so that you can get maximum benefit from them. This will mean bringing together your reflections on your own practice, using examples and case notes where appropriate. You will need to demonstrate to your supervisor that you have reflected on your own practice and that you have begun identifying areas for development. If you can provide evidence through case notes and records to support this, this will help your supervisor to work with you to develop your practice.

Appraisal

This is different from supervision; it may take place with your usual supervisor or it may be with a more senior manager or someone who specialises in appraisals. It normally takes place at 12-monthly

There should be a regular, uninterrupted session with your supervisor.

intervals and is only about you and your practice, not directly about the people you support. You will have the opportunity to discuss your work since your last appraisal and to look at how you have progressed towards any of the goals you identified last time. One of the key areas will be your professional training and development, and you will be able to look at the training you think you are going to need in order to achieve your goals.

In-house or external training and development

One of the other formal and organised ways of reflecting on your own practice and identifying strengths, weaknesses and areas for development is during formal training opportunities. On a course, or at a training day, aspects of your practice and areas of knowledge that are new to you will be discussed, and this will often open up avenues that you had not previously considered. This is one of the major benefits of making the most of all the training and education opportunities that are available to you. Some training may be organised in-house by your employer, perhaps through the training department if you work for a large employer, through a local national training provider, or through your supervisor or line manager in smaller organisations. Formal training can be very useful for developing your career and helping you to gain the knowledge and skills to move ahead. Formal training can be:

- single days on specialist areas
- ongoing courses with several sessions
- attendance at college or a training provider for formal qualifications.

Formal training and development are not the only ways you can learn and expand your knowledge and understanding. There are plenty of other ways to keep up progress towards the goals you have set yourself.

Case study

Identifying opportunities to improve practice

Emil is a support worker in a unit for young adults with disabilities, run by a leading charity. He was aware that his knowledge of disability legislation was not as comprehensive as it ought to be and he felt uncertain about answering some of the questions that the young people put to him.

Emil raised this issue with his line manager, who immediately found that training days were provided by the local authority that would help Emil to learn about the relevant legislation. Following his training days, Emil felt far more confident, as not only had he learned a great deal during the course itself, but also he had been given some handouts and been informed about useful textbooks and websites.

1. How will Emil benefit personally from taking this training?
2. How will those he works with benefit?
3. Are you confident about your knowledge of legislation relating to your own work? If not, what steps are you taking to improve it?

Not everyone learns best from formal training. Other ways people learn are from:

- being shown by more experienced colleagues
- working and discussing issues as a team or group
- reading textbooks, journals and articles
- following up information on the Internet
- making use of local library facilities or learning resource centres
- asking questions and holding professional discussions with colleagues and managers.

Reflect

Write down the different ways of learning that you have experienced. Have you, for example, studied a course at college, completed a distance learning programme or attended hands-on training sessions? Tick the learning methods which have been the most enjoyable and most successful for you.

Here is a checklist of ways of learning that you might find useful:

- watching other people
- asking questions and listening to the answers
- finding things out for yourself
- going to college and attending training courses
- studying a distance learning course or a course on the Internet.

How could you use this information about how you best like to learn in order to update your workplace skills?

Can you identify the different ways in which you could learn in this centre?

3.2 and 3.3 Agreeing a personal development plan and who should be involved, and drawing it up

A personal development plan is a very important document as it identifies your training and development needs. Also, because the plan is updated when you have taken part in training and development, it also provides a record of participation. A personal development plan should be worked out with your supervisor, but it is essentially *your* plan for *your* career. You need to think about what you want to achieve, and discuss with your supervisor the best ways of achieving your goals.

There is no single right way to prepare a personal development plan, and each organisation is likely to have its own way. However, it should include different development areas, such as practical skills and communication skills, the goals or targets you have set — such as being competent in working with people with **dementia** — and a timescale for achieving them. Timescales must be realistic; for example, if you were to decide that you needed to achieve competence in dementia in six months, this would be unrealistic and unachievable. You would inevitably fail to meet your target and would therefore be likely to become demoralised and demotivated. But if your target is to attend a training and development programme on dementia during the next three months and to work with two people with dementia by the end of the following three months, those goals and targets would be realistic and you would be likely to achieve them.

When you have set your targets, you need to review how you are progressing towards achieving them — this should happen every six months or so. You need to look at what you have achieved and how your plan needs to be updated.

Key term

Dementia – a disease that affects the brain, especially the memory

Development plans can take many forms, but the best ones are likely to be developed in conjunction with your manager or workplace supervisor. You need to consider carefully the 'areas of competence' and understand which ones you need to develop for your work role. Identify each as either an area in which you feel fully confident, one where there is room for improvement and development, or one where you have very limited current ability. The headings in Table 3 are suggestions only.

Development plan		
Area of competence	Goals	Action plan
Time management and workload organisation	Learn to use computer recording and information systems	Attend two-day training and use study pack. Attend follow-up training days. Use computer instead of writing reports by hand
Review date: 3 months		
Professional development priorities		
My priorities for training and development in the next 6 months are:		IT and computerised record systems
My priorities for training and development in the next 6 to 12 months are:		As above and single assessment training
Repeat this exercise in: 6 months and review the areas of competence and priorities		

Table 3: A sample development plan.

Once you have completed your plan, you can identify the areas on which you need to concentrate. You should set some goals and targets, and your line manager should be able to help you ensure they are realistic. Only you and your line manager can examine the areas of competence and skills that you need to achieve. This is a personal development programme for you and you must be sure that it reflects not only the objectives of your organisation and your job role, but also your personal ambitions and aspirations.

Training and development

This section of your plan helps you to look at what you need to do in order to reach the goals you recorded in the first section. You should make a note of the training and development you need to undertake in order to achieve what you have identified.

Goals	Development needed
Short term	
Medium term	
Long term	

Table 4: Short-, medium- and long-term goals.

Milestones and timescales

In this section you should look at the development you have identified in the previous section and plan some timescales. Decide what the milestones will be on the way to achieving your goal. Make sure that your timescales are realistic.

Development	Milestone	By when

Table 5: Development milestones.

Reviews and updates

This section helps you to stay on track and to make the changes which will be inevitable as you progress. Not all your milestones will be achieved on target – some will be later, some earlier. All these changes will affect your overall plan, and you need to keep up to date and make any alterations as you go along.

Milestone	Target date	Actual achievement/revised target

Table 6: Targets for milestones.

The style of plan you use is up to you and your supervisor. However you do it, the important thing is to make sure that you do one and that you continue to use it. In this way you can keep you career on track and have a record of the training and development you have undertaken.

4. Be able to develop knowledge, skills and understanding

There is little point in reading articles, watching TV programmes and attending training days if your work practice is not updated and improved as a result. With the enormous pressures on everybody in the health and social care services, it is often difficult to find time to keep up to date and to change the practices you are used to. Any form of change takes time and is always a little uncomfortable or unusual to begin with. So when we are under pressure because of the amount of work we have to do, it is only normal that we tend to rely on practices, methods and ways of working which are comfortable, familiar, and can be done swiftly and efficiently.

You will need to make a very conscious effort to incorporate new learning into your practice. You need to allocate time to updating your knowledge, and incorporating it into your practice. You could try the ways on the following pages to ensure that you are using the new knowledge you have gained.

New knowledge is not only about the most exciting emerging theories. It is also often about mundane and day-to-day aspects of your practice, which are just as important and can make just as much difference to the quality of care you provide for the people you support. It is also about taking your practice forward by developing your knowledge across a range of situations.

Case study

Identifying your own training needs

Meena works as a care worker at a big, busy day centre and meets the families of people of all ages. One day she was chatting to the daughter of one of the people at the centre and mentioned the problem of teenage pregnancy, expressing her disapproval of the extreme youth of some new mothers. 'It's funny you should say that,' replied the woman, 'but my daughter Louise is pregnant. I'm not that happy – she's only 16 – but what can you do?' Meena felt embarrassed, but decided she needed to be better informed on the issue. She got in touch with the local family planning clinic and spoke to the manager, explaining that she would like to learn more about the sexual health services available to young people. She arranged to spend some time on a self-directed work experience placement at the clinic, and is now a volunteer there, helping to run the crèche. In her reflective diary she writes:

> Really tired tonight. All day at work and then two hours at the clinic. Spent half an hour with a young girl who was crying because her dad has threatened to kick her out. Helped her fill in some forms and arrange to see social services. All this is making me more aware, and I hope a better all-round carer.

1. What benefits do you think will come from Meena's self-directed training?
2. Who will benefit from her new experience?
3. How can training help to overcome prejudice?

> ### Doing it well
>
> ## Applying new skills and knowledge in practice
>
> - Plan out how you will adapt your practice on a day-to-day basis, adding one new aspect each day. Do this until you have covered all the aspects of the new information you have learned.
> - Discuss with your supervisor and colleagues what you have learned and how you intend to change your practice, and ask for feedback.
> - Write a checklist for yourself and check it at the end of each day.
> - Give yourself a set period of time, for example, one month, to alter or improve your practice, and review it at the end of that time.

4.1 and 4.2 Show how a learning activity and reflecting on a situation has improved your knowledge, skills and understanding

Everything you do at work is part of a process of learning. Even regular tasks are likely to be important for learning because there is always something new each time you do them. A simple task like taking someone a hot drink may result in a lesson — if, for example, you find that they tell you they do not want tea, but would prefer coffee this morning, thank you! You will have learned a valuable lesson about never making assumptions that everything will be the same.

Learning from working is also about using the huge amount of skills and experience which your colleagues and supervisor will have. Not only does this mean they will be able to pass on knowledge and advice to you, but you have the perfect opportunity to discuss ideas and talk about day-to-day practice in the service you are delivering.

Finding time to discuss work with colleagues is never easy; everyone is busy and you may feel that you should not make demands on their time.

Most supervision will take place at scheduled times but you may also be able to discuss issues in the course of hand-over meetings or team meetings, and other day-to-day activities. Use supervision time or quiet periods to discuss situations which have arisen, problems you have come across or new approaches you have noticed other colleagues using.

Using your mistakes

Everyone makes mistakes — they are one way of learning. It is important not to waste your mistakes, so if something has gone wrong, make sure you learn from it. Discuss problems and mistakes with your supervisor, and work out how to do things differently next time. You can use reflective skills in order to learn from situations which have not worked out the way you planned.

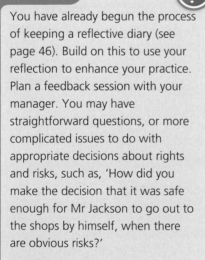

Reflect

You have already begun the process of keeping a reflective diary (see page 46). Build on this to use your reflection to enhance your practice. Plan a feedback session with your manager. You may have straightforward questions, or more complicated issues to do with appropriate decisions about rights and risks, such as, 'How did you make the decision that it was safe enough for Mr Jackson to go out to the shops by himself, when there are obvious risks?'

Try discussing such issues with different experienced colleagues – you may be surprised at what you learn.

It is important that you consider carefully why things turned out the way they did and think about how you will ensure that they go according to plan next time. There are real people on the receiving end of our mistakes in care, and learning how not to make them again is vitally important.

Using your successes

Talking to colleagues and supervisors is equally useful when things work out really well. It is just as important to reflect on why something worked, so that you can repeat it.

Personal and professional development

Personal development is to do with developing the personal qualities and skills that everyone needs in order to live and work with others, such as understanding, empathy, patience, communication and relationship-building. It is also to do with the development of self-confidence, self-esteem and self-respect.

If you look back on how you have changed over the past five years, you are likely to find that you are different in quite a few ways. Most people change as they mature and gain more life experience. Important experiences such as changing jobs, moving home, illness or bereavement can change people.

Professional development is to do with developing the qualities and skills that are necessary for the workplace. Examples are teamwork, the ability to communicate with different types of people, time management, organisation, problem solving, decision making and, of course, the skills specific to the job.

Continuing professional development involves regularly updating the skills you need for work. You can achieve this through attending training sessions both on and off the job, and by making the most of the opportunities you have for training by careful planning and preparation.

It is inevitable that your personal development and your professional development are linked — your personality and the way you relate to others are the major tools you use to do your job. Taking advantage of every opportunity to train and develop your working skills will also have an impact on you as a person.

How to get the best out of training

Your supervisor will work with you to decide on the types of training that will benefit you most. This will depend on the stage you have reached with your skills and experience. There would be little point, for example, in doing a course in advanced micro-surgery techniques if you were at the stage of having just achieved your First Aid certificate! It may be that not all the training you want to do is appropriate for the work you are currently assigned to — you may think that a course in advanced therapeutic activities sounds

Key terms

Personal development – developing the personal qualities and skills needed to live and work with others

Professional development – developing the qualities and skills necessary for the workforce

fascinating, but your supervisor may suggest that a course in basic moving and handling is what you need right now. You will only get the best out of training and development opportunities if they are the right ones for you at the time. There will be opportunities for training throughout your career, and it is important that you work out which training is going to help you achieve your goals.

Can you think about the different types of training you have attended?

Case study

Choosing appropriate training

Michelle is a healthcare support worker in a large hospital, on a busy ward. She was very aware of the fact that she lacked assertiveness in the way she dealt with both her colleagues and with many of the people she supported. Michelle was always the one who agreed to run errands and to cover additional tasks that others should have been doing. She knew that she ought to be able to say 'no', but somehow she could not, and then became angry and resentful because she felt she was doing far more work than many others on her team.

Her supervisor raised the issue during a supervision session and suggested that Michelle should consider attending assertiveness training. Although initially reluctant, Michelle decided to take the opportunity. After six weeks of attending classes and working with the supportive group she met there, Michelle found that she was able to deal far more effectively with unfair and unreasonable requests from her colleagues and to deal in a firm but pleasant way with the people she supported.

1. What difference is Michelle's training likely to make:
   a) to the people she supports
   b) to herself?
2. Have you ever said 'yes' to extra work or additional responsibility when you wanted to say 'no'? How did this make you feel?
3. What could you have done about it?

Doing it well

Training

Make the most of training by:

- preparing well
- taking a full part in the training and asking questions about anything you do not understand
- collecting any handouts and keeping your own notes of the training.

How to use training and development

You should work with your supervisor to prepare for any training you receive, and to review it afterwards. You may want to prepare for a training session by:

- reading any materials which have been provided in advance
- talking to your supervisor or a colleague who has attended similar training, about what to expect
- thinking about what you want to achieve as a result of attending the training.

Think about how to apply what you have learned to your work by discussing the training with your supervisor later. Review the ways in which you have benefited from the training.

Reflect

Think about the last training or development session you took part in and write a short report.

1. Describe the preparations you made beforehand so that you could benefit fully from it.
2. Describe what you did at the session. For example, what and how did you contribute, and what did you learn? Do you have a certificate to show that you participated in the session? Do you have a set of notes?
3. How did you follow up the session? Did you review the goals you had set yourself, or discuss the session with your supervisor?
4. Describe how you have used what you learned at the session. For example, how has the way you work changed, and how have the people you support and your colleagues benefited from your learning?

4.3 Showing how feedback from others has developed your knowledge, skills and understanding

You will also need to be prepared to receive feedback from your supervisor. While feedback is likely to be given in a positive way, this does not mean that it will be uncritical. Many people have considerable difficulty in accepting criticism in any form, even where it is intended to be supportive and constructive. If you are aware that you are likely to have difficulty accepting criticism, try to prepare yourself to view feedback from your supervisor as valuable and useful information that can add to your ability to reflect effectively on the work you are doing.

Your response to negative feedback should not be to defend your actions or to reject the feedback. You must try to accept and value it. A useful reply would be: 'Thank you, that's very helpful. I can use

Activity 7

Constructive criticism

Ask a colleague, or if you do not feel able to do that, ask a friend or family member, to offer some constructive criticism on a task you have undertaken – a practical activity such as cooking a meal, or work you have undertaken in the garden or in the house, would be suitable.

If you are able to practise receiving feedback on something that is relatively unthreatening, you are likely to be able to use the same techniques when considering feedback on your working practices.

that next time to improve.' If you are able to achieve this, you are likely to be able to make the maximum use of opportunities to improve your practice.

On the other hand, if criticism of any kind undermines your confidence and makes it difficult for you to value your own strengths, you should ask your supervisor to identify areas in which you did well, and use the positive to help you respond more constructively to the negative feedback.

4.4 Show how to record progress in relation to personal development

When you have identified the areas in which you feel competent and chosen your target areas for development, you will need to design a personal development log which will enable you to keep a record of your progress. This can be put together in any way that you find effective.

In your plan, you may wish to include things as varied as learning sign language, learning a particular technique for working with people with dementia, or developing your potential as a future manager by learning organisational and human resources skills. You could also include areas such as time management and stress management. All of these are legitimate areas for inclusion in your personal and professional development plan.

Getting ready for assessment

LO1

This unit is all about how you develop your skills and knowledge and improve your own practice, but for this outcome you need to show that you understand what you need to do in order to be a competent care and support worker. You may be asked to prepare a presentation or an assignment that will demonstrate to your assessor that you know how competence is judged and that standards that are used as the basis for deciding competence. You will not be expected to know the National Occupational Standards off by heart! But you will need to show that you know how they influence qualifications and form a basis for assessing competence.

LO2–4

These outcomes will be assessed as you demonstrate that you can do the essentials of personal development. You will have to show your assessor that you can reflect on your work – this may be through keeping a reflective journal for a period of time. If you do this, you will need

to write your views about the work you have done and to show that you can think about what went well and what went badly, and suggest some reasons for this. Alternatively, your assessor may ask you questions about the work you have been doing and you will need to be able to talk about your work and your thoughts about areas that are going well and areas for improvement.

Your own personal development plan will show your assessor that you understand how to prepare one and how to maintain it and keep it up to date. Your assessor will want to see it, whether it is paper based or kept electronically. You need to be able to show that you are able to develop and improve your practice; this will mean providing evidence that you have attended training and that you are making use of supervision and the learning opportunities in your own workplace. You will also have to provide your assessor with evidence, either through witness testimony or through questioning of how your practice has changed as a result of new learning and skill development.

Further reading and research

The introduction to this section highlights your duty to make sure that the service provided is the best it can possibly be. In order to do this it is essential that you are constantly reflecting on your practice and striving to develop the way you work. Here are some suggestions of further reading and research to help you to do this.

- www.gscc.org.uk (General Social Care Council (GSCC) – training and learning)
- www.dh.gov.uk (Department of Health – human resources and training)
- www.skillsforcare.org.uk (Skills for Care – workforce development for UK social care sector)
- www.skillsforhealth.org.uk (Skills for Health – workforce development for UK health sector)
- www.cwdcouncil.org (Children's Workforce Development Council)
- www.scie.org.uk (Social Care Institute for Excellence)
- Hawkins, R. and Ashurst, A. (2006) *How to be a Great Care Assistant*, Hawker Publications
- Knapman, J. and Morrison, T. (1998) *Making the Most of Supervision in Health and Social Care*, Pavilion Publishers
- Shakespeare, P. *Learning in Health and Social Care*, journal, Blackwell Publishing

Unit SHC 23

Introduction to equality and inclusion in health, social care or children's and young people's settings

This is a core unit that is common to several qualifications in related areas of work, both in adult and children and young people's work. This is because ensuring that people are treated equally and that people are not left out is vitally important if support and services are to be provided fairly to all people in need.

This unit will help you to understand how you can work in a way that makes sure that everyone is able to use support services. You will also find out about how discrimination impacts on people's lives and how to make sure that you are not letting your own prejudices influence the way you work.

In this unit you will learn about:

1. the importance of diversity, equality and inclusion
2. how to work in an inclusive way
3. how to access information, advice and support about diversity, equality and inclusion.

1. Understand the importance of diversity, equality and inclusion

1.1 What is meant by diversity

Diversity is about difference, and the value of diversity is the richness and variety that different people bring to society.

'All apples are red.' That statement is clearly silly. Of course they are not — some are green, some are yellow. When it comes to people, everyone is different. There are so many ways in which people differ from each other, including, for example:

- appearance
- gender
- race
- culture
- ability
- talent
- beliefs.

Imagine how boring life would be if everyone was exactly the same. Whole societies of identical 'cloned' people have been the central theme of many films, and it is clear immediately how unnatural that seems. However, we are not always very good at recognising and valuing the differences in the people we meet.

You can see that the statement 'all apples are red' is not right.

Different sorts of diversity

You can think about diversity in different ways. There are specific differences between people, all of the features that make each of us an individual, and there are broader differences as you can see from the list above. Both of these are important so you need to take account of each of them, and value the contributions made by different perspectives, different ways of thinking and different approaches.

Activity 1

Valuing differences

This exercise is best done with a group of colleagues, but you can also do it on your own.

1. List all the cultures and nationalities you can think of. Write them down. Next to each one, write something that the culture has given to the world. For example, the Arabs gave us mathematics, the Chinese developed some wonderful medicines, and so on.
2. Next, think about the groups of people you support. Note down the special angle of understanding each group can bring to society. For instance, someone who is visually impaired will always judge people on how they behave, not on how they look. Older people can often bring a different perspective to a situation based on years of experience and understanding. It is worth making some notes on each of the ideas you have. You may need to do some research and may find some fascinating information in the process.
3. When you have done this, be honest with yourself about whether you have really appreciated and valued the differences in both individuals and cultures. How do you think your practice could be different because of thinking about diversity?

Key term

Discrimination – treatment of one group or person in a less or more favourable way than another on the basis of race, ethnicity, gender, sexuality, age or other prejudice

Reflect

The London Marathon has a separate wheelchair event. It would not be possible for disabled competitors to race among the huge numbers of runners, but over the same course the wheelchair athletes are actually faster than the able-bodied runners. It is just a question of getting to the appropriate starting line, by recognising that people who use a wheelchair are not going to be able to run, but if they compete in their wheelchairs, then they can have a fair chance.

1.2 What is meant by discrimination

Discrimination is the result of unequal or excluding behaviour. It describes the disadvantage that people experience because of being unfairly treated or being excluded from society. People can be refused access to society, services, employment or education because of discrimination. Racial discrimination has some very famous examples such as the apartheid regime in South Africa and the segregation laws in the southern states of America.

Can you see how this race makes these wheelchair competitors more equal?

Discrimination on the basis of disability can be found in many places where disabled people have no access or are required to use a different entrance to non-disabled people. Education can often be difficult to access because the necessary support may not be available. Employers may also be reluctant to employ people with a disability because they are not prepared to make the adjustments necessary to enable someone to work.

Gender discrimination is still evident. Although the situation has improved considerably in the past 10 years, women's earnings are still around 20 per cent less than men's (source: Annual Survey of Hours and Earnings 2009) and there are still fewer women in senior positions. For example, out of 650 Members of Parliament, only 143 were women following the 2010 election. A report from the World Economic Forum looking at 600 companies across 20 countries showed that fewer than 5 per cent had women chief executives (source: World Economic Forum Gender Gap Report 2010). Out of the top 100 companies in the UK, only 12 per cent of board members were women. In the public sector, women make up 65 per cent of the workforce, but only 30 per cent of senior management and 21 per cent of Chief Executives (source: Local Government Association 2009).

It is easy to apply the same principles to a job. Someone who has impaired vision or is in a wheelchair can do a job just as well, or perhaps better, than someone who is able-bodied, provided they are allowed the opportunity. That means removing physical barriers such as steps or narrow doorways, and installing equipment that allows someone with impaired vision to 'read' documents.

1.3 Ways in which discrimination may deliberately or inadvertently occur in the work setting

Generalisations and stereotypes

It is often easy to make broad, sweeping statements that you believe apply to everyone who belongs to a particular group. It is the exact opposite of valuing diversity, by saying that everyone is the same. This is the basis of prejudice and discrimination, and you need to be sure that you are not guilty of making generalisations and thinking about people in stereotypes. People are often discriminated against because of their race, beliefs, gender, religion, sexuality or age. Treating everyone the same will result in discrimination because some people will have their needs met and others will not. In order to prevent discrimination, it is important to value diversity and treat people differently in order to meet their different needs.

Direct discrimination is, for example, where someone is refused a job because they use a wheelchair. Indirect discrimination would be where they are told they can have the job but the work must be carried out on the first floor and there is no lift.

Activity 2

Generalisations

Complete the following sentences.

- Police officers are…
- Teenagers are…
- Nurses are…
- Politicians never…
- West Indians are all…
- Asians always…
- Men all…
- Women are…
- Americans are…

You can probably think of plenty of statements that you make as generalisations about others. Think about how easy you found it to come up with statements for each of the examples. How do you think these generalisations could affect the way you work?

Key term

Stereotyping – making negative or positive judgements about whole groups of people based on prejudice and assumptions, rather than facts or knowledge about a person as an individual

Stereotypes

One of the main causes of discrimination is the fear and lack of understanding of others that is spread because of **stereotyping**. Prejudice is what makes people think in stereotypes and, equally, stereotypes support prejudice. Stereotypes are an easy way of thinking about the world. Stereotypes might suggest that all people over 65 are frail and walk with a stick, that all black young people who live in inner cities are on drugs, that all Muslims are terrorists, or that all families have a mother, father and two children. These stereotypes are often reinforced by the media or by advertising. Television programmes will often portray violent, criminal characters as young and black, and older people are usually shown as being dependent and unable to make a useful contribution to society.

Activity 3

Stereotyping in adverts

Next time you watch television, note down the number of adverts for cars that show trendy, good-looking young business people with a wealthy lifestyle. The advertisers attempt to convince us into believing that buying a particular brand of car will make us good-looking and trendy, and give us the kind of lifestyle portrayed.

1. How many people do you know with those particular makes of car that are anything like the people in the adverts?
2. How many do you know who wish they were?

What effect do stereotypes have?

The effect of stereotypes is to make you jump to conclusions about people. How many times have you felt uneasy seeing a young man with a shaved head walking towards you? You know nothing about him, but the way he looks has made you form an opinion about him. If you have a picture in your mind of a social worker or someone in the police force, think about how much the media influences that — do they really all look like that?

What do you instantly think about these people, just from looking at pictures of them?

Labelling

Labelling is slightly more complex than stereotyping, and happens when someone thinks the factor which people have in common is more important than the hundreds of factors which make them different.

For example, the remark 'We should organise a concert for older people' makes an assumption that being older is what is important about the people concerned, and that somehow as you grow older your tastes become the same as all other people your age! It would be much better to say, for example, 'We should organise a concert for older people who like music from the shows' or 'We should organise a concert for older people who like opera.'

It's not funny

'Have you heard the one about...?'

Telling jokes at the expense of particular groups of people is just displaying prejudices. If someone has stereotypes about people being mean, stupid or dangerous because of their nationality, they fail to treat people as individuals and fail to recognise that there are individuals everywhere and that all people are different. Of course, some people will be just as the stereotype portrays them — but a lot more will not be. Avoiding stereotypes and the discrimination that they promote is essential if you want to succeed in social care.

Reflect

Stop yourself every time you make a generalisation and look at the prejudice that is behind it. Reflect on why you think the way you do, and do something about it. The next time you hear yourself saying, for example, 'Social workers never understand what is really needed', 'GPs always take ages to visit' or 'People who live here wouldn't be interested in that', stop and think what you are really doing.

It may be true in some cases, but not necessarily all.

Perhaps most of the people you support would not be interested in something you suggested, but some might. You cannot make that assumption. You need to ask. You need to offer people choices because they are all different. Do not fall into the trap of stereotyping people based on factors such as gender, age, race, culture, dress or where they live.

1.4 How promoting equality and inclusion reduces the likelihood of discrimination

Avoiding stereotypes at work

It is a key part of your job to find out the personal beliefs and values of each person you support. Think about all the aspects of their lives, such as:

- diet
- clothing
- personal hygiene
- worship
- language
- relationships with others.

It is your responsibility to find out — not for the person to have to tell you. It will be helpful for you, and for other support workers, if this type of information is kept in the personal record.

Poverty and inequality

On a worldwide scale, poverty is defined by the World Health Organization as living on less than US$1 a day. There is little doubt that in many undeveloped countries, there are millions of people who suffer great hardship and live in very real poverty. This is 'absolute poverty'. In a society such as ours in the Western world, poverty takes on a different meaning and in the UK it is 'relative poverty', which means that people are poorer than the majority of society.

People living in poverty are far more likely to experience the conditions which will lead to ill health and a greater need for the health and care services than those in higher social groupings who are likely to live in better conditions. Some of the most obvious effects of poverty are poor housing, a poor diet, the likelihood of living in a poor area or neighbourhood with poor-quality local facilities. Socio-economic factors are a major cause of inequality, for example:

- infant and childhood death rates are significantly higher among children whose families have low incomes
- children from poorer families are four times more likely to die in accidents as those from families with higher incomes
- children in poverty have poorer attendance records at school and are less likely to continue into further education
- the highest incidents of mental health problems occur among people who live in poverty
- nutrition and eating habits show that poorer people tend to eat less fruit and vegetables and less food which contains dietary fibre. There is evidence that the diets of poorer families tend to lack choice and variety and often contain inappropriate foods such as crisps, sweets and soft drinks
- only 44 per cent of babies born to mothers with low incomes are breast fed, compared with 81 per cent of babies born to mothers in higher-income families.

Poverty is not the only cause of inequality; it can also result from issues around race, gender or disability. For example, there is a much higher incidence of coronary heart disease and diabetes among the Asian population of the UK where the death rate from heart disease can be up to twice as high as that of the general population. There also seems to a link between race and educational achievement. Government figures show that Chinese and Indian students are more than twice as likely to obtain five or more passes at GCSE than those from African-Caribbean or black African ethnic backgrounds (source: Office of National Statistics 2007).

Gender, disability and age can also be causes of inequality. This can be made significantly worse by the effects of poverty – very large numbers of older people live on very low incomes. Over 30 per cent of pensioners entitled to higher levels of income through income support do not claim it and as a result have a lifestyle of severe deprivation.

Poverty and deprivation are among the underlying causes of inequality in the UK. This is then reinforced by attitudes such as racism, sexism and discrimination against people with disabilities. If such attitudes go unchallenged, then inequality will continue.

Anti-discriminatory practice

Anti-discriminatory practice is what underpins the social care practice. For you to carry out your practice in an anti-discriminatory way, much of what you do in your day-to-day work must be based on anti-discriminatory practice. You are likely to find that you have come across these ideas before, but perhaps not in these terms or in this context. You will need to understand the terms because you will hear them used regularly and they have important implications for your practice.

Activity 4

Anti-discriminatory practice

Find an example of each of the aspects of practice given in Table 1 (next page). The examples can be from work, from other parts of your life or from fiction. For each example, look at how you could work in a way that is anti-discriminatory.

Your day-to-day practice and attitudes are important in how effective your anti-discriminatory practice will be. There is little point in supporting someone to challenge stereotyping and then returning to your own work setting ready to organise all the 'ladies' for a sewing afternoon!

Term	Description
Stereotyping	This is when whole groups of people are assumed to be the same — for example, 'these sort of people', 'old people love a sing-song' or 'black people are good athletes'.
Discrimination	This is the process of treating people less favourably based on a feature of themselves over which they have no control. Disabled people find it hard to get a job because employers are reluctant to take them on; research has shown that people with Asian names or from certain areas are told that job vacancies have been filled even though they have not; and women still do 90 per cent of the world's work, earn 10 per cent of the world's income and own 1 per cent of the world's wealth.
Anti-discrimination	This is about positively working to eliminate discrimination. It is about more than being against discrimination, you must ensure through your practice that you protect people from discrimination by identifying it and taking steps to eliminate or minimise it wherever you can.
Oppression	This is the experience which results from being discriminated against. People who are oppressed are being prevented from receiving equal treatment and exercising their rights. They often lose self-belief and self-confidence, and find it difficult to see a way out from the oppression.
Anti-oppression	This is about the practical steps you can take to counteract oppression. You will need to make sure that people have all the information and support they need to know what rights they have and how to exercise them. This may mean finding out about what they are entitled to and the ways in which they can be helped, setting up appointments for them and providing written information; it can also mean offering emotional support. It also means recognising when people are being oppressed and denied their rights, either by another person or by an organisation and working to challenge this, or supporting the person to challenge it for themselves.

Table 1: Terms related to anti-discriminatory practice.

Case study

Understanding different attitudes

Tai is in her mid-30s and has a busy job in an international finance company. She is from a Chinese family who have lived in a large city and run a restaurant for the past 40 years. Her parents have now retired from the restaurant and have both suffered from ill health in the past year. They are too frail to continue caring for themselves without support. Tai's brothers are busy running the family business and Tai has decided to stop working in order to care for her parents. Her English friends and work colleagues are horrified that she is prepared to give up such a good career to do this. The local social services department has offered to provide domiciliary care for Tai's parents, but the family have refused, explaining that it will not be necessary. Tai is having difficulty making her non-Chinese friends, colleagues and even social services understand her view that she is willing to do this for her parents and that their welfare is a greater priority than her career.

1. Can you see where the key differences are between the attitude of Tai and the attitudes of many non-Chinese families?
2. Would you encourage Tai to give up her job? Why?
3. How are the attitudes of her friends discriminatory?
4. How do you think they may make Tai feel?
5. What should the role of social services be in this situation?

Functional skills

English: Writing

Answer the case study questions in a clear and concise manner using an appropriate format. Present all your written work in a logical sequence using language that is fit for purpose. As you complete each question, check your written work for accuracy of spelling, punctuation and grammar.

Definitions of inclusive practice are varied, but broadly, it is about ensuring that there are no barriers that would exclude people, or make it difficult for them to participate fully in society, because of an illness or a disability. Traditionally, we have developed separate worlds in order to meet people's needs — for example, separate workshops, education groups, living accommodation for people with mental health needs or any type of disability have kept people out of mainstream society. Older people have been separated with clubs, day centres and residential accommodation on the assumption that separate is best — but increasingly, we have come to see that separate is not equal, and we should have an inclusive society that everyone can enjoy.

Now, we ask a different question about how we organise society. We do not ask, 'What is wrong with this person that means they cannot use the leisure centre or the cinema?' but, 'What is wrong with the cinema or the leisure centre if people with disabilities cannot use it?'

Inclusive practice is about providing the support that people want in order to live their lives as fully as possible. Examples of inclusive practice are:

- providing a ramp to give wheelchair access to a building
- providing information in a range of languages and in audio format.

Ensuring that systems and processes for obtaining support are easy to use and access allows people to work out the support they need and find the best way to put it in place.

Overall, practising in an inclusive way means constantly asking, 'What changes need to happen so that this person can participate?' and then doing whatever is within your area of responsibility to make those changes happen.

2. Be able to work in an inclusive way

2.1 Legislation, codes of practice and policies and procedures relating to equality, diversity, discrimination and rights

Discrimination is a denial of rights. Discrimination can be based on issues such as race, gender, disability or sexual orientation. The main Acts of Parliament and Regulations relating to equality and human rights in England, Scotland and Wales (Northern Ireland has its own equality legislation) were the:

- Equal Pay Act 1970
- Sex Discrimination Act 1975
- Race Relations Act 1976

- Disability Discrimination Acts 1995 and 2005
- Special Educational Needs and Disability Act 2001
- Employment Equality (Religion or Belief) and (Sexual Orientation) Regulations 2003
- Employment Equality (Age) Regulations 2006
- Racial and Religious Hatred Act 2006
- Equality Act 2006.

All of these Acts and Regulations have been superseded by a single Equality Act that came into force on 1 October 2010. The Equality Act 2010 covers all the present pieces of legislation and includes requirements on public bodies to consider how to deal with inequalities in health, education, employment and achievement.

The Equality Act 2010 provides a new Act to protect the rights of people and equality of opportunity. It makes the legislation simpler as there is now just one Act. Broadly, the Act covers:

- the basic framework of protection against direct and indirect discrimination, harassment and victimisation in services and public functions, premises, work, education, associations and transport
- changing the definition of gender reassignment, by removing the requirement for medical supervision
- levelling up protection for people discriminated against because they are perceived to have, or are associated with someone who has, a protected characteristic, so providing new protection for people like carers
- clearer protection for breastfeeding mothers
- applying the European definition of indirect discrimination to all protected characteristics
- extending protection from indirect discrimination to disability
- introducing a new concept of 'discrimination arising from disability', to replace protection under previous legislation lost as a result of a legal judgement
- applying the detriment model to victimisation protection (aligning with the approach in employment law)
- harmonising the thresholds for the duty to make reasonable adjustments for disabled people
- extending protection from third-party harassment to all protected characteristics
- making it more difficult for disabled people to be unfairly screened out when applying for jobs, by restricting the circumstances in which employers can ask job applicants questions about disability or health
- allowing hypothetical comparators for direct gender pay discrimination
- making pay secrecy clauses unenforceable
- extending protection in private clubs to sex, religion or belief, pregnancy and maternity, and gender reassignment

Doing it well

Providing support for rights

- Hold regular staff meetings and have a regular item on your agenda about rights.
- Ensure that people are fully aware of complaints procedures and know how to follow them.
- Make sure that you know your organisation's policies and guidelines designed to protect and promote people's rights.
- Ensure that you share with your colleagues any information that relates to people's choices, preferences and rights.
- Make sure that you discuss choices and preferences with people.
- Support people to maintain independence together with other rights if necessary.
- Never participate in or encourage discriminatory behaviour.

- introducing new powers for employment tribunals to make recommendations which benefit the wider workforce
- harmonising provisions allowing voluntary positive action.

2.2 Interaction with individuals that respects their beliefs, culture, values and preferences

You also need to support your colleagues to work in ways that recognise and respect people's beliefs and preferences. Your work setting should be a place in which diversity and difference are acknowledged and respected. You need to set a good example and to make it clear that behaviour such as the following is unacceptable:

- speaking about people in a derogatory way
- speaking to people in a rude or dismissive way
- undermining people's self-esteem and confidence
- patronising and talking down to people
- removing people's right to exercise choice
- failing to recognise and treat people as individuals
- not respecting people's culture, values and beliefs.

If you find that you have colleagues who are regularly practising in a discriminatory way, you need to seek advice from your manager or supervisor.

How to recognise your own prejudices

One of the hardest things to do is to acknowledge your own prejudices and how they affect what you do. Prejudices are a result of your own beliefs and values, and may often come into conflict with work situations. There is nothing wrong with having your own beliefs and values – everyone has them, and they are a vital part of making you the person you are. But you must be aware of them, and how they may affect what you do at work.

Think about the basic principles that apply in your life. Here are some examples.

- You may have a basic belief that people should always be honest. Then think about what that could mean for the way you work – might you find it hard to be pleasant to someone who you found had lied extensively?
- You may believe that abortion is wrong. Could you deal sympathetically with a woman who had had an abortion?
- You may have been brought up to take great care of disabled people and believe that they should be looked after and protected. How would you cope in an environment that encouraged disabled people to take risks and promoted their independence?

Activity 5

Values

1. Make a list of the things you believe in as values, such as honesty, caring about others and so on. Then make a second list of how they could affect your work.
2. Examine whether they do affect your work – you may need the views of a trusted colleague or your supervisor to help you with this.

This activity is very hard, and it will take a long time to do. It is often better done over a period of time. As you become more aware of your own actions, you will notice how they have the potential to affect your work.

Recording the results of this activity over a period of time may be useful when you are being assessed on this unit.

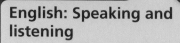
Exploring your own behaviour is never easy, and you need good support from either your supervisor or close friends to do it. You may be upset by what you find out about some of your attitudes, but knowing about them and acknowledging them is the first step to doing something about them.

As a support worker, it will be easier to make sure that you are practising effectively if you are confident that you have looked at your own practice and the attitudes that underpin it. Remember that you can ask for feedback from people you support and colleagues too, not only from your supervisor.

Beliefs and values of others

Once you are aware of your own beliefs and values, and have recognised how important they are, you must think about how to accept the beliefs and values of others. The people you work with are all different, so it is important to recognise and accept that diversity.

Respect for different people

If you are going to make sure you always respond to people in a respectful way which ensures they are valued, you need to understand what happens when people are not valued or respected. It is also important that you recognise the ways in which good practice helps to protect people from discrimination and exclusion.

Case study

Dealing with prejudice

Garth is a care worker in a residential setting for adults with disabilities. He is gay but had never discussed his sexual orientation at work and it was not mentioned at the time of his appointment. His sexual orientation only became known when the parents of one of the residents spotted him in a photograph of a gay pride event printed in a national newspaper.

Garth had always been a popular member of staff and had an excellent work record, with appraisals which showed that his skills and abilities were developing and progressing. However, following the discovery that he was gay, the atmosphere in the setting began to change. Two of the residents complained about being cared for by someone who was gay and said they were not prepared to have Garth provide them with any

personal care. Both of these residents were young men in their late 20s and their action was supported by their parents. Comments and jokes at Garth's expense began to circulate within the setting, particularly when he was on duty.

Garth felt that he was being unfairly discriminated against and intended to obtain the support of his trade union.

1. What are Garth's rights in this situation? Consider the Employment Equality (Sexual Orientation) Regulations.
2. What are the rights of the residents in this sort of situation? How do rights and responsibilities balance here?
3. How could this be approached by management?

People should make choices about how they want to live their lives. For some people, choices may be about things like how they will spend their Direct Payments or Individual Budget and the people they will choose to employ. For others, choices may be more limited as in some of the suggestions in Table 2. The ability to make choices of any sort is an important part of exercising rights and being valued.

Functional skills

English: Reading

Read through the case study on the previous page carefully to extract the information you need to answer the set questions. Extend your knowledge of different texts by finding a copy of the Employment Equality Regulations and using information from it to expand on your answers. By doing this you will develop your skills of extracting relevant information from a variety of texts and using it for a purpose. If you need clarification of words, use a dictionary or talk to others to find your answers.

Support service	Choices
Personal hygiene	• Bath, shower or bed bath • Assistance or no assistance • Morning, afternoon or evening • Temperature of water • Toiletries
Food	• Menu • Dining table or tray • Timing • Assistance • In company or alone

Table 2: Examples of choices available in support services.

Doing it well

Valuing diversity

- The wide range of different beliefs and values that you will come across are examples of the rich and diverse cultures of all parts of the world.
- Value each person as an individual. The best way to appreciate what others have to offer is to find out about them. Ask questions. People will usually be happy to tell you about themselves and their beliefs.
- Be open to hearing what others have to say – do not be so sure that your values and beliefs and the way you live are the only ways of doing things.

- Think about the assets which have come to the UK from people moving here from other cultures, including music, food and entertainment, and different approaches to work, relaxation or medicine.
- Think about language. The words and expressions you use are important. Avoid using language that might suggest assumptions, stereotypes or discrimination about groups (see Table 3).

Area	Examples of negative language
Disability	Some words such as 'handicapped' can suggest the discriminatory assumption that disabled people are damaged versions of 'normal' people. In general, people prefer to be called 'disabled people' rather then 'people with a disability'. The term 'disabled people' is used to show that people are disabled by the environment and the society in which they live and by the barriers that prevent them from participating.
Race	Some words and phrases may be linked to the discriminatory idea that certain ethnic groups (white groups) are superior to others. For example, the 'play the white man' means to play fair, and there are words that are associated with slavery in the past.
Age	Some words and phrases make fun of older people. Do not address an older person as 'pop' or 'granddad' unless you are invited to do so. Terms such as 'wrinklies' or 'crumblies' are offensive.
Gender	Some words and phrases are perceived as implying that women have a lower social status than men. Addressing women as 'dear', 'petal' or 'flower' may be understood as patronising or insulting. There is also the instance of always referring to people in high status roles as 'he' – often heard when talking about doctors or lawyers.
Sexuality	Gay and lesbian people often object to being catalogued using the biological terminology of 'heterosexual' and 'homosexual'. Use the terminology that people would apply to themselves.

Table 3: Language that might suggest assumptions, stereotypes or discrimination.

As we have seen, promoting equality and rights is supported by the practical steps you can take in day-to-day working activities to give people more choice and more opportunities to take decisions about their own lives. Much of this will depend on your work setting and the particular needs of the people you support. Respecting people and valuing them as individuals is always going to be an important factor in promoting self-esteem and therefore well-being.

2.3 How to challenge discrimination in a way that promotes change

There may be occasions when you have identified a person's rights and given them access to the information needed. However, they may not be able to exercise those rights effectively. There can be many reasons why people miss out on their rights, including:

- their rights may be infringed by someone else
- there may be physical barriers
- there may be communication barriers
- there may be emotional barriers.

Advocates

When you need to support people to maintain a right to choice, control and independence, it may be important to involve an outside advocate. An **advocate** is someone who argues a case for another person. They try to understand a person's perspective and argue on their behalf. Your organisation may have procedures and advice to assist you in gaining the services of people who will act as advocates for people.

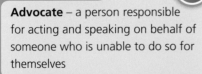

Key term

Advocate – a person responsible for acting and speaking on behalf of someone who is unable to do so for themselves

Case study

The right to make choices

Mrs Sullivan lives alone on just her state pension. She has never claimed any pension credit, although there is no doubt she would be entitled to it. She struggles to survive on her pension and, by the time she has paid all her bills and fed the cat, there is little left for herself. She eats very little and is reluctant to turn the heating on. Despite being given all the relevant information by her home care assistant, Mrs Sullivan will not claim any further benefits. She always says, 'I shall be fine. There are others worse off than me – let it go to those who need it.'

1. What are Mrs Sullivan's rights?
2. Should action be taken on her behalf?
3. Would the situation be different if she had a son or daughter with a learning disability who lived with her? Would her rights and responsibilities still be the same?
4. What would your responsibilities be if you were a support worker for Mrs Sullivan?

You may also need to defend people's rights in a more informal way during your normal work. For example, people have a right to privacy, and you may need to act to deal with someone who constantly infringes upon that by discussing other people's circumstances in public. You will have to balance the rights of one person against another, and decide whose rights are being infringed. You may decide that a right to privacy is more important than a right to free speech.

Overall, the key to **active participation** is ensuring that you:

- do as much as possible to support only the parts of people's lives that they really cannot manage for themselves
- provide support that will encourage them to take control and make decisions that enable the maximum possible participation in every aspect of their lives.

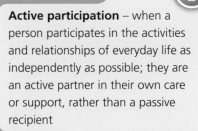

Key term

Active participation – when a person participates in the activities and relationships of everyday life as independently as possible; they are an active partner in their own care or support, rather than a passive recipient

Reflect

A person's right to rest may be infringed by someone who shouts all night. How would you balance the rights of one person not to be disturbed against the rights of another not to be given medication that only benefits others?

Doing it well

Reducing discrimination

Think about language. The words and expressions you use are important.

- Do not use words that degrade people with problems or disabilities, for example, words that are used as an insult such as 'spaz' or 'crip'.
- Avoid language that is racist or could cause offence, and think about expressions such as 'play the white man' that suggests that white people are somehow superior.
- Older people should not be referred to as 'grannies' or 'wrinklies'. It is not acceptable to call an older person 'pop' or 'grandad' unless you are invited to do so.
- Avoid using offensive terms to describe sexual orientation. Always try to find out the terms which people find acceptable.
- There are many words and expressions that help to reinforce discrimination against women. Think before using 'like a fishwife' or 'he's a right old woman'.

Encourage people you support to take part in society fully and achieve their full potential.

- Do not assume that older people are only capable of quiet activities that do not involve too much excitement.
- Avoid the temptation to overprotect and thus encourage dependence.
- Support people to challenge barriers that stand in their way.
- If you work with people with disabilities, try to think of ways you can show employers what people are capable of achieving.
- Try to work with the local community. If you work in a facility that is surrounded by neighbours, make sure that they get to know both the people being supported and staff. Knowledge removes the fear that lies behind prejudice.
- Encourage people to behave assertively and to develop confidence in their own abilities.
- Refuse to accept behaviour that you know is discriminatory.
- Do not participate in racist or sexist jokes and explain that you are not amused by 'sick' jokes about people with disabilities or problems.
- If you are uncertain what to do in a particular situation, discuss the problem with your supervisor.

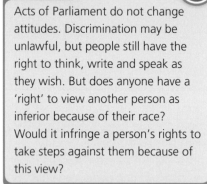

Reflect

Acts of Parliament do not change attitudes. Discrimination may be unlawful, but people still have the right to think, write and speak as they wish. But does anyone have a 'right' to view another person as inferior because of their race? Would it infringe a person's rights to take steps against them because of this view?

3. Be able to access information, advice and support about diversity, equality and inclusion

3.1 and 3.2 Situations in which additional information, advice and support may be needed, and how and when to access it

Your workplace will have policies and information about diversity and equality; there will be an inclusion policy. This is always a good starting point if you need to find out more information. Your supervisor will also be able to provide you with advice and signpost you to further information if there is something you are unsure about.

The Equality and Human Rights Commission (www. equalityhumanrights.com) has a statutory remit to promote and monitor human rights; and to protect, enforce and promote equality across the seven 'protected' grounds:

1. age
2. disability
3. gender
4. race
5. religion and belief
6. sexual orientation
7. gender reassignment.

They are able to provide a wide range of resources, advice and guidance about all areas of equality and rights. They produce guidance documents about legislation, particularly the Equality Act 2010, and you can download these from the website above or request a hard copy.

There are likely to be local sources of information such as the Citizens Advice Bureau, Welfare Rights or Law Centres. Local libraries also have plenty of information available both online and in hard copy.

If you need to talk to someone and your supervisor cannot help, then your trade union is likely to have an equalities officer who will have current knowledge about how to handle equality issues.

Knowing where to go and whom to ask when you need information and advice is important. If you are unsure or have tried a few places without success, do not give up. You owe it the people you support to develop your knowledge and understanding so that you can pass on advice and encourage people to insist on being treated equally and to be able to access their rights.

Doing it well

Respecting diversity

- Remember that stereotypes can influence how you think about someone.
- Do not rush to make judgements about people.
- Do not make assumptions.
- Everyone is entitled to their own beliefs and culture. If you do not know about somebody's way if life – ask.

Getting ready for assessment

LO1 and LO3

These outcomes will require you to show your assessor that you understand why equality, diversity and inclusion are important. This could be through a presentation or an assignment, or your assessor may undertake a professional discussion with you. You will need to show that you understand the consequences of discrimination for people who experience it. You are also likely to have to show your assessor that you know about the laws around equality, diversity and inclusion, and how people can access support and information about their rights.

LO2

Your work will be observed for this outcome, probably at the same time as observations for other units, and you will need to show that you understand how to work in an inclusive way. This will mean showing that you always deal with people as individuals and do not make assumptions based on stereotypes. Asking people about personal preferences and making sure that plans are person-centred will be an important part of showing that you work inclusively.

Legislation

- Disability Discrimination Acts 1995 and 2005
- Employment Equality (Age) Regulations 2006
- Employment Equality (Religion or Belief) and (Sexual Orientation) Regulations 2003
- Equal Pay Act 1970
- Equality Act 2006
- Equality Act 2010
- Race Relations Act 1976
- Racial and Religious Hatred Act 2006
- Sex Discrimination Act 1975
- Special Educational Needs and Disability Act 2001

Further reading and research

- www.cqc.org.uk (Care Quality Commission)
- www.dh.gov.uk (Department of Health)
- www.equalities.gov.uk (Government Equalities Office)
- www.gscc.org.uk (General Social Care Council (GSCC))
- www.legislation.gov.uk (Government legislation website)
- Burgess, C., Shaw, C. and Pritchatt, N. (2007) *S/NVQ Level 2 Health and Social Care: Easy Steps*, Heinemann

Unit SHC 24

Introduction to duty of care

In this unit you will learn about how having a duty of care affects all your work and is the basis for being a professional care and support worker. Your duty of care does not mean that you should make all the decisions for people. On the contrary, your duty of care involves being able to balance people's rights to take risks and participate in life, ensuring that the risks are not placing people in danger or in harm's way.

This is a small unit, but it is important that you have a clear understanding of your duty of care and how it affects your practice.

In this unit you will learn about:

1. the meaning of duty of care
2. dilemmas that may arise about duty of care and the support available for addressing them
3. how to respond to complaints.

1. Understand the meaning of duty of care

1.1 The term 'duty of care'

A duty of care means that all health and social care professionals, and organisations providing health and care services, must act in the best interests of the people they support. They also have to do everything in their power to keep people safe from harm and exploitation. As a care professional, you must ensure that you do not do something, or fail to do something, that causes harm to someone. You have a professional duty of care to act only within your own competence and not to take on something you are not confident about.

Your duty of care underpins everything that you do; it is what underlies the Codes of Practice and it should be built into your practice on a day-to-day level. Exercising your duty of care is also a legal requirement, and is tested in court in the event of a case of negligence or malpractice. This is not to suggest that you should always be worried about being sued, but you do need to recognise that you are responsible for the welfare of a vulnerable person and this brings with it certain duties.

It is no defence to say any of these things.

The responsibility to make sure that you have the knowledge and skills to do the task required is yours as much as your employer's. If you know that you cannot do something, then you must say so. In the same way, if you are asked to carry out a task that you know you cannot do safely because you do not have the equipment, then you must say so.

Functional skills

English: Speaking and listening

Have a discussion with staff at work about their understanding of the term 'duty of care'. Ensure that you take an active role in the discussion by contributing your opinions and picking up on points made by others. Speak clearly at all times and use appropriate language when speaking.

Activity 1

Understanding duty of care

Ask three colleagues and three people who do not work in health and social care to tell you what they understand by the term 'duty of care'. Make a note of all the answers – check if there is a difference between the understanding of people who work in social care and people who do not. Then check if there are differences in your colleagues' views about what it means.

If there are some differences, you could suggest to your manager that it is discussed at a team meeting.

Key term

Risk – the likelihood of a hazard's potential being realised

1.2 How duty of care affects your work role

People have a right to expect that when a professional is providing support, they will be kept safe and not be neglected or exposed to any unnecessary **risks**. The expression is that we 'owe' a duty of care to the people we work with. 'Owe' is a useful word to describe the nature of the duty of care because it is just like a debt: it is something that you must pay as part of choosing to become a professional in the field of social care.

Having a duty of care towards the people you work with is not unique to social care; all professions who work with people have a duty of care. This includes doctors, teachers, nurses, midwives and many others. Other professionals, such as lawyers, architects and engineers, also have a duty of care, and although it may be a little different in the workplace, the principles remain the same.

Thinking about the duty of care that you owe to people is helpful when you are planning your work. It makes you consider whether what you were planning to do is in the best interests of the person you are working with. This is not only about physical risks; you also have a duty of care to treat people with dignity and respect.

Functional skills

English: Writing

Answer the questions in Activity 2 in full sentences that have been checked by proofreading for errors in grammar, punctuation and spelling. Lay out your work using a suitable format and present your information in a logical sequence.

Reflect

Can you see how a duty of care will apply to your own work role? You may like to try Activity 2 in relation to the tasks you perform at work.

Activity 2

The effects of duty of care on your role

Try out the following scenarios. How does your duty of care in each situation affect what you do?

1. You are helping someone to have a bath. What do you need to check and how will you carry out your duty of care?
2. You are accompanying a mildly confused person on a shopping trip. What will you need to think about and what steps will you need to take to exercise your duty of care?
3. You are supporting someone to complete benefit claim forms. What will you do to make sure that you have carried out your duty of care? What could go wrong?
4. You are passing on a message to someone's relative. What must you think about?
5. You are on duty in a residential setting when the fire alarm goes off. What is your duty of care?

What is the duty of care when helping to fill in forms?

2. Be aware of dilemmas that may arise about duty of care and the support available for addressing them

2.1 Dilemmas that may arise between the duty of care and a person's rights

Potential conflicts or dilemmas

Exercising a duty of care is not about wrapping people in cotton wool or preventing them from taking any risks. Just participating in everyday life involves risks – for example, crossing the road is a risky business. There has to be a balance and you need to consider risks.

You do have a duty of care for the people you support, but they also have the right to make their own choices and to reach decisions about actions they want to take. Sometimes there can be a conflict between a person's rights and your duty of care. Having a duty to act in someone's interests and also needing to ensure that they are not placed in harm's way can be very hard to balance with encouraging people to take control of their lives and to make choices and decisions about their lives. The following three case studies give some examples of the sorts of dilemmas you may come across.

Case study

Backpacking in Australia

Kevin is 24. He has a mild learning disability and has always been protected by his parents. He wants to go backpacking around Australia with a friend whom he has met at the restaurant where he works. His parents are opposed to it, but his brother and sister are supportive.

1. What are the issues for you, as Kevin's support worker?
2. What should you do?
3. What is your duty of care here?
4. Can anything be done to stop Kevin? Should it be?

Case study

Stopping medication

George has a long history of schizophrenia. He has been living in the community for over 10 years and is doing well with regular medication. He has now decided that he does not want to continue with his medication because he has read that putting chemicals into your body may be harmful.

1. What is your duty of care here?
2. Who else may have a duty of care?
3. What can you do?

Case study

Buying a scooter

Olga is 75 years old. She has severe osteoarthritis, poor vision and uses a hearing aid. She has recently decided to purchase a mobility scooter in order to be able to get out more. You are concerned about her safety and the safety of others if she takes the scooter out on the road.

1. What can you do?
2. What is your duty of care?

These case studies are very different and you can see that your role would be very different in each of the circumstances. They are quite extreme situations, but they illustrate some of the difficulties and dilemmas that you may face.

Of course, many situations will not be nearly so difficult to deal with; the day-to-day situations may be around someone choosing to eat a poor diet or to drink too much. You have a duty of care to make sure that people know how and why they should follow a healthy lifestyle, but you cannot force them to do so.

It is important to make sure that you give information about risks and consequences to people in a way that they can understand. This means thinking about:

- the level of the language used
- the use of graphics where that will help
- the use of 'easy read' documents
- providing information in different languages, including sign language
- providing information verbally
- providing information in large print or Braille.

There is no point in giving people the information they need to make decisions if it is not in a form that can be easily understood. After giving people information, you should check that it has been understood. Once you are sure that the information you have given about the possible consequences of actions is understood, then people have a right to make their own decisions.

There are some circumstances in which you can and should take action, regardless of the wishes of the person concerned. These are if someone is planning to do something that:

- is criminal or illegal
- will deliberately harm them
- represents a serious risk to others.

In any of these circumstances, you must quickly seek advice from your manager.

The vast majority of people you work with will be in a position to take their own decisions about what they do in their lives. In order to exercise your duty of care, you must ensure that any decisions and choices people make are based on understanding the consequences and potential risks of what they want to do. Your role is not to prevent people from doing what they want, but to make sure that they know the possible results.

This can result in some very finely balanced decisions, especially where there are concerns about someone's capacity to understand the possible risks and consequences from their actions. The question of capacity to make decisions is highly complex and must be considered carefully. It is very easy to make the assumption that because someone has dementia, or has a learning disability or a long-term mental health problem, they lack the capacity to make decisions about important issues affecting their own life. If you think about it, the capacity to make a decision can often depend on how much help we have.

For example, if a government minister has to choose between two different highly advanced fighter aircraft to commission for the RAF, they will ask for help from experts across the aviation industry, from experienced civil servants from the relevant departments, and from the pilots and senior officers who are going to use the aircraft. The minister will make the final decision — but lacks the *capacity* to make the decision alone, and so uses lots of help and support.

Similarly, most of us, if asked to make a choice between two different types of central heating system, would need to ask for help from experts before deciding — we would lack the capacity to make the decision without advice and help.

So remember — capacity is relative to what has to be decided and depends on the circumstances.

Mental Capacity Act 2005

The Mental Capacity Act sets out a framework for supporting people to make decisions, and lays out the ways in which people can be supported. The Act is underpinned by five key principles.

1. A presumption of capacity — every adult has the right to make their own decisions and must be assumed to have capacity to do so unless it is proved otherwise.
2. The right for people to be supported to make their own decisions — people must be given all appropriate help before anyone concludes that someone cannot make their own decisions.
3. People must retain the right to make what might be seen as eccentric or unwise decisions.
4. Best interests — anything done for or on behalf of people without capacity must be in their best interests.
5. Least restrictive intervention — anything done for or on behalf of people without capacity should be the least restrictive of their basic rights and freedoms.

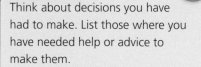

Reflect

Think about decisions you have had to make. List those where you have needed help or advice to make them.

The Act sets out clearly how to establish if someone is incapable of taking a decision; the 'incapacity test' is only in relation to a particular decision. No one can be deemed 'incapable' in general simply because of a medical condition or diagnosis. The Act introduces a new criminal offence of ill treatment or neglect of a person who lacks capacity. A person found guilty of such an offence may be liable to imprisonment for a term of up to five years.

2.2 Where to get additional support and advice about dilemmas

Your first port of call if you are unsure about how to respond to a dilemma between your duty of care and a person's rights is your manager. They should be able to advise you about the best approaches to take and give you the opportunity to discuss both sides of the dilemma.

If you are a member of a professional association or a trade union, they will also be able to offer advice about the uncertainties you may have about whether you are effectively exercising a duty of care towards the people you support.

3. Know how to respond to complaints

3.1 Why it is important that individuals know how to make a complaint

and

3.2 The main points of agreed procedures for handling complaints

'Agreed procedures' means the policies and procedures of the organisation you work for.

If you work as a personal assistant to one person, then this will not be something you will come across in your own workplace, but knowing about it is valuable in case you need to support your employer to make a complaint against another organisation at some time.

Your organisation should have a complaints policy, and it should be publicised and information on it readily available in the form of leaflets, posters, complaints form, web-based and printed.

All public service organisations are required to have a complaints procedure and to make the procedure readily available for people to use. Part of your role may be to support people in making complaints or in handling complaints made to you. You may support people:

- directly, by supporting them in following the procedure
- indirectly, by making sure that they are aware of the complaints procedure and are able to follow it.

There are principles of good complaint handling produced by the Local Government Ombudsman and the Health Service Ombudsman. They are as follows.

1. Getting it right.
2. Being customer focused.
3. Being open and accountable.
4. Acting fairly and proportionately.
5. Putting things right.
6. Seeking continuous improvement.

How complaints are approached can make all the difference between people being satisfied and feeling that they have been listened to, and people still feeling that their issues have not been recognised and that nothing will change.

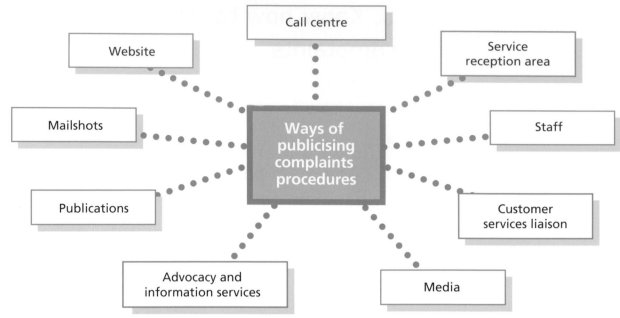

Ways of publicising complaints procedures.

Local authorities and NHS organisations need to:

- make sure that the complaints procedure is publicised
- offer to discuss a complaint as soon as it is received
- investigate complaints thoroughly and efficiently
- write to the person who made the complaint, explaining how it has been investigated and the outcome
- remind people of their rights to refer complaints to the relevant Ombudsman if they are not satisfied
- make sure that a senior manager is designated as being responsible for dealing with complaints and for sharing information about lessons that can be learned
- make sure that the person complaining has all the support they need in order to understand the procedure
- produce an annual report with information about the numbers and type of complaints received and how things have improved as a result.

3.3 Your role in responding to complaints as part of your duty of care

You may be asked by a senior manager to provide information for the investigation of a complaint. You must do so promptly, because there will be a time limit for responding to the complaint. You must give clear and honest information. It is unlikely that you will be asked for an opinion; it is usually just factual information that is needed. Do not give your opinion unless you are specifically asked for it; just stick to the facts. If you cannot remember some aspects, then say so – do not make up or guess what you cannot recall. You will find out if the result of the investigation means that lessons have been learned and practice has been changed.

Case study

Investigating a complaint

Tracey has a learning disability; she had been supported by a job coach in a work placement. She had been struggling to manage the till in the shop where she was working, and her job coach had shouted at her in front of customers and other members of staff. Tracey had come home very upset and her mother had subsequently complained to the service manager. She listened to Tracey's mother and spoke to Tracey. She apologised about Tracey having been upset and promised to look into the complaint. When she spoke to the manager concerned, she found that there had been concerns about this particular coach's attitude previously. It was agreed that the coach would undertake some additional training and Tracey would have a new coach allocated to her. The service manager met with Tracey and her mother and told them what would happen – they were satisfied with the result.

1. Was Tracey's mother right to complain on her behalf?
2. How did the service manager demonstrate good practice in dealing with the complaint?

If a complaint is made to you, then you should:

- make sure the person understands how to use the complaints procedure
- explain to them how it works and when they can expect to receive a response
- offer support in following the procedure if necessary
- advise your manager that the complaint is being made.

Do not:

- attempt to resolve complaints yourself
- discuss the complaint with the person it is about
- discourage people from making complaints
- promise that you will 'sort it out'
- discuss the complaint with colleagues or anyone other than your manager.

Reflect

Although it is not always easy to hear them, complaints are important because they help everyone to improve the service they provide. Try to think about a complaint by putting yourself in the complainant's shoes and seeing how an incident or a service has made them feel. This is a good start to learning lessons about how to make your practice, and the performance of the service, better.

Getting ready for assessment

For this unit you will need to show your assessor that you understand the concept of having a duty of care towards the people you support. You may have to produce an assignment or a presentation, or your assessor may hold a professional discussion about what a duty of care means. You will need to show your assessor that you realise having a duty of care can involve dilemmas, especially when you have to balance your duty of care with someone's rights to take risks and do what they want. It is better if you can give some examples of this from your own work. If you do not have any personal examples, then you can always give examples you have heard about from colleagues.

This unit also requires that you know how to deal with complaints. You may not be in a position to deal with many complaints directly, but you do need to understand the importance of complaints, how to handle them and how to learn from them.

Legislation

- Mental Capacity Act 2005

Further reading and research

- www.cwdcouncil.org.uk (Children's Workforce Development Council)
- www.dh.gov.uk (Department of Health)
- www.gscc.org.uk (General Social Care Council (GSCC))
- www.skillsforcare.org.uk (Skills for Care)
- www.skillsforhealth.org.uk (Skills for Health)

Unit HSC 024

Principles of safeguarding and protection in health and social care

In this unit you will look at some of the most difficult issues that support workers face. Working in social care means coming to terms with the fact that some people will be subjected to abuse by those who are supposed to care for them. Knowing what you are looking for, how to recognise it and how to respond, is the best possible contribution to protecting people from harm and abuse. You need to know how society handles abuse, how to recognise it and what to do about it.

If you can learn always to think about the risks, always to be alert to potentially abusive situations, and always to listen and believe when you are told of harm and abuse, then you will provide the best possible protection for people you support.

In this unit you will learn about:

1. **how to recognise signs of abuse**
2. **how to respond to suspected or alleged abuse**
3. **the national and local context of safeguarding and protection from abuse**
4. **ways to reduce the likelihood of abuse**
5. **how to recognise and report unsafe practices.**

1. Know how to recognise signs of abuse

Recognising risks

Many different factors will place people at risk, and it will not always be possible for you to protect everyone from everything, neither is it desirable. There are many situations in which you will have to balance the rights of someone to place themselves in potential danger in order to take control over their own lives. This does not necessarily mean that every disabled person you work with will want to take up wheelchair rock climbing, but the element of risk can equally apply to a vulnerable adult with deteriorating memory function who wants to go out alone on a shopping trip. There is undoubtedly a significant risk, but this needs to be balanced against the importance of empowerment, dignity and control.

There are vital differences between danger, harm and abuse. You need to know how each relates to what you do.

- **Danger** is about the possibility or risk of abuse.
- **Harm** is about the results and consequences of abuse.

Have you thought about the balance between protection and restriction?

Whether your job role means that you are responsible only for your own work, or whether you have some responsibility for the work of colleagues, you will need to give some thought to your role in protection. There are also likely to be differences depending on your working environment, for example, the dangers and risks presented in someone's own home will be different from those in a residential or healthcare setting. Clearly, the three concepts of abuse, danger and harm are interlinked; someone who is abused may be in danger and will be suffering harm – but not everyone who is exposed to danger is being abused, and people can be harmed through accident or carelessness rather than deliberate abuse.

Abusive situations

Abuse may happen just once, or it can be ongoing – either situation should be viewed just as seriously. If abuse has happened once, the risks of it happening again are far higher. It may be physical, sexual or emotional abuse. Deliberate neglect or a failure to act is also abuse, as is a vulnerable person persuaded to enter into a financial arrangement or a sexual act to which they have not given or cannot give informed consent.

A wide range of people, including family members, friends, professional staff, care workers, volunteers or other people, may abuse vulnerable adults.

Abuse may take place within the person's own home, nursing, residential or day care facilities or hospitals. Incidents of abuse can be either to one person or to a group of people at a time. Some instances of abuse will constitute a criminal offence – for example, assault, rape, theft or fraud. The person responsible for this can then be prosecuted, but not all abuse falls into this category.

1.1 Different types of abuse

Abuse can take many forms. These are usually classified under five main headings:

- physical
- sexual
- psychological
- financial
- institutional.

1.2 Signs and symptoms of abuse

Warning signs of harm or abuse

The following are indications for which you should consider harm or abuse as a possible cause. However, each of them can be the result of something other than abuse – so they are far from being foolproof evidence, but they do act as pointers to make you look at the option of abuse being the answer. You and your colleagues will need to use other skills, such as observation and communication with other professionals, in order to build up a complete picture.

Different types of abuse have different remedies in law, and some have no legal remedies, but are dealt with through other policies, procedures and guidelines.

Signs of possible abuse in adults

Abuse can often show as physical effects and symptoms. These are likely to be accompanied by emotional signs and changes in behaviour, but this is not always the case.

Any behaviour changes could indicate that the person is a victim of some form of abuse, but remember that they are only an indicator and will need to be linked to other factors to arrive at a complete picture.

Physical abuse includes:

- hitting
- slapping
- pushing
- pinching
- force feeding
- kicking
- burning
- scalding
- misuse of medication or restraint
- catheterisation for the convenience of staff
- inappropriate sanctions
- a carer causing illness or injury to someone in order to gain attention for themselves (this might be associated with a condition called fabricated and induced illness, or FII)
- refusing access to toilet facilities
- leaving people in wet or soiled clothing or bedding.

Potential indicators of physical abuse include the following. Any of these factors are not evidence of abuse — they are a warning indicator only.

- Multiple bruising or finger marks (especially in well-protected areas such as eye sockets, inner arms or thighs).
- Fractures — especially twisting fractures — and dislocations — especially when accompanied with bruising or finger marks.
- Scratches or cuts.
- Pressure ulcers and sores or rashes from wet bedding/clothing.
- Black eyes or bruised ears.
- Welt marks — especially on the back or buttocks.
- Scalds or cigarette burns.
- A history of unexplained minor falls or injuries or a history of accidental overdoses/poisonings.

- Explanations not consistent with the injuries.
- Clinical interventions without any clear benefit to the person.
- Deterioration of health without obvious cause.
- Loss of weight.
- Inappropriate, inadequate or soiled clothing.
- Withdrawal or mood changes.
- Carer's resistance to allowing people to visit.
- Reluctance by the vulnerable adult to be alone with the alleged abuser.

Sexual abuse

Sexual abuse, whether of adults or children, can also involve abuse of a position of power. Children can never be considered to give informed consent to any sexual activity of any description. For some adults, informed consent is not possible because of a limited capacity to understand its meaning. In the case of other adults, consent may not be given and the sexual activity is either forced on someone against their will or the person is tricked or bribed into it.

Physical signs	Behavioural signs
• Bruises, scratches, burns or bite marks on the body	• Provocative sexual behaviour, promiscuity
• Scratches, abrasions or persistent infections in the anal/genital regions	• Prostitution
	• Sexual abuse of others
• Pregnancy	• Self-injury, self-destructive behaviour including alcohol and drug abuse, repeated suicide attempts
• Recurrent genital or urinary infections	
• Blood or marks on underwear	• Behaviour that invites exploitation and further physical/sexual abuse
• Abdominal pain with no diagnosable cause	• Disappearing from home environment
	• Aggression, anxiety, tearfulness
	• Reluctance by the vulnerable adult to be alone with the alleged abuser
	• Frequent masturbation
	• Refusal to undress for activities such as swimming/ bathing

Table 1: Potential indicators of sexual abuse (any of these factors are not evidence of abuse — they are a warning indicator only).

Sexual activity is abusive when informed consent is not freely given. This might involve one person using services who is abusing another more vulnerable person. It is important to recognise the difference between the freely consenting sexual activity of adults who also happen to be supported by social care services, and those situations where abuse is taking place because someone is exploiting their position of relative power. The key is the capacity to give informed consent.

Sexual abuse includes:

- rape and sexual assault
- masturbation
- indecent exposure
- penetration or attempted penetration of intimate areas
- sexual harassment
- involving a vulnerable adult in pornography
- enforced witnessing of sexual acts or sexual media
- participation in sexual acts to which the vulnerable adult has not consented, or could not consent, or was pressured into consenting.

Psychological abuse

All forms of abuse also have an element of psychological abuse. Any situation which means that someone becomes a victim of abuse at the hands of someone they trusted is, inevitably, going to cause emotional distress. However, some abuse is purely psychological — there are no physical, sexual or financial elements involved.

Psychological abuse includes:

- emotional abuse
- bullying
- threats of harm or abandonment
- ignoring
- shouting
- swearing
- deprivation of contact with others
- humiliation
- blaming
- controlling
- intimidation
- coercion
- harassment
- verbal abuse
- deprivation of privacy or dignity
- lack of mental stimulation.

Potential indicators of psychological abuse include the following. Any of these factors are not evidence of abuse — they are a warning indicator only.

- Carer seeming to ignore the vulnerable person's presence and needs.
- Reports from neighbours of shouting, screaming, swearing.
- Reluctance by the vulnerable adult to be alone with the alleged abuser.
- Cared-for person fearful of raised voices, distressed if they feel they may be 'in trouble'.

- A culture of teasing or taunting which is causing distress and humiliation.
- Referring to the cared-for person in a derogatory way.
- No valuing of basic human rights, for example, choice, opinion, privacy and dignity.
- Cared-for person being treated like a child — infantilisation.

Financial abuse

Many adults are very vulnerable to financial abuse, particularly those who may have a limited understanding of money matters. Financial abuse, like all other forms of abuse, can be inflicted by family members and even friends as well as care workers or informal carers, and can take a range of forms.

Financial or material abuse includes:

- theft
- fraud
- exploitation
- pressure in connection with wills, property, inheritance or financial transactions
- the misuse or misappropriation of property, possessions or benefits.

Potential indicators of financial abuse include the following. Any of these factors are not evidence of abuse — they are a warning indicator only.

- Someone not being allowed to manage own financial affairs.
- No information being given where consent has been given to act.
- Family unwilling to pay, from relative's funds, for services, although relative has sufficient capital/income.
- Person not made aware of financial matters.
- Enduring power of attorney set up without consulting a doctor where the vulnerable adult is already confused.
- Other people moving into person's property.
- Family regularly asking for money from personal allowance.
- Very few or no personal possessions.
- Unusual and unexplained change in spending pattern.
- Unexplained shortage of money despite a seemingly adequate income.
- Unexplained disappearance of personal possessions or property.
- Sudden changing of a will.

Neglect

Neglect happens when care is not given and someone suffers as a result. There are broadly two different types of neglect: self-neglect and neglect by others.

Self-neglect is different from abuse by others, but it is still a situation that can place people at risk of harm and, potentially, place them in danger. People neglect their own care for a range of reasons; the most common are:

- increasing infirmity
- physical illness or disability
- memory and concentration problems
- sensory loss or difficulty
- mental illness and mental health problems
- learning difficulties/disabilities
- alcohol and drug misuse problems
- a different set of priorities and perspectives.

However, what may appear as self-neglect may be an informed lifestyle choice, and it is important that you do not attempt to impose your standards and values on those who have made a decision to live in a particular way. Decisions in these situations are very difficult and a balance must be achieved between safeguarding and protecting people who are vulnerable, and making sure that you are not removing people's ability to choose to live as they wish. Obviously, where someone has a deteriorating mental or physical condition, then you can, and should, act in order to protect them. A deliberate choice to follow a particular way of living is an entirely different matter.

Neglect by others occurs when either a support worker or a family or friend carer fails to meet someone's support needs. Neglect can happen because those responsible for providing the support do not realise its importance, or because they cannot be bothered, or choose not, to provide it. As the result of neglect, people can become ill, hungry, cold, dirty, injured or deprived of their rights. Neglecting someone you are supposed to be supporting can result from failing to undertake support services, for example:

- not providing adequate food
- not providing assistance with eating food if necessary
- not ensuring that someone receives support with personal care
- not ensuring that someone is adequately clothed
- leaving someone alone
- not supporting someone with mobility or communication needs
- failing to maintain a clean and hygienic living environment
- failing to obtain necessary medical/healthcare support
- not supporting social contacts
- not taking steps to provide a safe and secure environment.

In some social care situations, support workers may fail to provide some support services because they have not been trained, or because they work in a setting where the emphasis is on cost saving rather than service provision. In these circumstances it becomes a form of institutional abuse. Unfortunately, there have been residential care homes and NHS trusts where people have been found to be suffering from malnutrition as the result of such neglect. Individual workers who are deliberately neglecting people in spite of receiving training and working in a quality caring environment are, fortunately, likely to be spotted very quickly by colleagues and supervisors.

However, family and friend carers are in different circumstances, often facing huge pressures and difficulties. Some may be caring for a relative reluctantly because they feel they have no choice; others may be barely coping with their own lives and may find caring for someone else a burden they are unable to bear. Regardless of the many possible reasons for the difficulties that can result in neglect, it is essential that any suspicions or concerns are investigated and followed up so that help can be offered and additional support provided if necessary.

As with self-neglect, it is important that lifestyle decisions made by people and their carers are respected. Full discussions should take place with people and their carers where there are concerns about possible neglect. Neglect and failure to care includes:

- ignoring medical or physical care needs
- failure to provide access to appropriate health, social care or educational services
- withholding the necessities of life, such as medication, adequate nutrition and heating.

Potential indicators of neglect include the following. Any of these factors are not evidence of abuse — they are a warning indicator only.

- Medical condition deteriorating unexpectedly or not improving as expected.
- Hypothermia or person cold or dressed inadequately.
- Supported person is hungry.
- Living environment is dirty and unhygienic.
- Risks and hazards in the living environment are not dealt with.
- Person has sores and skin rashes.
- Unexplained loss of weight.
- Clothes or body dirty and smelly.
- Reluctance by the vulnerable adult to be alone with the alleged abuser.
- Delays in seeking medical attention.

Discriminatory abuse

Discriminatory abuse includes:

- racist and sexist abuse
- abuse based on a person's disability
- harassment, slurs or similar treatment
- abuse related to age, gender or sexual orientation
- abuse directed towards religion.

It is also the case that discriminatory abuse can underpin other forms of abuse — particularly physical or psychological.

Potential indicators of discriminatory abuse include the following. Any of these factors are not evidence of abuse — they are a warning indicator only.

- Exclusion from activities based on inadequate justifications.
- Restricted or unequal access to healthcare and medical treatment.
- Person is not supported in challenging discrimination.
- Unnecessary barriers restrict participation.
- Person experiences fear, withdrawal, apathy, loss of self-esteem.
- Many of the emotional indicators are similar to other forms of abuse.

Institutional abuse

Institutional abuse is not just confined to large-scale physical or sexual abuse scandals of the type that have been publicised regularly in the media. Of course this type of systematic and organised abuse has happened in residential and hospital settings, and must be recognised and dealt with appropriately so that people can be protected. However, people can be abused in many other ways in settings where they could expect to be supported, cared for and protected.

Abuse is not just carried out by individuals; groups, or even organisations, can also create abusive situations. It has been known that groups of care workers in residential settings can abuse those in their care. Often people will act in a different way in a group than they would alone. Think about teenage 'gangs', which exist because people are prepared to do things jointly which they would not think to do if they were alone. Many of the types of abuse described here can also be identified in their individual categories of physical, sexual or psychological abuse.

Abuse in a care setting may not just be at the hands of members of staff. There is also abuse which comes about because of the way in which an establishment is run, where the basis for planning the systems, rules and regulations is not the welfare, rights and dignity of the residents or patients, but the convenience of the staff and management. This is the type of situation where people can be told when to get up and go to bed, given communal clothing, only allowed medical attention at set times and not allowed to go out.

The key factor in identifying institutional abuse is that the abuse is accepted or ignored by the organisation, or that it happens because an organisation has systems and processes that are designed for its own benefit and not those of the people using the service. For example:

- people in residential settings are not given choice over day-to-day decisions such as mealtimes or bedtimes
- freedom to go out is limited by the institution
- privacy and dignity are not respected

- personal correspondence is opened by staff
- the setting is run for the convenience of the staff
- excessive or inappropriate doses of sedation/medication are given
- access to advice and **advocacy** is restricted or not allowed
- complaints procedures are deliberately made unavailable.

Patterns and nature of abuse

Patterns and the nature of abuse vary and can take place in different ways.

Serial abuse is where the perpetrator seeks out and 'grooms' vulnerable adults (sexual abuse and some forms of financial abuse usually fall into this pattern). These are often, but not always, criminal offences and are committed by people who deliberately prey on vulnerable people. This can range from the confidence trickster who poses as an official in order to gain entry to an older person's home to the abuser who will 'befriend' someone with mental health problems through an Internet chat room, and later subject them to abuse or assault. It can also include those criminals who attempt to commit fraud or threaten vulnerable people in connections with wills, property or other financial assets.

Situational abuse is a result of pressures building up and/or because of difficult or challenging behaviour. This type of 'acute' and immediate abusive situation normally results in physical abuse, although it can result in verbal or emotional abuse and sometimes in neglect where a carer no longer seeks out necessary medical treatment or other support.

Long-term abuse may occur in the context of an ongoing family relationship, for example, domestic violence, or where a family member with a physical or a learning disability is humiliated and belittled, or where an older relative has all their money and belongings gradually taken from them over a period of time. Neglect of someone's needs because others are unable or unwilling to take responsibility for their care is also likely to take place over a long period of time.

Institutional abuse arises from poor standards of care, inadequate staffing, lack of response to people's complex needs, staff with inadequate knowledge, skills, understanding and expertise. This can also involve unacceptable treatment programmes including overmedication, unnecessary use of restraint, and withholding food, drink or medication.

Risk factors

People can be abused for many reasons, and it is important in highlighting any contributing factors, to make it clear that the factors alone do not mean that abuse is taking place. It is quite possible to have any or several factors in place and for there to be no abuse –

How vulnerable do you think this woman is to strangers visiting?

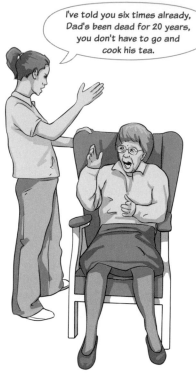

I've told you six times already, Dad's been dead for 20 years, you don't have to go and cook his tea.

Can you see how stress builds up in some situations?

equally, there may be no obvious factors but, nonetheless, abuse is happening.

Some of the factors that are known to contribute to the risk of harm and abuse of adults by family and friend carers are:

- poor communication between supported person and carer — this could be because of a medical condition or a social/relationship issue
- challenging behaviour by the supported person
- carer being young or immature
- carer feeling unable to carry on
- strong feelings of frustration on the part of the carer
- carer and supported person having a history of a troubled relationship
- carer having an alcohol or drug dependency
- carer believing that the cared-for person is being deliberately difficult or ungrateful
- caring role not having been taken on willingly
- carer having had to make major lifestyle changes
- carer having more than one caring responsibility — for example, young children and an older relative
- supported person being violent towards the carer
- carer having disturbed sleep
- carer and supported person being socially isolated
- financial or housing pressures
- delays or insufficient resources to provide adequate support
- isolated older people without family support or contact — particularly in relation to financial abuse.

Case study

Caring at home

Sunita is 48 years old. She has Parkinson's disease, which has recently begun to develop very rapidly. Her mobility has become very limited and she cannot be left alone because she falls frequently. The number of personal care tasks she can carry out has decreased significantly, and she is almost totally dependent on her husband for care.

Sunita has two grown-up sons who live and work considerable distances away. They both visit as often as they can, but are not able to offer any regular caring support. Sunita's husband has given up his career as a ranger in the local country park, a job he loved, in order to look after Sunita. She is very reluctant to go out

because she feels people are looking at her. She is very angry about the way Parkinson's has affected her, and has alienated many of the friends who tried to help initially, by being uncooperative and refusing much of the help they offered.

1. How could you try to relieve some of the pressures in this situation?
2. Are there any warning signs in this situation that would make you aware of the possibility of abuse? If so, what are they?
3. Can you think of a situation where you may have missed some signs like these?

Reflect

Look at your workplace. Do any of the points opposite apply? If any of these are the case in your workplace, you need to be aware that people can be put under so much stress that they behave abusively. Remember that abuse is not just about physical cruelty.

If none of these things happen in your workplace, then try to imagine what work would be like if they did. Sit down with a colleague, if you can, and discuss what you think the effects of any two of the items in the list would be. If you cannot do this with a colleague, you can do it on your own by making notes.

Functional skills

English: Speaking and listening

Use the list in the Reflect feature to initiate a group discussion. Choose a minimum of two points as a basis for the discussion. You will need to take an active role as a participant and to present your ideas clearly.

Doing it well

Recognising abuse

If you want to be effective in helping to stop abuse, you will need to:

- believe that abuse happens
- recognise abusive behaviour
- be aware of when abuse can happen
- understand who abusers can be
- know the policies and procedures for handling abuse
- follow the person's support plan
- recognise likely abusive situations
- report any concerns or suspicions.

Abuse by professionals

Some of the factors which are known to contribute to the risk of harm and abuse by professional support workers can include:

- poor-quality staff training
- lack of knowledge and understanding by staff
- inadequate staffing numbers
- lack of investment in continuing professional development
- little or no staff support or supervision
- low staff morale
- lack of opportunity for care workers to form a relationship with someone
- organisational culture which fails to treat people with dignity and respect as individuals
- culture of bullying of staff members by management.

Recognising the signs

You have looked at several examples showing possible signs and symptoms that may alert you to abuse or harm. One of the most difficult aspects of dealing with abuse is to admit that it is happening. If you are someone who has never come across deliberate abuse before, it is hard to understand and to believe that it is happening. It is not the first thing you think of when someone has an injury or displays a change in behaviour. However, you have to accept that abuse does happen and is relatively common. Considering abuse should be one of the options when someone has an unexplained injury or a change in behaviour that has no obvious cause. That does not mean it will be abuse, or that you should start formal reporting procedures — it means that you should always consider it as a real possibility.

Victims of abuse often fail to report it for a range of reasons. They:

- are too ill or too frail
- do not have enough understanding of what is happening to them
- are ashamed and believe it is their own fault
- have been threatened by the abuser or are afraid
- do not think that they will be believed
- do not believe that anyone has the power to stop the abuse.

Given the fact that relatively few victims report abuse without support, it is essential that those who are working in care settings are alert to the possibility of abuse and are able to recognise possible signs and symptoms.

Abuse can take place at home or in a formal care setting. At home, it could be a family or friend carer who is the abuser, or it could be a neighbour or regular visitor. It can also be a professional support worker who is carrying out the abuse. This situation can mean that abuse goes undetected for some time because of the unsupervised nature of a support worker's visits to someone's home.

In a residential social care setting, abuse may be more likely to be noticed, although some of its more subtle forms, such as humiliation, can sometimes be so commonplace that they are not recognised as abusive behaviour.

Up to this point, we have looked at abuse by professional support workers and by family and friend carers. But remember that in residential or hospital settings, abuse can occur between residents or patients, and it can also happen between visitors and residents or patients. People can also abuse themselves.

Case study

Appropriate ways to care

For the past five years, Julie, aged 43, had been a senior support worker in a residential unit for people with a learning disability. She loved her job and was very committed to the residents in the unit. She was very concerned for the welfare of the people she supported and did everything she could for them. Many of them had been in the unit for many years and Julie knew them well. The unit was not very large and had only a small staff who were able to work very closely with the resident group.

Julie and the other staff were concerned that the residents could easily be taken advantage of, as some were not able to make effective judgements about other people and potentially risky situations.

Regular mealtimes were arranged so that everyone could share the day's experiences and talk together, and bedtimes and getting-up times were also strictly adhered to. The staff found that this was a good way of keeping the residents organised and motivated.

Residents did not go out into the local town in the evenings because of the potential safety risk, but the staff would plan evenings of TV watching, choosing programmes that they thought would interest the residents. Sometimes simple games sessions or walks in the local park were arranged.

A new manager was appointed to the unit, and Julie and the other staff were very surprised to find that the new manager was horrified by many of these practices, and wanted to make major changes.

1. What changes do you think the manager may have suggested?
2. Why do you think those changes may be needed?
3. Do you consider that Julie and the other staff members were practising in the best way for the residents?
4. Think about, or discuss, whether this situation was abusive.

Self-harm

The one abuser it is very hard to protect someone from is the person themselves. People who self-harm should have the risk identified in their plan of care, and responses to their behaviour will be recorded. You must ensure that you follow the agreed plan for provision of care to someone who has a history of self-harm. It is usual that a person who is at risk of self-harm will be closely supported and you may need to contribute towards planned activities or therapies.

2. Know how to respond to suspected or alleged abuse

2.1 and 2.2 What to do if there are suspicions or someone alleges that they are being abused

If someone makes an allegation of abuse to you, the first and most important response is that *you must believe what you are told*. One of the biggest fears of those being abused is that no one will believe them – do not make this fear into a reality.

This is often harder than it sounds. If you have never been involved with an abusive situation before, it is hard to believe that such cases arise and that this could really happen.

You must reassure the person that you believe what you have been told. Another common fear of people who are being abused is that it is somehow their fault. You must therefore also reassure them that it is not their fault and that they are in no way to blame for what has happened to them.

When someone tells you about abuse or neglect, try not to get into a situation where you are having to deal with a lot of detailed information. After reassuring the person that you believe them, you should report the allegation immediately to a senior colleague and hand over responsibility. This may not always be possible because of the circumstances or location in which the allegation takes place, or because the person wants to tell you everything once they have begun to talk. If you do find yourself in the position of being given a great deal of information, you must be careful not to ask any leading questions – for example, do not say, 'And then did he punch you?' Just ask, 'And then what happened?' Use your basic communication and listening skills so that the person knows they can trust you and that you are listening. Make sure you concentrate and try to remember as much as possible so that you can record it accurately.

Remember that people tell you about abuse because they want it to stop. They are telling you because they want you to help make it stop. You cannot make it stop if you keep it secret.

Confidentiality

In general, of course, the right of every person to confidentiality is a key part of good practice. However, abuse is one of the few situations where you may have to consider whether or not it is possible to maintain this. You will always need to be clear, when someone alleges abuse, that you cannot promise to keep what they tell you confidential. This is not always easy; very often, when someone tells you about abuse they have suffered, they will start by saying, 'If I tell you something, will you promise not to tell anyone?' You cannot guarantee this, so do not make this promise — it is one you cannot keep. It is never acceptable to tell someone one thing and do another, so you must be clear from the start about what your responsibilities are, and make it clear that you may have to share what you are told with others. You can, however, reassure someone by saying, 'I can't promise not to say anything to anyone, but I can promise you that I will only tell people who will help you.' You can also promise that although some information may have to be shared, it will be shared on a 'need to know' basis, and only among those agencies directly involved in any investigation.

However, vulnerable adults are not children, and if they absolutely refuse to allow you to share information, it is very difficult for you to do so — beyond the absolute necessity to share the information with your manager. All efforts then have to go into trying to encourage the person to agree to sharing the information and pursuing an investigation. However, if there is no question of capacity (see page 87), then you may have to accept that you can only monitor matters carefully.

There can be some circumstances in which it is necessary for you to break confidentiality; for example, if someone discloses that an officer in charge in a residential care home is systematically stealing from the people living there. You would be justified in breaking the confidentiality of one person in order to protect other vulnerable people. However, this must only be done in discussion with your line manager, and any decisions taken must be fully recorded, giving reasons why it is necessary. You must also make sure that the person concerned knows to whom you have talked and why.

Why is it important for you to be clear that you may have to share what you are told with others?

The Data Protection Act 1998 (see page 240) requires you to ensure that any written information is kept securely. Information about abuse or potential abuse is very sensitive and it is important that people have their right to privacy and confidentiality respected. Information must be kept in a secure situation, password protected if it is kept electronically and with any hard copies securely in a locked cabinet. Make sure that only essential and necessary information is kept, and that it is used for the abused person's benefit and in their best interests.

How do you respond?

According to organisations promoting good practice in safeguarding vulnerable adults, there are four key priorities in responding to concerns or allegations of abuse:

- Priority 1: Protect
- Priority 2: Report
- Priority 3: Preserve
- Priority 4: Record and refer.

Priority 1: Protect

The first and most important concern is to ensure that the abused person is safe and protected from any further possibility of abuse. Make sure that any necessary medical treatment is provided, and give plenty of reassurance and comfort so that the person knows that they are now safe. Even if the abuse happened a long time ago, or has been going on for a long period, the process of making an allegation can be very distressing as well as being a huge relief, so lots of warm, kind and caring support is vital. When you find out, or suspect, that someone is being abused or neglected, you have a responsibility to take action immediately. Concerns, suspicions or firm evidence all require an immediate response.

Action to protect may mean taking someone to a safe place, or removing the alleged perpetrator. It may mean getting medical assistance or contacting trusted family or friends to provide support.

Priority 2: Report

You must report any abusive situation you become aware of to your line manager, or the named person in your workplace procedures for the Protection of Vulnerable Adults. You may have formal reporting procedures in place in your organisation, or you may simply make an initial verbal referral. However, it will be essential that you make a full, written report as soon as you can after the event. In the meantime, the checklist on the next page may help you to recall details you will need later, and make sure that you have done everything you need to.

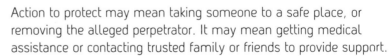

Functional skills

English: Writing

You will be practising your skills of writing and presenting information in a logical and concise way. Proofread your work to ensure accuracy of punctuation, spelling and grammar. By producing a report, you will be using a range of sentence structures, including complex ones, and ordering paragraphs to communicate effectively.

Checklist

Disclosure/observation made by . . . .

Date . . . .

How? . . . .

To whom? . . . .

Action taken by . . . .

What action? . . . .

If no action, reasons . . . .

Vulnerable adult seen?   Yes / No

When seen (date and time) . . . .

Who saw the vulnerable adult – list all . . . .

Consultations/information sharing/notification – health

GP?   Yes / No

District nurse?   Yes / No

CPN?   Yes / No

Consultations/information sharing/notification – Social Services

Community team?   Yes / No

Hospital team?   Yes / No

Police?   Yes / No

Housing/supporting people?   Yes / No

Provider agencies?   Yes / No

Other . . . . Yes / No

Medical examination?

When? . . . .

Where? . . . .

By whom? . . . . Yes / No

All action recorded?   Yes / No

Reasons for non-action recorded?   Yes / No

Telephone conversations confirmed in writing?   Yes / No

Strategy meeting?   Yes / No

Date of meeting . . . .

Priority 3: Preserve

Preserve any evidence. If this is a potential crime scene, you must be very careful not to destroy any potential evidence. If an incident of physical or sexual abuse is recent and there is likely to be forensic evidence, then you must preserve it carefully until the police arrive and take over. For example:

- do not clear up
- do not wash or clean any part of the room or area in which the alleged abuse took place
- do not remove bedding
- do not remove any clothes the abused person is wearing
- do not allow the person to wash, shower, bathe, brush hair or clean teeth
- keep other people out of the room or area.

If financial abuse is alleged or suspected, ensure that you have not thrown away any papers or documents that could be useful as evidence. Try to preserve as much as possible, in order to hand it over to those investigating the allegations.

The evidence for other types of abuse is different. Sadly, neglect speaks for itself, but it will be important to preserve living conditions as they were found until they can be recorded and photographed. This does not include the person concerned; bearing in mind Priority 1, any treatment and medical attention needed must be provided immediately. Make sure that you explain to any doctor or paramedic that the situation may result in a prosecution, so they should record any findings carefully in case they are later required to make a statement.

Psychological or discriminatory abuse is likely to be dependent on witnesses and disclosure from the abused person, rather than physical evidence.

Priority 4: Record and refer

Any information you have, whether it is simply concerns, hard evidence or an allegation, must be carefully recorded. You should write down your evidence or, if you are unable to do so for any reason, you should record it on audio tape and have it transcribed (written down) later. It is not acceptable to pass on your concerns verbally without backing this up with a recorded report. Verbal information can be altered and can have its meaning changed very easily when it is passed on. Think about the children's game of Chinese Whispers – by the time the whispered phrase reaches the end of its journey, it is usually changed beyond all recognition.

Activity 2

Concerns about an abuse situation

Write a report on concerns about an abuse situation that could occur in your workplace. If you are aware of abuse situations that have happened, you could report on one of them, making sure you do not use people's real names or any other information that could identify them. If not, make up the details. State to whom, in your workplace, you would give the report.

Your workplace may have a special report form for recording causes for concern or allegations. If not, you should write your report, making sure you include:

- everything you observed
- anything you have been told – but make sure that it is clear that this is not something you have seen for yourself
- any previous concerns you may have had
- what has raised your concerns on this occasion.

Record what has happened. This is vitally important, as you may need, at some stage to make a formal statement to police, or other investigation team. Initially, however, you should make sure that you have recorded all the key details for your own organisation. You may also need to make a referral to another agency, for example, the police or social services. You will need to record all of the following information carefully, including a detailed account of what actually happened, what you saw or were told, and who said or did what.

Be clear that you do not mix fact and opinion, and make sure that you state clearly what you actually know because you have seen or heard it yourself, and identify what you have heard from others as this is hearsay or third party evidence and it is important that others know how reliable your information is. For example:

> Mrs James was crying when I arrived.

This is a fact.

> Mrs James should not have been living there with him – everyone is aware of his bad temper.

This is an opinion.

> Mrs James had been upset earlier in the morning when her neighbour had visited.

This is hearsay from the neighbour, and not a fact that you have witnessed first hand. This type of information can be useful in a report, but you must identify it as hearsay, for example: 'Mrs James's neighbour told me that she had been upset earlier in the morning when she had visited.'

If you do have to make a formal statement or produce a report that will be used in court, you cannot include any hearsay, and must only report facts which you have seen or heard for yourself.

If you need to make a referral to another agency you will need to include all the information shown opposite.

Referral information

Details of abused person

- Name
- Address
- Telephone number
- Date of birth
- Gender
- Ethnic background (including principal language spoken)
- Details of any disability (including any communication needs)
- GP
- Details of carers and any significant family members, neighbours, friends
- Details about home/accommodation
- Reasons for concerns with details of any incidents, etc.
- Details of alleged abuse including information about suspicions, specific information
- Details of any immediate action taken to make safe and protect
- Details of any medical examination/treatment
- Whether the person has agreed to/is aware of referral being made
- The mental capacity of the person – how this has been decided
- Details of any other professional/agency involved
- Details of other agencies copied in to referral (Commission for Social Care Inspection, Police, Primary Care Trust, Hospital Trust, etc.)
- Details of the alleged abuser
- Background information or history

How to reduce individual risks

The types of attitude change needed to ensure whole communities see that taking responsibility for the well-being of its vulnerable members is a good thing is going to take time. In the meantime, vulnerable people still need to be safeguarded and protected. Whatever your role, and regardless of your work setting, you will be able to have an impact in reducing the risks of harm and abuse for vulnerable adults.

No one can guarantee to prevent abuse from happening — human beings have always abused each other in one form or another. However, using the information you have about possible abusive situations, you are now able to work towards preventing abuse by recognising where and how it can happen.

Working with carers

The 2001 census identified that there were 6 million carers in the UK. This was 12 per cent of the adult population. The increasing number of older people, along with the policy of empowering people to remain active in the community for longer, means that the number of carers is forecast to rise by over 50 per cent to almost 9.5 million by 2037, which is less than 30 years away.

Try to ensure that people in stressful situations are offered as much support as possible. A carer is less likely to resort to abuse if they feel supported, acknowledged and appreciated. Showing caring and understanding of a person's situation can often help to defuse potential explosions. If you work directly with carers, you might express this by saying, 'It must be so hard caring for your mother. The demands she makes are so difficult. I think you are doing a wonderful job.' Such comments, although simple and straightforward, can often help a carer to feel that they do have someone who understands and has some interest in supporting them. So many times the focus is on the person in need of care and the carer is ignored. If your role involves the management and support of colleagues who are working directly in the community, you can ensure that there is an awareness and focus on carers and meeting their needs.

How carers are supported in law

The first National Strategy for carers — Caring for Carers — was introduced in 1999. Since April 2001, carers have had further rights under a new law: the Carers and Disabled Children Act 2000. This entitles carers to an assessment of their needs if they wish. This can be done when the person they care for is being assessed, or separately. The carer can, with guidance from a social worker or care manager, assess themselves.

The Carers (Equal Opportunities) Act 2004 came into force in England on the first of April 2005. The Act gives carers new rights to information and ensures that work, life-long learning and leisure are considered when a carer is assessed. The Work and Families Act 2006 extends the right of carers to request flexible working.

Working alongside carers is an essential part of protecting vulnerable adults. Even if there are no immediate concerns, working with carers to make sure that they are accessing their rights and having the support they are entitled to reduces the risks that an abusive incident can develop out of anger and frustration.

Supporting carers in the community

Some situations require much more than words of support, and giving practical, physical support to a carer or family may help to reduce the risk of abuse. The extra support provided by a professional carer can do this in two ways: first, it can provide the additional help which allows the carer to feel that they are not in a hopeless never-ending situation; and second, it can provide a regular opportunity to check someone where abuse is suspected or considered to be a major risk.

When resources are provided within the community rather than at home, this also offers a chance to observe someone who is thought to be at risk. Day centres and training centres also provide an opportunity for people to talk to staff. Here they will feel that they are in a supportive environment where they can talk about their fears and worries, and be believed and helped.

Situation	Solution
Carer needs to be able to access breaks when necessary	Either regular or flexible breaks can be arranged. Some areas operate voucher schemes so carers can organise breaks when it suits them; others have regular planned breaks.
Carer needs aids, equipment and adaptations	Physical environment can be adapted to make caring easier. Hoists, ramps, accessible bathrooms, electronic equipment can all make the caring task easier.
Carer needs support to work or undertake training	Carers can be provided with support for the cared-for person while they are at work and they can be helped to undertake training courses in order to return to work.
Carers need some time and interests for themselves	Carers can be provided with support while they are involved in leisure activity. Advice and information about opportunities as well as practical support is available.

Table 2: Identifying situations where carers need support.

Vulnerable carers

Remember that sometimes, it is the carer who is the vulnerable person. For example, an older parent caring for a son or daughter with mental health problems, or who exhibits challenging behaviour, may be very much at risk. It is important to look at the whole picture when carrying out a risk assessment, and to offer support and protection to any vulnerable adult who is at risk.

Case study

Identifying vulnerable people

Mrs Clarke is 75 years old. She is quite fit, although increasingly her arthritis is slowing her down and making her less steady on her feet. She has been a widow for 15 years and lives with her only son, Ronnie, who is 51. When Ronnie was 29, he had a motorcycle accident. This caused brain damage, from which he has never fully recovered. His speech is slow and he sometimes has problems in communication. His coordination and fine motor skills have been affected, so he has problems with buttons, shoelaces and writing. Ronnie also suffers from major mood swings and can be aggressive. Mrs Clarke is Ronnie's only carer. He has not worked since the accident, but he goes to a day centre three days each week. Mrs Clarke takes the opportunity to go to a day centre herself on those three days because she enjoys the company, the outings and activities.

Recently, Mrs Clarke has had an increasing number of injuries. In the past two months she has had a grazed forehead, a black eye, a split lip and last week she arrived at the day centre with a bruised and sprained wrist. She finally admitted to the centre staff that Ronnie had inflicted the injuries during his periods of bad temper. She said that these were becoming more frequent as he became more frustrated with her slowness.

Despite being very distressed, Mrs Clarke would not agree to being separated from Ronnie. She was adamant that he did not mean to hurt her. She would not consider making a complaint to the police. Finally, Mrs Clarke agreed to increasing both her and Ronnie's attendance at their day centres, and to having some assistance with daily living.

1. What action can be taken?
2. What action should be taken?
3. Whose responsibility is this situation?

This kind of situation may cause a great deal of concern and anxiety for the care workers, but there are limits on the legal powers to intervene and there is no justification for removing Mrs Clarke's right to make her own decisions.

Activity 3

Mrs Clarke and Ronnie

Imagine that you are the support worker to Mrs Clarke and Ronnie. Your work involves regular visits to their house to monitor the effectiveness of the care package and provide support. One day you arrive to find Ronnie screaming at Mrs Clarke and hitting her.

1. What would your immediate actions be?
2. Write a report covering the incident, including your actions.
3. To whom would you give your report?
4. Who else would need to be informed of this incident?

Consent

A key issue in the protection of vulnerable adults is one of consent. Vulnerable adults have a fundamental human right to decide how and with whom they live. A person who is able to make decisions for themselves is entitled to refuse protection and to limit what you are able to do. In general, any action you take in relation to protecting a vulnerable adult must be with their consent.

The issue of gaining consent before taking any action does not only apply to reporting abuse, it also applies to providing evidence for any prosecution and to having any medical examination to record and confirm any injuries or other forensic evidence. If you are faced with a situation where it is clear that abuse has taken place and the vulnerable person is refusing to make a complaint, or to undergo a medical examination, then your only way forward is to try to give them as much clear information as possible and then to refer the situation to your line manager for consideration as to whether any further action is possible.

The steps you can take are limited; there is no legislation that gives vulnerable adults a right of protection as there is for children.

Reasons for refusing consent

There are many reasons why people refuse to agree to any further action being taken. If you can find out the reason, you may be able to provide the information and support that people need. Some of the reasons include those shown in Table 3.

Reason for refusal	Information to give
Fear of reprisals from the abuser	Reassure that it will be possible to make sure that there is no need to have contact with the abuser, and the person can be protected.
Belief that it is own fault	Emphasise that it is *never* the fault of the survivor, give information and reassurance about rights and state that abuse is against the law. Confirm that abusers are bullies and criminals.
Fear that services will be withdrawn	Reassure that a complaint against a professional is taken very seriously, and that services are a right. No one will remove services because of a complaint. Assure that service provider is on the side of the survivor, not the abuser — even if the abuser is the employee.
Fear of medical examination	Ask medical staff to explain procedure and to reassure. Explain why it is important to provide evidence, and show types of evidence that can be found from examination.
Fear of police investigation/court appearance	Explain support available for police interviews and for court appearances.

Table 3: Possible reasons for refusing consent, and how to respond to these.

Important difference

A refusal to undergo medical treatment following injuries is an entirely different situation to refusing to undergo a medical examination. If you are faced with someone who has been injured and is refusing treatment, then you must refer the matter to a doctor immediately, so that a decision can be made on the best way forward depending on the nature and severity of the injuries. This is not a decision for you to make without medical support.

3. Understand the national and local context of safeguarding and protection from abuse

Both nationally and locally, the protection of vulnerable adults forms part of the Safeguarding Adults agenda. Local authorities now have Safeguarding Adults Boards. These mirror the Local Safeguarding Children Boards, except that they do not have the statutory basis and powers of the Children's Boards. The local boards are responsible for delivering a multi-agency response to safeguarding adults and to ensure that all the partner agencies are recognising and acting on safeguarding issues at a strategic and an individual level. For example, late-night transport or street lighting may be a strategic issue for safeguarding adults, but it is equally important that systems are in place to deal with individual allegations. The local boards will have members from social services, the voluntary sector, police, housing and health as a minimum, and possibly other areas such as leisure, transport and highways. They are also responsible for conducting Serious Case Reviews when someone has died as the result of abuse and there are lessons to be learned.

Empower and protect

Current thinking in relation to policy for vulnerable adults is to focus less on someone as 'having a problem' which needs to be resolved, and more on empowering vulnerable people in their role as citizens. If people are contributors to decision making and are a valued and recognised vital part of a community, then abuse is less likely to occur, or if it does, people feel more able to report it and to take steps to stop it. Even the term 'vulnerable adults' tends to make people sound as if they have no power and are a target for bullies. It also sounds as if people need to be protected from harm and risk — and they do.

This type of policy change will take time to come into effect; if you have been around in the sector for many years, you may remember a time when rights, dignity, choice and anti-discriminatory practice were unheard of. Now all of these form a vital part of good practice and everyone understands how essential they are. The same thing will happen to the concept of empowerment as a means of protection, and it will become the basis for reducing the incidence of abuse and protecting vulnerable people from it.

If you take a direct comparison with child abuse, you can see that for over 20 years, the focus was on risk analysis, individual intervention and the removal of children into 'care'. Sadly, this often replaced one type of abuse with another. The 'Quality Protects' initiative in the late 1990s began a change in attitude and professionals began to recognise that improving the quality of children's services was an effective means of safeguarding against abuse, but it was the introduction of Sure Start and Connexions which really made it clear that children and young people are an integral part of society and that there has to be a 'whole system' — rather than separate parts just working together. The 2006 White Paper 'Our Health, Our Care, Our Say', quickly followed by 'Putting People First', set out the agenda for empowering people to take control of their services and support. This is moving rapidly and, by 2011, everyone who uses social care services will have the option to choose what services they want and how and by whom they want them delivered.

Being strong, informed and active citizens is a good protection against abuse.

Information is power

Giving people information and making sure that they are aware of their rights is very important. It is surprising how often a vulnerable adult who has been in an abusive situation did not even realise they were being abused, or that there was anything that could be done about it. After all, you have to be able to recognise abuse before you can report it!

Ways to empower vulnerable adults

For people to feel that they are able to take control and deal with difficulties, they need to have the means to do so. Many of the changes that need to be made will be outside your area of responsibility, and need to be undertaken by organisations at a strategic level. However, your own practice can make a huge contribution, and you can make suggestions and gain agreement to make improvements.

- Awareness of abuse of vulnerable adults must be part of all information that goes out. It should be available in a wide rage of formats – print, audio, Braille, appropriate languages, in picture format, large print and plain language.
- Information should be available about what abusive behaviour is, how to recognise it and how and where to report it.
- Information should be available everywhere, leaflets in all communications sent out by the agency, posters in libraries, leisure centres, schools, hospitals, churches, community centres, cinemas, pubs as well as in places providing services for vulnerable adults.

Knowledge is power – it makes people strong and less vulnerable.

- Reporting of abuse must be easily accessible — one easily remembered free telephone number or a 'one stop shop' in a central place.
- Publicity could be carried out through local newspapers, TV programmes and radio programmes.
- Involvement of survivors of abuse in policy-making forums can assist in looking at how to improve responses.
- Involvement of vulnerable adults in decisions about how services are planned and commissioned can raise their profile.

Case study

Reporting concerns

Kathy works in a post office in a small Midlands market town. She has known Mrs Morris for many years and always stops for a chat when she collects her pension. Kathy also sees her at the local church every week. Mrs Morris has always been active in the local community and is very friendly and sociable.

Mrs Morris's son and daughter-in-law have recently moved into her house. They have just moved from another part of the country and are not working. Mrs Morris had never spoken much about her son Paul, and Kathy was quite surprised when she mentioned he was moving in — Mrs Morris just said that he had had a bit of trouble where he was, but did not seem keen to talk about it. After Paul moved in, Mrs Morris did not come to church or to the post office for a few weeks. Eventually Paul came in to collect his mother's money. When Kathy asked how she was, Paul said that she was very confused and unable to look after herself any more. Kathy was surprised and sad, as Mrs Morris had always been so well and such an active person.

A few weeks later, Kathy was walking past Mrs Morris's house and saw Paul and his wife carrying boxes out of the house. Mrs Morris was watching through the window and crying, obviously unhappy about what they were doing. Kathy was very concerned and asked what was going on. Paul shouted at her that he was having to cope with looking after his mother who was too confused to communicate and was unable to go out, and that he was doing his best and Kathy should mind her own business.

Kathy left because she was quite frightened by his aggression, but she still felt that something should be done.

1. Should Kathy report her concerns and, if so, to whom?
2. How could she find out what Mrs Morris wants?
3. Is abuse everyone's business?

Legislation

There are laws that provide the basis for dealing with abuse of vulnerable adults. The legislation is not as clear-cut as it is for the protection of children, and there are no specific laws in England that deal exclusively with abuse, although the situation is different in Scotland.

Table 4 identifies some of the laws, regulations and guidelines that can be used in abusive situations.

Act of Parliament/regulation/guideline	Use	Type of abuse
Criminal Justice Act 1998	Criminal prosecution by police for assault.	Physical
Civil action by the victim	For assault, battery or false imprisonment.	Physical
Care Standards Act 2000	Regulation of residential and nursing homes – S10 – cancellation of Registration, S11 – emergency cancellation, for breach of regulations. However, it is the driving up of quality as a result of this Act which offers the best protection against abuse.	Institutional
Sexual Offences Act 2003	Police prosecution for rape, indecent assault and other sexual offences. This Act has greatly increased the protection for people with a learning disability or mental health problems because it has defined 'consent'.	Sexual
Family Law Act 1996	Can provide injunctions and non-molestation orders.	Physical, sexual, psychological
Offences Against the Person Act 1861	Prosecution by the police for more serious offences of actual bodily harm or grievous bodily harm.	Physical
No Secrets (England) and In Safe Hands (Wales)	Guidance documents that set out how local authorities must work jointly with other agencies to make local arrangements to safeguard and protect vulnerable adults.	All
Safeguarding Vulnerable Groups (Scotland) Act 2006	Sets up vetting and barring scheme for people who work with children and vulnerable adults in England and Wales.	All
Protection of Vulnerable Groups (Scotland) Act 2007	Sets up a vetting and barring scheme for people who work with vulnerable adults in Scotland.	All in Scotland
Adult Support and Protection (Scotland) Act (ASPA) 2007	Gives local authorities in Scotland the power to enter premises where they suspect abuse is taking place, and there are also powers to remove perpetrators and ban them from returning to the premises.	Physical, sexual
Criminal Injuries Compensation scheme	Can provide payments for survivors of abuse that was the result of a criminal act.	Physical, sexual, financial if criminality proven
Mental Capacity Act 2005	A criminal offence to ill-treat or neglect a person who lacks capacity.	Physical, sexual, neglect
Police and Criminal Evidence Act 1984 S17	Gives police emergency powers to enter premises if they believe there is danger to 'life and limb'.	Physical
Mental Health Act 1983	S37 is about the powers of a local authority, relative or court to take out guardianship of a vulnerable adult.

S115 is about the powers of entry and inspection for Approved Social Workers.

S117 is about providing after care for people with mental health problems.

S135 is about powers to remove people to a 'place of safety'.

S127 is about the ill-treatment of patients with mental health problems. | All |

Act of Parliament/ regulation/guideline	Use	Type of abuse
Protection from Harassment Act 1997	Provides protection from harassment and from fear of violence.	Psychological
Theft Act 1968	Police prosecution for theft.	Financial
National Assistance Act 1984 S47	Local authority has responsibility for matters to do with protection of property.	Financial
Fraud Act 2006	Has made it an offence to abuse a position of trust.	Financial
Office of the Public Guardian	Supports and promotes decision making for people who lack capacity.	Financial

Table 4: Acts of Parliament that relate to abusive situations.

Vetting and barring

Both England and Scotland now have legislation that sets up vetting and barring schemes that are designed to ensure that people who are unsuitable to work with vulnerable adults, or with children, are prevented from doing so.

In England, the Act set up the Independent Safeguarding Authority (ISA), which oversees the registration of people working, or who want to work, with vulnerable adults or children. There are different levels of activity, for those who work or volunteer occasionally with vulnerable groups, and those who work with them on a day-to-day basis. Criminal records checks are undertaken on everyone who works or volunteers, and anyone found to have a record of offences will be barred from working with vulnerable groups.

Information about people who have been barred is circulated to employers so that they do not take on someone unsuitable. Under the Act it is an offence for an employer to employ someone they know has been barred. (For more information, see www.isa-gov.org.uk)

Recognise the importance of whistleblowing

Abuse by professional carers

Responding to an abusive situation in your own, or another, workplace can be very difficult. There may be many reasons why you feel that you should not intervene.

- It will mean problems with colleagues — you will make yourself unpopular.
- It could jeopardise promotion — no one will trust you again.
- You might be wrong.

You may feel that you should leave matters to sort themselves out. You should not and they will not.

'Blowing the whistle' about an abusive situation among colleagues is never easy, but you have an absolute duty to do so; there are no if and buts.

The government has recognised this, and following several well-publicised cases, passed the Public Interest Disclosure Act 1998. This protects whistleblowers and ensures that you cannot be victimised by your employer for reporting abuse or any other illegal acts. The Act protects people making disclosures about:

- a criminal offence
- the breach of a legal obligation
- a miscarriage of justice
- a danger to the health or safety of any person
- damage to the environment
- deliberate covering up of information tending to show any of the above five matters.

The basis for being protected by the Act is that the worker is giving information that they 'reasonably believe tends to show that one or more of the above matters is either happening now, took place in the past, or is likely to happen in the future'.

It is important to realise that you must have reasonable belief that the information tends to show one or more of the offences or breaches listed above. You may not actually be right – it might be discovered on investigation that you were wrong – but as long as you can show that you believed it to be so, and that it was a reasonable belief in the circumstances at the time of disclosure, then you are protected by the law.

If you believe that your line manager will not take action, either because of misplaced loyalty or an unwillingness to confront or challenge difficult situations, then you must make a referral to a more senior manager. You must keep moving through the management chain until you reach the person you consider able and willing to take action. If there is no one within your own organisation, then you must make a referral to an outside agency.

Contact your local authority and make the referral to the social services department.

If you believe that the abuse you are aware of is potentially a criminal offence, such as physical or sexual assault, theft or fraud, then you should refer the matter to the police. At the same time, you should refer to the Care Quality Commission or inspectorate for the UK country in which you work.

How is this investigated?

Each local authority must have a multi-agency Local Safeguarding Adults Board for the protection of vulnerable adults. This committee is responsible for setting out procedures and policies, identifying and protecting those at risk, and ensuring each agency has an appropriate response to abuse. It is likely that the procedure for your workplace in relation to abuse by a professional carer will involve:

- immediate suspension of the person accused
- investigation by police if appropriate
- investigation led by an independent agency
- disciplinary procedures following the outcome of any police or protection investigation.

Case study

Abuse by a care professional

Mr Patel is 89 years old and has lived alone in his three-bedroomed house since his wife died several years ago. He has impaired sight and hearing, and mobility is limited after a recent fall in which he hurt his back. He has had twice-weekly visits from a physiotherapist from the local Primary Care Trust, for the past month. Mr Patel has daily social care support from a private provider contracted by Social Services.

Selina has been Mr Patel's support worker for the past year. She has noticed that over the past few weeks he is losing weight and that his meals, which are delivered daily, are largely uneaten. Mr Patel will only say that he is feeling a bit down and has not felt very hungry recently.

One day, Selina arrives at the door and hears someone shouting, 'Get on with it – you are not trying at all, you are so lazy.' As Selina walks into the hall, the physiotherapist looks shocked to see her and says that she is just leaving. After she leaves, Selina tackles Mr Patel and asks if everything is going well with the physio's visits. He says that there is a long waiting list for physio and he is very lucky to have anyone.

1. What can Selina do?
2. What barriers may she face in trying to deal with this issue?
3. Is this abusive behaviour?
4. How would you try to empower Mr Patel?

When the organisation abuses

You may want to blow the whistle about the way an organisation is run, or the quality of a service. You could find yourself working in an organisation where standards are not being met and vulnerable people are being abused because of the policies and procedures of the organisation rather than through the behaviour of any particular person. There may be a policy of overmedication, or vulnerable people may not be given sufficient food. People could be left in wet or soiled clothing or bedding, or the organisation may have a policy of restricting rights or freedoms. There is further information about institutional abuse on page 102. In this situation, you should contact your local inspectorate or the Local Safeguarding Adults Board.

Public Concern at Work is a national organisation that provides legal advice to those concerned about malpractice at work. The service is free and strictly confidential. (For more information, see www.pcaw.co.uk)

Challenging the potential for abuse

All abusive behaviour is unacceptable. However, there are other sorts of behaviour that you may come across which you may not be able to define directly as abusive, but which is certainly close to it — or could lead to an abusive situation if not dealt with.

Generally, you can define behaviour as unacceptable if:

- it is outside what you would normally see in that situation
- it does not take into account the needs or views of others
- people are afraid or intimidated
- people are undermined or made to feel guilty
- the behaviour is likely to cause distress or unhappiness to others
- someone is threatening violence
- someone is subjecting another person to unwelcome sexual harassment
- someone is playing loud music in a quiet area, or late at night
- there is verbal abuse, racist or sexist innuendo
- a person is spreading malicious gossip about someone
- someone is attempting to isolate another person.

Unacceptable behaviour from colleagues

You may come across unacceptable and oppressive behaviour in your colleagues or other professionals in your workplace. While you may see or hear a colleague behaving in a way which is not abusive as such, it may be oppressive and unacceptable. This can take various forms such as:

- speaking about people in a derogatory way
- speaking to someone in a rude or dismissive way
- humiliating people
- undermining people's self-esteem and confidence
- bullying or intimidation
- patronising and talking down to people
- removing people's right to exercise choice
- failing to recognise and treat people as individuals
- not respecting people's culture, values and beliefs.

In short, the types of behaviour that are unacceptable from workers in care settings are those which simply fail to meet the standards required of good-quality practitioners. Any support worker who fails to remember that all people they support are individuals, and that all people have a right to be valued and accepted, is likely to fall into behaving in an oppressive or unacceptable way.

All of these types of behaviour are oppressive to others and need to be challenged, whether it is behaviour by colleagues, visitors, carers or those being supported. You can probably think of many other situations in your own workplace that have caused unhappiness. You may have had to deal with difficult situations, or have seen others

Activity 4

Unacceptable behaviour

Ask three colleagues in your workplace to state one behaviour that they would find unacceptable in:

1. someone who was being supported
2. a colleague.

Compare the six answers and see if they have anything in common. Find out from your supervisor about the type of behaviour that is challenged in your workplace, and behaviour which is allowed.

deal with them, or perhaps you have wished that you had done something to challenge unacceptable behaviour.

The effects of abuse

Abuse can devastate those who experience it. It causes people to lose their self-esteem and their confidence. Many adults and children become withdrawn and find it hard to communicate. Anger is a common emotion among people who have been abused. It may be directed against the abuser, or at those people around them who failed to recognise the abuse and stop it happening.

One of the greatest tragedies is when people who have been abused turn their anger against themselves, and blame themselves for everything that has happened. These are situations that require expert help, and this should be available to anyone who has been abused, regardless of the circumstances.

Some of the behaviour changes that can be signs of abuse can become permanent, or certainly very long-lasting. There are very few survivors of abuse whose personality remains unchanged, and for those who do conquer the effects of abuse, it is a long, hard fight.

The abuser, or perpetrator, also requires expert help, and this should be available through various agencies, depending on the type and seriousness of the abuse. People who abuse, whether their victims are children or vulnerable adults, receive very little sympathy or understanding from society. There is no public recognition that some abusers may have been under tremendous strain and pressure, and abusers may find that they have no support from friends or family. Many abusers will face the consequences of their actions alone.

Support workers who have to deal with abusive situations will have different emotional reactions. There is no 'right way' to react. Everyone is different and will deal with things in their own way. If you have to deal with abuse, these are some of the ways you may feel, and some steps you can take that may help.

Shock

You may feel quite traumatised if you have witnessed an abusive incident. It is normal to find that you cannot get the incident out of your mind, that you have difficulty concentrating on other things, or that you keep having flashbacks and re-enacting the situation in your head. You may also feel that you need to keep talking about what happened.

Talking can be very beneficial, but if you are discussing an incident outside your workplace, you must remember the rules of confidentiality and never use names. This way of talking does become second nature, and is useful because it allows you to share your feelings about things that have happened at work while maintaining confidentiality.

These feelings are likely to last for a fairly short time, and are a natural reaction to shock and trauma. If at any time you feel that you are having difficulty, you must talk to your manager or supervisor, who should be able to help.

Anger

Alternatively, the situation may have made you feel very angry, and you may have an overwhelming urge to inflict some damage on the perpetrator of the abuse. While this is understandable, it is not professional and you will have to find other ways of dealing with their anger. Again, your supervisor or manager should help you to work through your feelings.

Everyone has different ways of dealing with anger, such as taking physical exercise, doing housework, punching a cushion, writing feelings down and then tearing up the paper, crying or telling their best friend. Whatever you do normally to express your anger, you should do the same in this situation (just remember to respect confidentiality if you need to tell your best friend – miss out the names). It is perfectly legitimate to be angry, but you cannot bring this anger into the professional relationship.

Distress

The situation may have made you distressed, and you may want to go home and have a good cry, or give your own relatives an extra hug. This is a perfectly normal reaction. No matter how many years you work, or how many times it happens, you may still feel the same way.

Some workplaces will have arrangements in place where workers are able to share difficult situations and get support from each other. Others may not have any formal meetings or groups arranged, but colleagues will offer each other support and advice in an informal way. You may find that work colleagues who have had similar experiences are the best people with whom to share your feelings.

There is, of course, the possibility that the situation may have brought back painful memories for you of abuse you have suffered in your own past. This is often the most difficult situation to deal with, because you may feel as if you should be able to help because you know how it feels to be abused, but your own experience has left you without any room to deal with the feelings of others. There are many avenues of support now available to survivors of abuse. You can find out about the nearest support confidentially, if you do not want your workplace colleagues or supervisor to know. Try www.stopitnow.org.uk or www.abuse-survivors.org.uk. Organisations such as your local Citizens Advice Bureau, health centre or library will also have contact details on posters and leaflets in case you do not want to ask.

There is no doubt that dealing with abuse is one of the most stressful aspects of working in social care. There is nothing odd or abnormal about feeling that you need to share what you have experienced and looking for support from others. In fact, most experienced managers would be far more concerned about a worker involved in dealing with abuse who appears quite unaffected by it than about one who comes looking for guidance and reassurance.

Dealing with abuse is difficult and demanding for everyone, and it is essential that you receive professional supervision from your manager. This may be undertaken in a regular supervision or support meeting if you have one. If not, it will be important that you arrange to meet with your supervisor, so that you can ensure you are working in the correct way and in accordance with the procedure in your setting.

Overview

Much of what you read about dealing with abuse may give you the impression that this is an area full of rules and procedures. It is, and for very good reasons. Abuse is extremely serious – it is potentially life-threatening. Systems and rules have been developed by learning from the tragedies that have happened in the past. Many of these tragedies occurred because procedures were either not in place or not followed. You must make sure that you and any staff you supervise know what the procedures are in your workplace and follow them carefully.

Working through this unit may make you feel as though abusive behaviour is all around you, and that vulnerable people are being hurt and frightened by carers all around you. Thankfully, the majority of carers and support workers do not abuse; they provide a good standard of care. And most vulnerable adults are not subjected to harm. However, while that may be comforting to know, it is the case that as more professionals develop understanding of abuse and are aware of how to recognise and respond to abuse, the less likely it is that abusers will be able to continue to harm vulnerable people.

Getting ready for assessment

This unit is about showing your assessor your knowledge and understanding of safeguarding and protection. For obvious reasons, your assessor is not likely to observe your practice. You are more likely to have to produce an assignment or a presentation to show that you can recognise abuse and know what signs to look for. You may have to describe these or find examples to illustrate them. Your assessor will also want to know that you are familiar with the legal basis for safeguarding and that you know what steps to take if someone makes allegations of abuse. You will need to be able to identify the legislation and to explain about how Local Safeguarding Children Boards work. There are some circumstances that make abuse more likely and you will need to show that you can identify what steps to follow to make abuse less likely to occur. One of the most difficult areas is to know how to 'blow the whistle' when you identify poor practice or even abuse among your colleagues. Your assessor will probably ask 'what if' questions to see if you understand what you need to do.

Doing it well

Dealing with abuse

- Feeling upset is normal.
- Talk about the incident if that helps, but respect the rules of confidentiality and miss out the names.
- Being angry is OK, but deal with it sensibly – take physical exercise, do the housework, cry.
- Do not be unprofessional with the abuser.
- If you are a survivor of abuse and you find it hard to deal with, ask for help.

Legislation

- Adult Support and Protection (Scotland) Act (ASPA) 2007
- Care Standards Act 2000
- Carers and Disabled Children Act 2000
- Carers (Equal Opportunities) Act 2004
- Criminal Justice Act 1998
- Data Protection Act 1998
- Family Law Act 1996
- Fraud Act 2006
- Mental Capacity Act 2005
- Mental Health Act 1983
- National Assistance Act 1984 S47
- No Secrets (England) and In Safe Hands (Wales)
- Offences Against the Person Act 1861
- Office of the Public Guardian
- Police and Criminal Evidence Act 1984 S17
- Protection from Harassment Act 1997
- Protection of Vulnerable Groups (Scotland) Act 2007
- Public Interest Disclosure Act 1998
- Safeguarding Vulnerable Groups Act 2006
- Sexual Offences Act 2003
- Theft Act 1968
- Work and Families Act 2006

Further reading and research

- www.abuse-survivors.org.uk (Abuse Survivors, support and information)
- www.cqc.org.uk (Care Quality Commission)
- www.isa-gov.org.uk (Independent Safeguarding Authority)
- www.pcaw.co.uk (Public Concern at Work)
- www.stopitnow.org.uk (Stop It Now, an organisation fighting sexual abuse against children)

Unit HSC 025

The role of the health and social care worker

This unit looks at your role as a professional care and support worker. The way in which you perform your role can have a major impact on a person's well-being and how they experience the services they need.

As a support worker, you have a range of responsibilities. Primarily you are responsible for delivering a quality service to the person you are supporting. You must do this by working in ways that your employer expects – of course, it may be that your employer is the person whom you support. You will also need to work in partnership with others, both professional colleagues and family or friends who are also providing support.

In this unit you will learn about:

1. working relationships in health and social care
2. how to work in ways that are agreed with the employer
3. how to work in partnership with others.

1. Understand working relationships in health and social care

1.1 Working relationships and personal relationships

Most people have a wide range of relationships with different people in different aspects of their lives. Relationships range from family to work colleagues. Each of the different types of relationship is important and plays a valuable role in contributing to the overall well-being of each of us as individuals. However, the needs and demands of different types of relationships are varied, as are the effects that relationships can have on a person's view of themselves and the confidence with which they deal with the world.

Types of relationships	Features of relationship
Family relationships	These are relationships with parents, grandparents, siblings and children. Depending on the type of family, they can be close or distant.
Sexual relationships	These relationships can be long term or short term, with a spouse or permanent partner, or shorter-term non-permanent relationships. The impact of sexual relationships is different from family relationships and more intense than the demands of a friendship.
Friendships	Friendships can be long term or can be short term but quite intense. Most people have a few close friends and a much larger circle of friends who are not quite so intimate or close. These may be friends who are part of a wide social circle but perhaps not close enough to share intimate details of someone's life. Close friends, on the other hand, are often the ones who are an immediate source of support in times of difficulty and the first person with whom good news is shared.
Working relationships	These can be relationships with employers or with work colleagues. Some may stray over the boundaries into friendships, but for most people the colleagues with whom they work are related in a different way to that in which they would relate to friends. For example, work colleagues may share very little information about someone's personal life even though they may have very close and regular day-to-day contact. It is perfectly possible to spend a great deal more time with work colleagues than with friends, but not be as close.

Table 1: Types and features of different relationships.

Family relationships

Family relationships are usually those that influence people most. For most children the type of relationship they have within the family where they grow up influences the rest of their lives and the kind of people they become. Primarily it is the relationship with their parents or main carers that is the most influential during childhood. For a growing child, relationships with parents and other extended family members, such as grandparents and siblings, provide the emotional security that is important in establishing a positive self-image and in developing confidence. As children grow through adolescence and into early adulthood, family relationships become less dominant as an influence; however, they remain significant for most people throughout their lives. It is notable that most major occasions in people's lives, such as weddings, christenings and coming-of-age birthdays, are regarded as 'family occasions', when members of the immediate and extended family are usually involved and invited to join the celebrations.

Sexual relationships

Most people who have a long-term sexual relationship would probably view that as being the most significant relationship in their lives. Even short-term sexual relationships can have a huge effect on someone and how they regard themselves and their general health and well-being. The physical closeness of a sexual relationship means that the dynamics involved are significantly different from other family relationships. Sexual partners are often close emotionally as a result of their intimate physical relationship. Sexual relationships can be long or short term, can be with an opposite or same-sex partner, and can be exclusive — with just one partner — or non-exclusive — where partners also have sexual relationships with others. These types of sexual relationships will obviously have different effects and will meet the needs of different people, possibly at different stages in their lives. For example, teenagers and young adults may have short-term and non-exclusive sexual relationships with a number of partners, but many will eventually develop a long-term exclusive relationship with one partner with whom they may remain for many years.

Friendship

Friends become increasingly significant as children grow. For very young children, pre-school individual friendships with other children, while important for their social development, are relatively insignificant as influences on their lives. Their relationships with other members of their family or their main carer are far more important. As children progress through school and into adolescence, their friendships become more important and have a huge influence on their behaviour. The ability to form friendships with others is an important skill and is a need that most human beings have. An inability of a child or young person to make friends or to be in a situation in which they feel they do not have friends, or are being bullied or excluded by others with whom they had hoped to be friends, can be extremely distressing and have a serious effect on the child's self-image and self-confidence. Adults too find it difficult to cope with being excluded and being unable to relate to others as friends. Most people, regardless of circumstances, need to have a close relationship with another person, through which they can share confidences, worries and joy.

Family structures

As recently as the early part of the last century, family structures were very different from how they are now. Less than a hundred years ago the most common family structure was an extended family with mother, father, grandparents, aunts and uncles living close to one another, if not in the same house. Children would move between different members of the family regularly and were equally at home being cared for by a range of relatives. Fifty years ago the most common family structure was a nuclear family, with mother, father and children living in the same house but not necessarily living close to other members of their family. While both nuclear and extended families are still quite common, there is now a much wider range of family structures and, as a result, a wider range of relationships and patterns of communication within families. Table 2 shows family structures and relationships within them.

Type of family	Features
Traditional extended family	Parents, grandparents, aunts, uncles, sisters, brothers, children, nieces and nephews living together or in close proximity.
Traditional nuclear family	Two parents and children living together. May or may not be close contact with other members of the family, but less likely than in an extended family.
Reconstituted family	Parents both have children from previous relationships, and then possibly children together.
Step-parent family	A family where one parent has children from a previous relationship and the other takes a step-parenting role.
Lone parent family	One parent bringing up children without a partner.
Cohabiting family	Unmarried partners who may also come into any of the categories above.
Same-sex family	Same-sex partners with or without children.

Table 2: Different types of family structure.

Families can be structured in different ways.

Working relationships

Effective working relationships are extremely important both to employees and to the organisations for whom they work. Businesses use techniques designed to encourage work colleagues to work well and effectively together. Usually, establishing good working relationships with colleagues requires an effective use of communication skills and a recognition of the value and significance of work undertaken by colleagues. For most people, having a good working relationship with colleagues is important, as it contributes significantly to overall job satisfaction. There are significant differences in a working relationship and the kind of personal relationships you may have with your friends or family. A working relationship is different because of:

- specific objectives and purpose
- boundaries
- professional codes of conduct
- employer policies and procedures
- time limits
- being in some cases a one-way relationship.

In a working relationship the reasons why you are involved with a particular person are clear. They will be in the **outcomes** of the support plan. This is different from choosing to be someone's friend, or having been born into a family. In a professional relationship, you are in a relationship with someone because it is your job. You will also have working relationships with colleagues and other professionals. In the same way, these are relationships that are necessary because they are part of your job and are in the interests of the people you support.

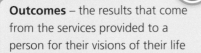

Key term

Outcomes – the results that come from the services provided to a person for their visions of their life

Professional relationships have clear boundaries; there are lines that you must not cross. For example, you should never invite someone you support to your home, nor should you visit them socially. You must not accept gifts or any payments, nor should you take gifts or give any of your own money to someone you are supporting. Sharing personal information can be difficult sometimes, especially as you will have a great deal of information about the people with whom you work. This can be especially difficult if you see them very regularly and they are friendly and show an interest in you. If people ask questions, it is almost impossible not to give some information. Sharing some basic information about yourself with someone who has a genuine interest is acceptable, but it is not acceptable to discuss any significant personal details about your life.

For example, telling someone that your daughter is sitting her GCSE exams is fine – even telling them the results if they ask is acceptable – but telling them about problems with your partner or that you think your son may be getting in with a bad crowd is not.

Professional codes of conduct set down by the regulators in each of the UK countries spell out how relationships are to be conducted. Following your code of conduct is a requirement of being a professional, and it is expected that everyone will practise in a way that stays within the code.

There is no written code of conduct for personal friendships or families, even though you may sometimes think that there should be! The way we conduct our personal relationships follows an unwritten code about how people behave towards each other, but it is not monitored by a regulator, nor a requirement of holding a professional position.

Reflect

Have you ever felt that you would like to become a personal friend of someone you support? Has there been a person with whom you have got on really well? How did you handle it? Do you honestly feel on reflection that you were totally professional and did not allow your personal feelings to cross the line a little? Think about what lessons you can learn from that experience.

Taking gifts is not permitted.

Your employer will have policies and procedures around what is acceptable; these are likely to follow the codes of conduct. However, if your employer is the person you support, it may be a little less formal and they may choose to have a more personal relationship.

In general, professional relationships are 'one way' in that you are not looking for anything back from the person you are supporting. There is no expectation that they will be supportive to you in return as you would expect from a friend or family member.

You are the person who is offering support; you are not looking for anything in return. In reality, of course, there are benefits that you will get, but they are in the area of job satisfaction, not personal friendship or support.

Information sharing is also one way in the other direction, as you are likely to know a great deal more information about the person you are supporting than they do about you.

1.2 Different working relationships

You have just been looking at how the relationship works with people that you support, but they are not the only working relationships you need to understand. You will also have relationships with colleagues both in your own organisation and in other organisations.

In any setting, it is not just the people using the services who have to be together for long periods of time – the staff have to learn to live together too! This may be the first time you have worked in a team with other colleagues, or it may be that you have moved to a new team that will function differently from the last place you worked – each team is different.

Teams take time to work well; they go through various stages as they settle down and every time a new team member arrives, things change. Not everyone will share the same views about how tasks should be undertaken and the right course of action on every occasion, and much will depend on how well the team is managed. However, some ground rules to make sure that you can work well with others can be used in most situations.

- Find out the ways in which decisions are reached and the team members who should be included.
- Always ask for advice and clarify anything you are not sure about.
- Do not assume that everything is the same in every workplace.
- Recognise that every team member, regardless of their role and status, has an essential contribution to make.
- Value the input of all colleagues and recognise its importance.
- Make sure that the way you work is not increasing the workload of others or hindering them in carrying out their work.

Most workplaces have a means of decision making – this could be planning and review meetings where decisions are made about service provision, staff meetings may be the forum for making decisions about general practice matters, or there may be specific staff development and training meetings for sharing best practice. Organised staff meetings run by a line manager or supervisor are the best place for airing differences about practice.

Supporting colleagues

'Supportive working relationships' is a very general term and can mean a great many things depending on the context and the purpose of the support. In the context of relationships with a work colleague in a team, support could mean:

- recognising when somebody is having difficulty in a particular area of work
- recognising when somebody is having difficulty in their personal life which may be affecting their work
- recognising and acknowledging when a colleague has worked particularly well
- noticing when people are overloaded with jobs to do and offering to lend a hand
- telling colleagues about information you have discovered or something you have seen or read which you know would be of interest to them
- making sure colleagues know of opportunities for training courses which you think are likely to interest them

Functional skills

English: Speaking and listening

Using the information you have gathered for Activity 1, have a discussion with other members of your team about the support that you give to each other. Ensure that you take an active role in the discussion but also take on board comments and opinions from other members of the team. Use appropriate language and present your points clearly.

Activity 1

Receiving and giving support

Keep a calendar for a week or two, or even a month. For each day, draw a stick figure which represents yourself. At the end of each working shift, draw arrows:

- outward from you for support which you have given to others in your team
- inward for the occasions when support has been offered to you.

None of the items may seem large, but a series of small actions of support is what is likely to contribute most effectively to successful teams.

At the end of each week, count up the arrows inward and the arrows outward. They should be in proportion to the people who work on the team, and you should be giving and receiving support in equal measure. If there are more arrows in than out, then you need to explore for yourself additional ways in which you can support colleagues. If there are more arrows out than in, then this is an item that could usefully be placed on the agenda at a team meeting.

- noticing when a colleague is nervous or unsure of a new task or procedure and offering help and encouragement
- noticing if a colleague is being made uncomfortable by the way in which they are being spoken to or treated by someone and offering to help if it is needed.

This list will make a contribution towards effective working relationships with other members of your team. If your team is working well, your colleagues will be doing the same thing for you and supporting you in your role.

Sometimes it is useful to offer a helping hand to a colleague who is supporting somebody.

2. Be able to work in ways that are agreed with the employer

2.1 The scope of the job

Working within the boundaries of your job is important. There are many different roles within social care, and your job should have a clear job description so that you know the areas for which you are responsible.

Usually, when an employer advertises a job, regardless of whether it is placed by a large local authority, a voluntary organisation, a private sector company or a person, there will be a job description that explains the requirements of the job. The job description will form part of your contract with your employer and is likely to include information about:

- the responsibilities of the role
- where the work is to be done
- who will supervise the work
- who the line manager is for the work
- any staff you will be responsible for.

It will also tell you the rate of pay for the job and the hours you will need to work. The job description will vary depending on the employer, but will probably look something the one below, which is for a care assistant in day services for people with a learning disability.

JOB DESCRIPTION: CARE ASSISTANT

Directorate: Adult and Community Services

Scale: Scale 2

Reporting to: Day Centre Officer

Responsible for:

Main purpose of role

- To provide practical help and support to people with special needs under the supervision of the senior member of the unit.
- To participate in plans to promote an environment conclusive to a high standard of care according to people's needs and wishes.
- You will be required to work in all areas of the Anytown Day Service including specialist areas with those who display severe challenging behaviour.

Key accountabilities:

To work within the Day Opportunities Policy, which is based upon 'ordinary life' principles for people with learning disabilities. This will involve at all times:

- ensuring that people are treated with dignity and respect
- ensuring that people have access to age-appropriate material and settings
- encouraging self-advocacy among people

- acting as an advocate on behalf of people where and when necessary
- providing opportunities for people to take calculated risks and practise learned skills as an aid to further learning
- linking people into ordinary community facilities in order to meet their support needs to promote the local authority's Equal Opportunities Policy
- maintaining confidentiality in line with local authority policy and procedure.

Specific responsibilities are to:

- assist people in meeting their physical and emotional needs
- assist, under supervision, the administration of medication to people as required
- assist in the implementation of their individual plans based on a needs-led day opportunities service
- communicate effectively with those needing support, carers and other professionals
- attend and participate in staff meetings
- attend relevant training courses to further personal development and/or to improve the service to those needing it
- record information as necessary in a clear and precise manner, and in accordance with departmental guidelines
- ensure a healthy and safe environment for those being supported, other staff and themselves.

Other duties are to:

- maintain personal and professional development to meet the changing demands of the job, participate in appropriate training activities, and encourage and support staff in their development and training
- undertake such other duties, training and/or hours of work as may be reasonably required and which are consistent with the general level of responsibility of this job
- undertake health and safety duties commensurate with the post and/or as detailed in the Directorate's Health and Safety Policy
- participate in the Council's emergency response arrangements as directed by the designated officer.

Contacts

In all contacts, the post holder will be required to present a good image of the Directorate and the Council as well as maintaining constructive relationships.

Internal: colleagues, managers

External: individuals, voluntary agencies, carers, members of the public, other statutory organisations, for example, Department of Health, Department of Education

Notes

The Council reserves the right to alter the content of this job description, after consultation to reflect changes to the job or services provided, without altering the general character or level of responsibility.

The duties mentioned in this job description must be carried out in a manner which promotes equality of opportunity, dignity and due respect for all employees and individuals, and is consistent with the Council's Equal Opportunities Policy.

Job description for a care assistant in day services for people who have a learning disability.

This description sets out very clearly what the employer expects of the person doing the job. If you applied for this job, you would be in no doubt as to what it entailed and what you would be required to do. Some jobs may be a little less formal. If you are working as a personal assistant for someone managing their own support, a description may be more like the one on the next page.

Job Description for Personal Assistant for D. F.

A Personal Assistant is employed to help me live my life the way I choose. Getting the right assistance when I need it allows me to lead my life independently. A Personal Assistant will enable me to do this by listening to what I want and following my instructions. It is therefore vital that an employee has good communication and listening skills.

The job involves assisting me with a variety of tasks. As for most people, my day varies, so it is difficult to list every task that is expected of a Personal Assistant.

After a period of familiarisation with the duties, you will be required to assist me with the following tasks, sometimes without close supervision. The post holder will therefore need to be able to work on their own initiative while at the same time being respectful of my wishes.

The post holder will work as part of a team and work on a rota so that I have support for 18 hours each day. This will involve evening and weekend working, and the ability to work well with other team members is essential as is the willingness to be flexible with working patterns.

The job involves moving and assisting/use of a hoist, etc. Previous experience is preferred, but training will be given if necessary. You do not have to be strong to do the job well, but general good health is important.

The job requires providing assistance with the following.

Personal tasks

- Assistance getting in and out of bed
- Assistance with showering/bathing
- Assistance with dressing and undressing
- Assistance with brushing hair and teeth
- Assistance with eating and drinking

Domestic tasks

- Preparing and cooking food
- Washing dishes and general cleaning of kitchen
- Laundry and ironing
- General cleaning and tidying of house
- Assistance with shopping

Social tasks

- Helping to go to pubs, cinema, theatre with or without friends
- Assistance when going out for a walk
- Helping to shop for pleasure
- Assistance with correspondence – phone calls/letter writing
- Assistance with other leisure activities, such as board games, music, reading

Other tasks

- Assistance to maintain upkeep of equipment, such as wheelchairs
- Assistance with gardening
- Driving
- Any other reasonable task

Pay: £7.56 per hour

Hours: 38 per week

Job description for a personal assistant to someone managing their own support.

Both of the examples show how employers make the scope of the job clear from the outset. There are good reasons for this; when an employer is planning how to deliver services, they will work out:

- what needs to be done
- how much of it needs to be done
- who needs to do it
- where they need to do it.

The answers to these questions give employers what they need to plan their workforce and ensure there are enough people doing the right jobs at the right level in order to be able to deliver services. You will have been recruited to do a particular job at a particular level, and other people will have been recruited to do different jobs at different levels. Everyone has their own area of responsibility and is accountable for what they do. If everyone started doing other people's jobs, there would be chaos.

The other reason for working within the agreed scope of your job is that you are working at the level for your experience and qualifications. Other job roles may require specialist knowledge or training, and you would not be able to do these jobs until you had been given the right training and gained relevant experience.

2.2 and 2.3 Agreed ways of working

Your employer identifies what you are to do in your job description, but sets out how it is to be done in the policies and procedures of the organisation you work for.

Policies will cover all the key areas of practice, such as the examples in Table 3.

Policy area	Sets out...
Equal opportunities	how the organisation ensures there is no discrimination in the way it works
Bullying and harassment	how the organisation will deal with staff found to be bullying or harassing other staff or those being supported
Confidentiality	the steps to be taken to ensure that people's information is kept as confidential as possible and only shared on a need-to-know basis
Data protection	how information will be handled to ensure compliance with the law
Supervision	how staff are to be given professional support and supervision
Environmental policy	how practice must look at the environmental impact of activity

Table 3: Key areas covered by policies.

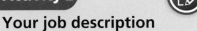

Activity 2

Your job description

Find the job description for your job. If you no longer have it, ask your line manager for a copy. Compare the information on your job description and see how well it matches up to the job that you do. Make notes about any differences and discuss the reasons for this with your manager.

Functional skills

English: Reading

Read your job description carefully to check the similarity and differences between it and the job you are doing. Make notes of the key differences between your actual job and the information on the job description. By doing this, you will have used the information contained in the written text and showed that you have understood the key points.

These examples of policies are just a few of the many that most employers will have in place. Policies will provide the broad outlines for the way you should work; they set out the boundaries rather than fill in the detail.

Detail is more likely to be found in procedures. Every employer will have procedures to go along with the policies. The procedures set out the detail of how to carry out day-to-day activities. For example, you are likely to find procedures for how to:

- deal with disciplinary issues
- deal with allegations of abuse
- assess and manage risk
- allocate resources
- respond to emergencies
- administer medication
- deal with a death
- handle an admission.

Can you see how each is important for doing your job?

Policies and procedures are an important way of knowing that you are working in the way your employer requires. Working within policy guidelines and following the laid-down procedures is a good indication that you are carrying out your job in the right way.

3. Be able to work in partnership with others

3.1 The importance of partnership working

In doing your job effectively, you could work in partnership with many different people. These may include, for example:

- colleagues in your workplace
- professional colleagues from other organisations
- the person you are supporting
- their informal support network.

Effective partnerships are about good teamwork, and in order to work well, they require some basic ground rules. These need to include agreements on the following.

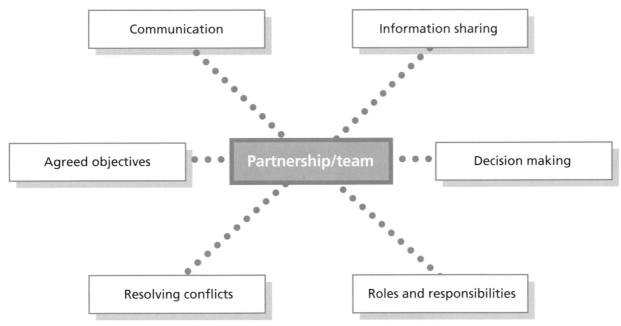

Can you see how there are many important aspects to effective team or partnership working?

Partnerships matter in delivering good-quality social care, because there are so many aspects involved in supporting people that no one person or organisation can deliver them alone. A support plan that will meet someone's needs requires cooperation and working together.

Having a shared purpose is a key part of good partnership working. Usually, the shared purpose will be the support of the person at the centre of the plan. Regardless of whether the partnership is all professionals in a multidisciplinary team or involves family and friends, an agreement on a shared purpose is the starting point.

A team has an agreed purpose. What other teams can you think of?

The circumstances in which groups can form are almost endless. However, if a group of people have a specific purpose that they are setting out to achieve, then that group becomes a team. For example, a group of friends who are a group because they all drink in a particular pub become a team when they enter the annual tug-of-war contest and attempt to win. Similarly, the quiz team develops or the football team develops. If people are a group because they all go to the same gym and talk to each other, but then decide to take on a neighbouring gym in a squash match, then they become a team.

3.2 Improving partnership working

There are certain key steps that will help to ensure that any partnership is able to work effectively.

Good communication

This is essential. Failure to maintain communication is fatal to partnership working. Having a partner find out about a course of action long after everyone else is likely to cause anger and mistrust, along with a loss of the goodwill that is so important for partnerships to work well. Ensure you keep everyone informed about actions and decisions that may be of interest or importance to the partnership.

Respecting and valuing the work of others

Nothing is more likely to make people fed up with working in partnership than feeling they are not appreciated or that their contribution to the partnership is not valued. Remember that all partners are essential; each person brings different skills, knowledge and experience. Make sure that you find out about the contribution of all of the partners and its importance to achieving the team objectives. Always acknowledge and show that you respect and value what people have to say.

> **Reflect**
>
> What is the difference between a gang and a team? Does a gang ever become a team?

Making clear decisions

All partners should feel confident that decisions being made within the team are following the agreed process. There is likely to be serious concern if partners feel that some decisions are being taken outside the team and that not everyone is being involved in the process. If people are not involved, then they will not take responsibility for the decisions and they may not be prepared to abide by them. If there is an agreed procedure for making decisions, then use it.

Functional skills

English: Writing

For Activity 3, present your information clearly and in an organised way using sufficient detail to cover the task. Proofread your work to check that spelling, punctuation and grammar are accurate, and that the language used is suitable.

Activity 3

Aims and objectives

1. Make a list of the aims and objectives of the organisation you work for. This should be contained in your organisation's mission statement or policy documents, or possibly a public plan or charter that your organisation has developed.
2. Then make a list of your own aims and objectives in your work. They may include things like wanting to give the best possible service to people, wanting to be of use to the people you support, or wanting to improve your skills and understanding of the area you work in.
3. Look at the people you support. What do they want from the service and what are their aims in terms of their own lives? How do they see that your support can assist them? Make a list of these aims.

When you have completed all three lists, compare them and see to what extent they match. You should check particularly how well the list of your aims and objectives fits with those of your organisation. Do not compare just the words on the list, but look at the overall effect of what you and your organisation want to achieve, and see how far they match.

3.3 and 3.4 Resolving issues and difficulties and getting support for working relationships

When you have begun to consider your relationship with the people in your team, you will need to work out how you deal with any problematic relationships. There are inevitably people in any team who do not get on with each other. Bear in mind that a working relationship does not require the same commitment or sharing of ideals, values and understanding as a personal friendship. In order to work with someone, it is sufficient that you recognise and value their contribution to the team performance and that you always communicate effectively and courteously when working. Although many teams socialise together, this is not an essential requirement for a successful team. The loyalty and camaraderie that is built up among good team members can be based purely on their performance at work and does not necessarily have to carry over into their personal lives. And remember — everyone working at the same time is not the same thing as everyone working together.

Activity 4

Improving working relationships

If you have to work with people with whom you feel you have little in common, try the following checklist to help view them in a more positive light.

1. List all the positive things and only the positive things about your colleague. For example…
   - Do they have a nice smile?
   - Are they very good with the clients?
   - Do they have a particular skill in one area of practice?
   - Are they good in a crisis?
   - Are they willing to accommodate swaps in shifts?
   - Are they good at organising?
   - Do they make good coffee?
2. Make a positive comment to your colleague at least once each day. This could range from 'Your hair looks nice today' to 'I have learned such a lot from watching you deal with…'
3. Ask questions about your colleague and try to find out more about them. This does not have to be on a personal level. Questions could be about their professional skills. You could try something like, 'Where did you learn to move people so well?' or take the trouble to find their opinions on current issues. Perhaps you could ask, 'What do you think about the new set of proposals for the shift rotas?'

4. Pick up on any comments that may lead to areas of common interest. For example, your colleague may comment about something they have done over the weekend, or they may make a reference to reading something or seeing a film or a play that you know something about. You should follow up on any of these potential leads which may allow you to find out more about the person.
5. Learn what you can, either by listening to others or by asking questions about the person's background and look at where their ideas and influences have come from. If you understand their culture, beliefs and values, it will be easier to see how and why they hold the opinions and views that they do.
6. Make a list of the positives that this particular colleague brings to the team.

Doing it well

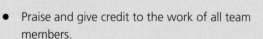

Team working

- Agree and share a common purpose, aims and objectives.
- Work on building relationships which value and respect all team members.
- Contribute to the planning process for all team activities.
- Make sure that all team members are involved in decision making.
- Respect and value diversity of each team member.
- Value working together and recognise the difference between working at the same time and working together.
- Support the goals agreed by the team.

- Praise and give credit to the work of all team members.
- Use your communication skills effectively when working with other members of the team.
- Ensure the team has dialogue and not debate.
- Work to identify and resolve conflicts within the team.
- Examine the way the team is operating and do not be afraid to initiate constructive and supportive criticism.
- Contribute to the growth and development of the team as a whole, the members of the team and yourself as an individual.

Asking for advice and support

Your manager or supervisor is your first line of support for partnership working. Your organisation may have set policies and procedures for setting up and working in a partnership. If so, these will need to be followed.

It is also likely that your manager will have experience of partnership working and will be able to share advice and their own experience. It is a sign of a mature and reflective worker that they know when to ask for advice and recognise when they need help. You will be working in the best interests of the people you support by making sure that you have the best possible guidance to work alongside others.

Getting ready for assessment

This is only a small unit, but it is important as it helps you to understand exactly what it is you need to do as a social care worker. Your assessor will be wanting you to show that you understand how working relationships operate. You may be asked to complete an assignment or a presentation where you show that you understand the nature of working relationships. One of the best ways to show this is by being able to discuss the different types of relationships that we all experience and showing how they differ from the ways we relate to work colleagues on a professional basis.

Your assessor is likely to observe how well you are able to work with others and to follow the policies and procedures of your employing organisation while they are observing other areas of practice. They will be looking for you to explain how and why you are doing things in ways that follow agreed procedures. They will also be looking for how well you work with others through being supportive and sharing information, knowledge and experience.

Further reading and research

- www.gscc.org.uk (General Social Care Council (GSCC))
- www.skillsforcare.org.uk (Skills for Care)
- www.skillsforhealth.org.uk (Skills for Health)

Unit HSC 026

Implement person-centred approaches in health and social care

This unit is all about how you put people at the centre of everything you do. Transforming the ways social care is planned and delivered has meant that services are now built around people's needs. People who want to use services no longer have to 'fit in' with whatever services happen to be available.

Person-centred working gives people more control over how, when and by whom their services are delivered. Planning is now in the hands of the person who is going to use the services, with support from social care professionals where necessary.

Social care services are there to fill in the gaps in social care needs that cannot be met by the person themselves or their informal support.

In this unit you will learn about:

1. person-centred approaches for care and support
2. how to work in a person-centred way
3. how to establish consent when providing care or support
4. how to encourage active participation
5. how to support the individual's right to make choices
6. how to promote individuals' well-being.

1. Understand person-centred approaches for care and support

1.1 Person-centred values

Unit HSC 024 has already looked at some of the key values that underpin work in this sector. These include:

- treating people as individuals
- supporting people to access their rights
- supporting people to exercise choice
- making sure people have privacy if they want it
- supporting people to be as independent as possible
- treating people with dignity and respect
- recognising that working with people is a partnership rather than a relationship controlled by professionals.

Treating people as individuals

This is about recognising that everyone is different and has their own needs. Not everyone likes doing the same things, eating the same things, reading the same things or wearing the same things. Just because a person is making use of support and care services does not stop them being a unique person with very particular needs. You will need to make sure that you do not make general assumptions about people. For example, not all older people like to play bingo or want to go out on coach trips. Some do and others do not. Not everyone wants to eat an evening meal at 5pm, or go to bed at 9pm, or get up at 7am. Some people do and others do not.

People can be excluded for many reasons.

You have looked at stereotyping in Unit SHC 23. Remember that thinking in stereotypes is the exact opposite of treating people as individuals.

Accessing rights

You have looked at rights in Unit HSC 024; this is about your role in ensuring that people are able to participate in society as full citizens and that they are not excluded from accessing their rights because they have a disability or because they are older or are seen as vulnerable in some way. You need to ensure constantly that people are not being prevented from exercising their rights because of issues such as physical barriers, complex paperwork, being made to feel a nuisance or the actions of other people.

Making choices

People have the right to choose how they live and what they want to do with their lives. They are also able to choose how they want their social care support to be delivered and to make choices about whom they want to deliver it and when.

Privacy

Everyone has a right to have some space where they can be alone if they wish. Sometimes they may want to be private just to have some time to themselves; on other occasions it may be because they are having personal care or medical treatment. It is also important that people have privacy if they want to talk to a professional and have confidential information to discuss.

Supporting independence

This is about supporting people to do as much as they possibly can for themselves. You need to make sure that you do not 'take over' and do things for people instead of allowing people to get on with their lives as they wish. Independence is also about managing risk so that people are able to participate in daily life and get on with living.

Dignity and respect

Everyone is entitled to be treated with dignity; this means all aspects of life from support with personal care to how people want to be addressed. It is also about listening to what people have to say and being interested in them.

Partnership

Social care is about working together with the person who uses the service being in control. It is no longer the professional who controls the money and the resources. This has made the whole relationship far more equal and means much more working together to plan for and achieve the outcomes that the person wants in order to improve their lives.

Can you see why having a private space is important?

1.2 Why it is important to work in a way that embeds person-centred values

The values that underpin your work have an impact on your day-to-day work. All the tasks for which you may provide support, including bathing, dressing, personal hygiene, preparing meals, shopping and general domestic tasks, will be done better if you take into account the person-centred values identified earlier — for example, providing services at a time and in a way that suits the person — not you, nor the system.

If someone decides they want a bath, even though you have gone there with the intention of supporting them to prepare a meal, they are quite within their rights to change their mind. Think about how often you change your mind about plans and end up doing something completely different. Just because someone needs some additional support to accomplish a task does not mean that they should lose control over that part of their lives. Being aware of all the person's values and making them a part of what you do each day will ensure that you are not guilty of imposing your choices on people or of robbing them of their rights to independence and choice.

1.3 Why risk-taking can be part of a person-centred approach

Everyone is entitled to take risks. We all take risks in our daily lives. Every time we get on a plane or cross the road, put money in a bank, take part in a sporting activity or plug in a toaster, we are taking risks.

We assess all of these risks and make sure that they are managed. For example, we know that there are stringent safety procedures in place for aircraft, we know that there are regulations for banks, and we take steps to maintain the electrical wiring in our houses so that we can reduce the risk of disaster when we use appliances.

We take risks every day.

Taking risks is part of being able to choose and being in control of your life, so you need to ensure that concern about risks is not getting in the way of people living their lives in the way they want to. Often, a risk assessment can make it possible for someone to do something that may seem unlikely in the first instance.

Case study

Reducing the risks

Alice, who has a learning disability, wants to move into a flat with a friend she has met at her work placement. A risk assessment will look at ways of reducing the risks to Alice from her move. The assessment may look at the steps that can be taken for Alice to increase her independence in the way she wants to. There could be a drop-in from a support worker and a link set up with a local supported living unit where Alice could go if she feels she needs support. It may be possible for a flat to be found through a housing association so that there are no concerns about the safety and the maintenance of the property.

1. What benefits do you think taking these steps will have for those who are concerned for Alice's safety and well-being?
2. What benefits do you think taking these steps will have for Alice?

Risk-taking is part of developing independence. If people never take risks then they will never find out what they are able to achieve and work out where their limits are.

Person-centred planning puts people at the centre of everything; it looks at what people can do and identifies what they want to achieve. Sometimes the things that people may want to achieve will involve risks, which is not a problem as long as they are not actually putting themselves in danger, or the dangerous activities can have the risks reduced in some way. Alternatively, some people may need to be encouraged to take some risks.

Case study

Encouraging someone to take risks

Henry, who is 75, was very active, despite having a visual impairment caused by macular degeneration. He always walked for at least a mile each day regardless of the weather. One day he slipped on some wet leaves and broke his hip. After his recovery, he was very reluctant to continue walking each day; he and his wife both felt it was too risky and so stayed indoors. This made him very depressed and put a strain on his relationship with his wife. Their support worker spoke to both of them about being prepared to take some risks in order to support Henry to get back to his daily exercise. Initially, the support worker went with Henry each day, but she gradually reduced her support, although Henry's wife would often go with him and found that she enjoyed the exercise too. After a couple of months, Henry was back to his usual daily walks.

1. Why was it important for Henry to take the risks involved with walking outdoors again?
2. How did the support worker help Henry to manage the risks?

1.4 How using an individual's care plan contributes to working in a person-centred way

Plans for how people want their support to be delivered are a vital part of person-centred working. People should be in control of their own plans and the planning process is a key way of ensuring that they are at the centre of any support provided.

Care/support plans are now developed by the person themselves, sometimes with support from family or friends. Plans are then agreed by the social worker or care manager. During the planning process, the person will:

- look at what they want to achieve and identify the outcomes they want
- work out what they can already do for themselves, or with the help of family and friends
- look at what services they need in order to fill the gaps
- identify how and when they need services to be provided.

The development of a support plan is the perfect example of how person-centred working operates.

Instead of offering people a 'choice' of what is currently available and finding what best fits their needs, person-centred working looks at someone's needs and builds the support package around them. One of the important aspects of person-centred planning is to look at what people are able to do for themselves and to ensure that services are not taking over aspects of a person's life that they could perfectly well manage without support.

Informal networks are also an important part of people's means of support and any additional professional support should only be to supplement, not replace, these.

Case study

The importance of informal networks

Pauline is 26 years old and has cerebral palsy; she requires support 24 hours a day. When she was working with Mike, her social worker, to develop her plan, she decided to hold the planning meeting in the pub one evening and invited all her friends. Her friends all joined in the planning to explain what they were able to do and finally, the whole group could look at where the gaps were and identify where professional support workers would be needed.

1. What benefits would this method of developing a support plan have for Pauline?
2. What benefits would it have for her friends?

2. Be able to work in a person-centred way

2.1 Finding out the history, preferences, wishes and needs of the individual

Person-centred working means that the wishes of the person are the basis of planning and delivering support and care services. Therefore, you must find out exactly what people want and expect from the care and support they are planning. Person-centred working means that service provision fits around the person — not the other way around.

If you are going to work with someone, it is important that you know as much about them as possible.

You have looked at ways to find out information about people in earlier units; there are various ways of doing this, but the most effective is always to ask the person concerned about whatever you want to know. Try to find time to sit down with someone and ask about their life. If they are able to tell you about their own history, you will learn a great deal and it will help you to offer support in the most appropriate ways. It is often easy to think about people, especially older people, as you see them now and to forget that their lives may have been very different in the past.

The following poem is said to have been found, after her death, in the locker of Kate, a geriatric patient in the early 1970s.

> What do you see, nurses, what do you see?
> What are you thinking when you look at me?
> A crabbit old woman, not very wise,
> Uncertain of habit with far-away eyes
> Who dribbles her food and makes no reply
> When you say in a loud voice, 'I do wish you'd try'
> Who seems not to notice the things that you do
> And forever is losing a stick or a shoe
> Who, unresistingly or not lets you do as you will,
> With bathing and feeding — the long day to fill.
> Is that what you're thinking? Is that what you see?
> Then open your eyes nurse — you're looking at me.
> I'll tell you who I am as I sit here so still
> As I use at your bidding, as I eat at your will.
>
> I'm a small child of ten with a father and mother
> Brothers and sisters who love one another,
> A young girl of sixteen with wings on her feet
> Dreaming that soon a lover she'll meet
> A bride soon, at twenty my heart gives a leap
> Remembering the vows that I promised to keep.
> At twenty-five now I have young of my own
> Who need me to build a secure happy home

Remember that people have had many life experiences.

A young woman of thirty, my young now grow fast
Bound to each other with ties that should last.
At forty my young ones now grown will soon be gone

But my memory stays beside me to see I don't mourn
At fifty, once more babies play round my knee
Again, we know children, my loved one and me.
Dark days are upon me as my husband is dead
I look at the future, I shudder with dread
For my young are all busy rearing young of their own
And I think of the years and the love I have known.
I'm an old woman now and nature is cruel
The body it crumbles, grace and vigour depart
There is now a stone where I once had a heart.
But inside this old carcass a young girl still dwells
And now and again my battered heart swells.
I remember the joys, I remember the pain
And I'm loving and living life over again
I think of the years — all too few — gone too fast
And accept the stark fact that nothing can last
So open your eyes, nurses, open and see
Not a crabbit old woman... look closer, see ME.

Finding out what people want

Person-centred working is about putting people in control of their lives. This may be a new experience for many people who have been using services for many years, but have always had to fit in with the system and the services that were available at the time. People often find it hard to think about what they want and you can help by offering prompts such as, 'Remember when you said you wanted to...', 'What sort of time do you want to get up?' or 'What about going out and meeting more people?'

Most workplaces will have a format for undertaking assessments, where people have the opportunity to identify:

- the goals they want to achieve
- what they are able to do for themselves
- areas where they need support.

Forms will vary between local areas, but are likely to cover:

- personal care
- nutritional needs
- practical aspects of daily life
- physical and mental health and well-being
- relationships and social inclusion
- choice and control
- risk
- work, leisure and learning
- travelling

Reflect

The poem above demonstrates clearly how easy it is to forget that everyone has a history and that people's lives will have been very different than their present circumstances. Can you think of a time when you may have forgotten this? Think about the people you support and be honest about how much you know about them. Do you really know about their history, what sort of lives they had? When they fell in love? Got married? Had children? What times were like then?

If you realise that you do not know enough about the history of the people you support, now is the time to change and start to ask questions. You may be surprised at the interesting lives people have had and how much they have done.

- caring/parenting
- social support
- unpaid carer support
- religious/cultural needs.

2.2 Applying person-centred values in day-to-day work

People and their needs should be at the centre of the support process. Your role is to make sure that people have every opportunity to state exactly how they wish their needs to be met. Some people will be able to share this information personally; others will need an advocate who will support them in expressing their views.

Seeing the whole picture

One of the essential aspects of planning care services is to have a holistic approach to planning and provision. This means recognising that all parts of a person's life will have an impact on their support needs and that you need to look beyond what you see when you meet them for the first time.

All of the following factors will directly affect someone and you must take all these into account when planning the best way to provide services – they include:

- health
- employment
- education
- social
- religious and cultural.

Health

The state of health of anyone has a massive effect on how they develop as a person and the kind of experiences they have during their lives. Someone who has always been very fit, well and active may find it very difficult and frustrating to find suddenly that they have restricted movement as the result of an illness such as a stroke. This may lead to them being difficult and expressing their anger against those who are providing support, or they may become very depressed and unhappy. Alternatively someone who has not enjoyed good health over a long period of time may be well adjusted to a more limited physical level of ability, but have compensated in other ways and be keen to follow and maintain intellectual activities.

Employment

Health is also likely to have had an impact on employment, whether making it possible at all or affecting the type of employment that people have. Whether or not people are able to work has a huge effect on their level of confidence and **self-esteem**. Employment may also have an effect on the extent to which people have socialised and

Key term

Self-esteem – how people value themselves

mixed with others. This may be an important consideration when considering the possible benefits of residential care where someone would have to live in a community with others, as opposed to care provided in someone's home environment. Income levels are related to employment and will have an effect on standards of living, the quality of housing, the quality of diet and the lifestyle which people are able to experience. Someone in a well-paid job is likely to have lived in a more pleasant environment with lower levels of pollution, more opportunities for leisure, exercise and relaxation and a better standard of housing. It is easy to see how all of this can affect someone's health and well-being.

Education

The level of education of anyone is likely to have affected both their employment and, in all likelihood, their level of income. It can also have an effect on the extent to which they are able to gain access to beneficial information about their health and lifestyle. It is important that the educational level of a person is always considered so that explanations and information are given in a way which in readily understandable. For example, an explanation about an illness taken straight from a textbook used by doctors would not mean much to most of us! However, if it is explained in everyday terms, we are more likely to understand what is being said. Some people may have a different level of literacy to you, so do not assume that everyone will be able to make use of written notes — some people may prefer information to be given verbally, or recorded on tape.

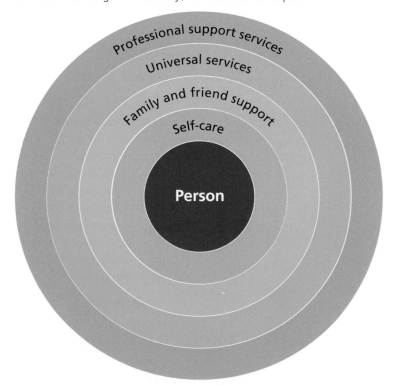

Person-centred support.

Social

The social circumstances in which a person has lived will have an immense effect on their way of life and the type of care provision that they are likely to need. The social classification of society is based on employment groups. However, the social groups in which people live are also about relationships with family and friends.

Religious and cultural

Religious and cultural beliefs and values are an essential part of the structure of the lives of all people. The values and beliefs of the community people belong to and the religious practices that are part of their daily lives are important in the planning of services. Any plan that has not taken account of the religious and cultural values of a person is doomed to fail.

Activity 1

Considering factors

Prepare a list of the different types of service provided by the setting in which you work. Remember to include all the aspects of the service you provide – if you work in residential care, you will need to list all parts of your service such as social activities, providing food, providing entertainment and personal care. if you work in a person's own home, you may need to list food preparation, cleaning, personal care and so on.

Make a note about the factors of a person's life you would need to take into account in order to provide a holistic assessment of their needs.

Record ways in which you may need to adapt the services you provide because of some of the factors you are taking into account.

3. Be able to establish consent when providing care or support

3.1 The importance of establishing consent when providing care or support

Giving consent for anything that is done to us is a basic human right. If we did not need to give consent it would mean that anyone could do anything to us. This is particularly important when it comes to medical or social care support. Much of the treatment or support that people receive is either invasive or personal.

Consent not only protects social care and health providers against legal challenge, it is also vital because of the rights of the person and the importance of recognising that people should determine what happens to them. Being able to give consent or not is also part of being treated with dignity and respect. There is nothing dignified about someone removing your underwear and sitting you on a commode without asking your permission. Neither is there anything respectful about someone sticking a needle in your leg without asking for your agreement or explaining why they are doing it.

Ensuring that people are in agreement with the support and care tasks that you need to undertake is just as important and is a key part of ensuring that you are working within person-centred values and the codes of practice for social care.

I'm just going to turn you over now, George – is that OK?

Not all consent is formal or written down.

As a broad principle, consent should be obtained before carrying out any kind of activity. Even something as simple as moving somebody or plumping their pillows should always be preceded by the question, 'Would you like me to plump your pillows?' In general, people need to provide consent for the provision of personal care. An overall agreement to the provision of care and support cannot be taken as a blanket consent to all activities; someone may not want the planned care on a particular day, so consent must always be obtained: 'Are you ready for your hair to be brushed?' or 'Do you want to go in the shower now?' are essential questions where agreement indicates consent.

Historically, areas of clinical practice has always 'acted in the best interests' of patients, and there are still many older people who believe that the doctor or nurse 'knows best', and who would not presume to question any medical suggestions about the way their treatment should proceed. As the traditional view of the power of medical practitioners has changed and it has become more common to question and challenge the opinions of doctors, nurses and other health workers, people have become more comfortable with the idea of being asked their views and being asked for their consent.

3.2 How to establish consent for an activity or action

If you are in the position where you are asked to obtain consent for an activity, you must take great care that you:

- answer any questions honestly and as fully as you can
- never attempt to answer a question that you are not sure of
- always refer the question on to somebody who has the knowledge to give the person a full answer.

Ensure that wherever possible you direct your information to the person concerned, even if there is a relative or friend with them. In most cases it is the person's consent that you must obtain, not that of their friend or relative. Where there is an issue of capacity to understand the information, then you should explain the procedure carefully to the person who is acting as an advocate. This could be a relative, friend or possibly a social worker or representative of the court if the person is subject to guardianship or a court order.

If, however, the person is capable of understanding but has difficulty with communication, then you must use the communication skills that you have learned (see Unit SHC 21) in order to provide the necessary information to make a decision. People who have sensory impairments should not be prevented from making their own decisions and asking their own questions by the limitations of either your time or communication skills.

Where there are language difficulties, an interpreter should be used as appropriate. You should always consider the nature of the consent being sought before a decision is made about whether or not to use a member of the person's family. It may be that in terms of either confidentiality or the nature of the procedure being discussed, it is not appropriate and the use of an interpreter is preferable.

When people are agreeing to potentially serious matters, such as medical treatment, sharing information, handing over control of part of their lives or changing accommodation, it is essential that they not only consent, but understand what it is they are consenting to and the implications of this. This is informed consent. Informed consent means that the person has full information about what is to happen, why it is to happen and the possible effects, both positive and negative. All the risks should have been explained so that a person is in a position to make a judgement about whether or not they wish to go ahead. Informed consent can be written, as in the case of somebody undergoing surgery, or it can be a verbal consent (for example, if somebody is having blood taken, then the procedure, the purpose of the blood test and what will be found out from the blood test could be explained to them before they agreed to it).

Implied consent

It is reasonable to assume that someone implies their consent to you taking their blood pressure if they present their arm when they see you arriving and taking out the blood pressure cuff. If somebody opens their mouth when you appear with a thermometer, it is reasonable for you to assume that they are implying consent to you taking their temperature. If people raise themselves up as you come to help them from a chair, you may assume that they consent. For these relatively minor and non-invasive procedures, implied consent is perfectly acceptable, as it would be very overcomplicated if consent to these types of activities had to be recorded on every occasion.

Written consent

This is most likely to be used in a clinical setting where there will be a form for written consent. This requires patients, or their relatives in the case of an emergency, to sign to say that they are willing for the named clinical procedure to be undertaken. Generally, written consent is likely also to be informed consent, as on most occasions the procedures will have been explained carefully before signing.

Written consent will also be needed if someone is agreeing to hand over control of part of their lives to someone else. For example, someone may decide to allow a relative to handle their finances because they are finding it too difficult. But doing this does not mean that they are incapable of making the decision or of understanding the consequences. In fact, that they know that they need someone else to do it could be said to show that they understand the issues.

Other major matters such as the transfer of property or moving home will also require written consent.

Verbal consent

Verbal consent is normally understood to exist when a person requests that a procedure be undertaken. For example, in a hospital, someone asking for pain relief who has been told, 'Yes, we will give you an injection for pain but it will make you sleepy', and the response is, 'Yes give it to me anyway', is taken to be verbal consent for the procedure and this consent must be recorded in the case notes. This could also apply, for example, to someone who is severely constipated and has asked for an enema, or to somebody who has requested that they be moved from the bed to the chair using lifting equipment.

3.3 Steps to take if consent cannot be readily established

You must not proceed with any care or clinical activity without consent. If someone refuses their agreement or changes their mind after having said 'yes', you must stop what you are doing.

It may be useful to repeat the information again just to be sure that any queries and concerns have been answered, but it is not your job to persuade someone or to put pressure on them to agree.

You must immediately report any refusal of consent or any reservations expressed by the person to your supervisor or to the clinical practitioner responsible for the procedure.

Your organisation will have procedures in place to deal with refusal of consent. Usually, this means that nothing further will be done, but sometimes, where there may be some doubt about a person's capacity to understand the consequences of a refusal, further assessments may be undertaken to decide whether it would be in someone's best interests to go ahead without agreement.

People have to give consent.

4. Be able to encourage active participation

4.1 How active participation benefits an individual

Supporting people to do things that they want to do and that they can do is your main role. Everyone should have the right to take a full part in society and play their part as a citizen.

Having active participation in society is important for people's self-esteem and their well-being. We can all identify with the feeling of having achieved something. It may be something quite small – finishing decorating a room, doing a tough workout in the gym, knitting a jumper, or something important like passing an exam or achieving your Health and Social Care Diploma! Achievement is not only about big things like winning a gold medal or swimming the Channel. Anyone who has children will know of the sense of achievement when they can tie their own shoelaces or count to 10.

We all participate in life because humans are not generally isolated creatures. We live with other people and usually live in communities alongside other people. In order to take part in community life and to make relationships with others, people may need support to get over some of the barriers.

Participation will mean different things to different people; it could be:

- having lots of mates and going to the pub
- going to the library or to the luncheon club
- maintaining contact with relatives and visiting neighbours
- being involved in sports
- going shopping or just getting out and about
- being on committees and political activity
- being involved in faith groups.

There are so many ways in which all of us are part of society, and you will need to work closely with the people you support to find out what they want to do and what assistance they need.

Participating in activities with others and achieving goals usually helps people to feel good about themselves and improves confidence and self-esteem. How we value ourselves is key to our sense of well-being. Feeling good and feeling confident are important ways of improving people's general and emotional health. There is more about this later in the unit.

Participation can mean many things.

Case study

Acting in somebody's best interests

Dennis is 27 years old; he has a learning disability and is in a work placement supported by a job coach. He likes sports and wants to spend more time playing football and doing athletics, which he enjoys. He has put together a support plan, but his parents think that it will all be too much for him and that he needs to come home and rest after a day at work.

Father: This plan is hopeless, he'll never do all this – you don't understand, it's just what he thinks he'd like to do.

Dennis: No, this is what I want, I like playing football and doing running. I'm not tired.

Father: You're just being silly son, I know it sounds good now, but you won't be able to do it. You know you like your evenings at home with me *and your mum.*

Dennis: No I don't.

Father: Don't be rude, Dennis. Do you see what I mean – he doesn't really know what he wants. I don't know why you people want to let him decide, it's just irresponsible.

Support worker: What do you think about that, Dennis?

Dennis: I want to do my plan.

Support worker: Mr Smith, this is about Dennis making decisions for himself and us helping him to do what he wants to with his life. I'm sorry if you don't agree, but I do think that Dennis has to try things his way. I think that your support is very important to him and it would be good if he could try this plan with your help.

Father: Well, we don't want to stand in his way – but I don't think you people really understand what he's like. We'll give it a go, but I'm not convinced.

Support worker: No, I understand that, but it has a better chance of working if you are backing it. What do you think, Dennis?

Dennis: Thanks Dad.

1. How do you think the initial response of the father would have made Dennis feel?
2. How does the support worker help the father to understand why doing things Dennis' way is preferable?
3. How do you think you would have acted in this scenario?

It is tempting to do things for people because this may be easier, quicker and less painful and it may seem that this would be the most helpful thing to do. In fact, doing tasks for people is far from helpful. It results in people being deskilled and increases dependency. This in turn decreases people's confidence, self-esteem and sense of well-being, thus resulting in people becoming more depressed and isolated. It is all a vicious circle.

Working with people to support them where there are things that they really cannot do for themselves is so much better than taking over and doing tasks for people and making them dependent on you.

4.2 Barriers to active participation

What gets in the way of active participation? There can be many things, for example:

- issues over physical access
- lack of information in accessible formats
- emotional barriers such as lack of confidence
- professional support staff taking over
- family carers who find it hard to let go.

Any combination of these barriers can mean that people do not participate in society as fully as they could and, as a result, lose out on so much that they could be doing.

4.3 Ways to reduce the barriers and encourage active participation

Issues over physical access

Where there are physical access issues for a public place, you may need to support someone to request information about access for disabled people, or possibly to make a complaint if there is no suitable access. For some people it may be that access is not just about a specific place, but more general in that their ability to walk is limited. In this case, you may need to support people to access transport or a disabled parking badge so that walking is reduced.

Lack of information in accessible formats

Information about facilities may be limited or only available in one format. You may need to support the person to request information in a format that is accessible for them, or you may be able to assist them to access information in other ways — for example, on the Internet.

Emotional barriers such as lack of confidence

Participation can be difficult for many people. They may lack confidence or have low self-esteem. They may believe that they are not able to make any efforts at participation and that no one would

Activity 2

Active participation plan

Think about someone with whom you work regularly. Identify a task or activity that is carried out for them. Why are they unable to do this task themselves? Work with the person to draw up an active participation plan to improve on this situation. This could be, for example, enabling them to carry out the task themselves or having more say in the way they are supported.

Functional skills

English: Speaking and listening

Practise your verbal communication skills by having a discussion with somebody you support about how to improve their ability to carry out a specific task or activity they are having difficulties with. Remember to use appropriate language and to speak clearly at all times. Show your ability to listen by picking up on points raised by the person and by making constructive suggestions to them to improve their ability to complete the task or activity.

respond if they did. You may need to encourage people by helping them to see the positive aspects of their lives, and reassuring them that they will not fail and that they have the ability to achieve. Using examples of other barriers they have overcome and previous achievements is a useful way of offering encouragement.

Professional support staff taking over

It may be, for example, far easier, less painful and quicker for you to put on people's socks or stockings for them. But this would reinforce the fact that they are no longer able to undertake such a simple task for themselves and remove the motivation to find a way to do it independently. Time spent in providing a 'helping hand' sock aid, and showing them how to use it, means they can put on their own clothing and, instead of feeling dependent, have a sense of achievement and independence.

It is tempting to undertake tasks for people you work with because you are keen to care for them and because you believe that you can make their lives easier. Often, however, you need to hold back from directly providing care or carrying out a task, and look for ways you can enable people to undertake the task for themselves.

Family carers who find it hard to let go

Families may want to protect people who they see as vulnerable and in need of care, and may have many concerns about the growing independence of loved ones who have always been dependent. Do not jump to the conclusions that families are being difficult or obstructive; usually people believe that they are doing their best for their relatives by protecting them and by reducing the risks. Working in partnership with people and their families to help them get used to new approaches and to see the benefits of active participation may be a slow process that needs to be taken gently, but the long-term benefits of people being able to participate in society as full citizens are worth the effort.

5. Be able to support the individual's right to make choices

5.1 Supporting an individual to make informed choices

Where people want to make choices about their lives, you should ensure that you do your best to help them identify any barriers they may meet and then offer support in overcoming these. If you are working with someone living in their own home, it is likely to be easier for them to make day-to-day choices about their lives. In some situations they may require help and support in order to achieve the choice, but it is generally less restrictive than a residential or hospital setting, where the needs of many other people also have to be taken into account.

For many people living in their own homes, the development of direct payments and individual budgets has meant a far higher level of choice and empowerment than was possible previously. This system means that payments for the provision of services are made to the person, who then employs support workers directly and determines their own levels and types of service. This changes the relationship between the person and the support workers, and puts the person in a position of power as an employer. Individual and personal budgets also give people the chance to control their lives. Here they have control over how resources are used and how money is spent, but do not have to be employers. You may need to offer some help initially, so people can get used to directing their own services.

The process of making choices can also be about simple things — it can just be a matter of checking with the person as you work, as in the illustration on the next page.

The worker in the example on the following page has offered Mrs Jones a choice about clothes. Mrs Jones has indicated that she is not happy with the choice offered, and she has also identified the possible barrier to having the clothes she wants. The care worker has looked for a way that the barrier may possibly be overcome. This process can be used in a wide range of situations.

You may be working with someone who is not able to fully participate in all decisions about their day-to-day life because they have a different level of understanding. This could, for example, include people with a learning disability, dementia or brain injury. In this situation, it may be that the person has an advocate who represents their interests and is able to present a point of view about choices and options. The advocate may be a professional one such as a solicitor, social worker or rights worker, or they could be a relative or friend. It is essential that you include the advocate in discussions, to make sure that the wishes of the person they are supporting are followed.

Doing it well

Supporting people to make choices

- Always ask people about their needs, wishes and preferences – whether this is the service they want and if this is the way they want to receive it.
- Ask if they prefer other alternatives, either in the service or the way it is delivered.
- Look for ways you can actively support people in achieving the choice they want.

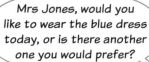

How do you think this interaction will have made Mrs Jones feel?

Information about choices

Earlier in this unit you looked at how to ensure people are able to give informed consent. Making informed choices is similar.

One of your key roles is to provide information to the person and their family about the choices they need to make. For example, it is not reasonable to expect a person to agree to 'attendance at a project' unless they have full information to make a choice. This will include information about:

- the exact nature of the project
- the location of the project
- the type of activities
- the general atmosphere and ethos of the project
- the number of people who will be attending
- what the transport arrangements will be.

These are just a few of the questions that someone may have about what will be provided. Informed choice requires full information.

This same principle applies to any choices that people have to make about, for example:

- accommodation
- money
- medical treatment
- support plans
- relationships
- leisure activities
- aids and adaptations
- education and learning.

All of us have the right to make informed choices about all aspects of our lives. For example, you would not purchase a house simply because the estate agents said, 'Oh, I have got a nice house for you.' You would want a great deal of information and to visit and look at the house for yourself, and to carry out extensive planning and questioning before you finally made that decision. Similarly, you would not buy a holiday or a car simply because somebody said to you, 'I have got a nice holiday here that I am sure would suit you.' You would want to ask questions about where, when, how much, what type of accommodation and so on.

Would you buy a property without finding out information about it?

Functional skills

English: Writing

This activity will give you the opportunity to write in an organised way. You will need to think about how you lay out your list and present it. When writing full sentences, ensure that you are consistent with tense, that spellings, punctuation and grammar are accurate, and that each sentence makes sense.

Activity 3

Providing choice

Think about a person with whom you have recently worked. Consider all of your actions and whether or not they were given a choice about how to live their lives. If you believe that they were given every possible choice, then list the ways in which you ensured that happened. If you believe that their choice was restricted in some way, identify the reasons why this happened and the steps you can take to ensure it is not repeated.

Exactly the same applies to people making choices about their lives. Your role is to make sure they have the information they need, and either get it for them or help them get it themselves.

Doing it well

Supporting people to make choices

- Communicate all information to people and their families clearly and in a way that can be understood.
- Make sure that their views are clearly represented to any forum where decisions are being taken or proposals being formulated.
- Support people to put forward their own views wherever possible.
- Clearly record information and options, and ensure that all of the relevant people involved receive them.

- Make sure that people and their families receive information in a form that they can access and understand.
- Ensure that the person has the opportunity to comment in their own time about options and in an atmosphere where they feel able to make adverse comments if necessary.
- Always provide people with the information they need to make informed choices, even if that is restricted by their circumstances.

5.2 Using agreed risk assessment processes to support the right to make choices

Risk assessments are used in several different ways in order to deliver safe and effective services that have people at the centre. Table 1 shows some examples.

Activity	Purpose of risk assessment
Moving and handling	Reduce risk of injury to worker and person being moved
Development activities	Reduce risk of injury to person undertaking the activity
Invasive treatment, managing open wounds	Reduce risk of infection
Finding appropriate resources for someone	Reduce risk of harm and abuse
Planning changes in support arrangements	Reduce risk of distress or concern

Table 1: Examples of risk assessments.

As you can see from the table above, risk assessments are carried out for various reasons, but they are always used in order to protect either the person using the services or the support worker, or both. Risk assessments should never be used as a reason to prevent people from making choices; they are there to protect and to ensure that risks are reduced.

Activity 4
Risky situations

Think about a time when you have said 'no' or advised against something because you thought it was too risky. If you are honest, could you have done a risk assessment? Think about people you currently support who may like to change their lives or get involved in something that might be risky. Plan out how the risks can be reduced so that it may be able to happen.

A good risk assessment allows people to make choices that are based on facts and on having the right information. It helps people to understand the consequences so that they are making informed choices.

5.3 Why your personal views should not influence an individual's choices

Choices that other people make are not *your* choices. Regardless of whether or not you agree or think that the choice is wrong, you should never let your own opinion influence what someone decides to do. It can be very tempting to try to influence someone to make a particular choice because you believe it will be of benefit, or because any other option is risky or unwise. You have to resist this temptation and simply give factual information about the options available.

You may be asked, 'What would you do if you were me?' As always, your answer has to be, 'Well I'm not you, so knowing what *I* would do won't be much help. Let's look at the options for *you*.'

You have learned in Unit SHC 22 about the influences on your own development and how factors in your life have resulted in you holding certain views and beliefs. These are your views and beliefs that have been shaped by your experiences; they are not necessarily right for others who have different backgrounds and different life experiences. Everyone needs to be able to make their own choices.

5.4 How to support an individual to question or challenge decisions concerning them

People who use social care services can find themselves the subject of decisions made by professionals. They may not agree with the decisions, but may not always feel able to challenge the decisions. Decisions could be about:

- accommodation
- support plan
- change in service provision
- assessment
- medication
- development activities
- personal care
- leisure time.

Although good practice is that people should always be in control of decisions, this does not always happen. Sometimes events just seem to take over, such as the closure of a facility or financial spending decisions, changes in family circumstances.

Decisions are made in all aspects of people's lives.

On other occasions it may be that the type of decision does not put the person in control, such as decisions on benefits, immigration status or employment issues. Or, of course, it could just be poor practice!

People can find it hard to challenge a decision that has been made for them. It can be difficult for a range of reasons — for example, people:

- feel intimidated
- lack the confidence to make a challenge
- do not believe that they have the right to challenge the decisions of professionals
- may have had poor experiences in the past when they challenged decisions unsuccessfully
- may simply not know how to go about it.

You can support people to overcome all of these barriers. You may be able to provide encouragement and also practical help and advice. The following case studies show two ways in which people can be supported in exercising their rights to question and challenge decisions.

Case study

Reviewing Tony's medication

Tony's doctor decided to change his medication. Tony was unhappy about this, but did not feel that he could argue with the doctor. Carole, his support worker, spent time with Tony to talk through his worries and encouraged him to write some notes explaining his concerns. She then agreed to go with Tony to see the doctor, but only as a support while he raised the issues. In the event, Carole did not need to say a word; Tony used his notes to explain to his doctor why he was unhappy and disagreed with the change. Even when the doctor got quite cross, Tony was still able to make his point.

1. How do you think Carole's method of supporting affected Tony's confidence?
2. If you were Tony's care worker, would you have been tempted to speak up when the doctor got cross? When do you think you should intervene in that sort of situation?

Case study

May's Attendance Allowance

May has been told that she will only be eligible for Attendance Allowance at the lower rate. She thinks this is unfair as her daughter has to help her in the night sometimes. Davinda, her support worker, explained that May could appeal against the decision. She told May where to get the forms to do this and explained that she could get help from the Welfare Rights office if she needed someone to support her to make the appeal.

May and her daughter visited the office and were very pleased at how helpful the officers were, but May did say to Davinda that she was sure they could not have managed the appeal on their own without support, as the process seemed pretty daunting.

1. What barriers was May facing?
2. How did Davinda support May to overcome these barriers?

Functional skills

English: Reading

When completing the questions following case studies, you will be practising your reading skills to use information from the text and to give suitable responses. When you give your answers, you will show that you have understood the facts and identified the relevant points.

6. Be able to promote individuals' well-being

6.1 How individual identity and self-esteem are linked with well-being

Identity/self-image

Key term

Self-image/self-concept – how people see themselves

Identity or self-image is about how people see themselves. Would you describe who you are in terms of what you do, for example, a support worker? Or perhaps in terms of your relationships with others, for example, a wife, a parent or a child? Have you ever described yourself as 'So-and-so's mum', or 'So-and-so's daughter'? You might think of yourself in terms of your hopes, dreams or ambitions. Or, what is more likely perhaps, all of these ways of thinking about yourself play some part.

Activity 5

Your self-image

Think about the number of different ways you could describe yourself. List them all. See how many relate to:

- other people – for example, someone's mum, sister, friend
- what you do – for example, care worker, volunteer at the youth club, gardener
- what you believe – for example, honest, loyal, a Christian, a Muslim
- what you look like – for example, short, brown hair, blue eyes.

You may be surprised when you see the greatest influences on how you view yourself.

Identify is about what makes people who they are. Everyone has an image of themselves, it can be a positive image overall or a negative one, but a great many factors contribute to an person's sense of identity. These will include:

- gender
- race
- language
- religion
- environment
- family
- friends
- culture
- values and beliefs
- sexuality.

All of these are aspects of our lives that contribute towards our idea of who we are. As a support worker it is essential that you take time to consider how each of the people you work with will have developed their own self-image and identity, and it is important that you recognise and promote this.

Reflect

Think about just one person you have worked with. Note down all the influences on their sense of identity. Have you really thought about it before? Think about the difference it may make to your practice now that you have spent some time reflecting about the influences that have made a person who they are.

You should ensure that you recognise that the values, beliefs, tastes and preferences which people have are what define them; they must be supported, nurtured and encouraged, not ignored and disregarded because they are inconvenient or do not fit in with the care system.

Self-esteem

Self-esteem is about how people value themselves — self-worth. It results from the way people feel about themselves. It is important that people feel that they have a valuable contribution to make, whether it is to society as a whole or within a smaller area such as their local community, workplace or own family.

Feeling good about yourself also has a great deal to do with your own experiences throughout your life and the kind of confidence that you were given as you grew up. All human beings need to feel that they have a valuable place and a valuable contribution to make within society.

The reasons why people have different levels of self-esteem are complex. The way people feel about themselves is often laid down during childhood. A child who is encouraged and regularly told how good they are and given a lot of positive feelings is the sort of person who is likely to feel that they have something to offer and can make a useful contribution to any situation. But a child who is constantly shouted at, blamed or belittled is likely to grow into an adult who lacks belief in themselves, or finds it difficult to go into new situations and to accept new challenges.

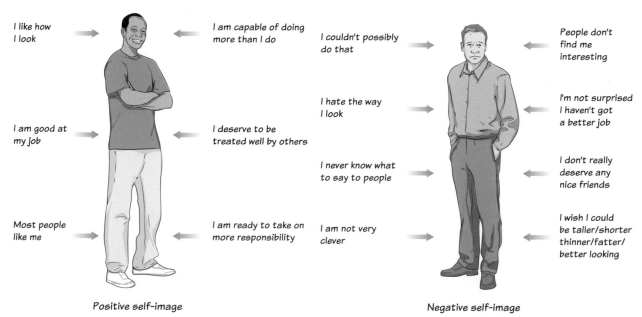

I like how I look

I am capable of doing more than I do

I am good at my job

I deserve to be treated well by others

Most people like me

I am ready to take on more responsibility

Positive self-image

I couldn't possibly do that

People don't find me interesting

I hate the way I look

I'm not surprised I haven't got a better job

I never know what to say to people

I don't really deserve any nice friends

I am not very clever

I wish I could be taller/shorter thinner/fatter/ better looking

Negative self-image

Do you see the factors that can influence how someone values themselves?

In the mid-1950s, a woman called Dorothy Law Nolte wrote this poem about how children are influenced during their early years.

> If a child lives with criticism, he learns to condemn...
> If a child lives with hostility, he learns to fight...
> If a child lives with fear, he learns to be apprehensive...
> If a child lives with pity, he learns to feel sorry for himself...
> If a child lives with ridicule, he learns to be shy...
> If a child lives with jealousy, he learns to feel guilt...
> But...
> If a child lives with tolerance, he learns to be patient...
> If a child lives with encouragement, he learns to be confident...
> If a child lives with praise, he learns to be appreciative...
> If a child lives with acceptance, he learns to love...
> If a child lives with honesty, he learns what truth is...
> If a child lives with fairness, he learns justice...
> If a child lives with security, he learns to have faith in himself and those about him...
> If a child lives with friendliness, he learns the world is a nice place in which to live.
>
> Dorothy Law Nolte

Not all the reasons for levels of self-esteem come from childhood. Many experiences in adult life can affect self-confidence and how people feel about themselves, for example:

- being made redundant
- getting divorced
- the death of somebody close
- the loss of independence, possibly having to go into residential care or into hospital
- the shock of being burgled
- having a bad fall, which results in a feeling of helplessness and a lack of self-worth
- being the subject of discriminatory or stereotyping abusive behaviour
- being the victim of violent or aggressive behaviour.

All of these experiences can have devastating effects. Very often, people will become withdrawn and depressed as a result, and a great deal of support and concentrated effort is needed to help them through these very difficult situations. People can be very vulnerable at these low points in their lives, and it is important that you make sure that you have followed the procedures in your organisation for assessing and managing the risk of self-harm where you are aware that someone is going through a period of very low self-esteem.

Self-esteem is also very closely tied into the culture we live in, and the values that particular culture has about what is important. For example, among a group of young car thieves, the person most admired might be the one who has stolen most cars, and the self-esteem of that person is likely to be really high because of this

Activity 6

Identifying criteria that trigger a risk assessment

Check your organisation's policies and procedures to identify the key criteria which will trigger a risk assessment for someone who has been showing low self-esteem and feelings of worthlessness.

admiration and approval; these are not values that would be shared by other people in the community! So never forget the influences of values and culture on self-esteem and on self-concept.

6.2 Attitudes and approaches to promote an individual's well-being

6.3 Supporting an individual in a way that promotes identity and self-esteem

and

6.4 Ways to contribute to an environment that promotes well-being

There are many practical ways in which people's needs can be met through the way in which you provide the services they need. Being recognised and valued as an individual is hugely important for people's self-esteem. When somebody either requests, or is referred, for a service, the assessment and planning cycle begins. Throughout the consultation and planning which follows, the person and their needs should be at the centre of the process. You will need to make sure that the person has every opportunity to state exactly how they wish their needs to be met. Some will be able to give this information personally, while others will need an advocate who will support them in expressing their views.

Feeling valued as an individual is vital to increasing self-esteem and making people feel good about themselves. After all, it is very hard to feel good about yourself, if you do not believe that anyone else thinks much of you. If you are able to feel that people respect and value you, then you are more likely to value yourself.

In your role as a care worker, you will come across situations where a little thought or a small change in practice could give greater opportunities for people to feel that they are valued and respected as individuals. For example, you may need to find out how someone likes to be addressed — do they consider that 'Mr' or 'Mrs' is more respectful and appropriate, or are they happy for a first name to be used? This, particularly for some older people, can be one of the ways of indicating the respect that is important for anyone who uses care services.

You will need to give thought to the values and beliefs which people may have, for example:

- religious or cultural beliefs about eating specific foods
- values about forms of dress which are acceptable
- beliefs or preferences about who should be able to provide personal care.

This will mean that you need to make sure that people have been asked about religious, cultural or personal preferences and those preferences are recorded so that all care workers and others providing care are able to access them.

There may already be arrangements in your workplace to ask for and record this information. If so, you must ensure that you are familiar with the process and that you know where to find the information for everyone you work with. If your workplace does not have arrangements in place to find out about people's choices and preferences, you should discuss with your line manager ways in which you can help to find this out.

Simple, open questions, asked politely are always the best way: 'Excuse me, Mr Khan, the information I have here notes that you are vegetarian. Can you tell me about the foods you prefer?'

Some information you can obtain by observation — for instance, looking at someone can tell you a lot about their preferences regarding dress. Particular forms of dress which are being worn for religious or cultural reasons are usually obvious; a turban or a sari, for instance, are easy to spot, but other forms of dress may also give you some clues about the person wearing them. Consider how dress can tell you about how much money people have or what kind of background they come from. Clothes also tell you a lot about someone's age and the type of lifestyle they are likely to have had. Beware, however — any information you think you gain from this type of observation must be confirmed by checking your facts. Otherwise it is easy to be caught out — some people from wealthy backgrounds wear scruffy clothes, and some people in their 70s wear the latest fashions and have face lifts!

Equally, be careful that you do not resort to thinking in stereotypes. Rather, work with people as individuals, and avoid making assumptions about them based on any of the factors that make them similar to others, such as:

- age
- gender
- race
- culture
- skin colour
- job
- wealth
- where they live.

All of these factors are important in giving you information about what may have influenced the development of each person — but they will never, on their own, tell you anything else about that person. The impact of stereotypical assumptions about people can result in very low self-esteem and a negative self-image. After all, if everyone assumes that just because you are 85 years old, you are too old to be interested in current affairs, or the latest sports news, you may decide that perhaps you are too old to bother; or, if employers keep refusing to give you a job because you live in an inner city, are 16 years old, male and black, you may well decide that it is not worth bothering to try any more.

Activity 7

Filling in a form

Look at the form, or other means of recording information, that is used in your workplace. Fill it in as if you were the person using the service. Now note down all the factors which make you who you are. For example, think about your:

- gender
- age
- background
- economic and social circumstances
- nationality
- culture
- religion
- sexual orientation
- food preferences
- entertainment preferences
- relaxation preferences
- reading material preferences.

Look at the form you have completed – would it tell anyone enough about you so that they could ensure
that all your needs were met and you did not lose parts of your life that were important to you? If not, think about what other questions you need to ask, note them down and make sure that you ask them to the people you support!

Functional skills

English: Writing

Filling in a form is a good way of practising writing accurately. Check that you use a suitable layout – for example, columns and bullet points as suggested for Activity 7.
Proofread your work to check that spellings, punctuation and grammar are accurate.

Doing it well

Putting person-centred values into practice

- Your key focus is the person you support.
- Services revolve around the person, not the other way around.
- Even in complex or difficult situation, the person is always at the centre.
- People must always be treated with dignity and respect.
- Make sure that people have all the support they need in order to make choices.
- Make arrangements for an advocate if necessary.

Getting ready for assessment

This unit is important because it is about the key aspects of how we deal with people who use social care services. The concept of person-centred working is at the heart of everything we do in social care. Most of the assessment for this unit is observation of your practice. Your assessor will want to be able to see that you have included all the aspects of person-centred working in the way you deal with the people you support. This means that you will need to let your assessor see that you support people to make their own choices about all aspects of their lives and actively participate in their own support. You will need to show this by the way you show that people are in control of their own support by being able to change their minds if they wish to and to decide what they want you to do for them. Your assessor will check that you get consent before undertaking any activity with anyone, and you can show this by always saying what you are going to do and checking that this is OK with the person.

As well as observing your practice, your assessor may ask questions or ask you to complete an assignment to show that you understand the principles behind person-centred working and why it is so important. You may also be asked to look at how this approach has changed how we think about the provision of social care support and how person-centred working is different from previous approaches.

Further reading and research

- www.alzheimers.org.uk (Alzheimer's Society)
- www.dh.gov.uk (Department of Health)
- www.legislation.gov.uk (Mental Capacity Act)
- www.nationalcareforum.org.uk (National Care Forum, Key principles of person-centred dementia care)
- www.nhs.uk (NHS Choices)
- www.opsi.gov.uk (Government legislation website)

Unit HSC 027

Contribute to health and safety in health and social care

Every workplace is governed by regulations and legislation to protect the health and safety of people who are supported and the workforce. You share part of the responsibility for maintaining the workplace in a healthy, safe and secure way, and knowing the key laws and guidelines that must be followed.

You must be aware of how to deal with risks such as moving and handling, disposal of clinical waste and the maintenance of hygienic conditions, and you must know how to deal with accidents and emergencies.

Working to support people can be stressful and demanding as well as rewarding, so it is important that you know how to recognise the signs of stress and how to deal with them.

In this unit you will learn about:

1. **own responsibilities, and the responsibilities of others, relating to health and safety in the work setting**
2. **the use of risk assessments in relation to health and safety**
3. **procedures for responding to accidents and sudden illness**
4. **how to reduce the spread of infection**
5. **how to move and handle equipment and other objects safely**
6. **how to handle hazardous substances and materials**
7. **how to promote fire safety in the work setting**
8. **how to implement security measures in the work setting**
9. **how to manage own stress.**

1. Understand own responsibilities, and the responsibilities of others, relating to health and safety in the work setting

1.1 Legislation relating to general health and safety in a health or social care work setting

The settings in which you work are generally covered by the Health and Safety at Work Act 1974 (HASAWA). This Act has been updated and supplemented by many sets of regulations and guidelines, which extend it, support it or explain it. The regulations most likely to affect your workplace are shown in the following diagram.

As you work through this unit, you will see how the different regulations under the Health and Safety at Work Act affect your day-to-day activity.

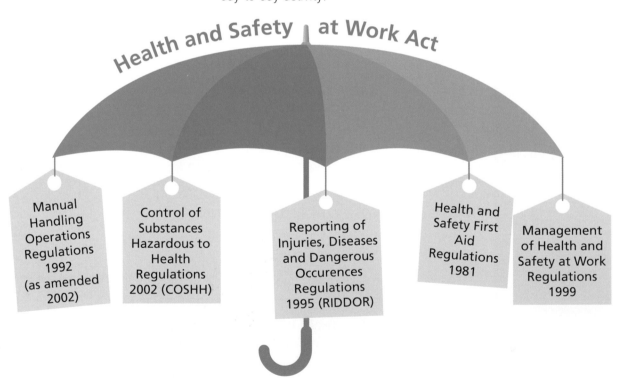

Health and Safety at Work Act

- Manual Handling Operations Regulations 1992 (as amended 2002)
- Control of Substances Hazardous to Health Regulations 2002 (COSHH)
- Reporting of Injuries, Diseases and Dangerous Occurences Regulations 1995 (RIDDOR)
- Health and Safety First Aid Regulations 1981
- Management of Health and Safety at Work Regulations 1999

Can you see how the Health and Safety at Work Act is the overall Act for many other regulations?

1.2 Health and safety policies and procedures agreed with the employer

and

1.3 Health and safety responsibilities of yourself and others in the work setting

It sounds very simple and straightforward: make sure that the place in which you work is safe and secure. However, when you start to think about it — safe for whom? From whom? Safe from tripping over things? Or safe from hazardous fumes? Safe from infection? Safe from intruders? Safe from work-related injuries? You can begin to see that this is a wide and complex subject.

You share the responsibility with your employer for your own safety and that of all the people you support.

There are many regulations, laws and guidelines dealing with health and safety. You do not need to know the detail, but you do need to know where your responsibilities begin and end.

The laws place certain responsibilities on both employers and employees. For example, it is up to the employer to provide a safe place in which to work, but the employee also has to show reasonable care for their own safety.

Employers have to:

- make the workplace safe
- prevent **risks** to health
- ensure that machinery is safe to use, and that safe working practices are set up and followed
- make sure that all materials are handled, stored and used safely
- provide adequate first aid facilities
- tell you about any potential **hazards** from the work you do, chemicals and other substances used by the organisation, and give you information, instructions, training and supervision as needed
- set up emergency plans
- make sure that ventilation, temperature, lighting, and toilet, washing and rest facilities all meet health, safety and welfare requirements
- check that the right work equipment is provided and is properly used and regularly maintained
- prevent or control exposure to substances that may damage your health
- take precautions against the risks caused by flammable or explosive hazards, electrical equipment, noise and radiation
- avoid potentially dangerous work involving manual handling and, if it cannot be avoided, take precautions to reduce the risk of injury
- provide health supervision as needed

Key terms

Risk – the likelihood of a hazard causing harm

Hazard – something that could possibly cause harm

- provide protective clothing or equipment free of charge if risks cannot be removed or adequately controlled by any other means
- ensure that the right warning signs are provided and looked after
- report certain accidents, injuries, diseases and dangerous occurrences to either the Health and Safety Executive (HSE) or the local authority, depending on the type of business.

As an employee, you have both rights and responsibilities in the workplace. Your rights are:

- as far as possible, to have any risks to your health and safety properly controlled
- to be provided, free of charge, with any personal protective and safety equipment
- if you have reasonable concerns about your safety, to stop work and leave your work area, without being disciplined
- to tell your employer about any health and safety concerns you have
- to get in touch with the Health and Safety Executive (HSE) or your local authority if your employer will not listen to your concerns, without being disciplined by them
- to have rest breaks during the working day, to have time off from work during the working week and to have annual paid holiday.

Your responsibilities are:

- to take reasonable care of your own health and safety
- if possible, to avoid wearing jewellery or loose clothing if operating machinery or using equipment
- if you have long hair or wear a headscarf, to make sure it is tucked out of the way (it could get caught in equipment or machinery)
- to take reasonable care not to put other people — fellow employees and members of the public — at risk by what you do or do not do in the course of your work
- to cooperate with your employer, making sure that you get proper training, and that you understand and follow the company's health and safety policies
- not to interfere with or misuse anything that has been provided for your health, safety or welfare
- to report any injuries, strains or illnesses you suffer as a result of doing your job (your employer may need to change the way you work)
- to tell your employer if something happens that might affect your ability to work (for example, becoming pregnant or suffering an injury); because your employer has a legal responsibility for your health and safety, they may need to suspend you while they find a solution to the problem, but you will normally be paid if this happens
- if you drive or operate equipment or machinery, to tell your employer if you take medication that makes you drowsy — they should temporarily move you to another job if they have one for you to do.

Activity 1

Health and safety policy

Find out where the health and safety policy is for your workplace and make sure you read it.

Both the employee and employer are jointly responsible for safeguarding the health and safety of anyone using the premises.

Each workplace which has five or more workers must have a written statement of health and safety policy. The policy must include:

- a statement of intention to provide a safe workplace
- the name of the person responsible for implementing the policy
- the names of any other people responsible for preventing particular health and safety hazards
- a list of identified health and safety hazards and the procedures to be followed in relation to them
- procedures for recording accidents at work
- details for evacuation of the premises.

1.4 Tasks that should not be carried out without special training

All manual handling needs to be carried out by people who have had training to do it. Employers are obliged to provide training in manual handling, and you have to attend it once a year. Training is not a one-off; it is important to be up to date with the latest techniques and equipment, as well as any changes in regulations. This area of work is very tightly controlled by legislation and regulations for very good reasons; moving people without proper training is dangerous both for them and for you. You will also need training for specific pieces of equipment — for example, if a new hoist is to be used in your workplace, no one will be able to operate it without training. You may think that it looks very similar to the last one you used and may be sure that it probably works in the same way — but you must have specific training on that particular hoist before using it. This applies to any piece of equipment that you have not used before.

Clinical tasks (including taking measurements like temperature or blood pressure) will require training, as does changing dressings or giving medication. There is more information about each of these in Unit HSC 2014.

1.5 How to access additional support and information relating to health and safety

You may find that you need some more information, or some further advice. Sometimes it may not always be clear what the best course of action may be. Health and safety is an important issue, and it is always better to ask for more help than to make a guess and get something wrong.

You may find that you need some additional help because you:

- are unsure about what legislation and guidelines apply
- do not know what action to take to ensure safety
- are concerned about a particular situation or person
- are unhappy about the risks from a piece of equipment or another hazard
- are unclear about who has responsibility.

Of course, your line manager is always your first choice for additional information or support, but if your manager is unavailable or unsure, and you cannot find what you need in your employer's policies, then the Health and Safety Executive (www.hse.gov.uk) should be able to provide any information you need.

Trade unions are also a good source of information about heath and safety issues, so you should always try asking your union steward if you need advice.

Reflect

Think about a time you have had to deal with a health and safety issue. Did you get all the information you needed? If so, think about how it helped you to take the right action. If not, think about how things could have been better.

If you have never had to deal with a health and safety issue, think about health and safety in your workplace and work out the different roles that people have to maintain health and safety. Can you see how you can play your part to make the workplace safer? Note down the actions you can take.

2. Understand the use of risk assessments in relation to health and safety

2.1 Why it is important to assess health and safety hazards

Risk assessment in health and social care is important for everyone whether they are employers, self-employed or employees, who are required by law to identify and assess risks in the workplace. This includes any situations where potential harm may be caused. There are many regulations that require risks to be assessed and some are covered by European Community directives. These include:

- Management of Health and Safety at Work Regulations 1999
- Manual Handling Operations Regulations 1992 (amended 2002)
- Personal Protective Equipment at Work Regulations 1992
- Health and Safety (Display Screen Equipment) Regulations 1992 (amended 2002)
- Noise at Work Regulations 1989
- Control of Substances Hazardous to Health Regulations 2002 (COSHH)
- Control of Asbestos at Work Regulations 2002
- Control of Lead at Work Regulations 2002.

There are other regulations that deal with very specialised risks such as major hazards and ionising radiation. However, these are not common risks in most workplaces.

There are five key stages to undertaking a risk assessment, which involve answering the following questions.

1. What is the purpose of the risk assessment?
2. Who has to assess the risk?
3. Whose risk should be assessed?
4. What should be assessed?
5. When should the risk be assessed?

The Management of Health and Safety at Work Regulations 1999 state that employers have to assess any risks which are associated with the workplace and work activities. This means all activities, from walking on wet floors to dealing with violence. Having carried out a risk assessment, the employer must then apply **risk control measures**. This means that actions must be identified to reduce the risks. For example, alarm buzzers may need to be installed or extra staff employed, as well as steps such as providing extra training for staff or written guidelines on how to deal with a particular hazard.

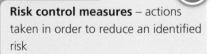

Key term

Risk control measures – actions taken in order to reduce an identified risk

How many potential hazards can you see?

Risks in someone's home

Of course, the situation is somewhat different if you work in a person's own home. Your employer can still carry out risk assessments and put risk control measures in place, such as a procedure for working in twos in a situation where there is a risk of violence. What cannot be done is to remove environmental hazards such as trailing electrical flexes, rugs with curled-up edges, worn patches on stair carpets or old equipment. All you can do is to advise the person whose home it is of the risks, and suggest how things could be improved. You also need to take care!

2.2 How and when to report potential health and safety risks

It is important that you develop an awareness of health and safety risks and that you are always aware of any risks in any situation you are in. If you get into the habit of making a mental checklist, you will find that it helps. The checklist will vary from one workplace to another, but could look like the one opposite.

Checklist for a safe work environment

Hazards	*Check*
Environment	
Floors	Are they dry?
Carpets and rugs	Are they worn or curled at the edges?
Doorways and corridors	Are they clear of obstacles?
Electrical flexes	Are they trailing?
Equipment	
Beds	Are the brakes on? Are they high enough?
Electrical or gas appliances	Are they worn? Have they been safety checked?
Lifting equipment	Is it worn or damaged?
Mobility aids	Are they worn or damaged?
Substances such as cleaning fluids	Are they correctly labelled?
Containers	Are they leaking or damaged?
Waste disposal equipment	Is it faulty?
People	
Visitors to the building	Should they be there?
Handling procedures	Have they been assessed for risk?
Intruders	Have police been called?
Violent and aggressive behaviour	Has it been dealt with?

Functional skills

Maths: Representing

Using the sections hazards and equipment from the information on this page, devise a chart which allows you to represent your findings – for example, for mobility aids:

1. Are they worn?   Yes / No
2. Are they damaged?   Yes / No

Using your answers, look at the ratio of yes answers to no answers and document your findings. Convert your answers to percentages, for example, 74% yes answers, 26% no answers.

In your workplace, you have a responsibility to report any unsafe situation to your employer. For example, if you come to use a piece of equipment – anything from a hoist to a kettle – and find that it is unsafe or needs repair, you must report it. It is not enough to assume that someone will notice it or to say, 'It's not up to me – that's a manager's job.' You have a share in the responsibility of making your workplace safe and secure.

However, there are some other situations which have to be reported officially, not just to your employer, and there are special procedures to be followed:

Reporting of Injuries, Diseases and Dangerous Occurrences (RIDDOR) Regulations 1995 (amended 2008)

Reporting accidents and ill-health at work is a legal requirement. All accidents, diseases and dangerous occurrences should be reported to the Incident Contact Centre. The Centre was established on 1 April 2001 as a single point of contact for all incidents in the UK. The information is important because it means that risks and causes of accidents, incidents and diseases can be identified, and any necessary risk assessments carried out. All notifications are passed on to either the local authority Environmental Health department, or the Health and Safety Executive, as appropriate.

Your employer needs to report:

- deaths
- major injuries
- accidents resulting in more than three days off work
- diseases
- dangerous occurrences.

These are monitored and recorded at a national level so that risks in different workplaces are understood and any trends can be identified.

2.3 How risk assessment can help address dilemmas between rights and health and safety concerns

If you work in someone's home or long-term residential setting, you have to balance the need for safety with the rights of people to have their living space the way they want it. It may be your workplace, but it is also the person's home.

Both you and the people you support are entitled to expect a safe place in which to live and work, but remember their rights to choose how they want to live.

Concerns for security can also create difficult situations. Of course people have a right to see whomever they wish, but there can be situations where there may be concerns about vulnerable people being exploited or placed at risk of harm. You cannot insist on the levels of security that people adopt in their own homes, but you can advise people of the risks of opening doors to strangers or inviting unknown people in.

People also need to assess the risks involved in doing the things they wish to do safely and without placing themselves at undue risk of harm. For example, someone with dementia may wish to go out shopping alone. This is potentially risky as they may become disoriented and be unable to find their way back. A risk assessment will help to look at the risks and the control measures that can be put in place in order to reduce the risks of the activity; for example, suggesting that a friend accompany the person, or cards with details of address and contact numbers be placed in pockets and bags and simple instructions with key landmarks are practised with the person prior to the trip.

What risks would you take into account? How can this be balanced with someone's rights?

A person with a visual impairment may be intending to take up a new exercise regime at a local gym. A risk assessment carried out with the person can identify any control measures needed such as liaison with the gym to ensure that they can provide the necessary support on using the equipment, offering a support worker if necessary and a review of travel arrangements.

Reflect

Effective risk assessments make it possible for people to do things. Risk assessments are not about restricting what people do, they are about making sure that it is done safely. The potential for health and safety concerns to limit people's activities and restrict their rights can be greatly decreased by good risk assessments that put sensible control measures in place to reduce the risks. Life is full of risks, and all people, regardless of age or ability, have the right to take risks in order to live as they wish. But a well carried-out risk assessment can make it less likely that any harm will result.

3. Understand procedures for responding to accidents and sudden illness

3.1 Different types of accidents and sudden illness that may occur

If accidents or injuries occur at work, either to you or to someone you are supporting, then the details must be recorded. For example, someone may have a fall or slip on a wet floor. You must record the incident regardless of whether there was an injury.

Your employer should have procedures in place for making a record of accidents — either an accident book or an accident report form. This is not only required by the RIDDOR regulations, but also by the inspection bodies in all UK countries.

Make sure you know where the accident report forms or the accident book is kept, and who is responsible for recording accidents. It is likely to be your manager.

You must report any accident in which you are involved, or have witnessed, to your manager or supervisor.

Any medical treatment or assessment which is necessary should be arranged without delay. If someone has been involved in an accident, you should check if there is anyone they would like to be contacted, perhaps a relative or friend. If the accident is serious, and you cannot consult the person — because they are unconscious — the next of kin should be informed as soon as possible.

Complete a report, and ensure that all witnesses to the accident also complete reports. You should include the following in any accident report:

* date, time and place of accident
* person/people involved — bearing in mind the Data Protection Act
* circumstances and details of exactly what you saw
* anything that was said by the people involved
* the condition of the person after the accident
* steps taken to summon help, time of summoning help and time when help arrived
* names of any other people who witnessed the accident
* any equipment involved in the accident.

Functional skills

English: Reading; Writing

Research examples of accident report forms. Choose a format that best fits the information you need to show for Activity 2. By doing this, you will be reading for a purpose and using information found in texts. Ensure that the layout you use for the form is suitable and that any information on it is clear and accurate in spelling, punctuation and grammar. Use suitable language at all times.

Activity 2

Designing an accident report

Imagine that your manager has asked you to design a new incident/accident report form for your workplace. They have asked you to do this because the current form does not provide enough information. The purpose of the new form is to provide sufficient information to:

- ensure the person receives the proper medical attention
- provide information for treatment at a later date, in case of delayed reactions
- give information to any inspector who may need to see the records
- identify any gaps or need for improvements in safety procedures
- provide information about the circumstances in case of any future legal action.

Think about how you would design the new report form and what headings you would include. Use the list above as a checklist to make sure you have covered everything you need.

Date: 24.2.11   **Time:** 14.30 hrs   **Location:** Main Lounge

Description of accident:

PH got out of her chair and began to walk across the lounge with the aid of her stick. She turned her head to continue the conversation she had been having with GK, and as she turned back again, she appeared not to have noticed that MP's handbag had been left on the floor. PH tripped over the handbag and fell heavily, banging her head on a footstool.

She was very shaken and although she said that she was not hurt, there was a large bump on her head. P appeared pale and shaky. I asked S to fetch a blanket and to call Mrs J, deputy officer in charge. Covered P with a blanket. Mrs J arrived immediately. Dr was sent for after P was examined by Mrs J.

Dr arrived after about 20 mins and said that she was bruised and shaken, but did not seem to have any injuries.

She wanted to go and lie down. She was helped to bed.

Incident was witnessed by six residents who were in the lounge at the time: GK, MP, IL, MC, CR and BQ.

Signed: **Name:**

Can you see how information about an accident is all in this report?

Types of accidents and sudden illness that may occur in a health or social care setting

It is important that you are aware of the initial steps to take when dealing with the most common health emergencies. You may be involved with any of these emergencies when you are at work, whether you work in a residential, hospital or community setting. There are major differences between the different work situations.

- If you are working in a hospital where skilled assistance is always immediately available, the likelihood of your having to act in an emergency, other than to summon help, is remote.
- In a residential setting, help is likely to be readily available, although it may not necessarily be the professional medical expertise of a hospital.
- In the community, you may have to summon help and take action to support a casualty until the help arrives. It is in this setting that you are most likely to need some knowledge of how to respond to a health emergency.

This section gives a guide to taking initial action in a number of illnesses or accidents that you may come across in your work. There are many others, but the general guidance given here may assist you in taking initial action until further assistance arrives in instances of:

- severe bleeding
- cardiac arrest
- shock
- loss of consciousness
- epileptic seizure
- choking and difficulty with breathing
- fractures and suspected fractures
- burns and scalds
- poisoning
- electrical injuries.

3.2 Procedures to follow if an accident or sudden illness should occur

Severe bleeding

Severe bleeding can be the result of a fall or injury. The most common causes of severe cuts are glass, as the result of a fall into a window or glass door, or knives from accidents in the kitchen.

Symptoms

There will be apparently large quantities of blood from the wound. In some very serious cases, the blood may be pumping out. Even small amounts of blood can be very frightening, both for you and the casualty. Remember that a small amount of blood goes a long way, and things may look worse than they are. However, severe bleeding requires urgent medical attention in hospital. Although people rarely bleed to death, extensive bleeding can cause shock and loss of consciousness.

Aims

- To bring the bleeding under control
- To limit the possibility of infection
- To arrange urgent medical attention

Action for severe bleeding

You will need to apply pressure to a wound that is bleeding. If possible, use a sterile dressing. If one is not readily available, use any absorbent material, or even your hand. Do not forget the precautions (see 'Protect yourself' below). You will need to apply direct pressure over the wound for 10 minutes (this can seem like a very long time) to allow the blood to clot

If there is any object in the wound, such as a piece of glass, *do not* try to remove it. Simply apply pressure to the sides of the wound. Lay the casualty down and raise the affected part if possible. Make the person comfortable and secure.

In a residential care setting, call for the senior registered nurse to assess the severity of the injury. They will make a decision regarding whether the wound is severe enough to call a paramedic.

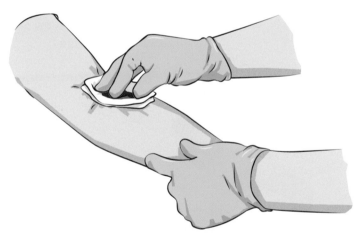

Would you know how to apply pressure to bleeding in an emergency situation?

Protect yourself

You should take steps to protect yourself when you are dealing with casualties who are bleeding. Your skin provides an excellent barrier to infections, but you must take care if you have any broken skin such as a cut, graze or sore. Seek medical advice if blood comes into contact with your mouth or nose, or gets into your eyes. Blood-borne viruses (such as HIV or hepatitis) can be passed only if the blood of someone who is already infected comes into contact with broken skin.

Ideally, wear disposable gloves. If this is not possible, cover any areas of broken skin with a waterproof dressing. If possible, wash your hands thoroughly in soap and water before and after exposure to blood. Take care with any needles or broken glass in the area. Use a mask for mouth-to-mouth resuscitation if the casualty's nose or mouth is bleeding.

Cardiac arrest

Cardiac arrest occurs when a person's heart stops. Cardiac arrest can happen for various reasons, the most common of which is a heart attack, but a person's heart can also stop as a result of shock, electric shock, a convulsion or other illness or injury.

Symptoms

- No pulse
- No breathing

Aims

- To obtain medical help as a matter of urgency

It is important to give oxygen, using mouth-to-mouth resuscitation, and to stimulate the heart, using chest compressions. This procedure is called cardio-pulmonary resuscitation — CPR. You will need to attend a first aid course to learn how to resuscitate; you cannot learn how to do this from a book. Giving CPR is very hard work and correct positioning is important, so you need the opportunity to try this out with supervision. On the first aid course you will be able to practise on a special dummy.

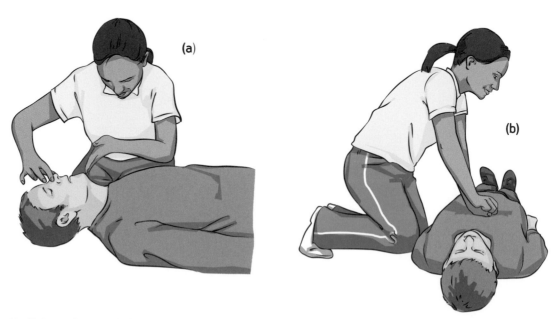

Mouth-to-mouth resuscitation (a) and chest compressions (b).

Action for cardiac arrest

Check whether the person has a pulse and whether they are breathing. If not, call for urgent help from a senior registered nurse who will assess the need for summoning emergency services.

Start methods of resuscitation if you have been taught how to do it. The pattern is two breaths then 30 chest compressions. Repeat this until help arrives if you have been trained to do it.

Shock

Shock occurs because blood is not being pumped around the body efficiently. This can be the result of loss of body fluids through bleeding, burns, severe vomiting or diarrhoea, or a sudden drop in blood pressure or a heart attack.

Symptoms

The signs of shock are easily recognised. The person:

- will look very pale, almost grey
- will be very sweaty, and the skin will be cold and clammy
- will have a very fast pulse
- may feel sick and may vomit
- may be breathing very quickly.

Aims

- To obtain medical help as a matter of urgency
- To improve blood supply to heart, lungs and brain

Action for shock

Summon expert medical or nursing assistance. Lay the person down on the floor. Try to raise the feet off the ground to help the blood supply to the important organs. Loosen any tight clothing.

Watch the person carefully. Check the pulse and breathing regularly. Keep the person warm and comfortable, but *do not* warm the casualty with direct heat, such as a hot-water bottle.

Raise the feet off the ground and keep the casualty warm.

Do not allow the casualty to eat or drink, or leave the casualty alone, unless it is essential to do so briefly in order to summon help.

Loss of consciousness

Loss of consciousness can happen for many reasons, from a straightforward faint to unconsciousness following a serious injury or illness.

Symptom

A reduced level of response and awareness. This can range from being vague and woozy to total unconsciousness.

Aims

- To summon expert medical help as a matter of urgency
- To keep the airway open
- To note any information which may help to find the cause of the unconsciousness

Action for loss of consciousness

Make sure that the person is breathing and has a clear airway. Maintain the airway by lifting the chin and tilting the head backwards.

Look for any obvious reasons why the person may be unconscious, such as a wound or an ID band telling you of any condition they may have. For example, many people who have medical conditions that may cause unconsciousness, such as epilepsy or diabetes, wear special bracelets or necklaces giving information about their condition.

Place the casualty in the recovery position (see below), *but not if you suspect a back or neck injury*, until expert medical or nursing help or the emergency services arrive.

Do not:

- attempt to give anything by mouth
- attempt to make the casualty sit or stand
- leave the casualty alone, unless it is essential to leave briefly in order to summon help.

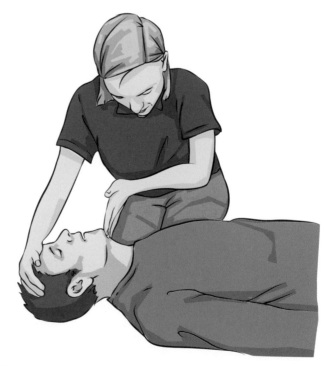

Open the airway.

The recovery position

Many of the actions you need to take to deal with health emergencies will involve you in placing someone in the recovery position. In this position a casualty has the best chance of keeping a clear airway, not inhaling vomit and remaining as safe as possible until help arrives. You should not attempt this position if you think someone has back or neck injuries, and it may not be possible if there are fractures of limbs.

- Kneel at one side of the casualty, at about waist level.
- Tilt back the person's head – this opens the airway. With the casualty on their back, make sure that limbs are straight.
- Bend the casualty's near arm as in a wave (so it is at right angles to the body). Pull the arm on the far side over the chest and place the back of the hand against the opposite cheek (**a** in the diagram).
- Use your other hand to roll the casualty towards you by pulling on the far leg, just above the knee (**b** in the diagram). The casualty should now be on their side.
- Once the casualty is rolled over, bend the leg at right angles to the body. Make sure the head is tilted well back to keep the airway open (**c** in the diagram).

(a)

(b)

(c)

The recovery position.

Epileptic seizure

Epilepsy is a medical condition that causes disturbances in the brain, which result in sufferers becoming unconscious and having involuntary contractions of their muscles. This contraction of the muscles produces the fit or seizure. People who suffer with epilepsy do not have any control over their seizures, and may do themselves harm by falling when they have a seizure.

Aims

- To ensure that the person is safe and does not injure themselves during the fit
- To offer any help needed following the fit

Action for epileptic seizure

Try to make sure that the area in which the person has fallen is safe. Loosen all clothing.

Once the seizure has ended, make sure that the person has a clear airway and place in the recovery position. Make sure that the person is comfortable and safe. Particularly try to prevent head injury.

If the fit lasts longer than 5 minutes, or you are unaware that the casualty is a known epileptic, call an ambulance.

Do not:

- attempt to hold the casualty down, or put anything in the mouth
- move the casualty until they are fully conscious, unless there is a risk of injury in the place where they have fallen.

Choking and difficulty with breathing

This is caused by something (usually a piece of food) stuck at the back of the throat. It is a situation that needs to be dealt with, as people can quickly stop breathing if the obstruction is not removed.

Symptoms

- Red, congested face at first, later turning grey
- Unable to speak or breathe, may gasp and indicate throat or neck — this is severe choking and requires immediate action

If a person can speak in answer to a question such as 'Are you choking?' then this is regarded a mild choking and they should be encouraged to cough.

Aims

- To remove obstruction as quickly as possible
- To summon medical assistance as a matter of urgency if the obstruction cannot be removed

Action for choking

1. Ensure any dentures are removed. Sweep the mouth with one gloved finger to clear any food, vomit or anything else from the mouth.
2. Try to get the person to cough. If that is not immediately effective, move on to step 3.
3. Bend the person forwards. Use the heel of the hand to give up to five blows sharply on the back between the shoulder blades (**a** in the diagram).
4. If this fails, use the Heimlich manoeuvre – also called 'abdominal thrusts' – *if you have been trained to do so*. Stand behind the person with your arms around them. Join your hands just below the breastbone. One hand should be in a fist and the other holding it (**b** in the diagram).
5. Sharply pull your joined hands upwards and into the person's body at the same time. The force should expel the obstruction.
6. You should alternate backslaps and abdominal thrusts until you clear the obstruction.

(a)

(b)

Dealing with an adult who is choking.

Fractures and suspected fractures

Fractures are breaks or cracks in bones. They are usually caused by a fall or other type of injury. The casualty will need to go to a hospital as soon as possible to have a fracture diagnosed correctly.

Symptoms

- Acute pain around the site of the injury
- Swelling and discoloration around the affected area
- Limbs or joints may be in odd positions
- Broken bones may protrude through the skin

Action for fractures

The important thing is to support the affected part. Help the casualty to find the most comfortable position. Support the injured limb in that position with as much padding as necessary — towels, cushions or clothing will do.

Take the person to hospital or call an ambulance. Do not:

- try to bandage or splint the injury
- allow the casualty to have anything to eat or drink.

Burns and scalds

There are several different types of burn; the most usual are burns caused by heat or flame. Scalds are caused by hot liquids. People can also be burned by chemicals or by electrical currents.

Symptoms

Depending on the type and severity of the burn, skin may be red, swollen and tender, blistered and raw or charred. The casualty is usually in severe pain and possibly suffering shock.

Aims

- To obtain immediate medical assistance if the burn is over a large area (as big as the casualty's hand or more) or is deep
- To send for an ambulance if the burn is severe or extensive. If the burn or scald is over a smaller area, the casualty could be transported to hospital by car
- To stop the burning and reduce pain
- To minimise the possibility of infection

Action for burns and scalds

For major burns, summon immediate medical assistance.

Cool down the burn. Keep it flooded with cold water for 10 minutes. If it is a chemical burn, this needs to be done for 20 minutes. Ensure that the contaminated water used to cool a chemical burn is disposed of safely.

Remove any jewellery, watches or clothing which is not sticking to the burn. Cover it if possible, unless it is a facial burn, with a sterile

Stop, drop, wrap, roll

If a person's clothing is on fire, STOP – DROP – WRAP – ROLL.

- *Stop* them from running around.
- Get them to *drop* to the ground – push them if you have to and can do so safely.
- *Wrap* them in something to smother the flames – a blanket or coat, anything to hand. This is better if it is soaked in water.
- *Roll* them on the ground to put out the flames.

or at least clean non-adhesive dressing. If this is not possible, leave the burn uncovered. For a burn on a hand or foot, a clean plastic bag will protect it from infection until an expert can treat it.

Do not:

- remove anything which is stuck to a burn
- touch a burn, or use any ointment or cream
- cover facial burns — keep pouring water on until help arrives.

Poisoning

People can be poisoned by many substances, drugs, plants, chemicals, fumes or alcohol.

Symptoms

Symptoms will vary depending on the poison.

- The person could be unconscious.
- There may be acute abdominal pain.
- There may be blistering of the mouth and lips.

Aims

- To remove the casualty to a safe area if they are at risk, and it is safe for you to move them
- To summon medical assistance as a matter of urgency
- To gather any information which will identify the poison
- To maintain a clear airway and breathing until help arrives

Action for poisoning

If the casualty is unconscious, place them in the recovery position to ensure that the airway is clear, and that they cannot choke on any vomit. Dial 999 for a paramedic.

Try to find out what the poison is and how much has been taken. This information could be vital in saving a life.

If a conscious casualty has burned mouth or lips, they can be given small frequent sips of water or cold milk. *Do not* try to make the casualty vomit.

Electrical injuries

Electrocution occurs when an electrical current passes though the body.

Symptoms

Electrocution can cause cardiac arrest and burns where the electrical current entered and left the body.

Aims

- To remove the casualty from the current when you can safely do so
- To obtain medical assistance as a matter of urgency

- To maintain a clear airway and breathing until help arrives
- To treat any burns

Action for electrical injuries

There are different procedures to follow, depending on whether the injury has been caused by a high- or low-voltage current.

Injury caused by high-voltage current

This type of injury may be caused by overhead power cables or rail lines, for example.

Contact the emergency services immediately. *Do not* touch the person until all electricity has been cut off.

If the person is unconscious, clear their airway. Treat any other injuries present, such as burns. Place in the recovery position until help arrives.

Injury caused by low-voltage current

This type of injury may be caused by electric kettles, computers, drills, lawnmowers and so on.

Break the contact with the current by switching off the electricity, at the mains if possible. It is vital to break the contact as soon as possible, but if you touch a person who is 'live' (still in contact with the current), you too will be injured. If you are unable to switch off the electricity, then you must stand on something dry which can insulate you, such as a telephone directory, rubber mat or a pile of newspapers, and then move the casualty away from the current as shown below.

For an electrical injury, move the casualty away from the current.

Do not use anything made of metal, or anything wet, to move the casualty from the current. Try to move them with a wooden pole or broom handle, even a chair. Alternatively, drag them with a rope or cord or, as a last resort, pull by holding any of the person's dry clothing that is *not* in contact with their body.

Once the person is no longer in contact with the current, you should follow the same steps as with a high-voltage injury.

Tasks that need training

The guidance above identifies situations where training is necessary, for example, carrying out CPR. This is important because you can do further damage to a casualty by attempting to carry out tasks you have not been trained for. Helping following an accident or sudden illness is about first aid, and you need to understand the actions you should take if such an emergency arises.

The advice in this unit is not a substitute for a first aid course, and will only give you an outline of the steps you need to take. Reading this part of the unit will not qualify you to deal with these emergencies. Unless you have been on a first aid course, you should be careful about what you do, because the wrong action can cause more harm to the casualty. It is always preferable to get suitably trained assistance if possible.

Only attempt what you know you can safely do. Do not attempt something you are not sure of. You could do further damage to the ill or injured person. Do not try to do something outside your responsibility or capability — summon help and wait for it to arrive.

What you can safely do

Most people have a useful role to play in a health emergency, even if it is not dealing directly with the ill or injured person. It is also vital that someone:

- summons help as quickly as possible
- offers assistance to the competent person who is dealing with the emergency
- clears the immediate environment and makes it safe — for example, if someone has fallen through a glass door, the glass must be removed as soon as possible before there are any more injuries
- offers help and support to other people who have witnessed the illness or injury and may have been upset by it. Clearly this can only be dealt with once the ill or injured person is being helped.

Summon assistance

In the majority of cases this will mean telephoning 999 and requesting paramedic assistance. It will depend on the setting in which you work and clearly is not required if you work in a hospital! But it may mean calling for a colleague with medical qualifications, who will then be able to make an assessment of the need for further assistance. Similarly, if you work in the residential sector, there should be a medically qualified colleague available. If you are the first on the scene at an emergency in the community, you may need to summon an ambulance for urgent assistance.

If you need to call an ambulance, try to keep calm and give clearly all the details you are asked for. Do not attempt to give information until it is asked for — this wastes time. Emergency service operators are trained to find out the necessary information, so let them ask the questions, then answer calmly and clearly.

Follow the action steps outlined in the previous section while you are waiting for help to arrive.

Assist the person dealing with the emergency

A second pair of hands is invaluable when dealing with an emergency. If you are assisting someone with first aid or medical expertise, follow all their instructions, even if you do not understand why. An emergency situation is not the time for a discussion or debate — that can happen later. You may be needed to help to move a casualty, to fetch water, blankets or dressings, or to reassure and comfort the casualty during treatment.

Make the area safe

An accident or injury may have occurred in an unsafe area — and that was probably precisely why the accident occurred there! Sometimes, it may be that the accident has made the area unsafe for others. For example, if someone has tripped over an electric flex, there may be exposed wires or a damaged electric socket. Alternatively, a fall against a window or glass door may have left shards of broken glass in the area, or there may be blood or other body fluids on the floor. You may need to make the area safe by turning off the power, clearing broken glass or dealing with a spillage.

It may be necessary to redirect people away from the area of the accident in order to avoid further casualties.

Maintain the privacy of the casualty

You may need to act to provide some privacy for the casualty by asking onlookers to move away or stand back. If you can erect a temporary screen with coats or blankets, this may help to offer some privacy. It may not matter to the casualty at the time, but they have a right to privacy and dignity if possible.

Make accurate reports

You may be responsible for making a report on an emergency situation you have witnessed, or for filling in records later. Concentrate on the most important aspects of the incident and record the actions of yourself and others in an accurate, legible and complete manner.

Dealing with a health emergency

On the way to lunch one Tuesday, Miss Shaw, who sometimes experiences incontinence, had a little accident in the main hallway. Another resident coming along behind called out, 'Oh look! She's done a puddle!' and stopped to stare. Miss Shaw, feeling embarrassed and distressed, turned quickly to go back to her room and slipped on the wet floor, falling heavily on her hip. The first staff member on the scene was Maria.

1. List the actions that Maria should take, in order.
2. Could this accident have been prevented? If so, how?
3. What follow-up actions or discussions would you recommend to the management?

How to deal with witnesses' distress – and your own

People who have witnessed accidents can often be very distressed by what they have seen. The distress may be as a result of the nature of the injury, or perhaps the blood loss. It could be because the casualty is a friend or relative, or simply because seeing accidents or injuries is traumatic. Some people can become upset because they feel helpless and do not know how to assist, or they may have been afraid and then feel guilty later.

You will need to reassure people about the casualty and the fact that they are being cared for appropriately. However, do not give false reassurance about things you may not be sure of.

You may need to allow people to talk about what they saw. One of the most common effects of witnessing a trauma is that people need to repeat over and over again what they saw.

What about you?

You may feel very distressed by the experience you have gone through. You may find that you need to talk about what has happened, and that you need to look again at the role you played. You may feel that you could have done more, or you may feel angry with yourself for not having a greater knowledge about what to do.

If you have followed the basic guidelines in this element, you will have done as much as could be expected of anyone at the scene of an emergency who is not a trained first aider.

4. Be able to reduce the spread of infection

4.1 The recommended method for hand-washing

The very nature of work in a social care setting means that great care must be taken to control the spread of infection. You will come into contact with a number of people during your working day — an ideal opportunity for infection to spread. Infection which spreads from one person to another is called 'cross-infection'. If you work in the community, cross-infection is difficult to control. However, if you work in a residential or hospital setting, infection control is essential. There are various steps which you can take in terms of the way you carry out your work (wherever you work), which can help to prevent the spread of infection.

You do not know what viruses or bacteria may be present in any person, so it is important that you take precautions when dealing with everyone. The precautions are called 'universal precautions' precisely because you need to take them with everyone you deal with.

Table 1: Wear gloves.

When	Why	How
Any occasion when you will have contact with body fluids (including body waste, blood, mucus, sputum, sweat or vomit), or when you have any contact with anyone with a rash, pressure sore, wound, bleeding or any broken skin. You must also wear gloves when you clear up spills of blood or body fluids, or have to deal with soiled linen or dressings.	Because gloves act as a protective barrier against infection.	Check gloves before putting them on. Never use gloves with holes or tears. Check that they are not cracked or faded. Pull gloves on, making sure that they fit properly. If you are wearing a gown, pull them over the cuffs. Take them off by pulling from the cuff — this turns the glove inside out. Pull off the second glove while still holding the first so that the two gloves are folded together inside out. Dispose of them in the correct waste disposal container and wash your hands.

Do you follow the correct procedure for putting on and taking off gloves?

Table 2: Wash your hands.

When	Why	How
Before and after carrying out any procedure which has involved contact with a person, or with any body fluids, soiled linen or clinical waste. You must wash your hands even though you have worn gloves. You must also wash your hands before you start and after you finish your shift, before and after eating, after using the toilet and after coughing, sneezing or blowing your nose.	Because hands are a major route to spreading infection. When tests have been carried out on people's hands, an enormous number of bacteria have been found.	In running water, in a basin deep enough to hold the splashes and with either foot pedals or elbow bars rather than taps, because you can re-infect your hands from still water in a basin, or from touching taps with your hands once they have been washed. Use the soaps and disinfectants supplied. Make sure that you wash thoroughly, including between your fingers.

1. Wet your hands thoroughly under warm running water and squirt liquid soap onto the palm of one hand.

2. Rub your hands together to make a lather.

3. Rub the palm of one hand along the back of the other and along the fingers. Then repeat with the other hand.

4. Rinse off the soap with clean water.

5. Rub in between each of your fingers on both hands and round your thumbs.

6. Dry hands thoroughly on a disposable towel.

Table 3: Wear protective clothing.

When	Why	How
You should always wear a gown or plastic apron for any procedure which involves bodily contact or is likely to deal with body waste or fluids. An apron is preferable, unless it is likely to be very messy, as gowns can be a little frightening.	Because it will reduce the spread of infection by preventing infection getting on your clothes and spreading to the next person you come into contact with.	The plastic apron should be disposable and thrown away at the end of each procedure. You should use a new apron for each person you come into contact with.

Have you worn these items of protective clothing before?

Table 4: Tie up hair.

Why
Because if it hangs over your face, it is more likely to come into contact with the person you are working with and could spread infection. It could also become entangled in equipment and cause a serious injury.

Table 5: Clean equipment.

Why	How
Because infection can spread from one person to another on instruments, linen and equipment just as easily as on hands or hair.	By washing large items like trolleys with antiseptic solution. Small instruments must be sterilised. Do not shake soiled linen or dump it on the floor. Keep it held away from you. Place linen in proper bags or hampers for laundering.

Table 6: Deal with waste.

Why	How
Because it can then be processed correctly, and the risk to others working further along the line in the disposal process is reduced as far as possible.	By placing it in the proper bags. Make sure that you know the system in your workplace. It is usually: • clinical waste – yellow • soiled linen – red • recyclable instruments and equipment – blue.

Table 7: Take special precautions.

When	How
There may be occasions when you have to deal with someone who has a particular type of infection that requires special handling. This can involve things like hepatitis, some types of food poisoning or highly infectious diseases.	Your workplace will have special procedures to follow. They may include such measures as gowning, double gloving or wearing masks. Follow the procedures strictly. They are there for your benefit and for the benefit of the other people you support.

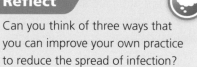

Reflect

Can you think of three ways that you can improve your own practice to reduce the spread of infection?

How many risks can you see?

4.2 Ways to ensure that your health and hygiene do not pose a risk to others

What you wear

You may not think that what you wear has much bearing on health and safety, but it is important. Even if your employer supplies, or insists on you wearing, a uniform, there are still other aspects to the safety of your work outfit.

There may be restrictions on wearing jewellery or carrying things in your pocket which could cause injury. This can also pose a risk to you — you could be accidentally stabbed in the chest by a pair of scissors or a ballpoint pen!

Many workplaces do not allow the wearing of rings with stones. Not only is this a possible source of infection, but also they can scratch people or tear protective gloves.

High-heeled or poorly supporting shoes are a risk to you in terms of foot injuries and very sore feet. They also present a risk to people you are helping, because if you overbalance or stumble, so will they.

Keeping food safe

Maintaining the safety and hygiene of food provided for people you support is an essential part of a safe and healthy environment. If you are preparing areas or equipment for people who are about to eat or drink, it is important that you follow basic hygiene procedures. This will also involve you knowing how to store and prepare food safely in order that people are able to eat it safely. Ensuring that food is not contaminated by bacteria is a matter which raises many questions, for instance:

Q   *What personal precautions do I need to make to ensure that I am hygienic?*

A   You must make sure that if you have long hair, it is tied back or covered. You should ensure that your nails are short and clean, and that you are not wearing any jewellery in which food could become trapped, such as rings with stones. You must ensure that you wash your hands thoroughly at each stage of food preparation and between handling raw food and cooked food, or raw meat and food which will not be cooked. You must always wash your hands after going to the toilet. Do not touch your nose during food handling or preparation.

Q   *What should I do if I have a cut or sore on my hands?*

A   You must wear a special blue adhesive plaster dressing. This is because no food is blue, and if the plaster should come off during food preparation it will be easy to locate.

Q   *How does food become contaminated?*

A   Food is contaminated by bacteria which infect food directly, that is, food which is not heated or chilled properly, or by cross-contamination, which is where bacteria are spread by somebody preparing food with unclean hands or equipment.

Q   *What are the main bacteria that cause contamination of food?*

A   Salmonella, campylobacter and e-coli are types of bacteria that can cause serious food poisoning in people who are old, ill or in young children.

Q   *How can infection and cross-contamination be avoided?*

A   Raw meat is a source of bacteria and you should be sure to use separate utensils and chopping boards or areas for raw food and for cooked food. For example, do not chop the raw chicken breasts and then chop the lettuce for the accompanying salad on the same chopping board or with the same knife. This is sure to give everybody who eats your salad a nasty dose of salmonella. You should keep separate chopping boards for meat and vegetables, and ensure that you use different knives. Remember to change knives and wash your hands between preparing different types of food.

Q   *Does it matter whether food is to be cooked or not?*

A   It is possible to kill bacteria by cooking food. But be careful with foods which are not cooked, such as salads or mayonnaise, that you are not using contaminated utensils to prepare them.

Q   *How hot does food have to be to kill bacteria?*

A   A core temperature of 75°C will kill bacteria. Hot food should be heated or reheated to at least this temperature.

Q   *How cold does food have to be to kill bacteria?*

A   By law, food should be stored at below 8°C. However, good practice dictates that food is stored below 5°C to be free from any risk of contamination with bacteria. A fridge with the door left open rapidly warms up to above 5°C or 8°C, and food can deteriorate quite quickly and become dangerous. Food in a fridge where the door has been left open or where the power has been cut off should be discarded.

Q   *What other safety steps should I take with the fridge?*

A   When you arrange food in a fridge, you should be sure that you put any raw meat on the bottom shelf to stop any moisture or blood dripping from the meat on to any of the foods stored below — moisture or blood from uncooked meat could be infected with bacteria. Fridges should be kept scrupulously clean and should be washed out regularly with an antibacterial solution. Do not allow particles of food to build up on the inside of the fridge. It is also important that the fridge does not become 'iced up', as this will make the motor work harder in order to keep it cold and could result in a warming of the fridge.

Q   What about 'best before' dates?

A   These are provided by the manufacturers to ensure that food is not kept by retailers beyond a date when it is safe to eat. Many manufacturers now include instructions about how soon the food should be consumed after purchase. These should be followed carefully. As a general rule, unless the manufacturer indicates otherwise, you should consume food by its 'best before' date in order to ensure that it has not begun to deteriorate.

5. Be able to move and handle equipment and other objects safely

5.1 Legislation that relates to moving and handling

Lifting and handling people is the single largest cause of injuries at work in health and care settings. One in four workers takes time off because of a back injury sustained at work.

The Manual Handling Operations Regulations 1992 require employers to avoid all manual handling where there is a risk of injury 'so far as it is reasonably practical'. Where manual handling cannot be avoided, then a risk assessment must be undertaken and all appropriate steps must be taken to reduce risks. Everyone from the European Commission to the Royal College of Nursing has issued policies and directives about avoiding hazardous lifting.

Provision and Use of Work Equipment Regulations 1998 (PUWER)

These Regulations require employers to ensure that all equipment used in the workplace is:

- suitable for the intended use and for conditions in which it is used
- safe for use, maintained in a safe condition and, in certain circumstances, inspected so that it continues to be safe
- used only by people who have received adequate information, instruction and training
- accompanied by suitable safety measures — for example, protective devices, markings, warnings.

The regulations also mean that where the risk assessment has shown that there is a risk to the workers from using the equipment, employers must ensure that equipment is inspected by suitably qualified people at regular intervals.

Lifting Operations and Lifting Equipment Regulations 1992 (LOLER)

These regulations came into effect on 5 December 1998 and apply to all workplaces. An employee does not have any responsibilities under LOLER, but under the Management of Health and Safety at Work Regulations, employees have a duty to ensure that they take reasonable care of themselves and others who may be affected by the actions that they undertake.

Employers do have duties under LOLER. They must ensure that all equipment provided for use at work is:

- sufficiently strong and stable for the particular use and marked to indicate safe working loads
- positioned and installed to minimise any risks
- used safely — that is, the work is planned, organised and performed by competent people
- subject to ongoing thorough examination and, where appropriate, inspection by competent people.

In addition, employers must ensure:

- lifting operations are planned, supervised and carried out in a safe way by competent people
- equipment for lifting people is safe
- lifting equipment and accessories are thoroughly examined
- a report is submitted by a competent person following a thorough examination or inspection.

Lifting equipment designed for lifting and moving loads must be inspected at least annually, but any equipment that is designed for lifting and handling people must be inspected at least every six months. If employees provide their own lifting equipment, this is covered by the regulations.

Doing it well

Manual handling

- Manual handling is a joint activity between you and the person being moved.
- Always use lifting and handling aids wherever possible.
- There is no such thing as a safe lift, so always be alert to risks.

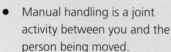

5.2 and 5.3 Principles for moving and handling equipment and other objects safely

On the rare occasions when it is still absolutely necessary for manual lifting to be done, there has to be a risk assessment and procedures put in place to reduce the risk of injury to the employee. This could involve ensuring that sufficient staff are available to lift or handle someone safely, which can often mean that four people are needed, or it may require the provision of specific equipment in order that the move can take place safely for all concerned.

The Health and Safety Executive is clear that this should be carried out jointly with the person concerned wherever possible and that there must be a balance between safety and the rights of the person. While you and your employer need to make sure that you and other staff are not put at risk by moving or lifting, it is also important that

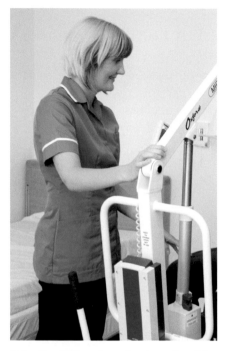

Using the right equipment reduces the risk of harm for everyone.

the person you are supporting is not caused pain, distress or humiliation. Groups representing people with disabilities have pointed out that blanket policies excluding any lifting may infringe the human rights of someone needing mobility assistance. For example, people may in effect be confined to bed unnecessarily and against their will by a lack of lifting assistance. A High Court judgement (A & B versus East Sussex County Council, 2003) found in favour of two women with disabilities who had been denied access to lifting because the local authority had a 'blanket ban' on lifting, regardless of circumstances. Such a ban was deemed unlawful under the Disability Discrimination Act 1995. It is likely that similar cases will be brought under the Human Rights Act 1998, which gives people protection against humiliating or degrading treatment.

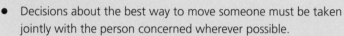

Doing it well

Moving someone

- Decisions about the best way to move someone must be taken jointly with the person concerned wherever possible.
- Encourage and support people to do as much as possible for themselves; only provide the minimum manual handling required.
- Make maximum use of aids to support people to move themselves.
- Your employer has a statutory duty to provide lifting and handling equipment, but it is your responsibility to use the equipment that is provided.
- You have a right to work safely, but people have rights to be moved with dignity and as safely as possible.

Case study

Using safe lifting procedures

Jo is a new care assistant at a day centre for adults with disabilities. She was trained to use a hoist as part of a moving and handling course in her previous job. Although there is a mobile hoist at the day centre, Jo has noticed that none of the staff use it. On several occasions she has seen people being manually lifted from their wheelchairs by the staff, working in pairs.

One morning Liz, a regular user of the centre, asked Jo to accompany her to the toilet. Jo knew that Liz would need to be helped from her chair on to the toilet, so she went to get the hoist. As she passed the other staff one

of them said, 'Oh, you don't want to bother with that thing. Liz isn't very heavy – it's much easier just to lift her yourself. Anyway, I don't think the hoist works any more.'

1. What should Jo do next?
2. If the hoist does not work, what should Jo do?
3. What could be the consequences of lifting incorrectly to the staff and to Liz?
4. What training and safety procedures would you recommend for this day centre?

6. Know how to handle hazardous substances and materials

6.1 Hazardous substances and materials that may be found in the work setting

Control of Substances Hazardous to Health (COSHH)

What are hazardous substances? There are many substances hazardous to health – nicotine, many drugs, even too much alcohol! The Control of Substances Hazardous to Health Regulations (or COSHH) apply to substances that have been identified as toxic, corrosive or irritant. This includes cleaning materials, pesticides, acids, disinfectants and bleaches, and naturally occurring substances such as blood, bacteria and other bodily fluids. Workplaces may have other hazardous substances that are particular to the nature of the work carried out.

The Health and Safety Executive states that employers must take the following steps to protect employees from hazardous substances.

Step 1: Find out what hazardous substances are used in the workplace and the risks these substances pose to people's health.

Step 2: Decide what precautions are needed before any work starts with hazardous substances.

Step 3: Prevent people being exposed to hazardous substances, but where this is not reasonably practicable, control the exposure.

Step 4: Make sure control measures are used and maintained properly, and that safety procedures are followed.

Step 5: If required, monitor exposure of employees to hazardous substances.

Step 6: Carry out health surveillance where assessment has shown that this is necessary or COSHH makes specific requirements.

Step 7: If required, prepare plans and procedures to deal with accidents, incidents and emergencies.

Step 8: Make sure employees are properly informed, trained and supervised.

Every workplace must have a COSHH file, which should be easily accessible to all staff. This file lists all the hazardous substances used in the workplace. It should detail:

- where they are kept
- how they are labelled
- their effects
- the maximum amount of time it is safe to be exposed to them
- how to deal with an emergency involving one of them.

Reflect

Hazardous substances are not just things like poisons and radioactive material – they are also substances such as cleaning fluids and bleach.

6.2 Safe practices for storing, using and disposing of hazardous substances and materials

Since April 2005, employers are required to focus on the following eight principles of good practice in the control of substances hazardous to health.

1. Design and operate processes and activities to minimise emission, release and spread of substances hazardous to health.
2. Take into account all relevant routes of exposure — inhalation, skin absorption and ingestion — when developing control measures.
3. Control exposure by measures that are proportionate to the health risk.
4. Choose the most effective and reliable control options which minimise the escape and spread of substances hazardous to health.
5. Where adequate control of exposure cannot be achieved by other means, provide, in combination with other control measures, suitable Personal Protective Equipment (PPE).
6. Check and review regularly all elements of control measures for their continuing effectiveness.
7. Inform and train all employees on the hazards and risks from the substances with which they work and the use of control measures developed to minimise the risks.
8. Ensure that the introduction of control measures does not increase the overall risk to health and safety.

If you have to work with hazardous substances, make sure that you take the precautions detailed in the COSHH file. This may be wearing gloves or protective goggles, or it may involve limiting the time you are exposed to the substance or only using it in certain circumstances.

The COSHH file should also give you information about how to store hazardous substances. This will involve using the correct containers as supplied by the manufacturers. All containers must have safety lids and caps, and must be correctly labelled.

Never use the container of one substance for storing another, and never change the labels.

Activity 3

COSHH

You must ensure that you and all staff know the location of the COSHH file in your workplace. Read the contents of the file, especially information about the substances you use or come into contact with, and what the maximum exposure limits are. You do not have to know the detail of each substance but the information you need should be contained in the COSHH file, which must be kept up to date.

Symbol	Abbreviation	Hazard	Description
	E	explosive	Chemicals that explode
	F	highly flammable	Chemicals that may catch fire in contact with air, only need brief contact with an ignition source, have a very low flash point or evolve highly flammable gases in contact with water
	T (also Carc or Muta)	toxic (also carcinogenic or mutagenic)	Chemicals that at low levels cause damage to health and may cause cancer or induce heritable genetic defects or increase the incidence of these
	Xh or Xi	harmful or irritant	Chemicals that may cause damage to health, especially inflammation to the skin or other mucous membranes
	C	corrosive	Chemicals that may destroy living tissue on contact
	N	dangerous for the environment	Chemicals that may present an immediate or delayed danger to one or more components of the environment

Table 8: Identifying hazardous substances.

The symbols above indicate hazardous substances. They are there for your safety and for the safety of those you care for and work with. Before you use any substance, whether it is liquid, powder, spray, cream or aerosol, take the following simple steps.

- Check the container for the hazard symbol.
- If there is a hazard symbol, go to the COSHH file.
- Look up the precautions you need to take with the substance.
- Make sure you follow the procedures, which are intended to protect you.

If you are concerned about a substance being used in your workplace that is not in the COSHH file, or if you notice incorrect containers or labels being used, report this to your supervisor or manager. They then have a responsibility to deal with the issue.

Dealing with hazardous waste

As part of providing a safe working environment, employers have to put procedures in place to deal with waste materials and spillages. There are various types of waste, which must be dealt with in particular ways. The types of hazardous waste you are most likely to come across are shown in Table 9 (next page), alongside a list of the ways in which each is usually dealt with. Waste can be a source of infection, so it is very important that you follow the procedures your employer has put in place to deal with it safely, in order to reduce the risks to you and to the people you support.

Type of waste	Method of disposal
Clinical waste — used dressings	Yellow bags, clearly labelled with contents and location. This waste is incinerated.
Needles, syringes, cannulas ('sharps')	Yellow sharps box. Never put sharps into anything other than a hard plastic box. This is sealed and incinerated.
Bodily fluids and waste — urine, vomit, blood, sputum, faeces	Cleared and flushed down sluice drain. Area to be cleaned and disinfected.
Soiled linen	Red bags, direct into laundry; bags disintegrate in wash. If handled, gloves must be worn.
Recyclable instruments and equipment	Blue bags, to be returned to the Central Sterilisation Services Department (CSSD) for recycling and sterilising.

Table 9: Types of waste and their disposal.

Reflect

Other people will have to deal with the waste after you have placed it in the bags or containers, so make sure it is properly labelled and in the correct containers.

7. Understand how to promote fire safety in the work setting

7.1 Practices that prevent fires from starting and spreading

Your workplace will have procedures that must be followed in the case of an emergency. All workplaces must display information about what action to take in case of fire. The fire procedure is likely to be similar to the one shown below.

Fire Safety Procedure

1. Raise the alarm.

2. Inform the telephonist or dial 999.

3. Ensure that everyone is safe and out of the danger area.

4. If it is safe to do so, attack the fire with the correct extinguisher.

5. Go to the fire assembly point (this will be stated on the fire procedure notice).

6. Do not return to the building for any reason.

   Important: Make sure that you know where the fire extinguishers or fire blankets are in your workplace, and also where the fire exits are.

Your employer will have installed fire doors to comply with regulations – never prop them open.

Your employer must provide fire lectures each year. All staff must attend and make sure that they are up to date with the procedures to be followed.

The Regulatory Reform (Fire Safety) Order 2005 requires that all businesses must have a person responsible for fire safety and for carrying out a risk assessment. The government recommends a five-step approach to a fire risk assessment.

1. Identify hazards: anything that could start a fire, anything that could burn.
2. Identify who could be at risk and who could be especially at risk.
3. Evaluate the risks and take action to reduce them.
4. Record what has been found out about hazards and the actions taken. Develop a clear plan of how to prevent fire and how to keep people safe if there is a fire. Train staff so they know what to do in the case of fire.
5. Keep the assessment under regular review and make changes if necessary.

Which extinguisher?

There are specific fire extinguishers for fighting different types of fire. It is important that you know this. You do not have to memorise them, as each one has clear instructions on it, but you do need to be aware that there are different types and make sure that you read the instructions before use.

All new fire extinguishers are red. Each one has its purpose written on it. Each one also has a patch of the colour previously used for that type of extinguisher.

Reflect

Do not be a hero! Never attempt to tackle a fire unless you are confident that you can do so safely, for example:

- you have already raised the alarm
- you have a clear, unobstructed route away from the fire in case it grows larger
- you are confident of your ability to operate the extinguisher
- you have the correct type of extinguisher.

Do you know what each fire extinguisher is for and where fire exits are in your place of work?

Type and patch colour	Use for	Danger points	How to use
Water *Red*	Wood, cloth, paper, plastics, coal, etc. Fires involving solids.	Do not use on burning fat or oil, or on electrical appliances.	Point the jet at the base of the flames and keep it moving across the area of the fire. Ensure that all areas of the fire are out.
Multi-purpose dry powder *Blue*	Wood, cloth, paper, plastics, coal, etc. Fires involving solids. Liquids such as grease, fats, oil, paint, petrol, etc. but not on chip or fat pan fires.	Safe on live electrical equipment, although the fire may re-ignite because this type of extinguisher does not cool the fire very well. Do not use on chip or fat pan fires.	Point the jet or discharge horn at the base of the flames and, with a rapid sweeping motion, drive the fire towards the far edge until all the flames are out.
Standard dry powder *Blue*	Liquids such as grease, fats, oil, paint, petrol etc. but not on chip or fat pan fires.	Safe on live electrical equipment, although does not penetrate the spaces in equipment easily and the fire may re-ignite. This type of extinguisher does not cool the fire very well. Do not use on chip or fat pan fires.	Point the jet or discharge horn at the base of the flames and, with a rapid sweeping motion, drive the fire towards the far edge until all the flames are out.
AFFF (Aqueous film-forming foam) (multi-purpose) *Cream*	Wood, cloth, paper, plastics, coal, etc. Fires involving solids. Liquids such as grease, fats, oil, paint, petrol, etc. but not on chip or fat pan fires.	Do not use on chip or fat pan fires.	For fires involving solids, point the jet at the base of the flames and keep it moving across the area of the fire. Ensure that all areas of the fire are out. For fires involving liquids, do not aim the jet straight into the liquid. Where the liquid on fire is in a container, point the jet at the inside edge of the container or on a nearby surface above the burning liquid. Allow the foam to build up and flow across the liquid.
Foam *Cream*	Limited number of liquid fires.	Do not use on chip or fat pan fires. Check manufacturer's instructions for suitability of use on other fires involving liquids.	Do not aim jet straight into the liquid. Where the liquid on fire is in a container, point the jet at the inside edge of the container or on a nearby surface above the burning liquid. Allow the foam to build up and flow across the liquid.
Carbon dioxide CO_2 *Black*	Liquids such as grease, fats, oil, paint, petrol, etc. but not on chip or fat pan fires.	Do not use on chip or fat pan fires. This type of extinguisher does not cool the fire very well. Fumes from CO_2 extinguishers can be harmful if used in confined spaces: ventilate the area as soon as the fire has been controlled.	Direct the discharge horn at the base of the flames and keep the jet moving across the area of the fire.
Fire blanket	Fires involving both solids and liquids. Particularly good for small fires in clothing and for chip and fat pan fires, provided the blanket completely covers the fire.	If the blanket does not completely cover the fire, it will not be extinguished.	Place carefully over the fire. Keep your hands shielded from the fire. Take care not to waft the fire towards you.

Table 10: Fire extinguishers.

7.2 Emergency procedures in the event of a fire in the work setting

and

7.3 The importance of maintaining clear evacuation routes at all times

In an extreme case it may be necessary to help evacuate buildings if there is a fire, or for other security reasons, such as:

- a bomb scare
- the building has become structurally unsafe
- an explosion
- a leak of dangerous chemicals or fumes.

The evacuation procedure you need to follow will be laid down by your workplace. The information will be the same whatever the emergency is: the same exits will be used and the same assembly point. It is likely to be along the following lines.

- Stay calm, do not shout or run.
- Do not allow others to run.
- Organise people quickly and firmly without panic.
- Direct those who can move themselves and assist those who cannot.
- Use wheelchairs to move people quickly.
- Move a bed with a person in, if necessary.

Functional skills

English: Speaking and listening

Use the questions on emergency situations as a basis for a discussion with your team at work. Ensure that everyone in the group has a chance to contribute to the discussion. Present your answers clearly and ask others to clarify any concerns that you may have. Show your listening skills by picking up on points made by others.

Activity 4

Emergency situations

1. Where are the main evacuation points in your workplace?
2. Which people use each one?
3. Do any people need assistance to reach evacuation points? If so, of what kind?
4. Who is responsible for checking your workplace is cleared in an emergency?
5. What are your personal responsibilities in an emergency situation?

8. Be able to implement security measures in the work setting

8.1 Agreed ways of working for checking the identity of anyone

and

8.2 Measures to protect security in the work setting

Most workplaces where care is provided are not under lock and key. This is an inevitable part of ensuring that people have choice and that their rights are respected. However, they also have a right to be secure. Security in a care environment is about:

- security against intruders
- security in respect of people's privacy and decisions about unwanted visitors
- security against being abused
- security of property.

If you work for a large organisation, such as an NHS trust, it may be that all employees are easily identifiable by identity badges with photographs. Some of these even contain a microchip which allows the card to be 'swiped' to gain access to secure parts of the building. This makes it easier to identify people who do not have a right to be on the premises.

In a smaller workplace, there may be a system of issuing visitors' badges to visitors who have reasons to be there, or it may simply rely on the vigilance of the staff.

Some workplaces operate electronic security systems, like those in the NHS where cards are swiped to open doors. Less sophisticated systems in small workplaces may use a keypad with a code number known only to staff and those who are legitimately on the premises. It is often difficult to maintain security with such systems, as codes are forgotten or become widely known. In order to maintain security, it is necessary to change the codes regularly, and to make sure everyone is aware.

Some workplaces still operate with keys, although the days of staff walking about with large bunches of keys attached to a belt are fast disappearing. If mechanical keys are used, there will be a list of named keyholders and there is likely to be a system of handover of keys at shift change. However, each workplace has its own system and you need to be sure that you understand which security system operates in your workplace.

The more dependent people are, the greater the risk. If you work with high-dependency or unconscious patients, people with a severe learning disability or multiple disabilities, or people who are very confused, you will have to be extremely vigilant in protecting them from criminals.

> **Doing it well**
>
> ## Protecting against intruders
>
> - Be aware of everyone you come across. Get into the habit of noticing people and thinking, 'Do I know that person?'
> - Challenge anyone you do not recognise.
> - The challenge should be polite. 'Can I help you?' is usually enough to find out if a visitor has a reason to be on the premises.
> - If a person says that they are there to see someone, do not give directions – escort them. If the person is a genuine visitor, they will be grateful. If not, they will disappear pretty quickly!
> - If you find an intruder on the premises, do not tackle them – raise the alarm.

Protect the security of yourself and others

Workplaces where most or all people are in individual rooms can also be difficult to make secure, as it is not always possible to check every room if people choose to close the door. A routine check can be very time consuming, and can affect people's rights to privacy and dignity.

Communal areas are easier to check, but can present their own problems; it can be difficult to be sure who is a legitimate visitor and who should not be there. Some establishments provide all visitors with badges, but while this may be acceptable in a large institution or an office block, it is not compatible with creating a comfortable and relaxed atmosphere in a residential setting. Extra care must be taken to check that you know all the people in a communal area. If you are not sure, ask. It is better to risk offending someone by asking, 'Can I help you?' or 'Are you waiting for someone?' than to leave an intruder unchallenged.

Case study

Checking visitors

Fitzroy works in a secure residential unit for older people with dementia. All the entry and exit doors to the unit are operated by a swipe card, and all staff and visitors are required to wear their identity pass visibly at all times. The visitor passes cannot open the doors.

One day Fitzroy sees Mrs Gregory, a resident, standing at the exit door with a man he does not recognise. The man has a swipe card and is about to open the door. Fitzroy quickly approaches and politely asks the man to identify himself. The man says he is Mrs Gregory's nephew and has come to take her out for a drive in his car. It is a cold day but Mrs Gregory is not wearing a coat.

1. Was Fitzroy right to challenge the man?
2. What should Fitzroy do next?
3. What might have happened if Fitzroy had not challenged the man?
4. What are the management issues in this case study?

Protecting people

If very dependent people are living in their own homes, the risks are far greater. You must try to impress on them the importance of finding out who people are before letting them in. If they are able to use it, the 'password' scheme from the utilities (water, gas and electricity) companies is helpful. There are many security schemes operated by the police in partnership with local authority services and charities such as Age Concern and Help the Aged, such as 'Safe as Houses' and 'Safer Homes'. These provide security advice and items such as smoke alarms and door chains to older people.

Every time you visit, you may have to explain again what the person should do when someone knocks on the door. Give them a card with simple instructions. Obtain agreement to speak to the local 'homewatch' scheme and ask that a special eye is kept on visitors. Contact your local crime prevention officers and make them aware that a vulnerable person is living alone in the house.

Restricting access

People have a right to choose who they see. This can often be a difficult area to deal with. If there are relatives or friends who wish to visit and the person does not want to see them, you may have to make this clear. It is difficult to do, but you can only be effective if you are clear and assertive. You should not make excuses or invent reasons why visitors cannot see the person concerned. You could say something like: 'I'm sorry, Mr Price has told us that he does not want to see you. I understand that this may be upsetting, but it is his choice. If he does change his mind we will contact you. Would you like to leave your phone number?'

I'm sorry, that is not something I can do. If your uncle does decide he wants to see you, I will let you know right away. I will tell him you have visited, but I can't do anything else.

Have you ever been asked to make an intervention that is outside your role?

Do not allow yourself to be drawn into passing on messages or attempting to persuade — that is not your role. Your job is to respect the wishes of the person you are caring for. If you are asked to intervene or to pass on a message, you must refuse politely but firmly.

There may also be occasions when access is restricted for other reasons, possibly because someone is seriously ill and there are medical reasons for limiting access, or because of a legal restriction such as a court order. In either case, it should be clearly written on the person's record and your supervisor will advise you about the restrictions. If you are working in a supervisory capacity, it will be part of your role to ensure that junior staff are aware of these restrictions.

Activity 5

Restricting access

Ask a colleague or friend to try this role play with you. One of you should be the person who has come to visit and the other the care worker who has to say that a friend or relative will not see them. Try using different scenarios – angry, upset, aggressive and so on. Try at least three different scenarios each. By the time you have practised a few, you may feel better equipped to deal with the situation if it happens in reality.

If you cannot find anyone to work with you, it is possible to do a similar exercise by imagining three or four different scenarios and then writing down the words you would say in each of the situations.

Security of property

Property and valuables belonging to people in care settings should be safeguarded. It is likely that your employer will have a property book in which records of all valuables and personal possessions are entered.

There may be particular policies within your organisation, but as a general rule you are likely to need to:

- make a record of all possessions on admission
- record valuable items separately
- describe items of jewellery by their colour, for example, 'yellow metal' not 'gold'
- ensure that people sign for any valuables they are keeping, and that they understand they are liable for their loss
- inform your manager if someone is keeping valuables or a significant amount of money.

It is always difficult when items go missing in a care setting, particularly if they are valuable. It is important that you check all possibilities before calling the police.

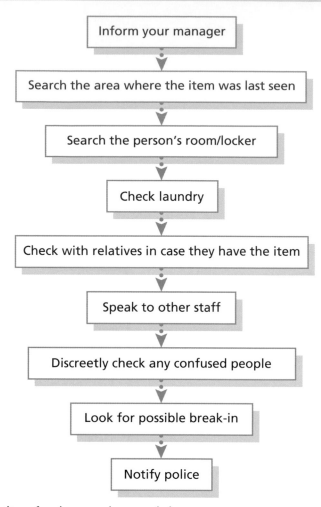

Action stages for when property goes missing.

8.3 The importance of ensuring that others are aware of your whereabouts

There is always an element of risk in working with people. There is little doubt that there is an increase in the level of personal abuse suffered by workers in the health and care services. There is also the element of personal risk encountered by workers who visit people in the community, and have to deal with homes in poor states of repair and an assortment of domestic animals! However, there are some steps that you can take to contribute to your own safety.

Steps to personal safety

- If you work alone in the community, always leave details of where you are going and what time you expect to return. This is important in case of accidents or other emergencies, so that you can be found and that someone will raise concerns if you are late returning.
- Carry a personal alarm, and use it if necessary.
- Ask your employer to provide training in techniques to combat aggression and violence. It is foolish and potentially dangerous to go into risky situations without any training.
- Try to defuse potentially aggressive situations by being as calm as possible and by talking quietly and reasonably. But if this is not effective, leave.
- If you work in a residential or hospital setting, raise the alarm if you find you are in a threatening situation.
- Do not tackle aggressors, whoever they are – raise the alarm.
- Use an alarm or panic button if you have it; otherwise yell – very loudly.
- Your employer should have a written 'lone-working' policy that identifies steps to be taken to protect staff working alone. Make sure that you have read and understood the policy.

Case study

Risk in the community

Karinda was a home-care assistant on her first visit to Mr West. She had been warned that his house was in a poor condition and that he had a large dog. She also knew that he had a history of psychiatric illness and had, in the past, been admitted to hospital compulsorily under the Mental Health Act.

When Karinda arrived on her first morning, the outside of the house was in a very poor state – the garden was overgrown, and it was full of rubbish and old furniture. The front door was half open and she could see that half the floorboards in the hallway appeared to be missing – there were simply joists and a drop into the cellar below. Mr West's dog was in the hallway growling and barking, and Mr West was at the top of the stairs shouting, 'Who are you? You won't get me out of here – I'll kill you first!'

1. What should Karinda do?
2. When should she go back?
3. What sort of risks need to be assessed?
4. If Mr West refuses to allow a risk assessment, or his house to be repaired, should Karinda go back in anyway?
5. Who should carry out the risk assessment?

9. Know how to manage own stress

9.1 Common signs and indicators of stress

All of us know somebody who appears to manage a workload and demands on their time that most of us would simply be unable to cope with; however, they appear to manage and in many cases to thrive very happily with what is apparently an extremely stressful situation. While the responses to stress are individual, so are (to a large extent) the effects. Stress can show itself in a number of ways.

Emotionally, stress can cause people to:

- feel tense, uptight, angry
- feel depressed, anxious, tearful, worthless
- be unable to cope, concentrate or make decisions
- feel tired and stretched to the limit
- be uninterested in everything, including sex
- contract respiratory disorders such as asthma and have chest pains.

Stress can cause:

- disturbance of sleep patterns
- disturbance of change in normal appetite
- feelings of anxiety
- loss of concentration
- quick temper or irritability
- low tolerance of disruption, noise or other disturbance.

Physically, stress can cause:

- tensing of the muscles
- headaches, migraines
- circulatory disorders such as high blood pressure, heart attacks, strokes
- digestive disorders such as ulcers
- menstrual problems
- increases in infections, such as cold sores or colds.

9.2 Circumstances that tend to trigger own stress

Stress means different things to different people. The sorts of things that can cause stress include:

- work pressures
- being in debt
- having relationship problems
- interrupted sleep.

Activity 6

Experiencing stress

Think of an occasion when you felt very stressed. Make a list of the feelings/emotions and physical symptoms you had at the time.

Stress is believed to be one of the major causes of time off work and of staff turnover. Stress at work can be caused by:

- poor working relationships
- the type of work that has to be done, especially in social care
- the hours spent at work, especially for shift workers
- a lack of career progression opportunities
- a fear of redundancy or retirement.

9.3 Ways to manage your stress

Stress is dealt with in a range of ways, depending on the underlying causes. It can be dealt with by physical means — that is, an immediate removal from the cause of the stress such as taking a break from work or respite from caring for a difficult, very ill or demanding relative, or by medical means such as taking drugs to reduce the physical effects of stress on the body and alter mood and responses. Another way would be to undertake a programme of relaxation exercises or meditation techniques in order to physically relax the body.

Everyone has their own way of coping with stress but sometimes coping mechanisms can make a situation worse! Things to avoid are:

- drinking alcohol
- smoking
- compulsive eating.

Behaviours like these might make matters feel better at the time, but in the long run can be very damaging to health.

Positive ways to deal with stress include:

- physical activity, for example, going for a walk, doing some gardening, punching a pillow — physical activity uses up the extra energy bodies produce when stressed
- talking things over, for example, with a friend or your supervisor — chatting about a problem often helps to identify what the real issues are and how to deal with them
- doing something to take your mind off the problem, for example, going to the cinema, reading a magazine, pampering yourself — escaping from a problem enables you to come back to it with a clear head and be more able to tackle things
- learning relaxation techniques — activities in which you learn to control your breathing can help to release the muscular tension that goes hand-in-hand with stress
- organising your time — do not take on more than you can handle and do things in order of their importance
- learning to shrug things off — raising your shoulders and lowering them uses up energy, leaving you feeling more relaxed; it also helps you get things into perspective — how important is what is causing the stress anyway?

Accessing support, advice and guidance

Anyone suffering from symptoms of stress which persist and who can see no way forward, should seek help.

Family and friends are usually the first people to look to for support. They have either 'got the T-shirt' or know someone who has been in your position, and can offer support and help.

If your stress is associated with work, talk things through with your supervisor. Some organisations employ people whose role includes talking people through their problems and guiding them in finding solutions. Often, stressful situations at work can be improved by some training to learn how to manage time more effectively, or in how to be more assertive so that it is easier to refuse to take on additional work that will cause stress or to deal with situations in which people feel that they have no control.

If the symptoms of your stress are seriously affecting your life, or if they have gone on for a long time, you should see your GP, who could treat your physical symptoms and perhaps refer you on to a suitably qualified therapist or counsellor.

Alternative therapies such as reflexology and aromatherapy can also be very valuable in helping to relieve stress.

Getting ready for assessment

This is essentially a very practical unit and most of the assessment will be through your assessor observing your practice. Some areas such as fire safety, dealing with accidents and dealing with emergencies cannot be observed, as they are unlikely to occur just when your assessor is there! You will have to show your assessor that you know how to deal with each of these situations – this could be through a question and answer session or through the completion of an assignment. You will need to be sure that you understand the main pieces of legislation that govern health and safety, and that you are familiar with the actions to take in emergencies and accidents.

Your skills in working safely will be observed by your assessor. They will be looking to make sure that you are taking all the steps to prevent the spread of infection, so how you dress, how you wash your hands, how you clean areas and how you use personal protective equipment will all be important areas to think about when you are being assessed.

Legislation

- Control of Asbestos at Work Regulations 2002
- Control of Lead at Work Regulations 2002
- Control of Substances Hazardous to Health Regulations 2002 (COSHH)
- Data Protection Act 1998
- Disability Discrimination Act 1995
- Health and Safety at Work Act 1974 (HASAWA)
- Health and Safety (Display Screen Equipment) Regulations 1992 (amended 2002)
- Human Rights Act 1998
- Management of Health and Safety at Work Regulations 1999
- Manual Handling Operations Regulations 1992 (amended 2002)
- Mental Health Act
- Noise at Work Regulations 1989
- Personal Protective Equipment at Work Regulations 1992
- Provision and Use of Work Equipment Regulations 1998 (PUWER)

Further reading and research

Workplace health, safety and security is an important and complex issue. This section has dealt with the key factors and below are details of opportunities to find out more.

- www.dh.gov.uk (Department of Health – health and safety, emergency planning)
- www.hse.gov.uk (Health and Safety Executive (HSE), tel: 0845 345 0055)
- www.healthandsafetytips.co.uk (Health and safety tips, tel: 01506 200109)
- www.neli.org.uk (National Electronic Library of Infection)
- www.nice.org.uk ((National Institute for Health and Clinical Excellence)
- www.nric.org.uk (National Resource for Infection Control)
- Bowmen R. C., Emmett R. C. (1998) *A Dictionary of Food Hygiene*, CIEH
- Hartropp, H. (2006) *Hygiene in Health and Social Care*, CIEH
- Horner J. M. (1993) *Workplace Environment, Health and Safety Management; A Practical Guide*, CIEH

Unit HSC 028

Handle information in health and social care settings

Increasing amounts of information are being recorded about people, so recording accurately, keeping information secure and being very clear about how it can be shared is very important.

In social care, we record very sensitive and personal information about people. We need to handle it in a way that protects people's privacy but also allows them to have the best possible support provided to meet their needs.

This unit will help you to understand how to deal with the different kinds of information that you will come across in your work.

In this unit you will learn about:

1. **the need for secure handling of information in health and social care settings**
2. **how to access support for handling information**
3. **how to handle information in accordance with agreed ways of working.**

1. Understand the need for secure handling of information in health and social care settings

1.1 Legislation about recording, storage and sharing of information

Key term

Data Protection Act 1998 – a law to ensure the safety of data held

All information, however it is stored, is subject to the **Data Protection Act 1998**, which covers medical records, social service records, credit information, local authority information and so on. Anything relating to a person, whether fact or opinion, is personal data. Data is the same thing as information in relation to the Act.

Anyone processing personal data must comply with the eight enforceable principles of good practice laid down in the Data Protection Act 1998. These say that data must be:

- fairly and lawfully processed
- processed for limited purposes
- adequate, relevant and not excessive
- accurate
- not kept for longer than necessary
- processed in accordance with the data subject's rights
- kept secure
- not transferred to countries without adequate protection.

'Processing' personal data means handling it in any way; gathering, recording, storing or sharing it. In practice, the Act means that you can only gather as much information as you need, you can only use it for the purpose you collected it, you must store it securely, and you cannot keep it after you have finished using it.

The Data Protection Act 1998 also gives people a right to see the information recorded about them. This means that people can see their medical records or social services files. Since January 2005, the Freedom of Information Act 2000 has provided people with a right to access general information held by public authorities, including local authorities and the National Health Service. This means that people are entitled to see their social care files, so remember this when you are entering information in people's notes. Personal information about other people cannot be accessed and is protected by the Data Protection Act.

The handling of information in the UK is monitored by the Information Commissioner's Office (ICO). This is an independent authority with responsibility for upholding information rights in the public interest. The ICO also has responsibility for promoting openness by public bodies and data privacy for people.

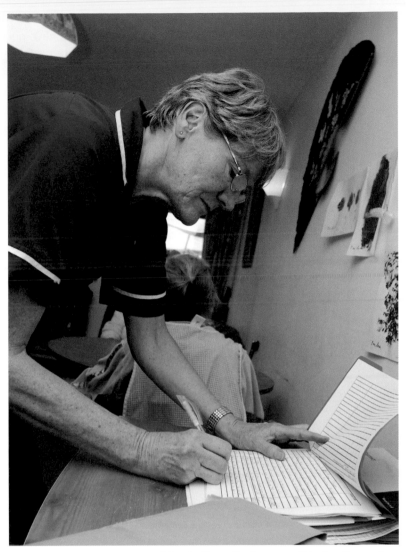

The Information Commissioner's Office is the authority responsible for all aspects of information.

1.2 Secure systems for recording and storing information

Once something is written down or entered on a computer, it becomes a permanent record. For this reason, you must be very careful what you do with any files, charts, notes or other written records. They must always be stored somewhere locked and safe. You should never take people's personal files outside your work premises if you work in a residential or hospital setting. There are many stories about files being stolen from cars or left on buses! However, if you are working in people's homes, it is likely that records may be kept there and completed by support staff who visit. You will need to take great care that the information is kept safe and not left lying around where casual visitors can see it.

Records kept on computers must also be kept safe and protected. Your workplace will have policies relating to records on computers, which will include access being restricted by a password, and the computer system being protected by a firewall against the possibility of people hacking into it. You are likely to find that there are security practices in place such as having to change your password regularly, and you may not be allowed to download any information from the Internet.

The information that you will be handling about the people you support will be very personal. It may contain details of medical history, details of family background and financial information. People need to feel confident that if they give these personal details, they will not be shared with everyone.

Computer record systems are secure and protected by a firewall.

Manual recording systems

Not all systems are electronic, although most are. Many large organisations will also keep paper-based files as a back-up to electronic records. Keeping information safe and confidential in a manual system is just as important as passwords and firewalls. Files are usually kept alphabetically, but in some places, such as hospitals, they may be allocated an index number. Systems for keeping paper files safe will vary, but they are usually kept in locked cabinets and may be in secure rooms.

Personal assistants

The kind of notes that you may keep if you are working as a personal assistant will be the information that your employer has decided needs to be recorded. This may include information for ensuring a clear handover to the next shift, or measurements that must be recorded for medical reasons. You may also need to keep records for the Direct Payments system, so that expenditure can be verified.

2. Know how to access support for handling information

2.1 How to access guidance, advice and information

There will be times when you are unsure about what to do with information. You may be uncertain about how to process or record something, or someone may have asked you for information and you are unsure about whether or not you should provide it.

The first place you should look for guidance is your supervisor or senior colleagues. They are the ideal people to ask for advice with regard to information in your workplace.

If you are looking for more general information or want advice about the legislation, then the Information Commissioner's Office (www.ico.gov.uk) is the place to contact. There are offices in all four countries of the UK. You will be able to find detailed information about how to ensure that you are complying with the law in the way that you are handling information.

Ask your manager about how to handle information if you are unsure.

2.2 Concerns over recording, storing or sharing information

If you are concerned that there are issues with how records are stored or how information is shared, then you must take action. Reporting concerns about something in the organisation you work for is never easy, but the place to start is with your line manager.

Your concerns may be straightforward and easily dealt with, or they may be more difficult, as these two examples show.

Example 1

You may be concerned that people's records are in an unlocked office. You raise it with your manager who explains that after everyone has gone home, the room is locked by the senior manager on duty.

✓ CONCERN DEALT WITH

Example 2

You may be concerned that night staff are not making notes of any incidents that happen. Your manager explains that very little happens during the night, so the night staff do not bother to record in the notes because they would have to unlock all the records and this would disturb people.

✗ CONCERN NOT DEALT WITH

Your next step would be to take this to a more senior manager or to the person within the organisation who holds responsibility for information. Ultimately, you have to take this concern to the director or chief executive of your organisation if you are unable to get the matter resolved in any other way.

Taking it further

When you do have concerns, and you are taking them to senior management, you should:

- put your concerns in writing
- be clear about dates, times and the exact nature of your concerns
- identify what steps you have already taken and the responses you have had
- involve your trade union or professional organisation in order to support you. (This would be a very unlikely step, as the vast majority of concerns can be dealt with through discussion with your management.)

If this still does not produce a satisfactory response, you can take the matter to the inspectorate for the country in which you work. Taking such action against your employer is very difficult and you should try all possible ways of addressing your concerns within the organisation in the first instance. People who do report their employer for any type of breach of the law or professional practice are protected against any

unfair treatment by the Public Interest Disclosure Act 1998. However, you must involve your trade union or professional organisation if you do have to take this action.

Step 4:
Take to inspectorate.

Step 3:
Take to director or chief executive.

Step 2:
Record your concerns and take to a more senior manager.

Step 1:
Discuss with your line manager.

Can you see how you can move through steps to resolve your concerns?

Case study

Dealing with concerns

Maria works in a supported living house for people with a learning disability. One of the people who used to live there and who has since moved on has asked for his personal files. Maria's manager asked her to change some of the entries she had made in the files and said, 'Well, he wouldn't really understand about some of the ways we work here. If you could just remove these pages and replace them without mentioning the use of restraint, that would make it much easier all round.'

Should Maria:

1. carry out her manager's request
2. refuse to change the file, but keep quiet about it
3. refuse to change the file and report it to the Information Commissioner's Office?

Give reasons for your answer.

3. Be able to handle information in accordance with agreed ways of working

'Agreed ways of working' means the policies and procedures that your employer has put in place to around handling information.

3.1 Keeping records that are up to date, complete, accurate and legible

Since the Access to Personal Files Act 1987, and subsequently the Data Protection Act 1998, people can see their personal files. This means that people can see their medical records or social services files from the date of the Act. People are only entitled to see information about themselves, and they cannot see any part of their record which relates to someone else.

The information that you write in files should be clear and useful. Do not include irrelevant information, and write only about the person concerned. Anything you write should be true and able to be justified. In general you should stick to the facts and not your opinion, as the two examples below show.

The purpose of a file is to reflect an accurate and up-to-date picture of somebody's situation, and to provide a historical record that can be referred to at some point in the future. Some of it may be required to be disclosed to other agencies. Any records must be signed and dated.

Doing it well

ACES

Always think about what you write, and make sure it is ACES:

- **A**ccurate
- **C**lear
- **E**asy to read
- **S**hareable.

Name: A. Potter

Mr P settling back well after discharge from hosp. Fairly quiet and withdrawn today. Son to visit in am. Report from hosp included in file – prognosis not good. Not able to get him to talk today; for further time tomorrow.

Name: J. Soane

Joe visited new flat today. Very positive and looking forward to move. No access problems; delighted with purpose-built kitchen and bathroom. Further visit from OT needed to check on any aids required. Confirmed with housing assoc. that Joe wants tenancy. Will send tenancy agreement – should start on 1st.

Need to check: housing benefit, OT visit, notify change of address to Benefits Agency, PACT team, etc., shopping trip with Joe for any household items.

Information should be clear and factual.

All information, however it is stored, is subject to the Data Protection Act 1998, which covers medical records, social service records, credit information, local authority information – in fact, anything which is personal data (facts and opinions about a person). The principles of data protection apply to all the records you keep.

The same principles apply whether you have handwritten notes in a case record or if you use an electronic system. Written communication may not be something you do very frequently. You may not write many formal letters, but as a support worker you will have to write information in records that could prove to be of vital importance.

The golden rule of good communication is to consider its purpose. If you are completing a support plan or record for someone, then that information needs to be there in order to inform the next support worker who takes over.

You need to record accurately any distress or worries you have tried to deal with, and any physical signs of illness or accidents. You may need to record fluid balances or calorie intake charts. It may be important to record visitors or any medical interventions.

Written records are no use unless they are legible. There is no point in scribbling something illegible in someone's notes. It is actually worse than not writing anything, because colleagues waste time trying to decipher what is there, and have to deal with the concerns raised by the fact that there was clearly something worth recording, but they have no idea what it was.

You also need to convey the message in a clear and concise way. People do not want to spend time reading a lengthy report when the main points could have been expressed in a paragraph. Equally, you need to make sure that the relevant points are there. Often bullet points can be useful in recording information clearly and concisely.

3.2 Agreed ways of working for recording, storing and sharing information

Choosing the best way to pass on information

Sometimes the method of communication is dictated by the circumstances. If the situation requires an immediate response, or you need to find essential information urgently, then you are unlikely to sit and write a long letter, walk down to the post office, put it in the post and wait until next week to get a reply! You are far more likely to pick up the telephone and see if you can contact the person you need to speak to, or send a quick email. Or you may choose to fax your request, or fax information in response to a telephone request from someone else. These methods are fast (almost instant) and relatively reliable for getting information accurately from one place to another.

Reflect

Think about the sort of information you would need to know. What things are important when handing over?

When choosing a method of communication, you have to take into account:

- who the information is for
- whether it is urgent
- whether it is confidential
- what type of information it is
- what the purpose of the information is
- whether there needs to be a written record
- who is sending the information
- whether there needs to be a record of the information having been sent.

There may be other occasions when, on the grounds of confidentiality, something is sent through the post marked 'Strictly confidential' and only to be opened by the person whose name is on the envelope. This method may be entirely appropriate for information that is too confidential to be sent by fax and would be inappropriate in a telephone conversation or an email.

Types of information

The types of information you wish to convey can vary from the simplest day-to-day information to the most complicated and detailed information on somebody's social and medical history, background, diagnosis and prognosis, support plan and finances.

Simple information

You may simply wish to communicate to a colleague that someone you are working with is probably not well enough to go out for a walk today. However, you have agreed with the colleague that you will go in with a cup of tea and see how she is feeling. You do not wish to shout the information in public, thus making the person the object of general interest, and you have agreed with your colleague that you will check the situation and give her a nod or a shake of the head to let her know. This is a very simple example of the way that information can be sent from one person to another by physical signals, without the need for words.

Two-way exchange

The information that you have to share may be the kind that requires a conversation with a colleague, or relative or the person concerned. The advantage of a verbal exchange of information is that it can be two-way, and you can receive information at the same time as you are sharing what you know.

Written information

Other information is of a nature that requires it to be written down. This could include detailed records about someone, or information that may need to be shared with more than one person and may be for inclusion in a person's health or care records. In this case you would probably choose to write the information and send it by fax, post or email.

Case study

Passing on information in different ways

Mr Shah had been receiving support in his own home for the past two years. His health and mobility had been deteriorating and he had found it increasingly hard to manage even with support. A review had been held at his home where Mr Shah, his social worker, the occupational therapist and the community nurse had all decided that his needs would best be met by a move into residential accommodation. His home carer had not been able to attend the review, and neither had his niece, who was a regular visitor. Following the review, Mr Shah's social worker passed on the following information:

Telephone call to Mr Shah's niece:

'Hello, Mrs Patel, this is Maria, your uncle's social worker. I promised your uncle I would call to let you know how the review went. Your uncle decided, and we all agreed, that he would be better to move into residential accommodation. He would quite like to go to Maidstone House, but if you and he decide you want to look at any others, I'll be happy to arrange it if you like. Of course, we will send you a copy of the review notes, but I wanted to let you know as soon as possible.'

Telephone call to home carer:

'Hi Sue – Maria. Mr S went for residential, as you hoped. He wants Maidstone House – I'll have to check vacancies, it's always really popular. I think he'd like you to carry on working with him until he goes in – he's very fond of you. I'll keep you up to date with progress.'

Email to Maidstone House:

Hi Jo

How are you – not caught up since that last training day – hope things are going well. What's your vacancy position? Can you let me know ASAP, I've got quite an urgent male admission if there's any hope??

Speak soon

Maria

Letter to GP:

Dear Dr Sida

Re: Mr W. S., 27 Miranda Street

Please find attached a copy of the review notes for records of the above gentleman who is a patient of yours. The plan is to arrange his admission to residential care as a matter of urgency. I will advise you of the date for admission.

Please do not hesitate to contact me if I can provide any further information.

Yours sincerely

Maria Perez

Social worker

1. Can you see the different styles of information giving and work out why each one was appropriate?
2. Would any of these styles have worked if they had been used with a different recipient?
3. Do you think that you have always used the most appropriate means of communication? Will this help you to think more carefully in future?

Activity 2

Recording types of information

Keep a record for a week of the types of information that come into and go out of your workplace. Note the methods used for different types of information. Ask people why they have chosen to pass on information in a particular way.

Functional skills

English: Writing; Reading

When writing information, it is important that you use the correct structures. You will need to learn how to take notes effectively, and to write letters, reports and case studies. Ensure that spellings, punctuation and grammar are accurate, and that the language is suitable. All your information should be written clearly and coherently.

Making a decision between these three means of communicating written information may be based on:

- availability of fax or email
- the nature and level of confidentiality of the information.

Doing it well

Considering the person receiving the information

One of the factors you must consider when choosing the best method of passing on information is the person who is going to receive it.

- Make sure that the method is appropriate for the person who will receive it.
- Do not send a letter to a person who is visually impaired unless you know they have a method of having it read.
- Do not attempt to pass on information by telephone to someone with hearing loss unless you are using an adapted telephone system.
- Use language that is at the right level for the person receiving it.

Sharing information

Personal information on people you support should only be shared on a 'need to know' basis.

It can be difficult when people claim to have a right or an interest in seeing a person's records. Of course, there are always some people who do need to know, either because they are directly involved in supporting the person or because they are involved in some other role. However, not everyone needs to know everything, so it is important that information is given on a 'need to know' basis. In other words, people are told what they need to know in order to carry out their role.

Relatives will often claim that they have a 'right to know'. The most famous example of this was Victoria Gillick, who went to court in order to try to gain access to her daughter's medical records. She claimed that she had the right to know if her daughter had been given the contraceptive pill. Her GP had refused to tell her and she took the case all the way to the House of Lords, but the ruling was not changed and she was not given access to her daughter's records. The rules remain the same. Even for close relatives, the information is not available unless the person agrees.

It is difficult, however, if you are faced with angry or distressed relatives who believe that you have information they are entitled to. One situation you could encounter is where someone believes that they have the right to be told about medical information in respect of their parent. Another example is where someone is trying to find out a person's whereabouts. The best response is to be clear and assertive, but to demonstrate that you understand that it is difficult for them. Do not try to pass the buck and give people the idea that they can find out from someone else. There is nothing more frustrating than being passed from one person to another without anyone being prepared to tell you anything. It is important to be clear and say something like, 'I'm sorry. I know you must be worried, but I can't discuss any information unless your mother agrees', or 'I'm sorry, I can't give out any information about where J is living now. But if you would like to leave me a name and contact details, I will pass on the message and she can contact you.'

I'm sorry, I understand that you are worried, but I can't give you any information unless your mother agrees.

Have you had to deal with relatives demanding information they should not have access to?

Proof of identity

You should always check that people are who they claim to be. It is not unknown for newspaper reporters, unwanted visitors or even a nosey neighbour to claim that they are relatives or professionals from another agency. If basic precautions are not taken to confirm their identity, then they may be able to find out a great deal of confidential information.

Doing it well

Sharing information

- Generally you should only give the information with consent.
- Only give people the information they need to know to do their job.
- Information should be relevant to the purpose for which it is required.
- Check the identity of the person to whom you give information.
- Make sure that you do not give information carelessly.

Checklist

In person: if you do not know the person who is claiming to have a right to be given information, you should:

- find out whether they are known to any of your colleagues
- ask for proof of identity – if they claim to be from another agency involved in providing care, they will have an official ID (identity card), otherwise ask for driving licence, bank cards, and so on.

On the telephone: unless you recognise the voice of the person, you should:

- offer to take the telephone number and call back after you have checked
- if various members of the family or friends are likely to be telephoning about a particular person, you could arrange a 'password'.

Case study

Sharing information with relatives of people you support

Mr Richardson is 59 years old. He is a resident in a nursing home, and he is now very ill. He has Huntington's disease, which is a disease causing dementia, loss of mobility and loss of speech. It is incurable and untreatable, and it is hereditary.

Mr Richardson was divorced many years ago when his children were very young and he has had no contact with his family for over 30 years. A young man who says he is his son comes to the nursing home in great distress. He is aware, through his mother, that his paternal grandfather died 'insane' and he has now heard about his father being in a nursing home. He is terrified that his father has a hereditary disease and that he also may have it. He also has young children and is desperate to know if they are at risk.

1. What can you tell Mr Richardson's son?
2. Does he have a right to know?
3. What do you think should happen?
4. Whose rights are your concern?

Who can see confidential records?

Every social care organisation will have a policy on confidentiality and the disclosure of information. You must be sure that you know what both policies are in your workplace.

The basic rule is that all information somebody gives, or that is given on their behalf, to an organisation is confidential and cannot be disclosed to anyone without the consent of the person.

Sharing information with consent

There are, however, circumstances in which it may be necessary to pass on information.

In many cases, passing information around is routine and related to the person's support. For example, medical information may be passed to a hospital, to a residential home or to a private care agency. It must be made clear to the person that this information will be passed on in order to ensure that they receive the best possible support.

The key factor to remember is that only information that is required for the purpose is passed on. For example, it is not necessary to tell the hearing aid clinic that Mr Smith's son is currently serving a prison sentence. However, if Mr Smith became seriously ill and the hospital wanted to contact his next of kin, that information would need to be passed on.

Each organisation should have a policy that states clearly the circumstances in which information can be disclosed. According to government guidelines (Confidentiality of Personal Information 1988) the policy should state:

- who the members of senior management designated to deal with decisions about disclosing information are
- what to do when urgent action is required
- what safeguards are in place to make sure that the information will be used only for the purpose for which it is required
- arrangements for obtaining manual records and computer records
- arrangements for reviewing the procedure.

Sharing information without consent

Sharing information without someone's agreement is always a difficult decision. You should always seek guidance from your manager in this situation and they will decide if it is necessary to pass on information.

There are several reasons why decisions about disclosing information without consent may need to be made, and the person involved should be informed at the earliest possible opportunity about what has been disclosed.

The person may be at risk; for example, you may have discovered that they have attempted to harm themselves and require urgent medical treatment.

Information may be required by a tribunal, a court or by the ombudsman. Ideally this should be done with the person's consent, but it will have to be provided regardless of whether the consent is given.

You may have to consider the protection of the community, if there is a matter of public health at stake. You may be aware that someone has an infectious illness, or is a carrier of such an illness and is putting people at risk. For example, if someone was infected with salmonella, but still insisted on going to work in a restaurant kitchen, you would have a duty to inform the appropriate authorities.

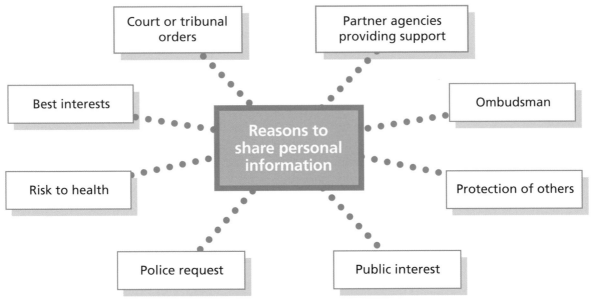

Reasons why it may be necessary to disclose information without consent.

There are other situations where you may need to give information to the police. If a serious crime is being investigated, the police can ask for information to be given, but information can only be requested in respect of a serious offence and it has to be asked for by a senior-ranking officer of at least the rank of superintendent. This means that if the local constable asks if you know whether Mr Jones has a history of mental health problems, this is not information you are free to discuss.

There may also be times when it is helpful to give information to the media. For example, an older, confused man, who wanders regularly, may have gone missing for much longer than usual. A description given out on the local radio and in the local paper may help to locate him before he comes to any serious harm.

Doing it well

Disclosure without consent

Disclosure without consent can be made:

- when it is necessary because of any legal requirement that has been placed on your employer
- when it is necessary to protect the best interests of the person concerned
- for social services purposes such as passing information to those undertaking the support of a person or to other departments/agencies
- for other purposes such as when required by police, courts or statutory tribunals
- when it is necessary to protect the public.

Getting ready for assessment

You will need to be able to show your assessor that you understand the reasons for careful handling of information. This may be through completing an assignment about how information is handled in your workplace. You will need to know how the legislation affects what you can and cannot do and how the Information Commissioner works. Your employer will have policies and procedures around handling information, and you must be able to show your assessor that you understand and work within these policies. Just producing your employer's policies on confidentiality and recording information is not enough; your assessor will want to know how you include these policies in your day-to-day practice.

Legislation

- Access to Personal Files Act 1987
- Confidentiality of Personal Information 1988
- Data Protection Act 1998
- Freedom of Information Act 2000
- Public Interest Disclosure Act 1998

Further reading and research

- www.ico.gov.uk (the Information Commissioner's Office)

Unit IC 01

The principles of infection prevention and control

Infection, even so-called minor infections, can be a major source of patient suffering leading to more serious infections, costly drug therapies and treatments, and possibly death. It is the responsibility of every care worker to understand their role in the prevention and control of infection, and to put standard precautions in place to reduce the risk of a person acquiring an infection.

This unit will focus on the principles of infection prevention and control, investigate laws and policies which relate to infection control, and explain the employer's and employee's responsibilities. You will consider your responsibilities in relation to the prevention and control of infection, and be able to demonstrate an effective hand-washing technique and the correct use of personal protective equipment (PPE).

In this unit you will learn about:

1. **roles and responsibilities in the prevention and control of infections**
2. **legislation and policies relating to prevention and control of infections**
3. **systems and procedures relating to the prevention and control of infections**
4. **the importance of risk assessment in relation to the prevention and control of infections**
5. **the importance of using Personal Protective Equipment (PPE) in the prevention and control of infection**
6. **the importance of good personal hygiene in the prevention and control of infection.**

1. Understand roles and responsibilities in the prevention and control of infections

1.1 Employees' roles and responsibilities in relation to the prevention and control of infection

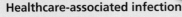
Over the past few years, there has been a dramatic increase in the number of patients developing **healthcare-associated infections** (HCAIs). As a care worker, you have a responsibility to take care of your own health and safety and that of others who may be affected by your actions such as the people you support, their family, friends and your work colleagues. The Health and Safety at Work Act 1974 requires workers to:

- take reasonable care for their own safety and that of others
- cooperate with the employer in respect of health and safety matters
- not intentionally damage any health and safety equipment or materials provided by the employer
- attend training provided by the employer
- use protective equipment provided by the employer.

When considering your responsibilities relating to infection within your work setting, you need to:

- think **prevention**
- think **control**.

Prevention of infection

You may have heard the term 'prevention is better than cure'; this is also true when it comes to infection. Preventing a person from acquiring an HCAI can save them from unnecessary discomfort, anxiety and exposure to high levels of antibiotic therapy, all of which could have serious consequences for people and their families. In 2000, the government identified that about 5,000 people die each year as a direct result of HCAIs. Your action could save lives.

The effects of infections are not just health-related; there is also a cost. The government identified that HCAIs may be costing the NHS a staggering £1 billion a year. This money could be better spent on developing cancer treatments, employing more staff or saving the taxpayer money.

One of the most important responsibilities care workers have in the prevention of infection is to adopt the practice of using standard precautions for all people. The principle of standard precautions is that all people are considered 'high risk'; that is, they are considered a high infection risk. This includes you!

You can help prevent infection by doing the following.

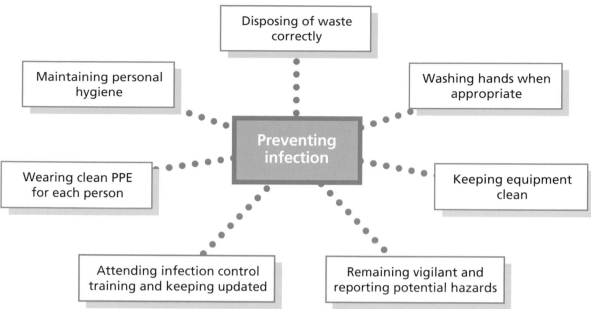

Preventing infection.

Activity 1

What are your responsibilities?

What are your responsibilities for the prevention and control of infection? Write a brief account and explain:

- why each responsibility is important
- how it contributes to the prevention and control of infection.

Functional skills

English: Writing

Write about your responsibilities for the prevention and control of infection at your place of work. Use a suitable format to present your information, and ensure that all your work is clear to read and provides sufficient facts to cover the task. Proofread your writing to ensure accuracy and that each sentence makes sense.

Control of infection

If a person acquires an infection, your responsibilities will focus on controlling and limiting the spread of the infection. The steps taken to help prevent infections will be maintained; you will already be treating all people as high risk, but with a confirmed infection outbreak, you will need to be more vigilant and record and report any changes in a person's condition.

1.2 Employers' responsibilities in relation to the prevention and control infection

There is a general duty of care placed on all employers under health and safety legislation, which gives employers the responsibility to protect employees from danger and harm, as far as is reasonably possible. For example, employers must:

- provide a safe workplace
- carry out risk assessments to assess the dangers of certain work activities
- provide training for staff
- provide personal protective equipment
- ensure regular health and safety checks are undertaken.

These responsibilities extend to employers protecting employees from the risks posed by biological hazards such as blood, body fluids and associated infections. Within your workplace, your employer will have put infection prevention and control policies and procedures in place for staff to adhere to. Your manager will have a good understanding of the general care of the people within the setting and will be able to respond appropriately in the event of a possible infection outbreak, such as moving them to a single room and arranging for swabs and specimens to be taken.

Care managers have a responsibility to the people within the care of the organisation and should undertake regular checks on the cleanliness of the setting, monitor hand-washing practice, know whom to contact in the event of an infection outbreak and report infections to the correct authority such as the Public Health Department.

2. Understand legislation and policies relating to prevention and control of infections

2.1 Current legislation and regulatory body standards which are relevant to the prevention and control of infection

We have already discussed the Health and Safety at Work Act 1974 (HASAWA) in relation to the responsibilities of employers and employees and their roles in protecting the health and safety of people within the workplace such as workers, patients and visitors, but, within the HASAWA there are regulations that have a relevance to the prevention and control of infection. These include the Control of Substances Hazardous to Health Regulations 2002 (COSHH) and the Reporting of Injuries, Diseases and Dangerous Occurrences Regulations 1995 (RIDDOR) .

Control of Substances Hazardous to Health Regulations 2002 (COSHH)

The COSHH Regulations focus on hazardous materials used within the workplace these include cleaning chemicals, disinfectants and, in care settings, body fluids such as urine and blood. The regulations explain how hazardous materials should be used in the workplace, how they should be stored, how they should be labelled and how to deal safely with a spillage. For care settings, this would include what to do in the event of a urine or blood spillage.

Reporting of Injuries, Diseases and Dangerous Occurrences Regulations 1995 (RIDDOR)

The RIDDOR Regulations provides employers with a legal requirement to record and report all accidents which occur in the workplace. These records must be kept for three years and need to be available for inspection by the Health and Safety Executive (HSE) if required. Needle stick injuries would also be reported under these regulations.

Activity 2

Can you smell gas?

Read the COSHH policy for your workplace and find out what it says about how to deal with a urine spillage. You will probably notice that the policy asks you to clean the spill with a detergent before using a bleach, or **sodium hypochlorite**, solution.

1. Why is this?
2. Would you use bleach, or sodium hypochlorite, directly on the spillage and why?

Key term

Sodium hypochlorite – the chemical name for bleach

Functional skills

English: Reading

In your place of work, you will need to read many policies. By doing this, you will have the opportunity to read a range of formal documentation. For many of the written tasks you have been set by your assessor, you will need to understand the texts and be able to extract and use information.

There are some incidents which must be reported directly to the HSE; these are:

- death or major injury
- injury resulting in an employee being off work for more than three days
- poisoning
- musculo-skeletal disorders including fractures
- skin conditions such as dermatitis and skin cancer
- lung disease such as those linked to asbestos and occupational asthma
- occupational cancers.

In 2007, the Department of Health launched the Saving Lives initiative to implement best practice, national guidance and the latest infection prevention and control policies to help reduce HCAIs throughout the NHS. The Department of Health also introduced the Health and Social Care Act 2008. This Act created the Care Quality Commission (CQC), which replaced the Healthcare Commission, the Commission for Social Care Inspection (CSCI) and the Mental Health Commission; it was designed to support improvements in the care given to patients. From 2009, certain NHS organisations were required to register with the CQC and made it a legal requirement to protect patients, workers and others from HCAIs.

A code of practice for the prevention and control of HCAI was produced under the Health and Social Care Act, which sets out how the NHS will attempt to prevent HCAIs. These include the 10 key criteria identified below.

1. Systems to manage and monitor the prevention and control of infection. These systems use risk assessments. They consider how susceptible service users are and any risks that their environment and other users may pose to them.
2. Provide and maintain a clean and appropriate environment in managed premises that facilitates the prevention and control of infections.
3. Provide suitable accurate information on infections to service users and their visitors.
4. Provide suitable accurate information on infections to any person concerned with providing further support or nursing/medical care in a timely fashion.
5. Ensure that people who have or develop an infection are identified promptly and receive the appropriate treatment and care to reduce the risk of passing on the infection to other people.
6. Ensure that all staff and those employed to provide care in all settings are fully involved in the process of preventing and controlling infection.
7. Provide or secure adequate isolation facilities.
8. Secure adequate access to laboratory support as appropriate.
9. Have and adhere to policies, designed for the person's care and provider organisations, that will help to prevent and control infections.
10. Ensure, so far as is reasonably practicable, that care workers are free of and are protected from exposure to infections that can be caught at work and that all staff are suitably educated in the prevention and control of infection associated with the provision of health and social care.

(Source: Code of practice for the NHS on the prevention and control of healthcare associated infections and related guidance, Department of Health, April 2010.)

If a healthcare organisation fails to comply with the code of practice, it could result in enforcement action by the CQC. From 2010/11 a revised version of the code of practice covering independent healthcare and social care will be prepared.

The Public Health (Control of Diseases) Act 1984 and the Public Health (Infectious Diseases) Regulations 1988 provide information on notifiable diseases such as cholera, dysentery, diphtheria and food poisoning, to name a few, and explains how outbreaks of these infections need to be dealt with, recorded and reported. The laws give GPs and healthcare managers the responsibilities to inform the local environmental health officer of any outbreak of a notifiable disease and for healthcare managers to ensure that they fully investigate the cause of any infectious outbreak.

Further legislation relating to the prevention and control of infection which you may find useful includes:

- the NICE Guidelines 2 2003
- the Hazardous Waste Regulations 2005
- the Food Safety Act 1990
- the Health Protection Agency Act 2004.

2.2 Local and organisational policies relevant to the prevention and control of infection

Every health or social care setting should have clear policies and procedures for the prevention and control of infection. These policies will be tailored to meet the requirements of each care setting and may include some of the following information:

- roles and responsibilities of key members of staff in the organisation such as infection control team members
- how to achieve best hand hygiene
- personal hygiene requirements
- how to apply standard precautions
- when and how to use personal protective equipment
- safe handling and disposal of sharps
- safe handling and disposal of clinical waste
- safe disposal of personal protective equipment
- managing blood and bodily fluid products and spills
- decontaminating equipment
- maintaining a clean clinical environment
- appropriate use and care of indwelling devices such as catheter care
- cleaning routines and requirements
- how to record and report accidents and incidents.

It may be difficult to apply all of these suggestions in each setting. For example, if you work in the community and have to work in a person's own home, you will be restricted on how clean you can keep

Activity 3

What does your policy say?

Read the infection prevention and control policy for your organisation. Identify your responsibilities under the policy. Can you think of how you would put your policy into practice? For example, how and where do you dispose of gloves once you have finished with them?

the environment you are working in. However, your workplace policy should reflect what standards should be expected for the area where you are required to work.

It is important for you to be familiar with the information in your organisations infection prevention and control policy. You will probably find that your organisation's policy contains information similar to the areas discussed above, but remember, it is your responsibility to read and follow your organisation's policy.

Case study

Refusing entry to visit people with infectious illnesses

Dusana is a care worker and works in the nursing unit of Rosenburg Hall nursing and care home. Over the last few days some patients and staff have been suffering from diarrhoea and vomiting. Results from specimens sent to the microbiology lab have come back and confirm an outbreak of the highly contagious norovirus, also known as the winter vomiting virus.

The infection control team have informed the charge nurse that the nursing unit has to be closed to all visitors, because this virus is very contagious. They also tell the charge nurse that all staff must follow the standard precautions policy when providing patients care and that effective hand-washing skills are very important.

During the evening shift, an angry relative demands to see their mother who is a patient on the unit and who has been confirmed as having the norovirus. The relative refuses to listen to Dusana and says that she does not have the right to prevent them from seeing their mother.

1. Is the relative right to say that Dusana does not have the right to refuse them entry to the nursing unit? Why?
2. How can the risk of the infection spreading be reduced?
3. What aspects of an infection control policy are important to consider in this situation?

3. Understand systems and procedures relating to the prevention and control of infections

3.1 Procedures and systems relevant to the prevention and control of infection

When looking at the prevention and control of infection, it can help you identify specific procedures and systems if you split the focus of the prevention and control measures into two areas, which are:

- the environment and equipment
- the people involved.

We will look at the procedures and systems relating to people later in the unit, but first we need to consider the environment and equipment in relation to the prevention and control of infection.

Care environments, and the equipment used within the care environment, will differ depending on the setting where you work. Environments within care settings can also differ depending on the activity being undertaken within that specific location. For example, in a hospital you will have wards, nursing stations, sluice and dirty utility areas, operating theatres, outpatient departments, storage areas and so on – these areas and the equipment used within them will need to be kept clean to reduce the risk of infection.

The level of cleanliness required will depend on the type of activities being undertaking. It is generally accepted that there are three levels of cleaning:

- general cleaning and decontamination
- disinfection
- sterilisation.

General cleaning and decontamination

General cleaning and decontamination is when dirt, dust and some micro-organisms are removed by using warm water, detergent and the physical action of cleaning. The purpose of cleaning is to change the environment, so bacteria cannot breed. This is achieved by removing physical debris such as body tissue and blood, where bacteria can breed and by drying the area or item. Drying is very important as bacteria cannot breed in a dry environment.

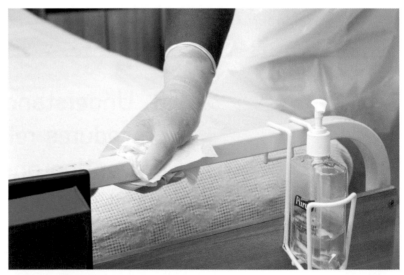

General cleaning is very important and its role in the fight against infection should not be underestimated.

Disinfection

Disinfection is a process taken after general cleaning which aims to further reduce the number of **pathogenic** organisms present on a surface. For example, once a work surface has been cleaned, a bleach or alcohol solution may be used to disinfect the surface. Unless there is a specific reason such as after a urine spill, there is no need to routinely disinfect ceilings, floors and walls. The process of disinfection will kill most micro-organisms, but will not destroy their resistant spores. This can only be achieved by sterilisation. Removing physical debris needs to be achieved before further disinfection and sterilisation can be effective.

Sterilisation

Sterilisation is the process of killing all micro-organisms and their resistant spores. All surgical equipment used during operations will go through the process of sterilisation to reduce the risk of infection, but even these items will have gone through the process of cleaning to remove physical debris such as blood and tissue before sterilisation. Many single-use items used within the care sector such as catheters and feeding tubes will also have been sterilised.

There are three main methods of sterilisation used for medical purposes.

- **Autoclaving** is one of the most common forms of sterilisation and is frequently used in hospital sterilising departments. Autoclaving is when steam (under pressure) is heated to between 134°C and 137°C to kill pathogenic organisms and their resistant spores.
- **Chemicals** can be used to sterilise equipment such as ethylene oxide gas, but this type of sterilisation has to be undertaken at specialist sterilisation centres. A more common form of chemical sterilisation used on a smaller scale involves the use of sodium dichloroisocyanurate solutions such as 'Milton', which is often used in maternity departments to sterilise feeding bottles and teats.
- Gamma **radiation** is a common form of sterilisation for single use items and for items that cannot withstand high temperatures.

Within your workplace, you will probably not be required to become actively involved in the sterilisation process, but the chances are you will be required to help clean the environment and disinfect equipment. You may have a cleaning rota which identifies daily, weekly and monthly cleaning activities, but you will need to follow your organisation's policies and procedures for cleaning and disinfecting. Some specific times when cleaning activities may have to be undertaken could include:

- between clinical activities, such as operations and clinical examinations
- between personal hygiene activities, such as cleaning the bath or disinfecting the toilet or commode
- at the end of the day, such as washing floors
- once a person has been discharged, such as cleaning the bed frame and mattress.

Activity 4

Your organisation's cleaning policy

What is your organisation's policy for cleaning? Find out what action you should take if you discover a piece of equipment that requires cleaning. What other systems are in place within your setting to prevent and control the spread of infection?

	After use	Daily	Weekly	Monthly
Toilet	✓			
Commode	✓			
Bath	✓			
Shower	✓			
Floors		✓		
Walls			✓	
Ceiling				✓
Bed frame			✓ or once discharged	
Cupboards				✓
Fridge			✓	
Dining table	✓			

Cleaning rotas can be useful, but everybody has a responsibility to keep the environment and equipment clean.

Many organisations now employ domestic staff who have specific responsible for undertaking general cleaning activities; however, you will still be required to undertake certain cleaning or disinfection tasks. For example, if you remove faulty equipment from service, which has been involved in patient contact, it is your responsibility to ensure the equipment is appropriately decontaminated before sending it for repair. Any equipment that has been decontaminated will need to be recorded according to your organisation's policy.

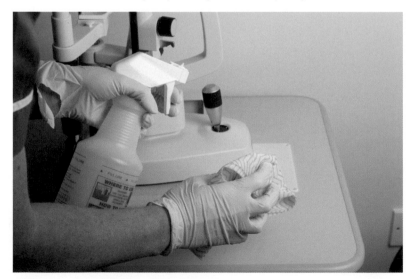

What does your organisation state should be worn when cleaning equipment?

3.2 The potential impact of an outbreak of infection on the individual and the organisation

The outbreak of an infection within a care setting can have serious consequences for both people and the care organisation. People who acquire HCAIs will require medical treatment to deal with the infection such as antibiotic therapy, but antibiotics can have side effects such as allergic reactions, diarrhoea and nausea. Some pathogenic organisms have become resistant to antibiotics causing the so-called superbug MRSA, which needs stronger antibiotics to fight it.

Unfortunately, the use of some antibiotics can also make people more susceptible to another increasingly common condition called Clostridium difficile (C. diff). C. diff can live harmlessly in the bowel alongside other naturally occurring bacteria; however, when a person takes antibiotics for an infection, the antibiotics will destroy the bacteria causing the infection and the naturally occurring good bacteria in the bowel, but the C. diff bacteria is very resistant and is not destroyed. This upsets the natural balance of bacteria in the bowel and enables the C. diff bacteria to increase in number and produce toxins that cause the symptoms of C. diff. These symptoms include diarrhoea, abdominal pains, nausea and, in severe cases, inflammation of the bowel.

The effects of a person acquiring MRSA or C. diff can at best be uncomfortable and at worst devastating and fatal. The effects of infections are not only physical; they can also have a mental impact because people who acquire infections often think they are 'dirty', which can lower their self-esteem. Some infections may require the patient to be isolated from others to help prevent and control the spread of infection. A person who has to be isolated from others may feel depressed because of the lack of social interaction. It is important, therefore, that care workers perform regular checks on isolated people to help reduce the risk of them becoming depressed.

For the organisation, an infection outbreak can prove to be an expensive affair with the cost of treatment and a prolonged stay in hospital; what's more it can ruin the organisation's reputation. If an investigation, conducted following the infection outbreak, identifies poor practice or negligence, the HSE has the right to prosecute people, which could result in a fine and/or imprisonment.

Every care worker has a duty of care to ensure that they minimise the risks of a person from acquiring an HCAI. The main way this can be achieved is by having an awareness of their responsibilities under the organisation's infection prevention and control policy, adopting safe practice including the use of standard precautions, effective hand-washing and attending regular training.

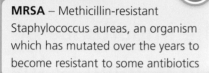

Key term

MRSA – Methicillin-resistant Staphylococcus aureas, an organism which has mutated over the years to become resistant to some antibiotics

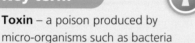

Key term

Toxin – a poison produced by micro-organisms such as bacteria

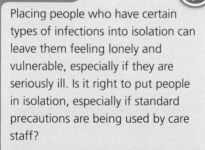

Reflect

Placing people who have certain types of infections into isolation can leave them feeling lonely and vulnerable, especially if they are seriously ill. Is it right to put people in isolation, especially if standard precautions are being used by care staff?

What are the possible positive and negatives of isolation nursing compared with the positive and negatives of not undertaking isolation nursing? Place yourself in the position of the person with an infection.

Activity 5

Your experience of infections in the care setting

Infections can have a massive impact on the person who has acquired the infection and the workplace.

1. What infections are commonly seen within the care setting where you work?
2. What systems are put in place to prevent infection?
3. What procedures are put in place to control the infection?

4. Understand the importance of risk assessment in relation to the prevention and control of infections

4.1 The definition of risk

Within the care setting, there are a number of hazards that have the potential to cause harm. Hazards that come from living organisms, such as humans, are called biological hazards or biohazards and include the organisms found in body fluids such as the HIV virus.

Once the biohazards within the workplace have been identified, the next step is to identify the risks that the biohazard could present. For example, if a patient had an MRSA infection, what is the risk of this infection spreading? The level of risk is rated as low, medium or high, depending on the severity of the hazard.

4.2 Potential risks of infection within the workplace

There is always a potential risk of infection wherever you work or wherever you go. For example, you expose yourself to the risk of food poisoning when you eat out, but this is normally a very low risk because there are stringent laws in place surrounding food hygiene and safety. However, the risk of acquiring an infection increases within the health and social care sectors because these sectors deal with many people who are more susceptible to the risk of infection due to their conditions. When considering the potential risks of infection, you will need to think about:

- the person being supported
- relatives, friends and visitors
- you the care worker
- the environment
- equipment.

This is the international symbol for biohazards.

The person receiving care

The person who is receiving care is likely to be at a high risk of acquiring an infection because of the following.

- **Age**: The very young and the very old often have a weaker immune system, and can therefore acquire infections more easily.
- **Immune status**: People who have a low immune status, such as people who have been receiving chemotherapy, have an increased risk of acquiring an infection, because their low immunity makes it more difficult to fight off infections.
- **Nutritional status**: People who are malnourished often have a weaker immune system, so are more susceptible to infection.
- **Skin integrity**: Patients who have been admitted to hospital following an accident, where they have open wounds as a result of trauma, or patients who have undergone surgery, have an increased risk of infection because the body's natural defence barrier against infectious agents, the skin, has been breached, allowing harmful pathogenic organisms to gain entry.
- **Invasive therapy**: The skin may also be breached because of invasive therapies, such as when a cannula is inserted into a patient's arm so intravenous fluids can be administered, or when catheters are inserted into a person's urethra, so urine can drain from the bladder. These invasive therapies give micro-organisms a direct route into the body.
- **Drug therapy**: People taking antibiotics can be at increased risk of acquiring an infection because the antibiotic can alter the level of normal bacteria living within the body – for example, C. diff. Chemotherapy drugs can lower the body's immune system and therefore expose the patient to a higher risk of acquiring an infection.

While people receiving care are clearly at a higher risk of acquiring an infection, they are also a high risk of spreading infections. People receiving care could have highly contagious blood-borne diseases such as Hepatitis B or HIV, or they could have MRSA, so it is important to remember to treat all people as high risk and use standard precautions when providing care to people.

Relatives, friends and visitors

Friends and relatives can be exposed to the risk of infection when visiting their loved ones in a care setting. For example, if there is an outbreak of the norovirus in the care setting, small aerosols containing the virus can enter the air when someone vomits and can be passed to another person. However, friends and relatives can also be risk factors and can bring infections into the care environment such as the common cold. While the cold is often harmless to fit healthy people, it can be fatal for people who have a weaker immune system.

Key term

Aerosol – a cloud of solid or liquid particles in a gas

You, the care worker

Like friends and relatives, care workers can be exposed to a number of potential infections within the workplace. These include the common infections such as:

- colds
- flu
- diarrhoea
- vomiting.

However, care workers often come into contact with patients' blood and body fluids, which can pose greater infection risks and may include the risk of acquiring hepatitis and HIV. Care workers may also be at an increased risk of acquiring scabies, which can be spread by touch.

Care workers may be exposed to infections spread through the air, such as tuberculosis and swine flu, although these are quite rare. Other airborne infections such as streptococcal infections are more common and can lead to sore throats and raised temperature.

As a care worker, you are a potential source of infection to the people you provide care for; because these people are at an increased risk of acquiring an infection, you will need to ensure you take precautions to minimise the risk of cross-infection. In particular, you must ensure that you take appropriate action if you become ill, because it may not be appropriate to go to work even if you just have a cold. You must check your organisation's sickness policy and inform your manager if you are sick. If you have suffered from diarrhoea, you should not return to work until you have been clear of symptoms for 48 hours. Even though you may feel you are letting your colleagues down, your actions could be saving someone's life.

The environment

The environment where people are being cared for and where you work must be kept as clean as possible. Bacteria and pathogenic organisms can live and breed in damp environments, and the resistant spores can remain dormant for a long time, such as those which cause C. diff. Some viruses such as HIV do not live outside the body for very long, but the hepatitis virus can survive for months, if conditions are right. Because some harmful pathogenic organisms are so resistant, effective cleaning is important. Particular attention should be paid to the bathroom, toilet, door handles and work surfaces, including those where food is served or prepared. Bed frames and mattresses need to be cleaned on a regular basis and bed linen changed frequently. Floors in clinical areas should be hard, so that they can be washed, and any spills can be cleaned quickly and efficiently.

Activity 6

Potential sources of infection

There are a number of potential sources of infection within the workplace. These sources depend on many things, including the type of workplace where you work.

1. Make a list of all the potential sources of infection which you come across during a routine day.
2. Share your list with a colleague and see if they agree with you or if they can add any more.

Now you know some of the potential risks for infection, you can start to think about what you do to reduce these.

Equipment

Equipment that comes in contact with people may also come in contact with blood or body fluid, so may harbour potential infectious agents. Equipment that does come in contact with patients should be disposed of in the appropriate manner. For example, 'sharps' such as needles and scalpel blades need to be disposed of in a sharps bin; catheters should be disposed of in yellow clinical waste bags. Equipment that is non-disposable, such as surgical instruments, pumps, commodes and so on must be cleaned and disinfected after use and, if appropriate, sterilised.

4.3 The process of carrying out a risk assessment

An infection control risk assessment, like other risk assessments, will identify the potential biohazards within the workplace, the risks these biohazards pose, who may be at risk and how the biohazard can be removed or reduced.

The HSE gives a five-step guide to risk assessment.

1. **Identify the hazard** – This step involves looking for and identifying the biohazards by inspecting the workplace, talking with employees looking at the types of activities taking place within the setting. For example, staff working in an operating theatre will be at a higher risk from biohazards than those working in a residential care home who will have a lower risk.
2. **Decide who might be harmed and how** – This will involve consideration of everyone in the workplace such as patients and visitors, not just care workers.
3. **Evaluate the risks and decide on precautions** – The risks arising from the identified biohazards need to be evaluated and a decision taken on the precautions required to minimise or remove the risk. This could include the use of standard precautions, PPE and cleaning schedules. If measures are already in place then the effectiveness of the measures need to be considered as to whether the existing precautions are adequate or if more are required.
4. **Record the findings and implement them** – The findings from the risk assessment need to be recorded and an explanation given on how the risks can be controlled to prevent harm. Care workers must be informed about the outcome of the risk assessment because they will need to implement the actions.
5. **Review the assessment and update if necessary** – The risk assessment must be reviewed from time to time and revised if necessary. For example, if new PPE becomes available, new infections are identified or work activities/processes change.

(source: Health and Safety Executive.)

4.4 The importance of carrying out a risk assessment

Under the Health and Safety at Work Act 1974, employers have a legal responsibility to protect the health and safety of their employees and anyone else using the workplace; in care settings this would include patients, friends and family. A risk assessment is one of the most important assessments an employer can undertake to protect these people as well as their organisation's reputation. The assessment identifies the risks in the workplace and the measures put in place to reduce the potential harm from these risks. In most cases straightforward measures can be put in place to control the risks — for example, ensuring adequate PPE is available for staff to use.

Health and safety legislation does not require employers to eliminate all risk, but does require them to protect people as far as is 'reasonably practicable'. Failure to undertake a risk assessment is not only illegal, but it also risks the health and safety of all people within the workplace, especially the most vulnerable people, the people you are providing care for.

5. Understand the importance of using Personal Protective Equipment (PPE) in the prevention and control of infections

5.1 Correct use of PPE

There are many different types of personal protective equipment (PPE) that can be used to protect people from harm. PPE is defined in the Personal Protective Equipment at Work Regulations as: 'All equipment (including clothing affording protection against the weather) which is intended to be worn or held by a person at work which protects them against one or more risks to their health and safety.'

Below is a list of the equipment used by care workers to protect themselves from the risk of acquiring an infection from a patient and to protect patients from acquiring an infection from the care worker.

- Uniforms
- Gloves
- Aprons
- Masks
- Visors
- Goggles
- Hats
- Shoes

Uniforms

Uniforms should be fresh every day; they should be loose-fitting to enable free movement. This is vey important in clinical areas such as emergency departments and operating theatres, where care staff are required to wear 'scrubs' (protective surgical clothing). This is because the friction caused by the action of the clothing rubbing on the skin can cause skin scales to be shed, and skin scales can carry bacteria which have the potential to spread infection. Any type of uniform should be worn fresh every day and should have short sleeves to prevent them from trailing in blood or body fluids. If travelling to and from work in a uniform, you should ensure the uniform is covered with another item of clothing, such as a coat or jacket.

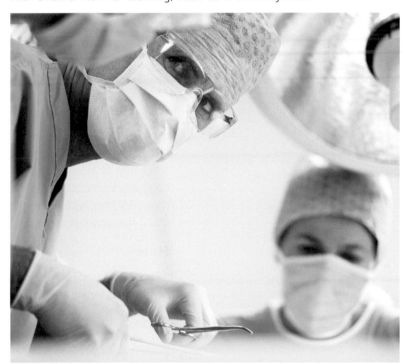

Some care settings require special uniforms to help reduce the risk of infection.

Gloves

Gloves should be worn only when having direct contact with a person or when dealing with blood, body fluids or items that could be contaminated by these. Wearing gloves when you do not need to can increase the risk of developing a latex allergy, as well as being an additional expense to the employer.

Aprons

Aprons should be placed over the uniform before undertaking activities involving blood, body fluids or liquids. Blue aprons should be used for food use only and white aprons should be used for all other activities. Once placed over the head, the apron should be secured by tying the waist ties behind the back. Aprons must be changed between patient contact.

Masks

If you need to use a mask, you should ensure that you do not touch the front of the mask during the donning process (the process of putting it on) as this may damage the mask's integrity. The mask should be used where there is a risk to the care worker of blood or body fluid aerosol. Most masks provide patients with some protection from airborne infections from the care worker reaching the patient, and this is why facemasks must never be worn round the neck, as the mask could harbour a large colony of bacteria from the care worker's respiratory tract. If the mask is worn round the neck between uses, there is the potential for the bacteria to spread.

Visors

Most non-disposable visors have an adjustable head strap so that the visor can be adjusted to ensure a comfortable fit for the wearer. Visors can also come attached to facemasks to provide full face protection from the risks of blood and body fluid aerosol.

Goggles

Goggles, like face visors, can protect the eyes from blood or body fluid splashes. Some goggles can be worn like glasses and have arms that fit around the ears; however, some people find this type of goggle uncomfortable as they can become loose and slide down the nose. Another type of goggle has an elasticated head strap which holds the goggles securely in place.

Hats

If hats/caps need to be worn, they should be securely fastened to the head by fastening the cap ties so that the hat fits tightly to the head.

Shoes

If special footwear is required, such as the type worn in ultraclean environments like operating theatres, then this should be provided by the employer and worn as required. These types of footwear also conform to antistatic regulations, which is extremely important when working in oxygen-rich environments.

5.2 Different types of PPE

Uniforms

In many care establishments, it is a requirement for staff to wear uniforms. Uniforms must be clean at the start of every shift and should be changed if they become soiled during the shift.

Gloves

There are many different types of gloves available on the market for care workers to use such as standard latex, nitrile and vinyl. Latex gloves are the most common gloves used within healthcare organisations, but as more people are becoming sensitive to latex and developing latex allergies, other gloves are becoming more popular. These include nitrile gloves, which come in a variety of colours and vinyl gloves.

Most gloves come in sterile and non-sterile packaging, depending on why they need to be used, and are available in small, medium and large sizes.

Gloves come in different sizes and are made from different materials.

Aprons

Plastic aprons can be placed over the uniform to help prevent the uniform from becoming soiled when performing activities such as personal care, toileting and wound care, and because plastic aprons are waterproof, they also provide protection when assisting people to have a bath or when handling body fluids.

Masks

These are disposable and come in three different types.

- The first is the most common type used and is made from paper. The mask forms a shield that may be pleated and has two ties for around the head and a flexible nose bridge.
- The second type of mask is similar to the first type but has ear loops instead of ties.
- The third type of mask has a moulded cup shape held in place by an elastic cord around the head.

Visors

Like facemasks, visors are not commonly used outside the clinical environment where they can be used to help protect the care worker from the risk of splashing from blood or body fluids.

Goggles

These can provide care workers with eye protection when dealing with blood or body fluids.

Hats/caps

Surgical hats can be either disposable or reusable. Disposable hats come in a range of colours and different sizes which can be adjusted to fit different size heads by securely fastening the ties at the back of the hat. Reusable hats are made from cotton material which can be laundered at high temperatures.

Shoes

Most care workers are required to wear sensible shoes that are not open-toed and do not have high heels. Within some clinical areas, special footwear may be required such as theatre shoes, clogs or boots; however, these types of footwear are only worn in specialist areas and you should follow your organisation's policy on footwear.

5.3 The reasons for use of PPE

Personal protective equipment is used to protect both care workers and the people receiving care. It is important to ensure that when using PPE, it is used correctly and for the purpose it was designed.

Uniforms are worn to reduce the risk of pathogenic organisms being transferred from the outside environment on the care worker's clothing to the patient, and to prevent any pathogenic organisms from the patient being transferred outside the care environment. This is why it is important not to go shopping in your work clothes.

Gloves form a physical barrier between the care worker's skin and all other surfaces including the patient's skin, blood and body fluids. Because gloves form a physical barrier, pathogenic organisms can not pass from one side to the other, so gloves provide protection for both the care worker and the person receiving care.

Like **gloves**, an apron also provides a physical barrier between the care worker and other surfaces, and provides similar protection. Blue aprons should only be used when undertaking activities involving food. White aprons should be used for all other activities; however, some organisations use red aprons for staff when working with patients who have highly infectious conditions.

Masks also form a barrier to protect healthcare workers from patients' blood or body fluid aerosols during surgical procedures, and in settings where bacteria or viruses may be present. The mask provides the patient with some limited protection, but to remain effective masks need to be changed regularly and must never be reused. The effectiveness of facemasks to prevent patients from acquiring infections is questionable, but they do provide some protection to staff.

Full face **visors** are another type of barrier protection and can be used when there is a risk to the care worker of blood or body fluid spray to their face and eyes.

The purpose of wearing **goggles** is to try to prevent blood or body fluids accidently getting splashed into the eyes.

Hats/caps are not commonly worn outside the operating theatre because research has shown that provided care workers keep their hair clean and tidy, the risk of infection is small.

It is important for shoes not to be open-toed, because this will reduce the risk of infection if blood or body fluids are spilt. It also provides the feet with some protection if an item is dropped on to them. In specific clinical areas it is important that the footwear is not worn outside that specific area, otherwise there is an increased risk of pathogenic organisms being carried back into the ultraclean environment on the soles of the shoes.

5.4 Current relevant regulations and legislation relating to PPE

There are legal duties and obligations in relation to PPE placed on employers. Under the Health and Safety at Work Act 1974, it is made clear that if items of PPE are required, then they must be provided free of charge by the employer; employees cannot be charged or be expected to contribute to the provision or maintenance of PPE required for them to carry out their work.

Under the Health and Safety at Work Act 1974, there are specific regulations which specifically address PPE. These regulations are:

- the Personal Protective Equipment at Work Regulations 2002
- the Management of Health and Safety at Work Regulations 1999
- the Control of Substances Hazardous to Health Regulations 2002 (COSHH)

These regulations ensure that where risks cannot be controlled by other means, then PPE is correctly selected and used. The Personal Protective Equipment at Work Regulations also place duties on employees to take reasonable steps to ensure that the PPE which is provided is used correctly and appropriately.

The Management of Heath and Safety at Work Regulations 1999 also relate to this area and require employers to identify and assess the risks to health and safety in the workplace. All risks must be minimised as far as reasonably possible. Where an activity involves a risk this could be minimised in a number of ways — one way is to wear PPE.

According to the Personal Protective Equipment at Work Regulations, PPE should be used as the 'last resort' to protect against risks to health and safety, and other control measures such as safe systems of work should be considered first. For example, after completing a risk assessment, employers should investigate if it is possible to do the job using methods that will reduce the risk of infection and will not require the use of PPE.

There are also regulations regarding the quality of PPE equipment and, since 1 July 1995, it has been a legal requirement that all new PPE must be CE marked. The CE mark certifies that the PPE has met the European Union (EU) consumer basic/minimum safety requirements.

5.5 Employees' responsibilities regarding the use of PPE

Section 7 of the Health and Safety at Work Act 1974 places a responsibility on employees to take reasonable care for their own health and safety and that of others who may be affected by their acts or omissions at work. This responsibility extends to PPE, which employees must wear to protect themselves and others, including patients. If an employee fails to wear PPE provided by the employer, they could be disciplined, unless it is proven that the PPE risks the health and safety of the employee, such as ill-fitting equipment.

Employees' specific responsibilities include:

- attending training provided by the employer relating to how to use PPE
- using PPE in accordance with the training
- taking reasonable care of all PPE provided by the employer
- returning PPE to the correct storage accommodation provided for it after use
- reporting to the employer any loss or obvious defect as soon as possible.

5.6 Employers' responsibilities regarding the use of PPE

Under the Health and Safety at Work Act 1974, employers have a general duty to ensure, as far as reasonably possible, the heath, safety and welfare at work of all employees. Employers also have a duty of care under the Personal Protective Equipment at Work Regulations 2002. These include the following requirements.

- Properly assessing the need for PPE and assessing PPE before it is used to ensure it is suitable. This will involve identifying the hazard and the types of PPE that could be used. For example, blood and body fluids splashes are hazards because there is a risk that these substances could get into the care worker's eye. The PPE options available are safety spectacles, goggles, visors or face-shields.
- Providing free PPE to employees. Employers cannot ask employees to pay for PPE; however, if an employee leaves and

does not return an item of PPE to the employer, the employer can deduct the cost of replacing the equipment from any wages owed, providing this information has been made clear in the contract of employment.

- Ensuring PPE is maintained and stored properly. Make sure equipment is well looked after and stored correctly. Maintenance may include: cleaning, examination, replacement, repair and testing. The wearer may be able to carry out simple maintenance (for example, cleaning), but more detailed repairs must be carried out by a competent person. All maintenance, repair and replacement cost are the responsibility of the employer.

- Providing employees with adequate information, instruction and/or training on its use. Training will include making sure that anyone using PPE is aware of why it is required, when it is to be used, repaired or replaced and its limitations. Employees must be trained to use the PPE properly and understand how to perform basic checks.

- Ensuring employees follow the training provide and that they use the PPE provided and fully investigate non-compliance.

(Source: Health and Safety Executive.)

5.7 The correct practice in the application and removal of PPE

To ensure the risk of infection and cross-infection are fully minimised, it is important that PPE is put on and removed correctly. Failing to remove contaminated PPE can result in infections spreading and defeats the purpose of using the equipment in the first place.

Uniforms

Uniforms should be fresh everyday and should be applied just before starting the shift, as this will help reduce the risk of pathogenic organisms from the outside environment being taken into the care setting. However, if you need to travel to work in your uniform, you should ensure that you keep your uniform covered with another item of clothing such as a coat, jacket or cardigan. Before putting on the uniform, you should ensure that you wash your hands and dry them thoroughly.

Uniforms should be removed at the end of the shift or after becoming contaminated with blood or body fluids. When removing a uniform, you should try to avoid touching the front of the uniform as much as possible, as this will reduce the risk of transferring pathogenic organisms from the uniform onto your skin. Once removed, the uniform should be placed in an appropriate place such as a laundry sack, until it can be taken away for laundering. Soiled uniforms should never be placed on the floor, as pathogenic organisms can be transferred from the uniform to the floor.

If you are required to launder your own uniform, you should be given instructions on the washing requirements which will normally involve washing at a temperature of at least 60°C and separately from your everyday clothes.

Remember to wash your hands after removing your uniform!

Gloves

Gloves should be applied to clean, dry hands. The gloves should be inspected before they are put on to straighten out folds and ensure there are no holes or tears. You should not blow into gloves before putting them on, because the moisture in your breath will help to provide a damp, warm environment for bacteria to breed. When putting on gloves, it is important to ensure that they are the correct size and that they fit properly. If you work in an environment where you need to wear a surgical gown, you may be taught the 'closed gloving technique', which will enable you to put sterile gloves on without touching the outside of the glove and pull the cuff of the glove over the cuff of the gown, so that the gown cuff ends up inside the cuff of the glove.

1. Check gloves before putting them on. Never use gloves with holes or tears. Check that they are not cracked or faded.

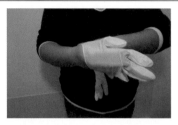

2. Pull gloves on, making sure that they fit properly. If you are wearing a gown, pull them over the cuffs.

3. Take them off by pulling from the cuff – this turns the glove inside out.

4. Pull off the second glove while still holding the first, so that the two gloves are folded together inside out.

5. Dispose of them in the correct waste disposal container and wash your hands.

When removing gloves, it is important to follow these important steps to reduce the risk of cross-infection.

- Grab the cuff of one glove with the opposite hand and pull down over the hand. This turns the glove inside out, so that the contaminated surface is away from you. Hold this glove in the hand which is still gloved.
- While still holding the removed glove, pull off the second glove by holding the cuff and pulling down over hand. While you do

this, you will wrap the first glove in the second glove and both gloves will be folded together with their contaminated surfaces facing inwards.

- Dispose of the gloves.
- Wash your hands.

Aprons

When putting on an apron, you should ensure you have washed and dried your hands before selecting the apron. The neck strap of the apron should then be placed over the head and the waist ties should be fastened behind the back. Once the apron has been secured, you can then put on your gloves and undertake the activity.

When removing an apron, it is important to reduce the risk of cross-infection by not touching the front of the apron. To remove the apron, you should pull at the neck strap and the waist strap until they snap, making sure that you keep hold of the apron so that it does not fall to the floor. The apron can then be scrunched up into a ball in your gloved hands. Once the apron is in a ball, it can be placed in one hand and the gloves can then be removed, as described on the previous page. The apron will end up securely enclosed in the gloves, which can then be disposed of.

Masks

Make sure your hands have been washed and thoroughly dried before selecting the mask. Once you have selected the mask, you can gently pull the mask open by pulling on the top and bottom of the mask from the middle, but remember not to touch the front of the mask. Place the mask over your face and gently squeeze the nose band area of the mask where it will sit on your nose. This will allow the mask to fit your nose better and will help to hold the mask in place while you tie it. You can tie the mask by grasping the top ties in your hands and pulling them behind your head. Then, gently but firmly, fasten the top ties behind your head, making sure they are tight enough to hold the mask in place. Fasten the bottom ties behind the back of your neck and make sure the mask feels secure. Finally, ensure the nose band is pressed firmly over the nose and make sure it feels comfortable before starting the activity.

When removing the mask, it is important not to touch the front of the mask and only handle the mask by the ties. The mask should be removed by untying the bottom tie then the top tie, and moving it away from your face by holding the ties. You can then dispose of the mask.

Visors

You should check the visor to ensure it is clean before placing it on your face. Once the visor has been placed on the head, you may be able to adjust the headband to ensure a more comfortable fit. If you are using a facemask with a fitted visor, you should fit the mask as described above.

When removing the visor, you should slide the visor up and away from your face. Once the visor has been removed, it should be cleaned and decontaminated as appropriate and then dried. Once the visor is thoroughly dried, it should be returned to the approved accommodation. If the visor is part of a disposable facemask, the mask should be removed and disposed of as described earlier.

Goggles

Like visors, goggles should be checked to ensure they are clean before they are placed on the face. Some goggles fit like spectacles, while others have a headband which can be adjusted to fit the head and around the eyes. The goggles should be adjusted so there is a firm seal around the eyes, but not too tight to be uncomfortable. Once the goggles have been removed, they must be cleaned and decontaminated as appropriate, and dried thoroughly. Once dried, the goggles should be returned to the approved accommodation.

Hats

According to most sources, theatre hats should be the first piece of clothing worn when preparing to enter the operating theatre department. Before selecting the correct size hat, hands should be washed and dried. The hat should be placed on the head, ensuring all the hair is covered. The hat can be secured into position by tying the hat at the back. Once the hat is ready to be removed, it can be pulled off the head by using the ties and disposed of.

Shoes

These should be the last item of clothing to put on because of the risk of cross-infection. Once shoes have been put on, hands should be washed and dried. Once removed, shoes should also be cleaned and decontaminated as required, not just left lying around!

5.8 The correct procedure for disposal of used PPE

Some PPE items such as uniforms, visors, goggles and footwear are non-disposable and should be cleaned, decontaminated, dried and stored in the appropriate accommodation ready for their next use. You will need to make sure that you are familiar with your organisation's policy for dealing with such items.

Masks, hats, gloves and aprons are all classed as clinical waste and are regarded as high-risk items; they should therefore be disposed of carefully to reduce the risk of cross-infection. This is regardless of whether the item has visible contamination or not. If clinical waste is generated in a person's own home, it still needs to be treated as clinical waste and must not be placed in domestic waste bags for household landfill sites.

The Hazardous Waste Regulations 2005 make it a legal requirement for organisations disposing of hazardous waste to be registered with the

Activity 7

Personal protective equipment

Different job roles and work environments will expose you to different infection risks. Your manager will have provided PPE to minimise some of these risks.

1. What PPE is available for you to wear in your workplace?
2. When should you wear this and how should it be used?
3. What are your responsibilities regarding using PPE?

Environment Agency. In 2006 the Department of Health Environment Agency introduced the Safe Management of Healthcare Waste, which incorporated a new European colour coding system for waste.

Colour	Waste
Orange	Infectious waste for alternative technology
Yellow	Infectious waste for incineration
Purple	Cytotoxic for incineration
Yellow/black	Offensive waste for suitably licensed facility
Black	As above for yellow/black

Table 1: It is your responsibility to find out what your workplace policy is for waste disposal and to follow the policy.

Activity 8

Your organisation's waste policy

Read the disposal of waste policy for your workplace.

Where should you dispose of gloves, aprons and masks?

Case study

Understanding the potential risk

Josh works as a care assistant at the Larks Residential Care Home for older people. Josh enjoys playing football and while playing a match last Sunday, he was involved in a nasty tackle and sustained a few cuts and grazes to his hands. One day, while on duty, Josh was asked to assist Mrs King to prepare for bed. She has poor mobility but manages with a walking frame. While Josh was assisting Mrs King into bed, she let go of her walking frame and misjudged the distance to the bed. She stumbled and fell to the floor, hitting her head as she did so.

Josh went to her assistance and noticed blood coming from her head; he put his hands into his pockets for his gloves and discovered that he has used them all. He decided Mrs King was of low risk, so grabbed a clean cloth and held it to her head. As he did this, a small amount of blood entered one of the cuts in his hands.

He summoned help and Mrs King was assisted back to bed. The incident was written in the incident book.

A few weeks later, Josh became unwell, developed a fever, had diarrhoea and vomiting, and generally felt he had flu-like symptoms. These lasted for a few days so he sought medical advice from his GP. Blood tests revealed that he had contracted Hepatitis recently. On investigation, it was discovered that he had contracted Hepatitis from Mrs King. He received a verbal warning for failing to comply with company policy.

1. How should have Josh dealt with this situation?
2. Was it right for Josh to be punished for being 'a good samaritan'?
3. Has Josh broken any laws?
4. Should Josh have known Mrs King was high risk and would this have made a difference?

Doing it well

Removing potentially infected PPE

- Avoid touching the contaminated surface.
- Remove the items before moving to the next patient.
- Place the items in the correct waste containers ready for collection.
- Decontaminate reusable equipment such as goggles and visors.
- Return decontaminated items to their correct storage accommodation.
- Inform your manager if any PPE is damaged or stock levels are low.

6. Understand the importance of good personal hygiene in the prevention and control of infections

6.1 Key principles of good personal hygiene

As a care worker, you are a role model and need to set a good example because you have a vital role to play in the prevention and control of infection; this starts with your own personal hygiene. You should ensure that you wash, shower or bathe and wear a clean uniform for work every day. Fingernails need particular attention because they can harbour bacteria, and you should ensure that they are kept short, clean and free from nail polish or false extensions.

Hair does not normally pose an infection risk if it is kept clean and should be washed on a regular basis. If you have long hair, it should be tied back away from your face and products such as hairspray should be avoided.

Jewellery should not be worn for work because items such as rings and watches can harbour bacteria and could scratch the patient. However, for some people it is unacceptable for them to remove their wedding ring, so most policies permit a single plain band ring. This should be the only exception and no other rings should be worn. Bracelets, necklaces, dangling earrings and facial piercings should also be removed to prevent the risk of cross-infection and to help prevent you from scratching the patient; it also makes you look professional!

You should take every opportunity to promote and encourage good personal hygiene for the people you provide care for. You should encourage people to wash their hands after toileting activities, and to wash every day. You should offer people the opportunity to bathe or shower, if it is appropriate to their condition.

Doing it well

Preparing for work

- Wash and ensure your face and hands are clean.
- Do not apply make-up too heavily, if you wear it.
- Ensure your uniform is clean.
- Check your nails are well trimmed, clean and free from polish.
- Keep your hair clean and, if it is long, tie it back.
- Remove jewellery, except for stud earrings and a plain-band wedding ring.

6.2 Good hand-washing technique

Hand-washing is the single most important aspect of the prevention and control of infection, yet it is still the most neglected practice undertaken by care workers. Poor and ineffective hand-washing can result in pathogenic organisms being transferred from one patient to another or from part of the patient to another, such as from an infected wound to a catheter site.

To reduce the risk of cross-infection, a good hand-washing technique is required because it is well known that effective hand-washing can significantly reduce the presence of pathogenic organisms on the hands.

It is easy to develop an effective hand-washing technique and dramatically reduce the spread of infection within the healthcare setting.

An effective hand-washing technique aims to remove dirt, organic material and pathogenic organisms such as those found in blood, faeces and respiratory secretions such as phlegm. The duration of the washing is extremely important because effective hand-washing involves both the physical action of rubbing the hands together and the chemical actions of the anti-microbial agent in the hand wash solution; hand-washing should not just be a quick rinse under the tap!

Once the hands have been washed, it is important that they are dried thoroughly with absorbent disposable paper towels, as the friction generated when drying is beneficial for removing any remaining bacteria on the hands. Hot air blowers and communal hand towels should be avoided as both these increase the risk of transferring pathogenic organisms back on to the hands.

6.3 The correct sequence for hand-washing

When washing your hands, it is important to have a sequenced, step-by-step approach to help reduce the risk of missing an area of skin. Before starting the hand-washing sequence, you must ensure you are fully prepared and have everything you need. Once you are ready to start, you should follow these steps.

1. Remove watches and rings.
2. Select the correct water temperature, as it needs to be comfortable enough for you to place your hands underneath without having to withdraw them because it is too hot or too cold.
3. Wet both hands.
4. Apply a full measure of hand wash solution, but not too much, and rub the palms of the hands together.

5. Rub one hand over the back of the other, remembering to rub in the spaces between the fingers.

6. Rub the finger tips together to clean the tips, the back and the front of the fingers.

7. Rub the finger tips in a circular motion against the palm of the opposite hand and then swap. If a wedding ring is being worn, pay attention to this area and ensure you wash under the ring.

8. Interlock the thumbs ensuring that the thumbs and the wrists have contact with the hand wash solution.

9. Once all the surface of the hands have been washed, ensure the hands are thoroughly rinsed to remove any soap residue, as this can make the skin sore and dry.

10. Depending on the type of hand-wash activity being undertaken, steps 4–9 may need to be repeated.

11. Turn taps off using the elbows or foot pedal; some modern taps turn on and off automatically when movement is detected by a motion sensor.

12. Thoroughly dry the hands on absorbent disposable paper towel.

See pages 213–214 for more on hand-washing.

6.4 When and why hand-washing should be carried out

Hand-washing activities must be performed regularly to help prevent and control the spread of infection, but there are certain times when it is recommended that care workers wash their hands. These are:

- before putting on a clean uniform or PPE
- before any **aseptic** procedure
- after patient contact
- after removing PPE
- after going to the toilet
- before handling food
- after finishing work.

Before washing your hands, you will need to consider the hand-washing method required for what you have just done or for what you are about to do. There are three types of hand-wash methods used within healthcare settings:

- routine hand-washing using soap
- disinfectant hand-washing using an anti-microbial agent
- aseptic hand-washing using a surgical scrub solution such as Hydrex or Betadine.

For example, if you have just assisted someone to the toilet and have removed your gloves, you will need to perform a routine hand-wash, but if you are going to assist during an invasive procedure such as cannulation, you will need to perform a disinfectant hand-wash.

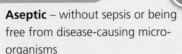

Key term

Aseptic – without sepsis or being free from disease-causing micro-organisms

Care workers who work in the community may not have access to soap and water to perform hand-washing activities. In situations such has these, you should use hygienic wipes to remove any physical debris from the hands and then apply an alcohol-based gel. Care workers working in the community should ensure that alcohol-based gel is applied prior to putting on and after removal of gloves. This should be done in front of the person being assisted, to help promote trust in the care profession.

6.5 Types of products that should be used for hand-washing

There are many different types of hand-wash solutions on the market and your employer will purchase the one which they believe best meets their requirements, but some general points to consider are discussed below.

General hand-washing soap

This type of soap is used for routine hand-washing and should be in a dispenser unit not a bar, because bars of soap harbour bacteria and can lead to the spread of infection. This type of soap has a minimal ability to destroy micro-organisms and is only useful for removing dirt, grease and loosely adhered micro-organisms.

Disinfectant hand-wash

Hand-wash solutions for disinfectant hand-washing procedures such as 2 per cent Chlorhexidine gluconate soap solution is commonly used in clinical areas for clinical purposes. It provides a significant residual activity and can be used for general and disinfectant hand-washing activities.

Surgical scrub solutions

Scrub solutions such as Povidone Iodine (Betadine) and 4 per cent Chlorhexidine gluconate (Hydrex) have a high residual activity and should only be used for aseptic procedures, as these solutions can lead to dry skin and irritations.

Alcohol gel

Hand gel containing 60–70 per cent alcohol kills 99.9 per cent of all bacteria and most gels contain moisturisers, emollients and skin protectors to help prevent the skin from drying out. These products are not a substitute for hand-washing, but can be used in the community where sinks and soap are unavailable immediately after direct patient contact. These gels are also effective in care environments and can be applied after routine hand-washing.

6.6 Correct procedures that relate to skincare

Maintaining healthy skin is an important step in the prevention and control of infection. However, constant washing and the wearing of gloves can cause the skin to dry out. To help prevent this, moisturising cream should be applied to the hands following routine hand-washing procedures. Gloves should not be worn when they are not required — for example, when completing paperwork. General skin care should also include ensuring any cuts or grazes are covered with an **occlusive** dressing prior to patient contact.

If you notice that your skin has started to become sore, you should report this to your manager, but you should not stop practising good hand hygiene practice. If the condition continues to worsen, you should contact your GP, who may refer you to a dermatologist for patch testing. Latex gloves are known to cause reactions, so close observation and reporting of any adverse reaction is extremely important. Any reaction to hand-wash solution, gel or after wearing gloves should also be recorded in an incident book or in accordance with workplace policy.

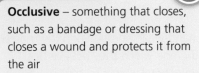

Key term

Occlusive – something that closes, such as a bandage or dressing that closes a wound and protects it from the air

Case study

Allergies to hand-wash products

Suzy works in a day procedure department at the local hospital. Her standards of care are very good and she always washes her hands between any patient contact. However, Suzy has recently noticed that the areas in between her fingers are becoming sore after wearing latex gloves, so she decides to stop wearing the gloves but continues to wash her hands between patient contact.

The sores on Suzy's hands do not improve and actually start to get worse. The skin between her fingers becomes itchy, has started to crack and weep fluid. Suzy decides to go and see her GP, who tells her that they think she has developed a contact dermatitis and refers her to a dermatologist. The dermatologist does a patch test and discovers that Suzy has an allergy to

Chlorhexidine, an anti-microbial agent used in some hand-wash products.

When Suzy returns to work, she explains what has happened to her manager, who asks her why she had not reported the symptoms sooner. Suzy's manager explains that there are alternative products available for Suzy to use and that these could have been used earlier if she had informed the trust sooner.

1. At what point should Suzy have informed her manager?
2. Was she right to stop using the latex gloves?
3. What risks do her hands pose to others?
4. Will Suzy be able to work in this acute setting and why?

Getting ready for assessment

LO1

This outcome requires you to demonstrate your knowledge of the responsibilities of employers and employees in relation to the prevention and control of infection to your assessor. You could demonstrate your knowledge by making a list of the employer's responsibilities and the employee's responsibilities.

LO2

For this outcome, your assessor will need to be satisfied that you know current legislation and policies relating to the prevention and control of infections. To demonstrate your knowledge, you could make a list of some key legislation and write a short account explaining how the legislation impacts on infection control. You could also read your workplace infection prevention and control policy and list the key points. There is no need to put a photocopy of the policy in your portfolio.

LO3

Your assessor will need you to demonstrate your knowledge of systems and procedures within your workplace that relate to the prevention and control of infection. This could include cleaning policies and procedures. To provide your assessor with this information, you could explain the cleaning regime adopted within your workplace and the role which you play. You also need to explain the potential impact an outbreak of infection could have on the person or the organisation. To help you to do this, you could look at newspaper articles about people who have suffered from MRSA or other infections; you may also find information on the Internet and discuss how the infection has changed their life. You could try to look at government papers to find out the potential cost to healthcare organisations when there are outbreaks of infections.

LO4

This outcome focuses on risk assessments and your assessor will want you to tell them what you think the term 'risk' means. They will want you to demonstrate an awareness of potential risks of infection within the workplace. You could do this my completing an infection audit, where you identify potential infection risks within your work area. The audit could be taken one step further by describing the steps carried out during a risk assessment. Finally, you could write a small report which explains why performing a thorough risk assessment is important.

LO5

This outcome will require your assessor observing you correctly selecting, putting on, removing and disposing of personal protective equipment (PPE). Your manager or a senior care worker may write a witness testimony to support the assessor's observation. You will also need to explain to the assessor why PPE needs to be worn and the responsibilities, relating to it. To do this you could list the PPE you are expected to use and explain the reasons for this. To describe responsibilities surrounding PPE, you could list your responsibilities and your manager's responsibilities or you could produce a poster or a spider diagram to show these responsibilities.

LO6

This outcome will require your assessor observing you washing your hands using an effective hand-washing technique. While you are washing your hands, you could explain to the assessor when you should perform hand-washing and describe each step of the procedure. You may also want to produce a hand-washing guide for a new member of staff. The guide could start by describing why personal hygiene is important for both staff and patient, and then list the times when hands should be washed, the products available to do this and the correct sequence for hand-washing. The guide good finish with some 'top tips' on hand health, where you can describe correct procedures for skincare, including any skincare products that could be applied to the hands.

Legislation

- Control of Substances Hazardous to Health Regulations (COSHH) 2002
- Food Safety Act 1990
- Hazardous Waste Regulations 2005
- Health and Safety at Work Act 1974
- Health and Social Care Act 2008
- Health Protection Agency Act 2004
- Management of Health and Safety at Work Regulations 1999
- NICE Guidelines 2 2003
- Personal Protective Equipment at Work Regulations 2002
- Public Health (Control of Diseases) Act 1984
- Public Health (Infectious Diseases) Regulations 1988
- Reporting of Injuries, Diseases and Dangerous Occurrences Regulations (RIDDOR) 1995

Further reading and research

- www.dh.gov.uk (Department of Health)
- www.hse.gov.uk (Health and Safety Executive)
- Serginson, E. and Torrance, C. (2004) *Surgical Nursing*, Bailliere Tindall
- Ayling, P. (2007) *Infection Prevention and Control*, Pearson Education

Unit HSC 2002

Provide support for mobility

Keeping mobile is extremely important for a person's health and for giving them a feeling of well-being. Keeping mobile through activities such as exercise has both physical and emotional benefits and can help to reduce the risks to health caused by immobility. You will need to know about how to maintain people's mobility, despite their age or infirmity, or the level of disability or difficulties they may experience. It is important that you are able to offer them encouragement and to help them to exercise to their maximum potential.

Mobility appliances help with walking and getting around, and can make a major difference to someone's life. Being able to stay mobile allows people to maintain their independence and avoid relying on human assistance. There is a world of difference between being able to go where you want, when you want to, even if you go there very slowly, and having to wait while someone else makes special arrangements.

In this unit you will learn about:

1. the importance of mobility
2. how to prepare for mobility activities
3. how to support individuals to keep mobile
4. how to observe, record and report on activities to support mobility.

1. Understand the importance of mobility

1.1 The definition of mobility

The term 'mobility' means different things to different people. For some people, mobility is being able to go out when they want to and where they want to. For others, mobility is being able to get from one place to another by any means to maintain their independence — for example, getting from the living room to the kitchen to make a cup of tea or going to the toilet on their own. Maintaining mobility is vital as people grow older. It can make the difference between an active old age and one spent sitting in a chair or shuffling around. Whatever mobility means to you, it is important that you check with people what mobility means for them.

1.2 How different health conditions may affect and be affected by mobility

There are many conditions that can affect a person's mobility as they become older and the joints of the body become worn. Not all mobility problems are caused by age; some people are born with health conditions that can affect their mobility. Mobility may also be affected following an accident or illness. Some people develop conditions that affect the muscles and ligaments connecting to bones, so they cannot move around easily. Some people may not be able to control their movements well, or the muscles may be too weak to support their weight.

Fractured bones

Throughout life, the bones in the body constantly change; this is because they are living structures that become damaged through everyday wear and tear. Most people's bones will repair themselves by growing new bone if they are damaged. If a bone is broken, it will probably need to be held in place, so that it mends in the right position, which might mean wearing an awkward plaster cast. It may take a while, but eventually the person will be back to normal, doing everything they did before. However, many older people, especially women, may suffer from **osteoporosis**, which can cause bones to break very easily and which may take longer to mend.

Arthritis

Arthritis is a painful condition where one or two joints become inflamed and swollen, become tender, warm to touch and painful on movement. There are two main types of arthritis:

- osteoarthritis
- rheumatoid arthritis.

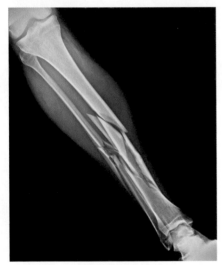

Activity 1

Considering mobility

Mobility can mean different thing to different people. Take a few moments to consider what mobility means to you, then ask your friends and colleagues what mobility means to them. Finally, ask somebody whom you support what mobility means to them. Are all your definitions the same? How would you define mobility?

Depending on age and health, broken bones may take longer to heal.

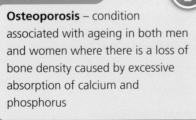

Key term

Osteoporosis – condition associated with ageing in both men and women where there is a loss of bone density caused by excessive absorption of calcium and phosphorus

Osteoarthritis is a degenerative condition where the cartilage covering the ends of the bone surfaces becomes worn and damaged. This may result in pain on movement because the bone surfaces may rub on each other. Joints commonly affected by osteoarthritis are the hip, knee and shoulder joints.

Rheumatoid arthritis commonly affects many smaller joints before affecting the larger joints, and results in varying degrees of deformity. The condition is also associated with muscle wasting at the joints. This condition does not only affect the joints, though, and many doctors now prefer to call it 'rheumatoid disease'.

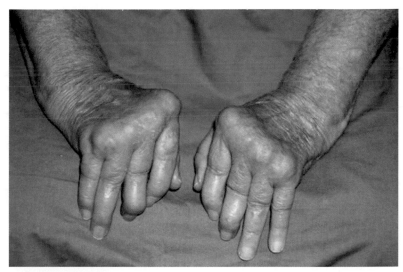

Severe arthritis of the hands can make it harder for a person to grip a walking stick or hold on to grab rails.

Cerebral palsy

Cerebral palsy is a condition that typically occurs at or shortly after birth, resulting in a range of mobility conditions ranging from clumsiness to severe muscle rigidity.

Muscular dystrophy

Muscular dystrophy presents in early childhood and is a muscle-wasting condition that results in loss of strength, increasing disability and deformity.

Stroke

A stroke is when the blood supply to part of the brain is cut off as a result of either a bleed or a clot leading to damage and/or death of brain tissue. As the brain controls everything the body does, damage to the brain will affect the body's functions. For example, if a stroke damages the part of the brain that controls how limbs move, mobility will be affected.

Multiple sclerosis

Multiple sclerosis (MS) is a progressive disease of the central nervous system where the protective sheath around the nerves, myelin, becomes damaged and interferes with the messages sent from the brain to the rest of the body. MS most commonly affects young adults. As the condition progresses people may experience mobility problems such as dizziness, muscle spasms and tremors.

Parkinson's disease

Parkinson's disease is an incurable disease which affects certain nerve cells in the brain. Damage of these cells can affect a person's mobility by causing tremors, slow movement and rigidity of the limbs.

Not all mobility problems are caused by age.

Amputation

Amputation of a limb can occur at any age for reasons such as disease or trauma from an accident. Amputation of a leg can make walking difficult, even with an artificial limb.

Operations

Operations can have a large impact on a person's mobility because of pain or because the patient may feel too frightened to move in case their stitches burst.

1.3 The effects that reduced mobility may have on an individual's well-being

People may have difficulty in moving around because of their age or health. Some people may not want to mobilise because it causes them pain or discomfort. However, sometimes a person's lack of mobility can cause other problems.

Effects of reduced mobility

Reduced mobility can lead to minor problems such as stiff, painful joints, weak muscles and weight gain from not being able to exercise. The effects of reduced mobility can create a vicious circle where it gets even harder to keep mobile and may lead to a person becoming immobile. Immobility can have serious implications and may cause other serious conditions such as **deep vein thrombosis** (DVT) or chest infections which can both be life-threatening.

> **Key term**
>
> **Deep vein thrombosis** (DVT) – a clot that forms in the deep veins of the body, usually the leg veins. If the clot moves it could get stuck in a blood vessel going to the lungs. If the clot is large enough, the patient could die

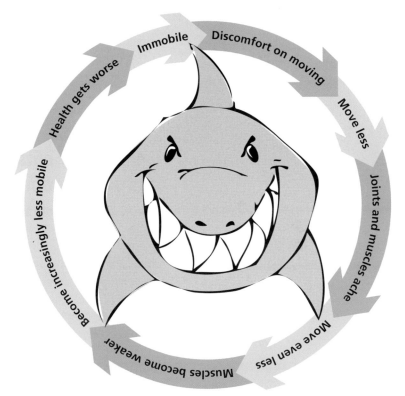

The more discomfort a person experiences, the less they want to move around. How might this create a vicious circle?

Whether you are employed in the health or social care sector, you will be required to work as part of the multidisciplinary team to help prevent people who have reduced or limited mobility from acquiring more serious conditions associated with immobility.

A mobility support plan should be completed for all patients with restricted mobility and any risks to the person should be identified. For example, risks from reduced mobility could include:

- chest infections
- urine infection
- swollen feet and ankles
- loss of independence
- wound infections
- pulmonary embolism
- deep vein thrombosis
- depression
- constipation
- pressure sores.

The person's mobility support plan should be followed and regular mobility activities completed to reduce the risks. These activities may include:

- getting out of bed and sitting in a chair
- regular turning of a patient who is unable to turn themselves
- use of specialised equipment such as triple wave pressure-relieving mattresses, surgical stockings and electronic or pneumatic calf stimulators
- gentle breathing exercises
- encouragement.

1.4 The benefits of maintaining and improving mobility

Properly designed mobility activities can have a range of benefits for people, both physically and psychologically. For example, if people are encouraged to undertake everyday activities such as getting up from a chair, walking across a room, washing, dressing, and going up and down stairs, they are more likely to keep their joints supple and less likely to become dependent on others. This is why it is important to encourage people to be as mobile as possible within the limits of their physical condition. People who have undergone surgical procedures also need to be encouraged to become mobile as quickly as possible following surgery, to reduce the risk of acquiring infections and to regain their independence.

Maintaining mobility does not have to mean a specially designed exercise programme; just remaining active will help. Moving around the house, preparing a meal or taking a walk are all valid forms of exercise which, as a care worker, you must encourage people to try to maintain. Maintaining their mobility can also help people to maintain their independence.

Improved social life

A person who is in pain may not want to talk very much. This can stop them from making friends and they may become lonely. Encouraging people to take part in fun mobility activities will help them to enjoy themselves. Working as a group may help people to talk with each other, and to develop friendships.

Disability does not have to mean no mobility. If a person feels healthy and is not in pain, then gentle exercise can help them to feel good about themselves. They may want to do more for themselves which will give them more independence. Being as independent as possible makes people feel good, as they will not feel a burden to others.

Some mobility activities such as exercise can be part of a formal programme which has been assessed by a physiotherapist, or it could be a specific form of exercise designed to increase mobility or to improve strength, stamina or suppleness. But more importantly, mobility activities should include the simple day-to-day activities that everyone carries out which involve some form of physical movement.

At its simplest, exercise is the contraction and relaxation of muscles in order to produce movement. These muscle movements use energy and raise the heart rate and breathing rate. These increased heart and breathing rates strengthen the cardiovascular system, while the movement itself tones and strengthens the muscles.

Case study

A healthy lifestyle

Strawberry Mill is a hostel for people with mental health problems. The effects of medication and the previous lifestyles of several residents have contributed to the fact that most of the residents (and staff) are unfit. At a house meeting, it was decided to start a fitness programme. The residents decided to call it 'Best Foot Forward'. It was decided to hold an exercise class every other evening, with a basic exercise video for everyone to follow. They also decided that everyone would walk to the shops instead of getting a lift or using the bus for just two stops, and that there would be a rota for taking the hostel dog for a walk, instead of leaving it to the officer in charge! Some residents also decided they would try to stop smoking and stop eating so many sweets and chocolates.

1. What would you expect to be the results of this programme?
2. What other activities could the group try?
3. How can they keep motivated to carry on?
4. What other benefits may come from this programme?

Maintaining and improving mobility can have many benefits, both physically and psychologically, including:

- more flexible joints
- better breathing
- reduced risk of infection
- improved cardiovascular system
- stronger muscles
- improved social life
- independence
- more confidence
- improved self-esteem
- less pain
- reduced embarrassment.

2. Be able to prepare for mobility activities

2.1 Agreeing mobility activities with the individual and others

When agreeing mobility activities with people, it is important to remember that they may already have a programme which has been devised by a physiotherapist, or another specialist such as an occupational therapist or even a doctor, to meet a specific outcome. If this is the case, the activity must be carried out exactly as it has been planned.

You must ensure that:

- the mobility activity is detailed in the plan of support and that it is followed accurately
- the person is given encouragement and support to follow the programme
- progress is carefully recorded, and achievement is recognised and celebrated
- any problems are immediately reported to your manager and to the professional who designed the programme.

If you are assisting a person to follow a programme designed by a physiotherapist, your role may be quite clearly defined. There may be times when you need to lend physical assistance or you may be required to assist in the case of exercise aids which are used as part of the programme. For example, someone who has had a stroke may be squeezing a rubber ball in their hand in order to strengthen the arm and hand muscles on one side of the body. Your job may be to count the number of repetitions of an exercise.

However, if you are simply trying to persuade someone to be more active by encouraging them to move from one room to another, or to start to mobilise following surgery, you will need to work with them to identify and agree the best ways they can keep mobile. You should encourage them to communicate their preferences about keeping mobile with other family members, friends and care professionals such as your line manager, fellow care workers and physiotherapists. You should also record this information on the support plan.

2.2 Removing or minimising hazards in the environment before a mobility activity

Before starting a mobility activity, you must ensure that a person can undertake the activity in a safe environment, and that a risk assessment has been carried out in relation to the activity and the person.

Doing it well

Risk assessments for activities

This will include checking:

- that the floor surfaces are safe and dry to reduce the risk of falls
- that there is nothing that can be tripped over or that could cause injury
- what support, if any, a person will need
- how many professional carers need to be involved with the activity
- the actions to be taken in an emergency.

If the activity is being carried out by a person sitting in a wheelchair, check that:

- the wheelchair is absolutely stable and steady
- the brakes are firmly on.

If the activity is being carried out by someone in bed, check that:

- it is stable and steady
- the bed brakes are firmly on.

If the activity is being carried out by someone following surgery, check that:

- catheter bags and drains are off the floor and out of the way of the patient's feet
- drip stands are stable, steady and free moving.

If the activity is being carried out by a person using a walking aid, check that:

- the aid is being used properly
- the aid has been measured correctly to make sure it is the correct size.

2.3 The suitability of an individual's clothing and footwear for safety and mobility

The clothes that a person wears must be appropriate for the activity they are about to undertake. It is no coincidence that the tracksuits and trainers worn by athletes for many years have now been adopted as regular wear by people relaxing or taking part in leisure exercise, as they are so comfortable and easy to wear.

Reflect

Think about how you make your work environment safe before undertaking mobility activities with the people you help to support. What do you do if you notice something is wrong or unsafe?

This type of clothing may be suitable for all kinds of people undertaking mobility activities. You will need to make sure that shoes are firm, comfortable and offer support, and that any exercise which involves standing or moving the feet is not carried out in loose or ill-fitting shoes or slippers, but in firm, well-fitting, well-supporting shoes with safe, non-slip soles. The correct clothing also helps to maintain people's dignity, as they need not fear that the exercise will involve them in exposing parts of themselves which they would rather keep covered!

2.4 The safety and cleanliness of mobility equipment and appliances

There are particular ways of using the various mobility appliances in order to get the maximum benefit from them. It is important that you ensure that people are using them in the correct way, because otherwise they are likely to cause injury or discomfort.

It is also important to explain to people how different floor surfaces and floor coverings affect the use and safety of appliances. Make sure that you check the risk assessment which will have been carried out in relation to the person and the use of the appliance. This will have been recorded in their support plan, and you should always make sure that the person is using the appliance in accordance with the risk assessment.

It is also very important to remember that each appliance should be cleansed with the appropriate cleansing agent to minimise the chances of cross-infection between use.

Walking sticks

Measuring a walking stick

To measure a stick correctly, you need to ask the person to hold it in the hand which is opposite to their 'bad side', if they have one. If the weakness or pain is not located in a particular side of the body but is more general, for instance spinal problems, the person should use the stick on the side of the body which they would normally use most – the right-hand side for right-handers, the left-hand for left-handed people.

You should ensure that the person's hand is at the same height as the top of their thigh when it is resting on the stick handle. The elbow should be slightly bent, but make sure that the shoulders are level and that one side is not pushed higher.

With an adjustable metal stick, you will be able to measure fairly easily by sliding the inner part of the stick up and down until the correct height is reached. The metal button will then snap into place in the guide holes.

With a wooden walking stick, you will need to measure the correct height and then the person responsible should saw the stick to the proper length, making sure that the rubber ferrule is firmly attached to the bottom of the stick. It is important that you check that the ferrule is in good condition because if it becomes worn or the suction ridges have become smooth, the stick is likely to slip when leaned on.

Do you check the safety and cleanliness of mobility equipment and appliances on a regular basis?

Key term

Ferrule – rubber foot on the bottom of a walking frame or stick

Quadrupeds or tripods

A quadruped should only be used for a person who has considerable difficulty in walking on one particular leg, either because of hip or knee degeneration or a stroke. It is not an appropriate aid for somebody who is generally unsteady.

Measuring a quadruped or tripod is exactly the same procedure as measuring a walking stick. Quadrupeds are made from metal and are adjustable. You should check that the three or four small ferrules, which are on the suction feet, are safe and not worn.

Walking frames

A person should be provided with a walking frame when they need considerable support from one or two care workers and are no longer steady on a walking stick or quadruped.

Measuring a walking frame

Walking frames are measured in the same way as walking sticks. They are usually adjustable in height between 28 and 36 inches (71 and 91 cm), although they do come in different sizes with a range of 3–4 inches (8–10 cm) alteration within each frame.

To reach the correct height, the person should stand against the frame, holding it and leaning slightly forward. The feet should be level with the back legs of the frame and the arms only slightly bent.

If a walking frame is too small, you will see the person hunched forward at the frame. If the elbows are very bent and the shoulders are hunched up, the frame is too tall.

You will also need to check that the ferrules are in good condition on each leg.

Functional skills

Maths: Analysing and interpreting

Measure the height of a person you support and calculate the height needed for their walking frame. Carry out this activity for a number of people and document your findings in an organised way. Use a minimum of five sets of calculations to work out the mean and range of the frames required for people in your workplace.

Putting yourself in someone else's shoes

Imagine you are a recipient of care. For example, you might be in hospital with a broken leg. Imagine the care team do everything for you: they wash you, place you on a bedpan when you want to go to the toilet, choose your meals, tell you what time to turn the light off and what time to go to sleep.

1. How would you feel about not being offered any choice?
2. How would you want to be treated?

3. Be able to support individuals to keep mobile

3.1 Promoting active participation during a mobility activity

Active participation is a way of working that recognises a person as an active partner in their own care or support, rather than just a passive recipient of care. It puts the person at the centre of their care and involves them in decisions taken about them. Before active participation, many users of care services felt that they were not being listened to and that paperwork was more important than the person.

An important aspect of active participation is to listen to what users of a service want and responding to their needs. People who use care services should not have their needs come second place to the needs of the service provider.

As a care worker, it is important to promote active participation throughout everything you do, including mobility activities. This can be achieved by offering people choice about the type of mobility activity they would like to be involved in, where they want to do the activity and at what time.

3.2 Assisting an individual to use mobility appliances correctly and safely

Mobility appliances will be recommended by an appropriate professional, either a physiotherapist or occupational therapist. This professional will have explained to the person how the appliances are to be used, and there will have been an opportunity to try them under supervision. However, you will need to reinforce the advice and continue to support people until they are confident and are using appliances correctly.

Using a walking stick

Depending on how much support a person needs, there are two generally recommended ways of using a walking stick. The method for a person who needs a considerable degree of support is as follows.

1. Move the stick forward, slightly to one side.
2. Take a step with the opposite foot, going no further forward than the level of the stick.
3. Take a step with the foot on the same side as the stick. This should go past the position of the stick. Then move the stick again so that it is in front of you, and repeat the sequence.

For a person who needs less support – for example, if they are just using a stick because of lack of confidence or are just generally a little unsteady – move the stick and the opposite leg forward at the same time. Then move the leg on the stick side forward past the stick. Repeat the sequence.

For a person who needs considerable support, walking with a walking stick may require some practice. You may find that there is a natural progression in people who are improving their mobility and that, as they get better, they will automatically begin to move their leg and the stick at the same time. They should be encouraged to do so.

If you need to provide physical support for somebody who is walking with a stick, you should give it from behind and you should support with one hand on each side of the pelvis, just below the person's waist.

If you find that you need to offer this kind of help on a regular basis, you should consider suggesting an increase in the degree of walking support the person is offered. It is far better for them to have a more supportive walking aid than to rely on help from a care worker.

Using a quadruped

The quadruped should be held in the opposite hand to the person's 'bad side'.

Move the quadruped forward, and then take a step with the opposite foot. Then take a step with the foot on the same side as the quadruped so that it is either at the same level or slightly in front of the quadruped, and then repeat.

If you find that someone's condition is improving and they have started to put the quadruped and the opposite leg forward together, rather than after each other, then they should be moved on to a walking stick, as the support offered by a quadruped is no longer needed.

Using a walking frame

It is important that a person follows the proper pattern of walking in order to get the maximum benefit from a walking frame. If there are difficulties, or if the person uses a frame in the wrong way, it can be quite dangerous and may cause a fall or other injuries.

Put the frame forward so that the person can lean on it with arms almost at full stretch. They should then take a step forward – if they have a 'bad side', step first with that leg; if not, then either leg.

The next step should be taken with the other leg walking past the first leg. Repeat the sequence.

It is essential that you ensure that the frame has all four feet on the ground at any point when the person is taking a step.

Offer additional assistance if it is needed. It should be offered from behind the person, as giving assistance under one arm is not possible when a person is using a walking frame.

A walking frame with wheels is also available in various styles. This means that the walking pattern is not interrupted in the way it is with an ordinary walking frame. This is very useful for people who are too confused to be able to cope with learning the walking pattern for an ordinary walking frame. It is also useful for people who have particular arm or shoulder problems, which mean they cannot lift a frame. The assessment of the suitable height for a frame with wheels is carried out in exactly the same way as for an ordinary walking frame.

Wheelchairs

Where an assessment has been made that a person requires a wheelchair, they are entitled to have a wheelchair of their own which will be correctly measured and assessed by a physiotherapist. Wheelchairs come in a range of sizes and styles. They include chairs which have to be pushed, chairs which people can propel themselves and electric wheelchairs. Many younger people with disabilities have very clear views about the types of wheelchair they will use, the amount of equipment and additions that they have on their wheelchair, the colours they are decorated in and the speed at which they travel around in them! Regardless of age, a person's choice of wheelchair style must be respected.

A person's choice of wheelchair style must always be respected!

Mobility scooters

Many people who want to be able to get out and about, but have mobility problems when outdoors, can use powered scooters to get around. Most large shopping centres have a 'shopmobility' centre where powered scooters can be borrowed or rented to make shopping easier. Similarly, many theme parks and large public attractions offer scooter facilities. Scooters can be very useful in supporting people in maintaining their independence and their ability to make local journeys without assistance.

The use of wheelchairs should not be seen as negative. Many people with disabilities have described how getting a wheelchair has increased their mobility to such a great extent that their lives have been significantly improved. They progressed from slow, painful movements with walking sticks, where everything was a tremendous effort, to suddenly being able to move themselves around al will.

The biggest problems experienced by wheelchair users are the result of other people's attitudes to them and the limited access available to most buildings. However, the Disability Discrimination Act 1995 does make it a requirement of all public buildings to be accessible to anyone who wants to use them, and this includes people with any type of disability. The Act adds the phrase 'where it is reasonable to do so', and so this will not be universal. But a large number of buildings have become more accessible than they have been, and all new buildings have to be accessible to all.

Activity 4

Wheelchair users

Wheelchair users can often find it difficult to access all the buildings they would like to. Look around the local area where you live.

1. How accessible are the buildings for users of wheelchairs?
2. Would making reasonable adjustments to these building improve accessibility?
3. Can you suggest how these buildings could be improved?

You could discuss your findings with wheelchair uses to see if they have experienced problems accessing the buildings you have identified.

3.3 Feedback and encouragement to the individual during mobility activities

One of the most significant factors which affects how well people carry out mobility activities is whether they feel confident. Supportive feedback and encouragement can play a major part in helping to build people's confidence.

Feedback to people undertaking mobility activities should be given during and after the activity. The feedback should be constructive and should identify how the person could improve the activity. For example, if a person is not using their walking stick correctly, then you need to provide feedback to them explaining how to improve the activity next time. However, you must ensure that you do not alter any aspect of the person's mobility plan. Giving constructive feedback and encouragement can promote people's confidence, and their dignity.

It may not be necessary for you to assist a person physically in order to give them support; it may be sufficient for you simply to be there offering verbal support and encouragement as they carry out the mobility activity. Your support and encouragement could range from going along to the local gym to support a person from your setting who plays in a wheelchair basketball team, to giving words of encouragement to someone following a stroke who is lying in bed trying to raise an arm by 2 or 3 inches.

If someone is having problems following the exercises they have been set because they are too difficult, too strenuous or are causing discomfort, you must report this immediately to the physiotherapist or to your supervisor.

Never advise anyone to do an exercise in a different way, even though it may seem to you that, if they simply moved a little to the left or to the right, or did it a little bit differently, it would be easier and less painful. You should never make such a suggestion, as you could cause injury, or further discomfort or pain to the person. Any difficulties should be reported to the professional who prepared the programme.

4. Be able to observe, record and report on activities to support mobility

4.1 Monitoring changes and responses during a mobility activity

It is essential that you regularly check the progress of anyone who is using any type of mobility aid or following an activity plan. You should never assume that any condition will remain static – just because somebody was walking well with a frame or a stick when it was given to them does not mean that it is still the most appropriate mobility aid for the person to use.

Whether a person is following a mobility plan or just attempting to improve their mobility, it is important to observe them and monitor for any changes in their mobility. The mobility support plan should state how progress will be monitored and it should identify the person's mobility goal. For example, if someone has begun to regain confidence or had a mobility aid as a temporary measure while recovering from an illness or injury, you should encourage them to move away from dependence on the aid as soon as possible.

If someone has been using a wheelchair temporarily following illness, you should encourage them with daily exercises to increase their mobility and stop the use of a wheelchair as soon as possible. If the use of the wheelchair is permanent, you should still record and monitor the progress of its use to ensure that there are no problems and the user is coping with adjusting to using the wheelchair.

4.2 Recording observations of mobility activity

Recording a person's progress on a mobility activity is important. The physiotherapist or other care professionals will want to regularly review the progress that is being made so that they can change and update the programme as necessary. Observations of mobility activities need to be detailed and kept up to date. You should take careful notes about how many times an activity or exercise has been repeated and whether there is any evidence that flexibility, suppleness or strength is improving as a result. If the aim is for the person to become generally more active, you should regularly note in their records the differences that a more active approach is making to their general level of fitness, alertness and mobility.

Reflect

Information contained in people's records needs to be accurate and kept as up to date as possible. Think about people that you complete mobility records for. What records do you complete and what information do you include?

Functional skills

English: Writing

Information in records needs to be presented in a logical sequence, using language that is fit for purpose. You need to write your report in a concise and factual way, and proofread it.

4.3 Progress and/or problems relating to the mobility activity including choice of activities, equipment, appliances and the support provided

Once a person's progress on mobility activities has been monitored and recorded, it is important to report any progress or problems to an appropriate person. This person may be your line manager or a care professional.

Doing it well

Reporting progress on people's mobility

- Ensure the report is factual based on what you have seen and what the person has told you.
- Include information about how well the person is doing with the planned activities and any improvement in their mobility or ability to cope with the activities.
- Be aware of any particular difficulty a person is having in using a mobility aid, and you should report any of those problems immediately. It could be that a reassessment will be needed and a different type or size of aid will need to be provided.
- Report any problems like shortness of breath, dizziness or pain following mobility activities without delay.

You may be required to report your findings in the person's mobility support plan; however, if there has been a problem with a piece of equipment or a mobility appliance, you may need to complete an incident form, especially if the person suffered from a fall as a result of faulty equipment. This is a legal requirement under the Reporting of Injuries, Diseases and Dangerous Occurrences Regulations 1995, which is part of the Health and Safety at Work Act 1974. If you notice any signs of damage or wear, you must immediately stop the person from using the aid. Report the fault at once and make arrangements for a replacement or repair.

Getting ready for assessment

LO1

Maintaining and improving mobility have a number of benefits to people. To show your assessor that you understand the benefits of mobility, you could draw a spider diagram to identify the possible benefits for people from the setting where you work. You could then write an account that describes the benefits you have identified in the spider diagram. Remember to maintain confidentiality.

LO2

For this learning outcome, you need to demonstrate to your assessor that you are able to prepare for mobility activities. To help you prepare for this assessment, think about the people you support. What mobility activities do you help them prepare for? How do you agree the mobility activity and how much support will you give? How do you ensure that the environment and mobility equipment and appliances are safe? You could reflect on the last time you prepared for a mobility activity and write an account for your assessor. You could also ask your line manager or other health professional, such as a physiotherapist, to write a witness testimony to support your account.

LO3

There is a variety of ways that you can use to support people during mobility activities. Your assessor will want to see that you are able to support people to keep mobile. To help prepare for this, you could produce a workplace guide on how to support people to keep mobile. You could also ask your line manager or a senior member of staff to write a testimony to support your knowledge.

LO4

This outcome requires you to be able to observe, record and report on activities to support mobility. You will need to show your assessor how you monitor, record and report your findings on mobility activities undertaken by people. You can prepare for assessment by identifying the records and reports that you complete for people so you can show your assessor. You do not need to photocopy these documents, as the assessor will be able to see them, although they should not read the confidential information contained within the report. You could write an account about how information contained within is used by the care team to review a person's care.

Legislation

- Disability Discrimination Act 1995
- Health and Safety at Work Act 1974
- Reporting of Injuries, Diseases and Dangerous Occurrences Regulations 1995

Further reading and research

- www.gscc.org.uk (General Social Care Council (GSCC))
- www.hse.gov.uk (Health and Safety Executive)
- www.mssociety.org.uk (Multiple Sclerosis Society)
- www.parkinsons.org.uk (Parkinson's UK)
- www.scope.org.uk (Scope)
- www.stroke.org.uk (The Stroke Association)

Unit HSC 2003

Provide support to manage pain and discomfort

In this unit you will learn about why people who you support may experience pain and discomfort. There are many reasons for this – every person is different in what they feel and how they would prefer to manage pain. You will learn how to support a person using an individualised and holistic approach to help to reduce their pain and discomfort.

The person's pain can change, so it is important that you know how to keep an eye on this.

In this unit you will learn about:

1. **approaches to managing pain and discomfort**
2. **how to assist in minimising individuals' pain or discomfort**
3. **how to monitor, record and report on the management of individuals' pain or discomfort.**

1. Understand approaches to managing pain and discomfort

1.1 The importance of a holistic approach to managing pain and discomfort

Pain is basically whatever the person who is suffering it feels it to be. Physical pain can be experienced as a result of disease or injury, or some other form of bodily distress. Childbirth, for example, is not associated with injury or disease, but can nevertheless be an extremely painful experience that is different for everyone who gives birth. But pain is not only physical; it can also be social, emotional and spiritual. It is therefore important that we consider areas other than physical pain and have a **holistic** approach.

Pain is caused by the transmission of the sensation of pain from the site of the injury, disease or stress along a pain pathway. It is transmitted through sensory nerve endings along nerve fibres to the top of the spinal cord and into the brain. There are thought to be different routes for pain pathways for acute pain, caused by an immediate injury, disease, inflammation or illness, and for chronic pain, which is long-standing and continuous.

The feelings linked with these types of pain are often described very differently. Acute pain may be described as a stabbing or pricking sensation, whereas chronic pain is more likely to be described as a burning sensation and is perhaps quite difficult to locate in one particular spot. Acute pain serves an essential purpose — it is the body's warning system that something is wrong or that there is an injury. But there is often no obvious purpose to chronic pain. It frequently cannot be cured; it can only be treated so that its effects are reduced as much as possible.

Emotions play a huge part in the experience of pain. If someone is afraid or tense, or has no knowledge of what is wrong, they are likely to experience more pain than someone who is relaxed and knows exactly what the cause of their pain is. Sometimes the fear of pain can make it worse; it can cause additional pain through anticipation. This is commonly seen in a person who has an illness or injury in which movement is extremely painful, and they react in anticipation of being moved. Social pain may also be evident — for example, if the person who is ill worries about paying bills and supporting their family, especially if their illness is long term. Spiritually, the person may feel guilt, regret and anger; this can be particularly difficult for the care worker to help to support a person suffering such emotions. Chaplains and other specialists can help spiritually, but care workers can also give vital support by using their effective communication skills and by just being there. It may be useful for care workers to have training in supporting people emotionally and spiritually.

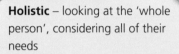

Key term

Holistic – looking at the 'whole person', considering all of their needs

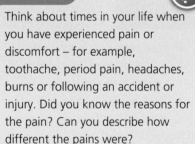

Reflect

Think about times in your life when you have experienced pain or discomfort – for example, toothache, period pain, headaches, burns or following an accident or injury. Did you know the reasons for the pain? Can you describe how different the pains were?

Case study

Supporting a person with different types of pain

Ferdik is Czechoslovakian. He works for a small local builder to support his wife and three children. Ferdik does not get paid from his employer if he does not work; he gets a reduced amount of money from the government for sick pay. He finds it difficult sometimes to express what he means, because his English speaking skills are limited.

Ferdik began to have abdominal pains and he was told he had **appendicitis**; he was admitted to hospital and had an emergency **appendectomy**. He was extremely frightened because things happened very quickly and at times he was not sure what was going on. After the operation, Ferdik experienced a lot of physical pain, he

was incontinent of urine and the sheets needed to be changed; this was very uncomfortable for him.

Because of the physical nature of Ferdik's job, it was clear that he would not be able to go back to work for some time. At times he appeared very quiet and frightened.

1. How could the care workers support Ferdik when changing his sheets to minimise the physical pain?
2. What other pain do you think that Ferdik was experiencing?
3. How can care workers support the holistic needs of people who suffer pain and discomfort?

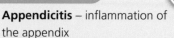

Key terms

Appendicitis – inflammation of the appendix

Appendectomy – surgical removal of the appendix

Palliative care – care that relieves symptoms, but does not cure

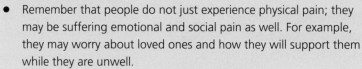

Doing it well

Supporting people with emotional and social pain

- Remember that people do not just experience physical pain; they may be suffering emotional and social pain as well. For example, they may worry about loved ones and how they will support them while they are unwell.
- Support people holistically by using effective communication skills, verbal and non-verbal, including active listening to help to support the person.
- Appropriate use of touch especially if a person is unable to communicate verbally can be very reassuring for them.

Having a personalised and holistic approach to a person's pain and discomfort needs good teamwork. For example, nurses and care workers may be able to help to support the person with physical pain, but support from the **palliative care** team or chaplain may contribute to the spiritual and emotional aspects. It must be remembered that the person themselves should be central to the assessment, choices, treatment and review.

1.2 Different approaches to alleviate pain and minimise discomfort

Before you use any equipment to alleviate pain, or undertake any moving or changing of positions, it is essential that you take note of the risk assessment your employer will have carried out in relation to use of any equipment. You must also carry out a risk assessment for the particular person before any movements or the use of any equipment. Even simple methods of alleviating discomfort, such as hot-water bottles, are not without risk, so it is vital that you protect the person and yourself by following the correct procedures and taking all necessary precautions.

The types of approaches to pain which are known to be effective are:

- drugs
- physical methods
- self-help methods
- alternative therapies.

Drugs

Drugs used for pain relief are classified as:

- analgesics (for example, aspirin, paracetamol)
- opiates (for example, morphine, heroin)
- anti-inflammatories (for example, ibuprofen)
- anaesthetic blocks (for example, epidural).

Drugs which are supplied on medical prescription for the relief of pain are likely to be **analgesics** or, in more extreme cases of severe or prolonged pain, may be opiates.

If additional pain relief is requested, you must refer this to your supervisor and through them to a medical practitioner who is able to prescribe additional drugs if necessary.

Physical methods

Physical methods of pain relief include:

- massage (superficial or pressure)
- vibration
- ice application (with massage)
- superficial heat or cold
- transcutaneous electrical nerve stimulation (TENS)
- transcutaneous spinal electroanalgesia (TSE)
- repositioning.

Self-help methods

Self-help methods of pain relief that have been found to be effective include:

- moving or walking about, if this is possible
- imagining oneself in a pleasant place and in comfort
- taking a warm bath
- taking some recommended exercise
- finding a task to distract from the pain
- having a conversation.

Alternative therapies

Often people get relief from having a massage or from using aromatherapy oils. The practice of reflexology can be a useful way of relieving pain, and many agencies and care settings have experts who visit on a regular basis to offer services like this.

Alternative therapies are increasingly being accepted by practitioners of mainstream Western medicine as having a valuable role to play in the reduction of pain and the improvement of general well-being.

Alternative therapies include:

- **aromatherapy** – the use of natural oils
- **homeopathic medicine**, which works by treating the illness or disease with minute quantities of naturally occurring substances which would cause the illness if taken in larger amounts – these may not be used in some care settings
- **reflexology** – specialised foot massage to stimulate particular areas of the feet which are said to be linked to parts of the body
- **acupuncture** – like the other treatments, this must be administered by an expert; it uses ancient Chinese medical knowledge about specific points in the body which respond to being stimulated by very fine needles, and is now being increasingly recognised by Western medicine and becoming available from the National Health Service in many places
- **yoga and meditation** – these work essentially on the emotional component of pain. Meditation works by dealing with the mental response to pain, whereas yoga combines both mind and body in an exercise and relaxation programme. Relaxation can often be a

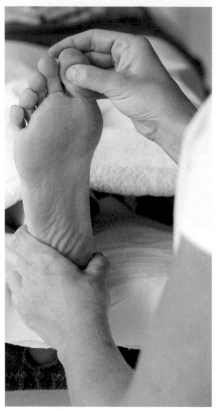

Do you know anyone who has found reflexology, aromatherapy or massage a useful relaxing technique?

key to relieving discomfort and to helping people cope. Pain is increased by muscles which are tense, so when people are able to find a relaxation technique that they can use when necessary, this can be extremely beneficial.

Alternative therapies should be used only where care professionals are in agreement that they may be used with a particular person.

Some people may prefer to use home remedies which have been used in their family for many years. This could be something like a hot drink or soup which is made in a particular way. Others may prefer to use alcohol or other drugs, such as cannabis, which is known to provide relief in some conditions and can be prescribed in specific circumstances. Requests for these forms of pain relief should be referred to your supervisor in the first instance.

Most methods of pain relief are not curative — they are not treatments or cures for any particular illness, disease or injury. They are palliative — they provide relief from the symptoms without curing the illness or disease itself. These palliative treatments may be offered alongside drugs which are designed to cure a particular condition.

For example, an infected wound may be treated with antibiotics to clear the infection and with painkillers to deal with the pain caused by the infection. In other conditions such as arthritis, terminal cancer, osteoporosis or other long-standing chronic conditions, the cause of the pain may not be curable, but the pain can certainly be relieved and strategies can be developed to help people to cope with it.

Case study

Working with a person who uses cannabis

Gabriel is 37 and has multiple sclerosis. He is currently living in a specialised unit as he is no longer able to care for himself. He hopes to be in the unit for a short time only until his medication and treatment regime is stable, then he plans to employ personal assistants using the direct payment scheme and live in an adapted bungalow.

In the meantime he is causing concern among the staff of the unit because he is a regular smoker of cannabis.

He finds that this is effective in relieving pain and discomfort, and says he intends to continue to use it.

The staff hold a review with Gabriel and his key worker to discuss the situation and how to respond.

1. What would you do in this situation?
2. Is Gabriel right to relieve his pain by any means necessary?
3. Can the unit support him in this?

Activity 3

Methods of relieving pain

Ask your friends and colleagues about their experiences of pain and discomfort, and what they do to relieve it.

Note the different types of pain, and different ways that each of them use to relieve the discomfort. How much do they vary?

Functional skills

English: Speaking and listening

Have a discussion with friends and colleagues about their experiences of pain and what they do to relieve it. Ensure that you make relevant and full contributions to the discussion and allow others in the group to respond to your points. Present your information clearly using appropriate language.

1.3 Agreed ways of working that relate to managing pain and discomfort

Information about the best ways to manage pain or enable someone to rest and sleep should be entered in the plan of care. You should always check the plan before starting to work with people to support them and make them comfortable, and make sure that you enter any new information so that colleagues can take appropriate action.

Do not forget that any information you enter into a plan of care is covered by the Data Protection Act 1998 (see Unit HSC 028) and you must take all necessary steps to keep information confidential.

Doing it well

Supporting people to manage pain and discomfort

- Be very clear about how a person's pain and discomfort should be managed and only use agreed and approved methods.
- Remember that team communication and a consistent approach are vital.
- If you are not sure, then read the support plan or ask your supervisor.
- If the person asks for something different from what is on the support plan – if they ask you to buy them some alcohol, for example – always check with your supervisor first. It may be absolutely fine for them to have some alcohol, but sometimes alcohol can affect how prescribed drugs work.
- If you have any concerns at all about how a person wants to relieve their pain, discuss this with your supervisor immediately.

2. Be able to assist in minimising individuals' pain or discomfort

2.1 How pain and discomfort may affect well-being and communication

We saw earlier in the unit how pain and discomfort can affect a person physically, socially, emotionally and spiritually. Pain can also have a huge effect on a person's ability to sleep and rest. There are several theories around the need for these two things. Some theories suggest that sleep is for the repair and renewal of the body, while other theories say it is for allowing our brains to organise and file all the things which have happened during the day and get the information into some kind of order. Some say that it is about escaping from the world and a chance to recharge our batteries. Whatever the reason for sleep and rest, pain and discomfort can certainly affect the amount and quality of sleep that we have.

Researchers have managed to keep volunteers awake for between 100 and 200 hours at a stretch, but after that time they tend to fall asleep anyway, regardless of what steps are taken to keep them awake. So it is clear that sleep is very necessary and that ultimately the body will ensure that it does sleep.

The physical effects of sleep deprivation are quite slight:

- slight changes in temperature
- insignificant changes in heart and breathing rate.

Most people deprived of sleep are still able to carry out physical tasks without any serious change in their ability to do so.

Emotional changes are more noticeable. People tend to become:

- irritable or anti-social
- very depressed
- suspicious almost to the point of paranoia
- very poor at carrying out mental tasks.

Memory can also be affected by lack of sleep. People's ability to recall things they learned before being deprived of sleep seem to be quite seriously affected.

2.2 Encouraging an individual to express feelings of discomfort or pain

Measuring pain

One of the important factors that you need to establish when somebody is experiencing pain is how much pain they are feeling. This is difficult because everyone experiences pain at a different level and it is not possible to have an objective measure of pain.

You need to be very clear that pain is about what a particular person experiences and cannot be measured against pain you suffer or anyone else may suffer. You cannot measure one person's suffering against another's, because each is a unique experience.

Several methods have been developed to try to measure pain, but one of the most effective is to ask the person to describe it to you on a scale of 1 to 10, with 1 being mild discomfort and 10 being the most excruciating pain they have ever felt. This will at least give you some idea of the level of discomfort the person is feeling and the sort of assistance they are likely to need.

Remember that this is not about comparing like with like. If two people have arthritis and one only puts their pain at 3 while the other puts it at 7, you cannot say that the person who rated their pain at 7 is a 'moaning Minnie' and that the one who put it at 3 is a 'wonderful, brave soul'. It is about individual experience and you need to react to the level at which that person describes their pain.

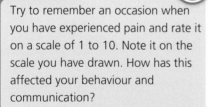

Reflect

Try to remember an occasion when you have experienced pain and rate it on a scale of 1 to 10. Note it on the scale you have drawn. How has this affected your behaviour and communication?

An example of a pain scale.

Because of people's beliefs, values and culture, they may not find it easy to say that they are in pain. This can result from a feeling that they do not want to make a fuss, be a nuisance or bother anyone. Many think it is somehow 'wet' or 'babyish' to ask for pain relief and that they should accept pain without complaining.

It is important that you create as many opportunities as possible for people to express their pain and that you contribute towards creating an atmosphere where people know it is acceptable to say that they are in pain and they want something done about it. You can help by:

- noticing when someone seems tense or drawn
- noticing facial expressions, especially if someone is wincing or looking distressed
- observing if someone is fidgeting or trying to move around to get more comfortable
- noticing when someone seems quiet or distracted
- checking when someone is flushed or sweating, or seems to be breathing rapidly.

All of these signals should prompt you to ask a person whether they are in pain and if any help or relief is needed. Even in the absence of any obvious signals, it is important to check regularly and ask if any of the people you work with are in pain or discomfort, or need any assistance.

You will need to be particularly aware of possible pain when you are providing care for people who are not able to communicate directly with you, including people who:

- do not speak English as a first language
- have speech or hearing difficulties
- have a severe learning disability or multiple disabilities
- are extremely confused.

You will need to be especially vigilant if you provide care for anyone who comes into these categories. In all of these cases, you may need to look for indications of distress and be able to react to those rather than waiting for the people to communicate directly in some way. If a person who is very confused is in pain, this can be difficult to detect because they may not be able to find appropriate words to communicate with you.

2.3 Encouraging an individual to use self-help methods of pain control

Sometimes even the simplest of methods can be effective in responding to and dealing with pain. It may be sufficient just to alter someone's position, or to provide them with a hot-water bottle or an ice pack. Sometimes a distraction, like getting them involved in an activity or talking to them, can help.

Many people who have long-term problems will have developed their own strategies for dealing with pain. You should make sure that you know what these are and what part you can play in making them effective. Self-management is always the most effective method of dealing with pain and discomfort, because it gives the person the maximum amount of control. People who feel out of control, and who do not have any information, experience a greater degree of pain than people who feel that they are in control and have a strategy that works for them to minimise their pain.

You should note down in the support plan each person's preferred way of dealing with discomfort and ensure you are able to offer them the assistance needed. Sometimes it can be a case of simply positioning a limb or feet on a pillow, raising the feet a little or helping the person to get up and move around, and this can make all the difference.

2.4 Assisting an individual to be positioned safely and comfortably

Pain will obviously be a hindrance to personal comfort, so it is important that you establish that the person is positioned as comfortably as possible and has had any treatments — for example, self-help or medication. If the person needs to be turned during the night, ensure that this is done as comfortably and quickly as possible, with minimum disturbance.

Positions for resting

While for many people the most comfortable position for resting and sleeping is to lie down in bed with their head supported by a pillow, this may not be the case for others. Everyone has their preferred position for sleeping. Some medical conditions may mean that people have to rest propped up or sitting in a chair. You will need to check with the person and their support plan if there are any reasons for ensuring that someone maintains a particular position; for example, a breathing problem, a stoma, a musculo-skeletal condition or a prosthesis may mean that someone cannot rest in a particular position. Above all, you will need to check with people themselves about positions in which they are comfortable, and positions which are not possible for them.

Reflect

Think about a time when you have had pain (you may think back to the examples that you gave on page 318). Did you use any self-help methods and were they effective?

Key term

Empathy – putting yourself in someone else's shoes; showing understanding and kindness

2.5 Carrying out agreed measures to alleviate pain and discomfort

Clearly the most natural response you will have to anyone in pain is empathy. This may seem obvious, but it is always worth restating that one of the most supportive responses to anyone in pain is to be empathetic and offer some TLC – tender loving care.

A person's support plan will include a strategy for dealing with any pain that they experience. This strategy will have been carefully planned by the whole team if the person you are caring for suffers from a condition known to involve pain.

Alternatively, someone may be suffering pain as a result of an accident or injury which is a sudden occurrence, and you may need to respond before a support plan has been drawn up. If this is the case, it is important that you offer sympathy and support, and immediately refer the person to your team manager or supervisor, who can arrange for a medical assessment to take place and appropriate pain relief to be prescribed.

Responses to pain are almost as varied as the people involved. Background, culture and beliefs have a great deal of influence on how we respond both to our own pain and to others who are experiencing pain. If you have been brought up with the view that you should 'get on with it' or 'not make a fuss', then you may find it difficult not to become exasperated with someone who constantly complains about the level of pain that they are experiencing. There may be a temptation to remind the person that 'there are plenty worse off than you' or that 'if you take your mind off it and think about something else, you will feel a lot better'. That type of response is largely unhelpful to someone who is suffering pain and does not know how to manage it. These are not acceptable responses from a care worker.

Being empathetic does not mean that you cannot offer suggestions and be constructive in advising a person about steps they can take personally to minimise pain. Empathy is about more than just patting someone's hand and agreeing that it must be awful; it includes offering practical help and ideas to improve things.

It is also important that you ask the person what help and support they would like you to give. It may be that they know from previous experience that a hot-water bottle, a change of position, a cushion or a walk around the garden will help to minimise the pain. Make sure that you ask the person what they would like to do before offering any of your own suggestions.

Activity 4

Guidelines for responding to people's pain

Find out the guidelines in your workplace for responding to people's pain; check the procedure that needs to be followed.

Find out the forms of pain relief which can be provided, and those which have to be referred for a medical opinion.

Functional skills

English: Reading

Read the guidelines in your place of work for how to respond to people's pain. Then check any written documentation on procedures that need to be followed before administering pain relief. By doing this, you will be skimming documents to pick out relevant information. Use the information you have found to ensure that you have sufficient knowledge to help people manage their pain. Make notes of the key points you have found out.

3. Be able to monitor, record and report on the management of individuals' pain or discomfort

3.1 Carrying out required monitoring activities relating to management of pain or discomfort

The person's pain and discomfort levels should be regularly monitored in accordance with their support plan. This will show if there are any changes and it will also give an idea if the pain-relieving methods are effective or not.

Measurements should be taken at times stated in the person's support plan. In some situations, pain scoring can help a nurse judge how much analgesic to give, so it is important to get it right. Always use the agreed pain measurement tool throughout, and follow the instructions and guidance accurately. If the person has difficulty using the numerical scales, then a visual 'face rating' scale may be suggested.

Sometimes it is necessary to measure pain when the person is at rest and then in movement. Knowing how painful it is for a person to move is very helpful, especially if they are undergoing activities such as physiotherapy or moving after they have had an operation.

A behaviour rating pain assessment tool may be used if it is not possible for the person to give a self-assessment score of pain themselves — for example, due to communication difficulties or lack of understanding.

If you have any difficulty assessing a person's pain, then it is important that you let your supervisor know; if you have difficulties, then others might too. Never be tempted to guess, because you may get it wrong.

3.2 Completing records in required ways

Records about a person's comfort, sleep and rest should be accurate and contain enough information so that other care workers can continue to support them. Statements like 'had a good night', 'comfortable night' or 'slept well' do not give enough information and they do not provide enough *accurate* information. How do you know that Mr Jones had a comfortable night — did he tell you or did he not use his buzzer at all? He may have been lying in bed awake, not wanting to be a nuisance and call you.

Never make assumptions about someone's comfort and sleep levels. You could ask the person or observe them and reflect this in your care records. For example, 'Mr Smith said that he had a good long sleep last night; he said that he woke once to use the toilet but he was soon back to sleep; he thinks that he had his usual 7 hours and feels refreshed this morning.'

If a person cannot tell you – for example, if they have communication difficulties – your care record could say, 'Mrs Khan appeared to have had a restful night and enough sleep; on observation for each check she appeared asleep. At 6.30 she called for help to use the commode.' This statement makes it clear that you can only assume by observation that Mrs Khan had a good night's sleep; you are not claiming that she definitely did.

Getting it right is important because it might affect the support and care that is given following periods of rest. For example, if you recorded that a person 'slept well' and he did not, then he may be encouraged to get up and dressed when he could do with more time resting. He may even have a fall as a result of being tired – therefore accurate and factual record keeping is vital.

Records should be written in a way that they are easy to understand by everyone, so avoid jargon and abbreviations. Remember that care records are legal documents and need to be treated as such.

Not completing records is as serious as completing them incorrectly. For example, if no care entry is made, it would be assumed that no care was given; this could be seen as neglect.

Activity 5
Record keeping

Good record-keeping skills are vital in care work, so refer back to Unit HSC 028 to find out how you need to record information properly.

So I can put you down 'slept well', Mr Wilson?

I had a terrible night, didn't sleep a wink, but didn't want to be a nuisance and call.

What negative consequences could this situation have?

Key term

Trend – a tendency or a development – for example, a person's pain score is getting higher or lower

Records support continuity of care. If a decision has been made to respond to a situation or to care for a person in a particular way – for example, if a person likes to have a hot malt drink or listen to music before going to bed – then other care staff are aware of this, thus ensuring continuity of care. Good clear records will also detect problems or difficulties early; this can be done by looking at **trends**. If a person's pain score is becoming higher, then there may be an underlying problem that needs to be taken further.

3.3 Reporting findings and concerns as required

We have discussed the importance of effective and accurate record keeping in relation to a person's physical comfort and rest, but it is important to know what to do with this information. It would not be helpful to just leave this information in the person's care notes. It is essential that you know what to do with the information and whom to share it with. It is also important that you know what information needs to be shared urgently with others.

Concerns that you will need to report and record

If a person is in pain, it is important to report this quickly, especially if it is a different type of pain. For example, if a person says that she has period pain (dysmenorrhoea) which she says is a dull nagging pain in her pelvic area, but then starts to complain of a 'stabbing' pain in her right side, this might be related to something completely different. This is why it is very important to get a good description of the pain.

It is not just worsening of pain that you need to report on; you may find that a person's pain gets better, and you must report this too. For example, if a person is using a Patient Controlled Analgesia pump but is feeling much better, it may be that it is time for their pain relief medication to be changed. Some people are worried about taking painkillers in case they become addicted to them. If this is the case, this needs to be reported so that the nurse or doctor can talk this through with the person.

People may not rest and not only because of physical pain; they may have things on their minds that are stopping them from relaxing, resting and sleep.

For example, Mr Chan may not be sleeping well at the moment because he is worried about his hospital appointment at the end of the week. People may worry when awaiting test results. Worry about money can also affect sleep and rest. It is important, if you discover that someone has something on their mind that could affect them resting and sleeping, to ask them if you can pass this information to your supervisor, because they may be able either to help or to find someone else who can.

> *I have not slept much at all the last few nights; I am worried about my hospital appointment at the end of the week. I will be getting my test results.*

Why does this sort of worry affect someone's relaxation, rest and sleep?

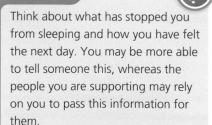

Reflect

Think about what has stopped you from sleeping and how you have felt the next day. You may be more able to tell someone this, whereas the people you are supporting may rely on you to pass this information for them.

If you discover a change in a person's condition that might affect their sleep and rest, you must report it to your supervisor. They may then need to pass this information on to others – for example, the GP.

Doing it well

Identifying changes in people's conditions

- Get to know people well so that you can quickly recognise when things are not right.
- Use effective communication skills – for example, observation and active listening skills.
- Report changes to people's conditions (for example, pain and discomfort) quickly to your supervisor or manager.
- Tell the person that you have reported their pain and discomfort; that way they will know that it is being taken seriously.
- Keep the team informed.

Getting ready for assessment

LO1

This learning outcome requires you to be able to demonstrate your knowledge and understanding of agreed and approved ways of working in relation to managing people's pain and discomfort. You may be asked to write some case studies on different approaches to managing pain and discomfort. Use examples from your work setting if possible, but you could also give examples of different approaches that have been used from other work settings if you can.

Assessors will be looking to see that you can understand the different approaches to manage pain and discomfort, but also to see that you can apply the knowledge that you have and that you support people as individuals.

LO2

You will need to demonstrate to your assessor that you can help to position a person safely and comfortably. Check with the person and their support plan to see how they would like or need to be positioned, and have pillows, cushions, blankets and so on ready. Remember that people's needs and preferences change, so your assessor will want to see that you take this into account. A witness testimony or reflective account supporting another person may be useful as well, to show that you can support people as individuals and respect their differences.

LO3

Your assessor will want to see that you complete records properly relating to people's pain and discomfort. You do not need to photocopy their records because you must respect confidentiality. Show your assessor the records that you have completed relating to a person's pain and discomfort. Records could be using pain-scoring tools, daily care records, support plans or other records specific to your workplace. You could also get a witness testimony from your supervisor to confirm that you do keep records properly relating to pain and discomfort. If you do not complete many records, then you could provide an example of a record that you could write in order to support the records that your assessor sees.

You also need to demonstrate your understanding of reporting findings and concerns. You may be asked to write a reflective account of a situation when you were concerned about somebody's pain; you may have observed that they were in pain even though you knew they had had painkillers (analgesia) or they were experiencing a different type of pain. Your assessor will need to see that you know whom to report concerns to, what to report and when.

Legislation

- Data Protection Act 1998

Further reading and research

- http://bnf.org/bnf/index.htm (British National Formulary (BNF))
- www.nhs.uk/CarersDirect/guide/bereavement/Pages/Accessingpalliativecare.aspx (NHS Choices)
- www.gscc.org.uk (General Social Care Council (GSCC))
- http://therapiesguide.co.uk (information on alternative and complementary therapies)

Unit HSC 2014

Support individuals to eat and drink

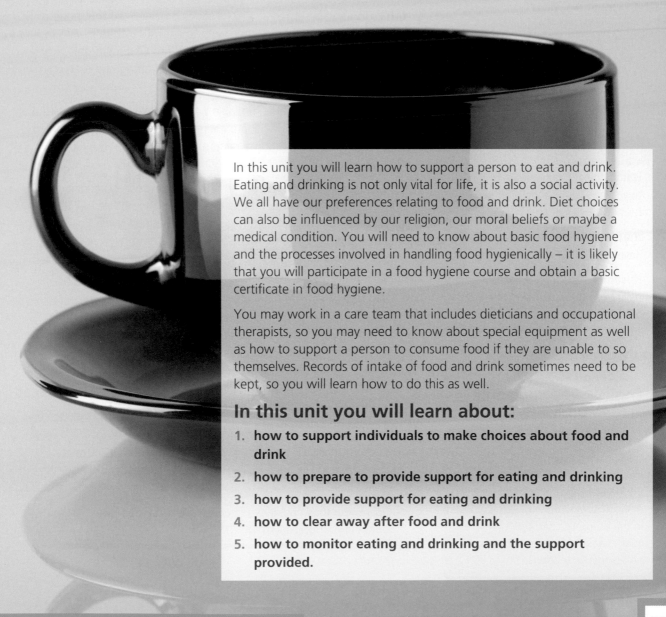

In this unit you will learn how to support a person to eat and drink. Eating and drinking is not only vital for life, it is also a social activity. We all have our preferences relating to food and drink. Diet choices can also be influenced by our religion, our moral beliefs or maybe a medical condition. You will need to know about basic food hygiene and the processes involved in handling food hygienically – it is likely that you will participate in a food hygiene course and obtain a basic certificate in food hygiene.

You may work in a care team that includes dieticians and occupational therapists, so you may need to know about special equipment as well as how to support a person to consume food if they are unable to so themselves. Records of intake of food and drink sometimes need to be kept, so you will learn how to do this as well.

In this unit you will learn about:

1. **how to support individuals to make choices about food and drink**
2. **how to prepare to provide support for eating and drinking**
3. **how to provide support for eating and drinking**
4. **how to clear away after food and drink**
5. **how to monitor eating and drinking and the support provided.**

1. Be able to support individuals to make choices about food and drink

1.1 Establishing with an individual the food and drink they wish to consume

It is important to give people some choice in the food they eat. This will make mealtimes more enjoyable. Just imagine being unable to prepare meals for yourself and having to sit down day after day to eat boring, unappetising or badly cooked food!

Choice should be offered in the type of food, the way it is cooked and the quantity of food that is provided. It may also be helpful, if possible, to vary the times at which food is provided, so that people can choose the time at which they wish to eat rather than having to fit in with the arrangements of their care setting. Of course, this is not easy as there are always considerations about staffing and running any care facility.

Knowing the types of food and drink a person likes will help to build a trusting relationship. Some people choose not to eat meat because of their concern for animals. Some people have foods that they just do not like.

Some people choose not to eat certain foods because of religious reasons. People from some groups will only eat food that has been prepared in certain ways depending on their religious laws. For example, meat from animals that have been slaughtered according to Muslim Law is halal. Meat for Sikhs must be Jhatka, while some Jewish people eat only kosher food.

It is likely that people's preferences will vary according to their life stage. For example, young children are likely to have quite different tastes from those of adults or older people. A meal of burger, chips and ice cream may be very attractive to a 10-year-old, and to a considerable number of adolescents, but may not be welcomed by an older person.

Key terms

Halal – meat from animals that have been slaughtered according to Muslim Law

Jhatka – meat from animals that have been killed with one stroke

Kosher – meat from animals that have been humanely slaughtered according to Jewish Law

Functional skills

English: Speaking and listening

Have a discussion with your colleagues and people you support about your food and drink preferences. Ensure that you make relevant comments and allow others in the group to contribute. Present your choices clearly and respond to points made by others.

Reflect

Think about how your food tastes have changed. Reflect back on the food choices that you made when you were a child and the choices that you make now. Have your tastes and preferences changed?

Compare your food and drink preferences to those of people that you support and your colleagues.

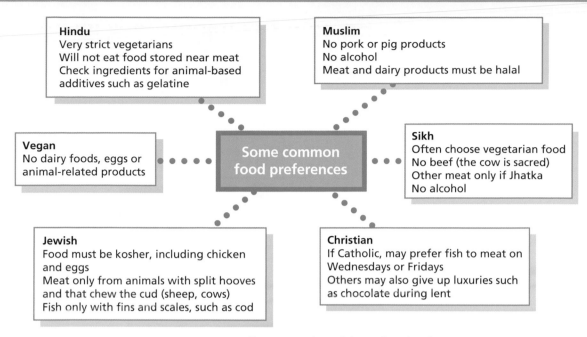

Hindu
Very strict vegetarians
Will not eat food stored near meat
Check ingredients for animal-based
additives such as gelatine

Muslim
No pork or pig products
No alcohol
Meat and dairy products must be halal

Vegan
No dairy foods, eggs or
animal-related products

Some common food preferences

Sikh
Often choose vegetarian food
No beef (the cow is sacred)
Other meat only if Jhatka
No alcohol

Jewish
Food must be kosher, including chicken
and eggs
Meat only from animals with split hooves
and that chew the cud (sheep, cows)
Fish only with fins and scales, such as cod

Christian
If Catholic, may prefer fish to meat on
Wednesdays or Fridays
Others may also give up luxuries such
as chocolate during lent

Always respect people's needs and preferences.

Doing it well

Respecting people's food preferences

- Ensure that you discuss people's religious preferences with them and support them in choosing suitable food and drink.
- Make sure these preferences are recorded in their support plans and are observed by everybody who is providing care for them.
- Discuss the personal likes and dislikes of each person with them and record these.
- Ensure that it is clear to any new member of the care team if there are particular types of food which a person does not eat or does not like.

1.2 Encouraging the individual to select suitable options for food and drink

It is important to know what a healthy and balanced diet is. Encouraging people to make suitable choices about what they eat is a very important part of supporting them. Some people may need to have a special diet for medical reasons, such as **diabetes**. Check people's support plans to find out about what their dietary needs are. A healthy balanced diet gives people all the nutrients in the right amounts for their age and gender. The amount of food taken in by a person needs to balance with the energy they use. If these are not balanced, the person will lose or gain weight. For example, an energetic teenager eats more than an older person who is not very active, because the teenager uses more energy.

Key term

Diabetes – a condition that affects the level of sugar in the blood

Do you eat the right amounts of food from the nutrition pyramid?

Everyone should eat a variety of foods, so that our bodies get all the nutrients that we need. This is especially important if people are recovering from an accident or an operation. The nutrition pyramid above typically shows the amount needed from each food group every day. If dietary choice permits, try to choose low-fat dairy foods and lean meat. Eat two portions of fish each week.

Alcohol should be kept within the recommended limits or, better still, to occasional use only. The long-term effects of too much alcohol include conditions that can cause serious damage to the liver, or the stomach. It can also lead to dementia.

It is important to encourage people to drink on a regular basis. For example, you could offer water, fruit squash, fruit juice and other drinks. However, too many sugary drinks, such as fizzy drinks, and drinks that contain high levels of caffeine should be avoided.

A lot of research has been carried out about what we eat. It has shown that too much salt is bad for you because it can lead to high blood pressure and heart disease. Research has also shown that eating enough fruit and vegetables can help to prevent some cancers.

A person who eats too much and does not exercise enough may become obese. This puts a huge strain on the body, and can lead to many other problems. Obesity has been linked to heart attacks, varicose veins and diabetes. It can also lead to low self-esteem, which means that the person does not feel good about themselves. Eating too much junk food can make the person feel sluggish because it can be filling, but does not contain many nutrients.

Recommended daily allowances

The government has suggested a recommended daily allowance (RDA) of many nutrients, such as salt, fat, protein, and so on. The RDA is the amount that an average man or woman needs every day of each nutrient in order to stay healthy. Some people may not need as much if they are not very active. But it is still very important that what they do eat is nutritious. If a person has a very small appetite, it is even more important that the little they do eat is very nourishing, and gives them what they need to stay well.

Make sure that you know what a healthy diet is so that you can support people to make healthy choices. If you help people to develop independent skills by supporting them to do their own shopping, point out the healthy options and alternatives. Healthy food can also be made appealing by presenting it nicely on the plate.

What can food manufacturers do?

Manufacturers must show the nutritional value of food items on the packaging. Food manufacturers and supermarkets use labels that show nutritional information in many different ways. Some are colour-coded, while others show the amount of each ingredient as a percentage. These can be the recommended daily allowance (RDA) or the guideline daily amount (GDA).

The Food Standards Agency's 'traffic light' system of food labelling is another system in use, and is becoming more popular. Colour-coded panels clearly show the levels of total fats, saturated fats, sugar and salt in foods such as ready meals. This can help people to make healthier choices at a glance.

- **Red** means eat this once in a while.
- **Amber** means this is fine to eat most of the time.
- **Green** means that this is a good choice at any time.

1.3 Ways to resolve any difficulties or dilemmas about the choice of food and drink

There can be many reasons why a person does not choose a healthy, balanced diet. They may not know what a healthy diet is. Diet can also be linked to social class because poorer people may not be able to afford good-quality food; however, with some thought it is possible to eat a healthy diet on a budget.

Busy lifestyles mean that some people eat a lot of processed or convenience foods, which usually contain a lot of salt and fat. Other people just do not want to follow the advice to eat well, because they feel that the unhealthy option tastes better!

Make sure that you know what a healthy diet is so that you can help people to make healthy choices. If you help them to develop independent skills by supporting them to do their own shopping, point out the healthy options and alternatives. You also need to know what the consequences of a poor diet choice might be. For example, obesity can lead to heart disease, varicose veins, diabetes and arthritis. High cholesterol and diets high in salt can lead to heart attacks and strokes. If you are aware of the consequences, this means that you can offer sound advice.

Long-term eating habits may take some time to change. You may therefore wish to suggest making small changes at a time, such as introducing more vegetables. Explain the benefits of making healthy choices, such as more energy and raised self-esteem. Effective communication skills with a positive outlook from you can be encouraging, and remember to be a good role model yourself.

Case study

Improving Kelly's food choices

Kelly lives in a flat with her three children. She does not work and has very little money to spend on food. Kelly tends to buy a lot of cheap, processed foods such as pies, sausages and beef burgers which fill the children up. She usually buys the children some sweets at the end of a shopping trip. She does not buy fresh fruit very often, because it is too expensive.

1. What are the potential health problems with Kelly's shopping list?
2. How could you support Kelly to help her to provide more healthy foods for her family?

1.4 How and when to seek additional guidance about an individual's choice of food and drink

People may be reluctant, or may even refuse, to eat certain types of food which have been noted in their support plan as a requirement for their condition – such as a diabetic diet, a weight-reduction diet or a gluten-free diet. This can cause difficulties in terms of being able to offer freedom of choice. You may feel that this places you, and other care staff, in a very difficult position.

If someone is determined to ignore medical advice and to follow a different diet, this should be reported and discussed among the care team and the medical staff responsible for the person's care. Ultimately you have little control over a diabetic who buys and eats chocolate bars and sweets. However, you do have a responsibility to provide full information and explanations, and to repeat the explanations regularly to the person, making every effort to persuade them to comply with the dietary requirements. If a person chooses, in full knowledge of the consequences, to ignore medical advice, then that is their choice.

The situation is different, however, for children, people who are compulsorily detained under the Mental Health Act 1983 or subject to guardianship, and older people who are very confused or severely demented. All of these situations require a high degree of tact, skill and understanding. It is important that you report immediately to your supervisor any difficulties involving a person's consumption of food and drink.

2. Be able to prepare to provide support for eating and drinking

2.1 The level and type of support an individual requires when eating and drinking

Most people can feed themselves, but some will need you to help them. They may have a physical problem such as a broken arm, or there may be another reason such as confusion or dementia. The level of support may be different even if two people have the same condition – for example, one person who has had a stroke might be able to feed themselves because they have some movement in their arm, while another may have no movement or strength at all and will need more support.

Your Code of Practice says that you must 'treat each person as a person and promote independence'. Always check to find out how much help each person needs. Giving too much help can take away a person's right to independence, and not giving enough help may lead to them not having enough to eat and drink.

If a person can tell you, then ask them how you can support them to eat and drink. It may be that just cutting food up into manageable chunks is enough to enable a person to eat their meal independently. It can be degrading to feed a person if they are able to feed themselves with a little support. Always check the person's support plan because this includes all of the care needs; helping to eat and drink will be one part of this. Remember, though, that needs sometimes change; the person's condition may improve and they may be able to do more for themselves, or their condition might have deteriorated and they will need more support. The support plan must accurately reflect changes.

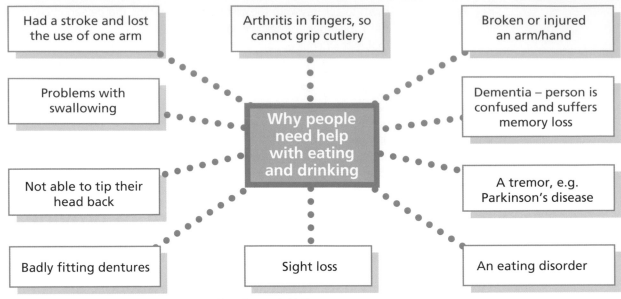

Had a stroke and lost the use of one arm	Arthritis in fingers, so cannot grip cutlery	Broken or injured an arm/hand
Problems with swallowing		Dementia – person is confused and suffers memory loss
Not able to tip their head back	Why people need help with eating and drinking	A tremor, e.g. Parkinson's disease
Badly fitting dentures	Sight loss	An eating disorder

Some reasons why people may need help with eating and drinking.

Professionals such as speech and language therapists and occupational therapists can give guidance about how much support a person may need when eating and drinking. If they are involved in the care of the person, then their advice should be easily accessible in the person's support plan.

2.2 Effective hand-washing and use of protective clothing when handling food and drink

All establishments where food is prepared and served are governed by the Food Safety (General Food Hygiene) Regulations 1995. These regulations set out the basic hygiene principles that must be followed in relation to staff, premises and food handling.

Under the regulations, all establishments must have effective food safety management measures (or 'controls') in place, to ensure that food is produced safely and that the health of people is not put at risk.

Handling food safely

Infection control is important when helping people to eat and drink. You will need to show that you can handle food hygienically. Food poisoning can spread very easily and quickly. Some people may be at risk of catching infections because they may already be unwell, and have a weak immune system. Older people can be more at risk too. Food poisoning can kill, so you must protect people.

If it is part of your job to prepare and handle food, then you need to follow some basic hygiene rules and have a Food Hygiene Certificate. This will show that you have had training in safe food handling.

Food poisoning is extremely unpleasant for the person who gets it. They can become very ill, and even die. Signs of food poisoning can include vomiting, diarrhoea and flu-like symptoms. Food poisoning occurs when there are dangerous bacteria on food when it is eaten. Effective hand-washing can dramatically reduce the risk of spread of infection and food poisoning.

Hand-washing

If hands are not clean, they can spread food-poisoning bacteria. A quick rinse will not make sure they are really clean, so it is important for all staff to know how to wash hands properly. Basic rules of hygiene must be followed to avoid the risk of contaminating food and drink. See pages 213 and 214 for the correct hand-washing procedure.

Have you used ultraviolet light to check how well you have washed your hands?

Doing it well

Handling or preparing food

- If you have long hair, tie it back.
- Wear a protective hat if working in a kitchen.
- Wear a protective apron.
- Wash knives and utensils well after using them on raw meat.
- Keep nails short and do not wear jewellery where germs can lodge underneath.
- Wash your hands thoroughly between each stage of food preparation.
- Wash your hands thoroughly after going to the toilet.
- Do not touch your nose during food handling or preparation.

2.3 Supporting the individual to prepare to eat and drink, in a way that meets their personal needs and preferences

Although the basic rules of hygiene must be followed to avoid the risk of contaminating food and drink, all of us have our own ideas about what is acceptable and hygienic practice in relation to food preparation and eating. For example, some people always wash their hands before starting a meal, whereas others never do. Others will wash in specific ways for religious or cultural reasons. It is important that you are aware of your own values and beliefs about hygienic arrangements for eating and drinking, and recognise that they are your own values and not necessarily those of others. You must never attempt to impose your own values on other people, but at the same time you do need to be aware of any situation where the values of others place people at risk of contamination, and be able to point this out in a tactful and positive way.

You will need to make sure that people are given the opportunity to wash their hands and go to the toilet before a meal. This can be time consuming if you are working with a group of people who need assistance, so make sure you start in plenty of time so that people are not rushed.

It is also important that people have the opportunity to complete any religious activities which may be important to them at mealtimes, such as saying a prayer, giving thanks or washing themselves.

People who need to have protective napkins should be provided with them before the start of the meal. You must take care that you do not patronise people or treat older people as if they were children by tucking bibs around their necks. Sometimes it is necessary to protect clothing, and for comfort and cleanliness to protect a person's neck and chest if they do have some difficulties in eating. It is far better to offer some kind of protection and allow people the dignity and independence of eating by themselves than to assist them to eat simply because they make a mess.

2.4 Suitable utensils to assist the person to eat and drink

The most important thing you need to do is to establish with the person whether they require your assistance. You should never impose help on a person — it is far better to encourage independence, if necessary through the use of specially adapted utensils, rather than to offer to provide assistance to eat or drink. Occupational therapists are trained to give advice on how people can remain independent. If necessary they can recommend equipment that might help. Some people would be perfectly capable of eating by themselves if they were given a minimal amount of assistance.

There are also special ways of helping people who have particular needs. For example, a visually impaired person is often able to manage to eat for themselves if you can help to prepare the plate of food in advance. If you arrange the food in separate portions around the plate and then tell the person, using a clock face as a comparison, that pie is at 12 o'clock, lettuce at 3 o'clock, tomatoes at 6 o'clock and so on, then this is often enough to allow the person to work out what they are eating and to enjoy the meal.

If you do need, because of additional requirements, to provide direct assistance to a person who has a visual impairment, you should try to avoid giving instructions like 'open', which could be patronising, to indicate that you are ready with the next mouthful of food. Perhaps a signal like a tap on the hand or saying 'OK' would be appropriate. You can agree with the person in advance what signal they would like you to use.

Arranging food in a clock face pattern can help people with visual impairment.

Activity 1

Understanding eating with a visual impairment

Sit down and practise being fed by a colleague. You could have a blindfold on or keep your eyes closed, to see what it is like to be visually impaired. Swap places and be the care worker feeding the other person. Think about the following.

● How did it feel to be fed?
● Was the speed right?
● Was the food given to you in the right combination?
● Was it the right temperature?

3. Be able to provide support for eating and drinking

3.1 Factors that help promote an individual's dignity, comfort and enjoyment while eating and drinking

As well as storing and preparing food, and making sure that people are being given a balanced and healthy diet, you also need to ensure that the environment is safe, hygienic and pleasant for people to eat food. The place where food is consumed in your work setting should be clean and attractive.

Doing it well

Providing a pleasant environment for eating

- Make sure that there are no unpleasant smells where people are eating.
- Turn the television off to avoid distractions or interruptions, and, if possible, have some quiet background music on.
- Ensure that the room is warm but not too hot. Remember that when people are sitting still they are more likely to feel the cold, so avoid draughts.
- Mealtimes should be a social event, so try to make sure that each person sits next to other people that they get on with.
- Keep the environment scrupulously clean and ensure that it can be used by everyone with or without assistance.
- Some people may not be able, or wish, to eat in the dining room. If they have their meal in their room, make sure that the food is still hot when it gets to them.

Some workplaces encourage care workers to sit down and eat with people; this can help to create a good homely feeling for all concerned.

There is no reason why people receiving meals in a care setting should not have exactly the same consideration about the presentation, the flavour, content and attractiveness of their food as in top restaurants where great trouble is taken with presentation. It is amazing what some careful presentation can achieve with the simplest meal in terms of making it more appetising, more attractive and more likely to be eaten and enjoyed.

3.2 Supporting the individual to consume manageable amounts of food and drink at their own pace

Mealtimes should be enjoyable and not rushed. If people need active support with feeding, make sure that you allow plenty of time. If food is offered and eaten too quickly, the food or drink may spill, or the person may develop indigestion or even choke. Rushing people can make them feel as if they are a nuisance and undervalued. We all eat at different paces. Do not be tempted to rush the person to finish their meal, nor be so slow that the person is waiting for the next mouthful.

Reflect

Think of a time when you have felt rushed when eating. You may have been in a restaurant and the staff were eager to clear the table ready for the next customers. Or you may have felt rushed on your lunch break because you needed to get back to work. How did being rushed make you feel as a person, as well as physically?

Doing it well

Helping a person to eat

- Sit down beside the person, slightly to one side and in front of them.
- Make sure that you leave enough time for them to chew or swallow each mouthful properly.
- Bear in mind that if someone is ill, they may take longer to eat. Make sure that you do not rush and find yourself hovering with the next spoonful before they have finished the last one.
- Offer the person regular drinks before, during and after the meal.
- Chat and keep an interesting conversation going but beware of asking a question just after you have placed some food in their mouth!

3.3 Providing encouragement to the individual to eat and drink

If someone is reluctant to eat or drink, you will need to talk with them and try to find out the reason for the problem. You will need to establish whether it is a physical reason. One of the most common causes of eating problems, particularly for older people, is badly fitting dentures. This can often be a source of difficulty for people eating, partly because it is physically difficult to eat and also because they could be embarrassed by the fact that their dentures do not fit properly and could fall out or become clogged with food. This is a problem that can be resolved very simply by making arrangements for the dentures to be properly fitted, perhaps by the use of denture adhesive.

If people have dental problems, a sore mouth or difficulty swallowing, you may need to provide food which has been liquidised or puréed to make it easier to eat.

Reluctance to eat may be due to an emotional problem to do with being unhappy, frightened or worried. In this case, you should use your communication and listening skills to try to find out the nature of the concerns and if there is anything you can do to assist. With reassurance or some greater involvement in settling in to a new care setting, or with some empathy and understanding, it may be possible gradually to improve the person's interest and appetite.

Identifying Mrs Maxwell's difficulties with eating

Mrs Maxwell is a resident at Sunnymead Residential Home for older people. She has worn dentures for many years. She enjoyed her food and had a good appetite. One day her upper dentures broke and the care staff made an appointment for her to see her dentist. Mrs Maxwell had a new set of dentures made, but she found them difficult to get used to. They made her mouth very sore, and gave her mouth ulcers.

Sasha noticed that Mrs Maxwell was eating very little at lunchtime and looked as if she was in pain while eating. She also noticed that Mrs Maxwell was starting to lose weight. Sasha spoke to her and it became clear what the problem was.

Sasha reported the problem to her supervisor who then made another appointment for Mrs Maxwell to see her dentist. Meanwhile, she agreed to have her food liquidised or puréed to make it easier to eat.

1. What might give you a clue that someone has a sore mouth when eating?
2. What effect could this have had on Mrs Maxwell if Sasha had not reported this to her supervisor?

Functional skills

English: Writing; Reading

When answering questions relating to a text, you are practising both reading and writing skills, as you have to extract relevant information to answer the questions and write coherently and clearly with appropriate detail to show that you have understood the meaning. You will need to lay out your information in a logical way and use suitable language to answer points. Proofread your work to ensure that it is accurate in spelling, punctuation and grammar.

3.4 Supporting the individual to clean themselves if food or drink is spilt

Sometimes people can spill food or drink despite being given support or equipment to be independent. If food is spilt the person may feel embarrassed, especially if there are other people nearby; they may consider themselves a nuisance. They may already feel childlike because they may need extra support with feeding. How you react to the situation is vital. Do not draw attention to the situation. Instead, discreetly offer the person a napkin and let them clean themselves if they are able; if they are not able to clean themselves then you should do it for them tactfully. Such situations can affect how a person feels about themselves. For example, if the care worker deals with the situation negatively and makes the person feel a nuisance, their self-esteem may be reduced, or they may be nervous about eating or drinking in the future. Professional care workers show empathy and sensitivity in such situations.

3.5 Adapting support in response to an individual's feedback or observed reactions while eating and drinking

Sometimes it is necessary to adapt the support that you give to help a person to eat and drink. For example, a person who is usually able to eat independently with minimal assistance may feel unwell and weak. Your observation skills at mealtimes will help you to notice if they need extra support. On the other hand, you may find that a person who usually needs a lot of support is more able to eat and drink with just minimal assistance. Remember to ask them if they feel that the level of support is right for them. How people feel can change on a daily basis, so you need to use your observation and effective communication skills, and adapt the support that you give when necessary.

Occasionally, you may find that a person has an allergic reaction to a particular food. Signs and symptoms of a serious allergic reaction include:

- redness of skin, nettle rash (hives)
- swelling of throat and mouth, difficulty in swallowing or speaking
- feeling sick, stomach pain, vomiting
- wheezing, severe asthma
- collapse and unconsciousness.

Anaphylaxis is very serious and needs treatment straight away, because it could lead to death. Immediate medical help should be called.

As a care worker, if you know that one of the people has such an allergy, make sure they have their medication with them at all times. Check expiry dates on their medication, too. Make sure that the allergy and what to do in the event of a reaction are written in the support plan.

Choking in adults

This is often caused by something stuck in the back of the throat (usually a piece of food). It is very frightening for the person who is choking. As with any other emergency, try to keep the person calm. Reassure them, so that they do not become more anxious.

Signs and symptoms of choking are:

- a red face at first, later turning grey
- coughing and distress (panicking)
- finding it difficult to speak and breathe
- holding the throat or neck.

Your aims are to:

- remove the item
- get medical help as soon as possible if it cannot be removed.

It is common for people to choke, especially if a person's swallowing reflex is impaired — for example, if they have had a stroke. It is possible for a person to die if emergency aid is not given when a person is choking. Emergency aid techniques cannot be learned from a book — try to attend a course on this.

Key term

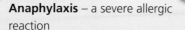
Anaphylaxis – a severe allergic reaction

1. If the person is breathing, lean forward and encourage them to cough. Remove the item if it is coughed up.

2. If they are unable to cough, stand beside them, support their chest and give up to five firm back slaps between the shoulder blades. Stop if the obstruction comes out.

3. If this does not work, try abdominal thrusts, starting by standing behind the person. Lean the person forward. Bring your hands around the front of the person, just below the breastbone. Make a fist with one hand, and grasp this fist with your other hand. Sharply pull your joined hands in an inwards and upwards movement. The force should get rid of the obstruction.

4. If it does not clear, try steps 2 and 3 up to three times.

5. If it still does not clear, then call for an ambulance straight away.

What to do if someone chokes.

This advice is not a substitute for a first aid course. Unless you have been on a first aid course, you need to be careful about what you do because doing the wrong thing could cause harm.

4. Be able to clear away after food and drink

4.1 Why it is important to be sure that an individual has chosen to finish eating and drinking before clearing away

The way in which you clear up is just as important as the way you present and serve food to people. Most of us have had the experience of being in a café or restaurant and having plates cleared away before you are ready to leave, or, even worse, having crumbs swept into your lap and the table wiped with a soggy cloth! It is important to be sure that people have chosen to finish their meal before you start clearing away. Clearing away when a person has not finished their meal does not demonstrate respect and it reflects negatively on the overall service, just as it would in a restaurant. Sometimes people will put their cutlery down and have a rest during a meal, and it may look like they have finished, but they may wish to continue eating after having a rest and digesting some of their food. Some hospitals have protected mealtimes, which means that nurses and care staff can concentrate on helping people to eat and drink. Non-emergency procedures do not take place during this time.

4.2 Confirming that the individual has finished eating and drinking

People may take their time for all sorts of reasons, and, although it can be frustrating if you are busy and need to get on with the next job, you should make sure that people can finish their meal at their own pace.

> **Doing it well**
>
> ### Allowing people to finish eating when they choose to
>
> - Always check with people that they have finished eating and drinking.
> - Ask the person if they have finished or whether they would like some more time to finish.
> - Let the person know that it is all right if they wish to continue eating and drinking.
> - Do not clear away until you are absolutely sure that they have finished.

Key terms

Dehydrated – not enough fluid in the body

Constipation – difficulty in passing faeces

Concentrated – strong

If the person is unable to tell you verbally, then you will need to use other methods of communication. If you take the food away before the person has finished, they may fall short of the valuable nutrients that they need and if they do not have enough to drink they may become **dehydrated**, which can lead to all sorts of problems such as headaches, infections and **constipation**.

Case study

Respecting people's eating habits

Suki is 32 years old and is a patient on an orthopaedic ward in the local general hospital. She had a car accident last week which she is slowly recovering from. Suki has limited use at the moment in both of her arms. She does not sleep well at night and tends to have naps during the day. She can manage to feed herself but she needs to use her left hand because her right arm was badly fractured (she is usually right handed). It takes Suki a long time to finish her meal but she is determined to be independent and do it herself. She often has a rest during her meal between courses, because her arm aches so much if she uses it a lot. Suki likes to save her dessert until later in the evening, when she feels hungry again.

The ward is very busy and there is a new member of staff, Karen, giving out the meals and drinks, and

collecting the trays afterwards. She likes to make sure that the ward is neat and tidy and free of clutter. Suki's tray is often taken away before she has had a chance to finish. Sometimes even full cups of drink are taken away before she has a chance to finish them. The ward has been very hot recently and Suki is getting headaches. Staff wonder if she is drinking enough because her urine is very **concentrated**.

1. What should Karen do if Suki is having a nap while she is clearing up the trays?
2. Why is it important for Suki to say that she has finished her meal?
3. What might happen if Suki's food and drinks continue to be taken away before she has finished?

4.3 Clearing away used crockery and utensils in a way that promotes active participation

Crockery, cutlery and other items from the table should be cleared and removed to the kitchen or designated area. Depending on the setting in which you work, this may be a trolley rather than an area for cleaning utensils. The cleaning may take place elsewhere and your role may be only to stack utensils in the proper sections of the trolley for removal.

Encouraging people to assist

Some people may want to clear away for themselves, or want to help you do this. If it is feasible and safe, you should encourage this as far as possible.

Whether people can help with the washing and putting away of dishes and utensils will depend on the setting. If you are working on a hospital ward, clearly it is not possible for people to do much about washing up and putting dishes away, but in a supported living environment, this is something that should be a normal part of everyday living.

Disposing of waste

Your workplace will have policies about the disposal of food waste. As with all waste disposal, you must comply with the set procedures as they are based on safe and hygienic practices to protect both you and the people you work with. Policies are likely to include:

- wearing an apron or other protective clothing
- following correct hand-washing procedures both before and after clearing away
- placing all leftover food in a marked bin for collection
- never reusing leftover food.

There may be policies about recycling, which will involve separating green waste from cooked food and meat, to be collected separately. Much will depend on the waste collection arrangements in your local area.

4.4 Supporting the individual to make themselves clean and tidy after eating or drinking

Just as you prepared the area for the person to eat, so you must support people to feel clean and tidy after they have eaten. This might be as simple as providing them with hand-washing facilities afterwards. Clothes might have become ruffled if a napkin has been tucked in. People may wish to have a toothpick, especially if they have had meat or food that can easily get stuck between their teeth.

Give them the opportunity to clean their teeth if they wish, remembering that some people may not wish to do so; do not impose your own values on others.

Support the person to feel as tidy as they did before they had their meal. They may wish to return to their room to freshen up and have a look in the mirror, maybe apply some lipstick and comb their hair.

Support people to feel and clean and tidy, as they did before their meal.

5. Be able to monitor eating and drinking and the support provided

5.1 The importance of monitoring the food and drink an individual consumes and any difficulties they encounter

Reporting and recording

It may be necessary for you to pass on information about how much people are eating and drinking, or if they are having problems. It is important not to ignore problems. Accurate record keeping is vital. Some people may need to have their food intake recorded, especially if they are at risk of malnutrition. People may be assessed to judge their risk of malnutrition. People who may be at risk could include those who:

- have difficulties with chewing and swallowing
- are unable to feed themselves
- are depressed
- may lose appetite because of tablets or medication they are taking.

If a person is at risk of malnutrition, then their dietary intake will be monitored and recorded. This will show problems early on and action can then be taken to prevent the situation getting worse.

It may be necessary to monitor fluid intake; usually urine output is recorded as well. Recording fluid intake and output can give a good indication about how well the heart and kidneys are working.

Difficulties eating and drinking need to be reported and recorded also, because if a person has difficulties eating and drinking (for example, swallowing), it may mean that their food needs to be prepared in such a way that they can consume it.

5.2 Carrying out and recording agreed monitoring processes

Reporting and recording

It may be necessary for you to pass on information about how much people are eating and drinking, or if they are having problems. It is important not to ignore problems. Accurate record keeping is vital. If records are not accurate, it can have an effect on the care that a person receives. For example, if fluid intake was not recorded when it should have been, or the quantity was not correct, then it might appear that there is something wrong when there is not, and the person may end up being treated for a problem that they do not have.

Doing it well

Filling in records

- Always fill in records properly, making sure that they are accurate and give enough information.
- Make sure that they are clear and easily understood.
- If you have problems filling records in, then ask your supervisor or a colleague to help you.

Functional skills

English: Writing

When recording information on a person you support, it is important that you follow the format used in your place of work. All the information recorded should have the appropriate amount of detail. Check your records for accuracy, use suitable language at all times and present the information using a logical sequence.

Activity 2

Record keeping

Good record keeping skills are crucial if accurate information is to be passed on about a person's consumption of food and drink. Accurate records should ensure that people receive the correct care and treatment.

Read the section in Unit HSC 028 (pages 246–255) to remind you how to record, store and share information properly.

You may need to add up and record at the end of the day the total intake. If you are unsure, ask a colleague to check. If you have made a mistake or forgotten to record something, always tell your supervisor — it is much safer to be honest.

Food and Drink Record Chart

Name: *Davina Jones*

Ward: *Women's Centre 1*

Date: *12 February 2011*

Is patient receiving a special diet? Yes / (No)

Please record all food and drink consumed, **giving details of type and quantity eaten**.

Small Yes / (No)

Women's Centre 1

Breakfast	Details	1/4	1/2	3/4	All	Energy	Protein
Cereal + Milk + Sugar (tsp)							
Egg					✓		✓
Bread/Toast (slices)			✓			✓	
Butter/Margerine/Jam/Marmalade		✓				✓	
Tea/Coffee + Milk + Sugar (tsp)					✓		
Other (*e.g. supplement*)							
Lunch							
Soup			✓			✓	✓
Cheese/Egg/Fish/Meat/Pulses							
Vegetables							
Potato/Rice/Pasta/Bread							
Dessert			✓			✓	✓
Drink							
Other (*e.g. supplement*)							
Supper							
Soup							
Cheese/Egg/Fish/Meat/Pulses							
Vegetables							
Potato/Rice/Pasta/Bread							
Dessert							
Drink							
Other (*e.g. supplement*)							
Before bed							
Drinks							
Cake/Biscuit							
Other (*e.g. supplement*)							
					Total		

A completed diet and fluid chart is one way to ensure that people are eating and drinking the right amounts.

5.3 Reporting on the support provided for eating and drinking in accordance with agreed ways of working

We discussed earlier why it is sometimes necessary to monitor and how to record people's eating and drinking intake, and difficulties they may be having. It is also necessary to pass on information about the type and level of support that has been provided for people when they are eating and drinking — for example, if you were assisting a person to eat their meal and you cut up the food for them and they ate independently, then you need to pass this information on. Equally if a person managed to eat completely independently, this should be reported too. Passing on information is necessary because any changes which might mean a problem or an improvement can then be clearly seen.

It may be necessary for you to complete people's care records with this information, but in some workplaces it is enough for you to pass on the relevant information to your supervisor and they will record it. You will need to find out the correct procedure for your workplace.

Legislation

- Food Safety (General Food Hygiene) Regulations 1995
- Mental Health Act 1983

Further reading and research

- www.dlf.org.uk (Disabled Living Foundation)
- www.food.gov.uk (Food Standards Agency)
- www.nutrition.org.uk (British Nutrition Foundation)
- www.nutritionsociety.org (Nutrition Society)
- www.rcn.org.uk (Royal College of Nursing)
- Lear, M. (2006) *Fox and Cameron's Food Science, Nutrition and Health*, Hodder Arnold
- Tull, A. (1997) *Food and Nutrition (Home Economics)*, Oxford University Press

Getting ready for assessment

LO1

You will need to provide evidence that you can describe different ways to resolve conflict about the food and drink that people choose. It could be that you are supporting a person who has diabetes and they insist on eating an unhealthy diet, or a person chooses to eat very little and you know that it is not enough for them to be healthy. You will need to give examples of different ways that the situation could be overcome. Ideally evidence should come from real workplace situations, in which case you could obtain a witness testimony from your supervisor. If this is difficult because you are not experiencing conflict with food choice, you could write a fictional account and give examples of what could be done.

LO2

Effective hand-washing is vital to reduce the risk of food poisoning. Your assessor will want to see that you are able to wash your hands properly when handling and preparing food. Practise washing your hands using the hand-washing guide on pages 213 and 214, and let your assessor know when you feel ready for assessment. Remember to wear protective clothing and equipment such as aprons and gloves when appropriate. If you have a basic Food Hygiene Certificate, this can be used to support your evidence for this outcome.

LO3

Eating and drinking should be a pleasurable experience, and it is important to be able to provide the appropriate support. You will need to describe to your assessor factors that can help to promote the person's dignity, comfort and enjoyment while they are eating and drinking. You will need to demonstrate that you are able to offer practical support while people are eating and drinking, and afterwards. Sometimes it is necessary to adapt the support that you give as a result of your observations and feedback from the person. You will

need to provide evidence that you are able to adapt to such changes; your assessor may suggest that you obtain a witness testimony or complete a self-reflective account.

LO4

It is important for the area to be cleared away properly after mealtimes. That means making sure that crockery and utensils are dealt with in the correct way. The procedure may differ depending on the area that you work in. Your assessor will want to see that you follow the correct procedure and involve people that you support as much as possible; again, the level of participation will depend on the area in which you work. Correct disposal of waste food from dishes will also need to be disposed of properly. Let your assessor know when you feel ready to be assessed.

LO5

This learning outcome is about the importance of monitoring the food and drink a person consumes and any difficulties they may have. You will need to explain to your assessor and give real examples if you can from the workplace. You can prepare for assessment by finding out if any people in your workplace have their food and drink intake monitored and if you are not sure why, then you could ask your supervisor. Your assessor may suggest that you write an account of your examples or they may ask you oral questions and then write down your answers.

You do not need to photocopy records that you have completed because you need to maintain confidentiality. Your assessor will, however, want to see records relating to monitoring eating and drinking activities; they may suggest that you obtain a witness testimony from your supervisor confirming that you can competently monitor and record eating and drinking activities.

Unit HSC 2015

Support individuals to meet personal care needs

In this unit you will learn how to support people to meet their care needs. Supporting personal care is more than just helping people to wash, bathe and use toilet facilities; it is about understanding why hygiene is important and how to be sensitive while respecting people's personal preferences and beliefs with regards to personal care. You will learn why people may need support with personal care and how to find out the level of support that they need.

Looking good can make you feel good too; you will explore how to support people to manage their personal appearance in ways that respect dignity, promote active participation and retain their individuality.

When you are helping people with hygiene, it is easy to spread germs. You will find out how to prevent this from happening, thus ensuring that you protect yourself and others from the spread of infection.

In this unit you will learn about:

1. **how to work with individuals to identify their needs and preferences in relation to personal care**
2. **how to provide support for personal care safely**
3. **how to support individuals to use the toilet**
4. **how to support individuals to maintain personal hygiene**
5. **how to support individuals to manage their personal appearance**
6. **how to monitor and report on support for personal care.**

1. Be able to work with individuals to identify their needs and preferences in relation to personal care

1.1 Encouraging an individual to communicate their needs, preferences and personal beliefs affecting their personal care

It is important to consider people's preferences; what they prefer may be very different to what you would like. There may be cultural considerations that you might need to think about too. If the person is unable to communicate their needs, preferences and personal beliefs very easily, you may need to give them more time or use other methods of communication to find out. Refer back to Unit SHC 21 to read about how to promote effective communication. You could ask family, friends or previous care providers for advice. Some people prefer a bath to a shower. You may feel that it is more practical to have a shower than a bath, but this may not be what they would like. Never impose your own views on others. Some people may wish to bathe or shower weekly and just have a daily wash; you need to respect their choices and views even if they conflict with what you believe.

As well as personal preferences, some people have religious or cultural needs regarding personal care. It is important that you find out about these and respect them, otherwise you could easily offend the person and their family without intending to do so.

Functional skills

English: Speaking and listening

Have a discussion with a group of friends or colleagues about the topics listed in Activity 1. Ensure that you take an active part in the discussion by picking up on points made by others and by making your own contributions clearly and using appropriate language.

Activity 1

Different opinions

Answer the following questions, then ask a friend or colleague to answer them as well. Compare your answers.

1. Do you prefer to shower or bathe?
2. Do you use bubble bath, soap or shower gel?
3. Do you have a preferred variety?
4. (If female) Do you shave, wax, sugar or use hair remover cream?
5. Do you use a particular shampoo and conditioner? If so, what variety?
6. Do you wear make-up?
7. Do you have a preferred brand of make-up, creams and so on? If so, what?

People from some cultures who need help with their personal care may prefer or insist on a care worker of the same gender. That means males for men and females for women. Where possible, you must respect their wishes to avoid causing offence and embarrassment. For example, a Jewish woman would accept help from a male care worker if necessary, but a Muslim or Hindu man would be very offended to be helped by a female care worker.

Here are some examples of cultural and religious preferences. Remember to ask the person how they would like you to help them.

- Many people prefer to wash in running water. If showers are not available, you should provide a basin and fresh water.
- Muslims and people of some other faiths perform special washing rituals before prayers.
- Some people prefer to wash themselves rather than using toilet paper. If bidets are not available, provide a jug of water.

1.2 Establishing the level and type of support and individual needs for personal care

The amount of help that people need with personal hygiene will differ. You must promote the person's independence so they can actively participate; that way they will feel that they still have some control over their own life. For example, a person with arthritis in their hands may find turning on the taps very difficult — you could consider simple changes to the taps or filling the basin for them. This small action could help the person to manage unaided. If the person can wash themselves all over, apart from their back, you could just help with what they are unable to do. Never be tempted to do more to save time. Remember to ask the person how much help they need.

There are many ways of helping people to manage their own hygiene and independence. An occupational therapist can help; they are specialists who can advise on changes and sometimes equipment to help people to be independent. The occupational therapist will assess the person's needs fully and make suggestions about what will really help them to manage with daily living tasks on their own. This may not necessarily mean the use of equipment; sometimes changes in the way people do things can be enough. It is advisable that people seek advice from professionals such as occupational therapists before purchasing any equipment, because it can be very expensive and may not even be suitable.

People should be encouraged to do as much for themselves as they can, but never forced to do things. Some people are nervous about getting in and out of the bath even with special equipment. They may be scared in case they slip and have a fall, or they may worry that powered equipment will not work properly. You will need to help to build the person's confidence and let them know that you will be there to help if needed.

Activity 2

Levels and types of support

Explore the different levels and type of support that is needed for the people you support. Have you used any of these before?

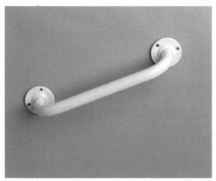

A range of equipment such as non-slip mats and handles is available to support people with personal care.

Reflect

Imagine that you are a patient in a hospital and you share a bay with five other people. There are people of the opposite sex on the ward in other bays. You have had an operation and are unable to manage your own personal care, so you need a care worker to help you.

How you would feel and how would you like the care worker to support you?

1.3 Agreeing with the individual how privacy will be maintained during personal care

Ideally people should be able to manage their personal care independently and in private; however, this is not always the case and they may need some degree of assistance. It should be agreed between the person and the care team how much the person can do unaided and unsupervised, and this should be clearly documented in the plan of care. The person should be fully involved in the decision. Sometimes it can be risky for the person to manage personal care for themselves unsupervised – for example, if they have had a stroke or at risk of slips or falls for other reasons. The person may wish to bathe completely in private and wish to take the risk of any resulting consequences; in such circumstances this must be clearly agreed between the person and then documented.

If support is needed and agreed, then the care worker must exercise great sensitivity. Try to empathise with the person's situation. Simple actions can maximise privacy and make all the difference – for example, knocking on the door before entering the room. It can be more difficult in a hospital setting where there may only be a curtain to maintain privacy, but you can make sure that there are no gaps and alert the patient by calling their name and asking permission to enter before opening the curtains, in order to avoid entering when they may be exposed.

If a person is being supported with personal care at home and they are unable to use their bathroom (for example, it may be upstairs and they have limited mobility), ensure that privacy is maintained, by preventing people outside from seeing the activity by closing curtains or blinds.

Modesty is greatly valued by some religions and cultural groups, such as Muslims. In order to avoid offence, talk to the person to establish the level of privacy they wish to have when personal care is being undertaken.

If a person requires full support by the care worker for personal care, then maximum privacy can still be maintained. If the care worker needs to help with an assisted wash or a blanket bath, ensure that the person remains covered as much as possible by not exposing them unnecessarily. You will need to ensure that you have extra towels or a warm sheet for this purpose.

Would you like an audience if you were having a bath?

2. Be able to provide support for personal care safely

2.1 Supporting the individual to understand the reasons for hygiene and safety precautions

When we are babies and small children, our personal care is supported by our parents or guardians. This can influence our habits and values. For example, some people bathe or shower daily while for others it may be weekly. Attitudes to the care of teeth, hair, shaving and nails can also differ. Those who have very little contact with other people may become less motivated to pay attention to personal hygiene — for example, a person with limited mobility living alone. While we must respect people's differences and attitudes to hygiene and not impose our own standards, health and social care workers have a responsibility to promote healthy and safe practice in relation to hygiene.

Skin is the largest organ of the body; it provides a protective covering. Any breaks to the skin leads to a risk of infection entering the body.

Key term

Epidermis – the outer layer of the skin

The outer layer (the **epidermis**) is constantly being renewed; cells are shed and replaced with new cells. The skin contains glands that produce sweat and sebaceous glands that produce an oily substance called sebum that maintains the waterproofing of the skin.

If skin is not washed and kept clean, dried sweat, dead skin cells and oily sebum build up; this creates a breeding area for a range of bacteria and also leads to body odour.

Care of the teeth is as important as care of the skin. It is recommended that teeth should be cleaned at least twice a day in order to remove particles of food which could decompose and lead to mouth infections, tooth decay and gum disease.

Hair can become greasy if not washed; however, as we get older our hair generally becomes drier and more brittle and it is particularly important to use a mild shampoo in this case. Hair must be thoroughly rinsed to remove shampoo and conditioner residues, which can lead to a dry, irritated scalp.

Be vigilant for head lice which can be easily spread between people who have close head-to-head contact. Head lice can be easily treated using preparations from the chemist or GP. Electronic nit combs are also available to kill head lice, thus avoiding the use of chemicals. Reinfection can be prevented by applying conditioner and combing through using a fine toothcomb. Well-conditioned hair makes it more difficult for the egg to latch on to the hair. Special head lice repellent sprays are also available.

Personal hygiene is not only about preventing the spread of infection, it improves the way we feel about ourselves. We usually feel better when we have had a shower or bath, washed our hair and cleaned our teeth. Care workers need to promote and demonstrate good hygiene practices, and be positive role models. Some people that you support may need to be sensitively reminded and educated about hygiene.

Case study

Supporting a person with poor personal hygiene

Keith is 30 and lives in a small residential home for people with learning disabilities. He refuses to wash; he sweats a lot and sometimes wets himself. Keith does not like to clean his teeth either; he has bad breath and tooth decay. Some of the other residents are unkind and refuse to sit near Keith because they say that he smells. He likes the company of other people and wants to join in with activities, but gets upset and does not understand why the other people will not talk to nor be near him.

Keith's family are upset when they visit, especially when they see other people are ignoring him.

1. Why do you think that Keith does not want to wash?
2. Why is it important to maintain good hygiene?
3. If you were supporting Keith, what would you do?

2.2 Protective equipment, protective clothing and hygiene techniques to minimise the risk of infection

Use hand gel on clean hands if your employer provides it.

Germs can spread very easily from one person to another, especially if they get onto your uniform; therefore, you must limit the spread of infection. You must use the correct precautions to stop infections from spreading.

Washing your hands and using personal protective equipment (PPE) such as gloves and aprons when supporting people with personal care can greatly reduce the spread of infection. Inform people you support that these universal precautions are in place to protect everyone from the spread of infection. Your organisation may provide hand gel for you to use after you have washed your hands; if they do, then you must use it. Hand gel should be applied to clean hands. Remember to cleanse your hands when you remove gloves and put them into the correct bin.

Never put dirty laundry such as soiled bedding or clothes on to the floor, because this unhygienic practice can spread infection. Instead, have the correct laundry bag at hand to use.

Always use people's own toiletries when helping them with personal care and never share personal items with others. Germs can harbour in creams, make-up, combs and so on; they can easily spread from person to person if shared. Sharing toiletries and equipment also compromises a person's individuality.

Your own hygiene should be of a high standard. Wear a clean uniform each day which has been laundered in a hot wash and wash uniforms separately from other household laundry. It is a good idea to have a separate uniform available to wear in case of spills or contamination. Never wear uniforms in public places such as supermarkets, because not only does it portray a negative professional image, but it also puts other people at risk of infection. Use changing areas if they are provided by your employer, otherwise go straight home to change.

Doing it well

Personal presentation and hygiene at work

- Tie your hair back if it is long enough.
- Make sure that your fingernails are clean and not too long.
- Keep jewellery to a minimum (check your workplace policy to find out what is allowed); jewellery can harbour and transmit germs.
- Do not wear strong perfumes and keep make-up to a minimum.
- Remember that if you smoke, the smell of stale smoke may be offensive to others, especially if they are feeling unwell.

Activity 3

Organisational policies and procedures

Refer back to Unit HSC 027 to remind yourself of your responsibilities about following organisational policies and procedures, including using PPE.

Activity 4

Reporting faulty or unsafe equipment

Find out how you should report faulty or unsafe equipment or facilities that are used for personal care.

2.3 How to report concerns about the safety and hygiene of equipment or facilities used for personal care

Facilities and equipment used for personal care should be in good working order, safe and clean. We all have a responsibility under health and safety law to ensure the safety of all people using the premises; be observant by not putting anyone at risk of danger or harm. Equipment should be checked regularly, and all electrical equipment needs to be tested and confirmed to be safe. You should become familiar with the correct working of equipment. That way you will recognise when things are not right.

You should check equipment before every use and not use anything that might cause harm; take the item out of use and report and record as per your local policy. Dripping taps can be a hazard. If hot water drips from a tap while a person is bathing, the person could suffer serious burns. Sharp edges on bath seats, for example, can cause skin tears.

Items such as dirty or unhygienic bath mats, commodes and bath hoists can easily spread infection. Unclean items should be reported to the appropriate person and cleansed thoroughly before use.

2.4 Ways to ensure the individual can summon help when alone during personal care

If people are alone during personal care, they must have the means of calling for assistance if needed. If a call system is available, make sure that it works and that the person knows how to use it. Never leave a person until you are absolutely sure that they are able to call for help if needed. People being supported in their own home without an electronic call system can be given a hand bell or simply call you, in which case you will need to be fully aware and listen carefully for their call and not be distracted by other things such as a radio or TV. Always be alert when a person is alone during personal care and check from time to time if you are concerned about them. You could agree a time at which you will return to see if they need further assistance. Always respond to calls quickly because many accidents occur in bathrooms; if a person is left without response to their call, they may attempt to do more than they are able and suffer a fall or other accident.

How would you feel if a person fell because you could not hear them calling for you?

2.5 Safe disposal of waste materials

Offensive hygiene waste is natural products of the human and animal population (not known to be infectious). Waste can include:

- urine
- faeces
- incontinence pads
- catheter and stoma bags
- sanitary items
- condoms
- sputum
- vomit
- blood.

Such waste should not pose a risk if it is properly wrapped, free from excess liquid and disposed of properly. If handled, however, there are risks, such as contracting gastrointestinal infections resulting in diarrhoea and vomiting. It is therefore vital that you know how to safely dispose of waste. Remember that other people have to deal with waste after you have put it into a bag or container. Organisations have a legal obligation to dispose of waste properly; make sure that you are fully aware of your workplace's procedures regarding waste disposal and do not overfill bags, as these can be a risk to moving and handling as well as splitting open and contamination. Do not overfill bins, as these can pose a risk to the environment and people by encouraging vermin.

It is important that waste is properly disposed of to keep people safe. Table 1 details where waste should be disposed of.

Waste	Disposal
Liquid waste such as urine, faeces, vomit, blood	Normal sewage system
Incontinence pads, sanitary items, wound dressings, used gloves	Yellow bag
Soiled foul linen	Red bag with inner dissolvable liner
Linen	White bag
Household waste	Black bag
Sharps	Yellow sharps box

Table 1: Correct methods of disposal for different types of waste.

When you handle any waste, remember to wear gloves and wash your hands.

3. Be able to support individuals to use the toilet

3.1 Providing support for the individual to use toilet facilities in ways that respect dignity

It can be embarrassing to have someone else supporting you to use toilet facilities. When going to the toilet, most of us would prefer to use our own toilet and do so in private. Unfortunately, this is not always possible. For example, a person may have had an operation and need some help for a short time, while others may have a long-term health problem that severely affects their mobility and they need longer-term care. You may feel embarrassed supporting people to use toilet facilities, but it will help the person if you treat all aspects of going to the toilet in a straightforward, natural way — after all, getting rid of body waste is a perfectly normal process and promoting continence is an essential part of a care worker's role.

Where possible the person should use the proper toilet facilities. Adapted clothing can help a person to be independent when using toilet facilities. Sometimes small changes can make all the difference, such as clothes that are easy to remove; elasticated waistbands and Velcro instead of buttons may help.

Doing it well

Supporting people to use toilet facilities

- Make the activity as private as possible in order to maintain the person's dignity and self-respect.
- Communicate with sensitivity, using appropriate language and terms to demonstrate a professional approach.
- Try to avoid other people hearing you when you discuss toilet issues.
- Some people prefer to have a care worker of the same sex to help them to use toilet facilities; although this is not always possible, ask the person if they have any particular preferences and respect these as much as possible.

Sometimes people may need to use portable toileting equipment such as a commode, bed pan or urinal. Toilet aids can help a person to be independent with toileting. Supporting people while using equipment in bed or in an area away from the bathroom can sometimes make it be more difficult to maintain dignity and privacy, but you must take every effort to make it as private and unembarrassing as possible. Make sure that doors or curtains are closed properly and that the person is free from interruptions. You may wish to provide an air freshener that can be used to eliminate unpleasant odours that can be embarrassing for the person. This is especially so if a person has a colostomy bag that is not a sealed unit and emits strong odours. It is best if the person is able to use the odour eliminator themselves; that way they will feel that they are in control. Remember to empathise with their situation.

If a person is embarrassed, then they may avoid going to the toilet. This can lead to many problems such as not asking for support to use the toilet, which may then lead to incontinence, urinary infections or constipation. Remember to ensure that the person can communicate their need to use the toilet, and exercise sensitivity at all times.

Key term

Empathise – have compassion for, understand

Reflect

Imagine that you are a patient on a busy hospital ward and you are unable to use the toilet. The care worker supports you and helps you to use a bed pan. The curtains are closed but you can hear everything that is happening on the other side.

How do you think you would feel?

3.2 Supporting individuals to make themselves clean and tidy after using toilet facilities

Support people to cleanse thoroughly after using the toilet to prevent them from becoming sore. Traces of urine and faeces that have been left can lead to soreness and infections. Make sure that there is enough toilet tissue and always wipe in the correct way (from front to back); this prevents traces of faeces being drawn towards the vagina and urethra, which could cause infections.

People in some cultures may wish to have running water to cleanse after using the toilet. If bidet facilities are not available, then a jug and water may suffice. Some people like to use moist toilet wipes after using the toilet. Females who are menstruating may wish to use feminine wipes that are gentle and non-irritant. Make sure that underwear is comfortable and help to replace pads if necessary, checking they are correctly positioned.

Hand-washing facilities should be available and people should be encouraged to wash hands thoroughly, as should the care worker who has assisted. Soap and water should be used and hands dried thoroughly afterwards using paper towels.

Doing it well

Supporting people with toileting

- Find out from the person how much support they need.
- Wear gloves and an apron.
- Wash the genital areas gently.
- If using water, make sure that it is warm, not too hot nor too cold.
- If using paper or wipes, make sure that the area is thoroughly clean and free from urine, faeces (and blood if menstruating).
- Wipe from front to back to prevent faeces entering the vagina or urethra.
- Dispose of waste properly and safely.
- Encourage the person to wash their hands and wash your own hands.

---

4. Be able to support individuals to maintain personal hygiene

4.1 Ensuring room and water temperatures meet individual needs and preferences for washing, bathing and mouth care

Areas where personal care is being undertaken should be warm and free from draughts. Prepare and warm the room beforehand by closing windows and ensure that heating is on. When a person is wet, they will feel the cold more readily because heat is taken from the body to evaporate the water. You can warm towels and clothes to take the chill off, but make sure that they are not too hot. Remember also that if you put towels on radiators, you will be preventing the warm air flow from the radiator into the room.

When running baths, run the cold water first; hot water can cause scalds, especially to vulnerable people. A number of serious scalds in the health and social care sector have been reported to the Health and Safety Executive, and guidelines about safe water temperatures and those who may be at risk have been issued. Older and younger people are more at risk of burns, as are people with circulation problems and diabetes. Those who are confused may not be able to judge or control the temperature of the water, and people with limited mobility may not be able to get out of the bath quickly enough if it is discovered that the water is too hot. Risk assessments should be carried out to establish whether a person is at risk of scalds, and measures then taken to reduce the risks.

Water should be at an appropriate temperature; the maximum set hot water temperature is recommended to be:

- 44°C for a bath
- 41°C for a shower
- 41°C for a washbasin
- 38°C for a bidet.

Always use a thermometer to check the temperature of the water and report water that is not within the recommended temperatures.

People may also need support to clean their teeth. Encourage people not to leave the tap running, as we all have a responsibility not to waste water.

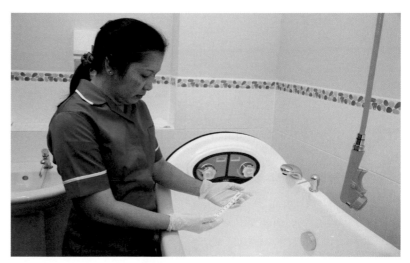

Do you always use a thermometer to check the temperature of the water?

4.2 Ensuring toiletries, materials and equipment are within reach of the individual

Keeping toiletries, materials and equipment to hand makes personal hygiene easier. If the person can reach things easily, it will help them to manage to wash and groom independently. Consider a toiletry bag that can hang in an easily accessible place. Make sure, though, that the area is not cluttered with things that are not needed, because this can be more of a hindrance, especially if things fall to the floor and the person tries to pick them up — this could cause an accident. Arrange things in an organised manner. Ensure that the person has their glasses or hearing aid to hand if they wear them, as well as

Key term

Prostheses – artificial parts of the body, such as, eyes, limbs or breasts

prostheses such as a false breast or limb. Explain where things are, then check that the person has everything they need before you leave them and that they know how to call you if necessary.

4.3 Supporting personal hygiene activities in ways that maintain comfort, respect dignity and promote active participation

People should be encouraged and supported to manage their own personal care so that they are as independent as possible. It is important to find out how much they can do independently; this should be in the support plan, but you still need to be observant because a person's condition and needs can change. People should be encouraged to participate actively; you help by giving the right level of support. Too little help may lead to the person feeling unable to cope, yet too much help will take away their independence. Even if the person can only do a little for themselves, then you must support them to do so. Never be tempted take over because it is quicker; this does not show respect or value for the person.

Offer the person the opportunity to use toilet facilities before they wash, bathe or shower, and help to minimise any levels of pain as far as possible. If a person is suffering pain, they are less likely to want to move or even wash. Ensure that prescribed painkillers have been given beforehand if appropriate.

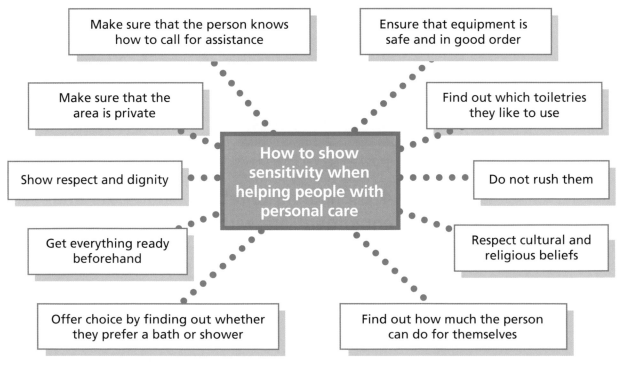

How to show sensitivity when helping people with personal care.

An occupational therapist can advise the person about how personal care can be managed as independently and as safely as possible. Sometimes the use of equipment or aids may be suggested. It is best if the person can try the equipment out before they commit to buy them, because it can be very expensive.

Activity 5

Equipment that allows independence

Ask an occupational therapist, research using the Internet or use catalogues to find equipment that could support a person to be independent with personal care.

If you have a Disability Resource Centre nearby, ask if you can visit to find out about the services they provide.

5. Be able to support individuals to manage their personal appearance

5.1 Supporting individual to manage their personal appearance in ways that respect dignity and promote active participation

Our individuality is very much expressed by our clothes, hairstyle, make-up, jewellery and perfume. Help people that you support to express their individuality. Find out what their preferences are. Do they have favourite brands of hair product, for example? If they are unable to tell you, ask their family and friends.

Respect and offer choice, even if the person cannot communicate very well. It can be confusing for some people to be given too much choice, so you could offer two options; this way, you are still respecting their right to choose. Ensure that people have access to a mirror to shave or apply make-up; a magnified mirror can help if a person is sight-impaired. A full-length mirror will enable the person to feel confident that their appearance is how they intend it to be.

Shaving

Check with men that you support to see if they prefer a traditional wet shave or a dry shave using an electric razor. Many men are very particular with how they like to shave.

Females may like to remove excess body hair; if so, you will need to ask them how this should be done. For example, do they shave, use hair removal creams, or visit a beauty therapist for wax or sugar treatments?

Supporting people to do as much as they can for themselves will help them to have control of their lives.

Nails

Remember to pay attention to fingernails and toenails. Care must be taken with toenails; many organisations have a policy that cutting of these must be carried out by a professional **chiropodist**. You can, however, care for nails by supporting the person to keep them clean and dry. After washing, fingers and toes should be dried very carefully using a soft towel. Do not pull toes apart or pass a flannel through them, because this can split and damage the skin. Trimming fingernails is easier after bathing because the warm water softens them.

Some people like to use foot or hand cream after washing; if you help to apply cream, it is best that you wear gloves.

Hair

The way we feel is sometimes reflected in our hair — for example, if we are feeling unwell, our hair may be dull and lifeless. Hair that is clean and styled can raise our self-esteem. People usually have particular preferences regarding styles and hair products that are used. Promote individuality and find out what the person likes; they may have a particular hairdresser they like to use. If so, find out if a visit can be arranged.

Key term

Chiropodist – a professional trained person who looks after feet

Choices

Do not impose your views on others — for example, you may think the clothes that a person has chosen to wear do not match. Remember, it is their identity, not yours, and you must respect this. However, if the person chooses to wear a thin summer dress on a winter day, you have a duty of care to protect them from harm. You may need to use gentle persuasion to encourage them to wear more suitable clothing.

As well as personal preferences, some people may have religious or cultural needs regarding how they dress. It is important that you find out about these and respect their wishes; if you do not, you may offend the person and their family.

Case study

Respecting Ethel's individuality

Ethel is 80 years old and lives in a residential home. She has always liked to be different and unique; her family describe her as eccentric.

Ethel likes to choose what to wear, and loves bright make-up. The colours of her skirts and jumpers often clash, or she wears her tops on the wrong way round. Other times, she chooses clothes that are unsuitable for the weather. For example, last week it was very cold, but Ethel wore a thin orange stripy blouse with bright purple trousers to go into town. People often turn, look

and sometimes laugh at her. The care workers are very worried and have tried to advise Ethel on what to wear. One care worker even hid a dress that she thought was inappropriate. A few care workers think it is funny and laugh at Ethel.

1. What are the care workers' concerns?
2. Is it right for Ethel to choose what she likes to wear?
3. What would you do in this situation?

Functional skills

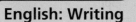

English: Writing

Use the case study to gather your information to answer the set questions. Ensure that each question is answered fully and that your answers are laid out using an appropriate format. Answers should be checked for accuracy of spelling, punctuation and grammar.

5.2 Encouraging the individual to keep their clothing and personal care items clean, safe and secure

When living with other people, it is easy for clothes and other items to get lost. You can help to avoid this by labelling clothing and equipment clearly. Support people to put clean clothes away neatly on hangers and in drawers. Combs and brushes should be kept clean with any hair in them removed. Encourage people to discard make-up or creams that are old because these can harbour germs and cause infections. Make-up can create stains that are difficult to remove from fabric; therefore, make sure that tissues are available and clothes are protected from any mess.

Razors should be clean and in working order. Make sure that foils are intact on electric razors and that safety razors used for wet shaves are clean and not blunt. Blunt and dirty blades could result in damaged skin, causing not only discomfort but a route for infection.

6. Be able to monitor and report on support for personal care

6.1 Feedback from the individual and others on how well support for personal care meets the individual's needs and preferences

Feedback from people is important when a service is provided. This enables health and social care workers and organisations to know what they are doing well and the areas that they could improve on. It can be uncomfortable sometimes to ask for feedback from others when you have carried out an activity, because you may be worried about what they might say. You could ask, 'What have I done well and what could I have done better?' Seeking informal feedback is a good way of developing your own knowledge and practice (see Unit SHC 22 for more on informal feedback).

Formal feedback is also sought from time to time. For example, when a patient is discharged from hospital services they are often asked to complete a questionnaire to measure their level of satisfaction. Registered care providers who are inspected by the Care Quality Commission also seek feedback from those who use the service; this aims to continually improve the quality of health and social care service provision.

All people should have equal access to give feedback. Therefore, if a person is unable to give feedback themselves (for example, if they have dementia), then it can be sought from their family, friends or advocates. Questions should be asked in a straightforward manner, both verbally and written, because this will maximise the accuracy of the responses.

6.2 Monitoring personal care functions and activities in agreed ways

Having an idea of what is normal for the person, and what is not, will help to prevent unnecessary discomfort or something more serious from developing. Each person is unique, and what is normal for one person may not be for another. You are more likely to be the one to notice changes because you probably support the person on a day-to-day basis, whereas your manager may not provide hands-on support in the same way.

What is normal for urine?

Urine should be clear and straw-coloured. However, in the morning it is usually stronger and may look more yellow or orange. There should be no pain on passing urine. If the urine is cloudy and smells

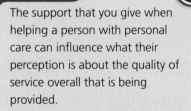

Activity 6

The support that you give when helping a person with personal care can influence what their perception is about the quality of service overall that is being provided.

Seek informal feedback from people you support with personal care and reflect on what you have done well and how you could improve the support that you give.

fishy, it may mean that the person has an infection. Ask them if they have noticed any change in their urine and tell them that you will need to report this to your supervisor, who may ask you to collect a urine sample to send off to be tested. (If you are not sure how to do this, ask your supervisor.)

You may have urine testing kits that use dipsticks. These can give an early clue as to whether there is an infection or not. These sticks can also show other things that are in the urine, such as blood or glucose.

Doing it well

Testing urine

- Always record the results clearly and accurately.
- Inform your supervisor and record the results even if they are normal; your supervisor may want to report your findings to the doctor.
- Remember to keep the person informed about what you are doing.
- Always ask for their permission before taking samples and testing.
- Remember it is their right to be involved in their care.

Key terms

Faeces – waste matter remaining after food has been digested, which is discharged from the bowel

Motion – an emptying of the bowel

Constipated – finding it difficult to pass faeces

What is normal for faeces?

Faeces should be brown, soft and formed. People will differ as to how often they pass a **motion**. As with urine, what is normal for one person may not be for another, so it is important to find out what is right for the person.

If faeces are hard, it may mean that the person is **constipated**. You need to encourage people to drink enough fluid to prevent them becoming dehydrated and to have a diet with enough fibre to prevent constipation (see Unit HSC 2014 for more about diet).

Bristol Stool Chart

Type 1	Separate hard lumps, like nuts (hard to pass)	Type 5	Soft blobs with clear-cut edges (passed easily)
Type 2	Sausage-shaped but lumpy	Type 6	Flufy pieces with ragged edges, a mushy stool
Type 3	Like a sausage but with cracks on its surface	Type 7	Watery, no solid pieces. Entirely Liquid
Type 4	Like a sausage or snake, smooth and soft		

The Bristol Stool Chart helps you to report accurately on the texture of faeces.

If you suspect that the person is constipated, report this to your supervisor. The GP may prescribe laxatives. These are medicines that can help people to open their bowels. You may need to record when the person has passed faeces and note the consistency and texture. You may have to record what they have eaten, when they ate and how much. It can help with early detection of constipation or to monitor **diarrhoea**. The dietician might need to recommend changes to the person's diet.

Women and menstruation

If you are looking after women of childbearing age, they may need help when they are menstruating (having their periods). You should always report any changes. Missed periods could mean a woman is pregnant, but there could also be other reasons such as stress or **anorexia**. It may mean that the woman is going through the **menopause**. Heavy periods could lead to the person becoming **anaemic**. There could be other medical reasons that need investigating for heavy periods. You must always report any bleeding after the menopause, as this will need to be investigated.

6.3 Recording and reporting on an individual's personal care in agreed ways

You may be asked to record and report on a person's personal care. When you have supported a person with any aspect of personal care (for example, with hygiene or toileting needs), it is important to record and report accurately on the support that you have given, as well as any changes you have noticed. Organisations have different records and ways of reporting, so you will need to become familiar with the procedures of your own workplace.

Accurate record keeping is vital and could have serious consequences if not done properly. For example, sometimes a person's urine output needs to be measured and recorded because they may have a kidney or heart condition – if the care worker did not record accurately, the person might end up having some treatment or medication that they do not need. If you forget to measure the amounts accurately or have difficulty doing so, it is best to be honest and tell your supervisor.

Key terms

Diarrhoea – liquid faeces

Anorexia – an eating disorder where the person does not eat enough

Menopause – when a woman's periods stop

Anaemic – not having enough iron in the blood

Case study

Being honest about recording and reporting

Tom is a healthcare assistant working on a busy male ward. He usually remembers to check to see if patients' urine output is to be recorded before he takes away urinal bottles.

Tom had been supporting Mr Jones with his personal care when, at the end of his shift, he realised that he should have measured and recorded Mr Jones' urine output; he had just disposed of the urine without measuring it. Tom did not get on very well with his supervisor and was worried about telling her.

1. If you were Tom, what would you do?
2. What might happen to Mr Jones because of Tom's carelessness?

Functional skills

English: Reading

This unit provides you with a number of opportunities to practise your reading skills. Some examples of this are researching new terminology, reading case studies and reviewing information listed in the websites provided to broaden your knowledge. When reading for information as part of a unit, it is important to identify the main points so that they can be used for your coursework. It is important that you understand what you are reading and, if necessary, that you use a dictionary to clarify unknown words. When you are given a set text to read for your place of work, ensure that you understand how you need to use it – for example, to extract information for a set purpose or to extend your knowledge on a topic.

Legislation

- Health and Safety at Work Act 1974

Further reading and research

- www.cqc.org.uk (Care Quality Commission)
- www.dh.gov.uk (Department of Health)
- www.hse.gov.uk (Health and Safety Executive)
- www.nhs.uk (NHS)
- www.nhsfife.scot.nhs.uk (NHS Fife: hot water management risk control measures for the prevention of scalds and burns)
- www.skillsforcare.org.uk (Skills for Care)
- www.skillsforhealth.org.uk (Skills for Health)
- Benson, S. (1994) *Handbook for Care Assistants*, 5th edition, Hawker, London
- Burgess, C., Shaw, C. and Pritchatt, N. (2007) *S/NVQ Level 2 Health and Social Care: Easy Steps*, Pearson Education

Getting ready for assessment

LO1

It is important to consider people's preferences when supporting them with personal care; it is therefore vital to encourage people to communicate (in their preferred way) their personal preferences, to provide the person with the right level and type of support, and to agree how privacy will be maintained. Evidence must come from a real work environment and activities. If it is not appropriate for assessor observation, it may be suggested that you obtain expert witness testimonies to provide evidence for this outcome.

LO2

Handling body waste and not disposing of it properly can increase the risk of the spread of infection. You will need to show your assessor that you can demonstrate safe disposal of a range of waste products. You will also need to explain why you disposed of the waste the way that you did. Your assessor may ask you to obtain a witness testimony of safe disposal of waste; this will provide evidence to your assessor of consistency of your performance.

LO3

This outcome requires you to be able to support people competently to use the toilet in a way that respects privacy, dignity and respect and to support them with cleansing afterwards. It may not be appropriate for your assessor to observe you in such sensitive situations, but nevertheless they will need evidence to prove that you are competent in these activities. Your assessor may therefore suggest that you obtain witness testimonies from your supervisor or manager.

LO4

This outcome requires you to be able to support people competently to maintain personal hygiene in a way that shows privacy, dignity and respect. It may not be appropriate for your assessor to observe you in such sensitive situations, but nevertheless they will need evidence to prove that you are competent in these activities. Your assessor may therefore suggest that you obtain witness testimonies from your supervisor or manager.

LO5

For this outcome you need to support people to manage their personal appearance. You will need to demonstrate how you promote independence while respecting people's choice and dignity. You will also need to show evidence of encouraging people to keep their personal care items clean and safe. Assessor observation is preferable, but if this is not possible, your assessor may suggest that you obtain witness testimonies from your line manager.

LO6

This outcome is about being able to monitor and report on support for personal care, which includes what is normal for the person and what is not. You work closely with the people that you support and you are more likely to notice when situations have changed. You will need to show your assessor that you notice changes in people and that you are able to record and report them properly according to your workplace's procedures. Your assessor may not be with you when you do notice changes with people's personal care, so they may suggest that you collect a witness testimony from your supervisor. You could also show your assessor records that you have completed relating to personal care, such as care records and input/output charts.

Glossary

Accessible — able to be obtained, used or experienced without difficulty

Accommodation — regarding eye sight, the process by which the eye changes optical power to focus on an object as its distance changes

Acquired — in terms of sensory loss, anything that is not present at birth but develops some time later

Acrylamide — a chemical found in starchy food that has been cooked at high temperatures — for example, crisps, chips or crisp breads

Active participation — when a person participates in the activities and relationships of everyday life as independently as possible; they are an active partner in their own care or support, rather than a passive recipient

Advocacy — acting and speaking on behalf of someone who is unable to do so for themselves

Advocate — a person who is responsible for acting and speaking on behalf of someone who is unable to do so for themselves

Aerosol — a cloud of solid or liquid particles in a gas

Anaemic — not having enough iron in the blood

Analgesic — a medicine used to reduce pain

Anaphylaxis — a severe allergic reaction

Anatomy — the physical structure of the body

Anorexia — an eating disorder where the person does not eat enough

Aphasia (or **dysphasia**) — a reduced ability to understand and to express meaning through words

Appendectomy — surgical removal of the appendix

Appendicitis — inflammation of the appendix

Aseptic — without sepsis or being free from disease-causing micro-organisms

Autistic spectrum — a spectrum of psychological conditions characterised by widespread abnormalities of social interactions and communication, as well as severely restricted interests and highly repetitive behaviour

Bariatric — a term used for a person whose weight exceeds 25 stone

British Sign Language (BSL) — a way of communicating with people who cannot hear, using hand signals instead of words

Chiropodist — a professionally trained person who looks after feet

Competence — demonstrating the skills and knowledge required by National Occupational Standards

Concentrated — strong

Congenital — present at birth

Constipated — finding it difficult to pass faeces

Constipation — difficulty in passing faeces

Contract — in terms of muscle function, get shorter

Data Protection Act 1998 — a law to ensure the safety of data held

Deep vein thrombosis (DVT) — a clot that forms in the deep veins of the body, usually the leg veins. If the clot moves it could get stuck in a blood vessel going to the lungs. If the clot is large enough, the patient could die

Dehydrated — not having enough fluid in the body

Dementia — a disease that affects the brain, especially the memory

Diabetes — a condition that affects the level of sugar in the blood

Diarrhoea — liquid faeces

Discrimination — treatment of one group or person in a less or more favourable way than another on the basis of race, ethnicity, gender, sexuality, age or other prejudice

Dosette box — a pill organiser; usually someone's medication for the day, part of the day, or for a whole week

Empathise — have compassion for, understand

Empathy — putting yourself in someone else's shoes; showing understanding and kindness

Epidermis — the outer layer of the skin

Faeces — waste matter remaining after food has been digested, which is discharged from the bowel

Ferrule — rubber foot on the bottom of a walking frame or stick

Generic — basic or common

Halal — meat from animals that have been slaughtered according to Muslim Law

Hazard — something that could possibly cause harm

Healthcare-associated infection — an infection that has been acquired as a result of treatment in any care setting

Holistic — looking at the 'whole person', considering all of their needs

Induction — a formal briefing and familiarisation for someone starting at an organisation

Jhatka — meat from animals that have been killed with one stroke

Kosher — meat from animals that have been humanely slaughtered according to Jewish Law

Learning style — how we learn — for example, by watching, doing, reading or seeing, or a combination of these

Legislation — laws

Menopause — when a woman's periods stop

Motion — an emptying of the bowel

MRSA — Methicillin-resistant Staphylococcus aureas, an organism which has mutated over the years to become resistant to some antibiotics

National Occupational Standards — UK standards of performance that people are expected to achieve in their work, and the knowledge and skills they need to perform effectively

Non-verbal communication — body language, the most important way in which people communicate

Occlusive — something that closes, such as a bandage or dressing that closes a wound and protects it from the air

Ombudsman — a public officer who investigates complaints about poor service or unfair or improper actions from public services

Osteoporosis — condition associated with ageing in both men and women where there is a loss of bone density caused by excessive absorption of calcium and phosphorus

Outcomes — the results that come from the services provided to a person for their visions of their life

Palliative care — care that relieves symptoms, but does not cure

Pathogenic — micro-organisms that have the potential to cause disease or infection

Personal development — developing the personal qualities and skills needed to live and work with others

Physiology — the normal functions of the body

Professional development — developing the qualities and skills necessary for the workforce

Prostheses — artificial parts of the body — for example, eyes, limbs or breasts

Risk — the likelihood of a hazard causing harm

Risk control measures — actions taken in order to reduce an identified risk

Sacrum — the bony part of the back located at the base of the spine

Self-esteem — how people value themselves; how much self-respect and confidence they have

Self-image/self-concept — how people see themselves

Sodium hypochlorite — the chemical name for bleach

Stereotyping — making negative or positive judgements about whole groups of people based on prejudice and assumptions, rather than facts or knowledge about a person as an individual

Toxin — a poison produced by micro-organisms such as bacteria

Trend — a tendency or a development — for example, a person's pain score is getting higher or lower

Vena cava — a large vein that returns blood to the right atrium of the heart

Legislation

This page lists all the legislation referenced in this book. For more information on any item, please refer to the index.

Access to Personal Files Act 1987

Adult Support and Protection (Scotland) Act (ASPA) 2007

Care Home Regulations 2001

Care Quality Commission (Registration) Regulations 2009

Care Standards Act 2000

Carers (Equal Opportunities) Act 2004

Carers and Disabled Children Act 2000

Children Act 1989

Confidentiality of Personal Information 1988

Control of Asbestos at Work Regulations 2002

Control of Lead at Work Regulations 2002

Control of Substances Hazardous to Health Regulations 2002 (COSHH)

Criminal Justice Act 1998

Data Protection Act 1998

Disability Discrimination Act 1995

Disability Discrimination Act 2005

Employment Equality (Age) Regulations 2006

Employment Equality (Religion or Belief) and (Sexual Orientation) Regulations 2003

Equal Pay Act 1970

Equality Act 2006

Equality Act 2010

Family Law Act 1996

Food Safety (General Food Hygiene) Regulations 1995

Food Safety Act 1990

Fraud Act 2006

Freedom of Information Act 2000

Hazardous Waste Regulations 2005

Health and Safety (Display Screen Equipment) Regulations 1992 (amended 2002)

Health and Safety at Work Act 1974

Health and Social Care Act 2008

Health and Social Care Act 2008 (Regulated Activities) Regulations 2010

Health Protection Agency Act 2004

Human Rights Act 1998

Lifting Operations and Lifting Equipment Regulations (LOLER)

Local Authority Social Services Act 1970

Management of Health and Safety at Work Regulations 1999

Manual Handling Operations Regulations 1992 (amended 2002)

Mental Capacity Act 2005

Mental Health Act 1983

National Assistance Act 1984 S47

National Minimum Standards for Care Homes for Adults (18–65)

National Minimum Standards for Care Homes for Older People (65+)

NICE Guidelines 2 2003

No Secrets (England) and In Safe Hands (Wales)

Noise at Work Regulations 1989

Offences Against the Person Act 1861

Office of the Public Guardian

Personal Protective Equipment at Work Regulations 1992

Police and Criminal Evidence Act 1984 S17

Protection from Harassment Act 1997

Protections of Vulnerable Groups Act 2007

Provision and Use of Work Equipment Regulations 1998 (PUWER)

Public Health (Control of Diseases) Act 1984

Public Health (Infectious Diseases) Regulations 1988

Public Interest Disclosure Act 1998

Race Relations Act 1976

Racial and Religious Hatred Act 2006

Reporting of Injuries, Diseases and Dangerous Occurrences Regulations (RIDDOR) 1995

Safeguarding Vulnerable Groups Act 2006

Sex Discrimination Act 1975

Sexual Offences Act 2003

Special Educational Needs and Disability Act 2001

Theft Act 1968

Work and Families Act 2006

Unit numbers by awarding organisation

Unit no. in Heinemann book	Unit title	Unit accreditation no.	Edexcel / NCFE unit no.	CACHE / OCR unit no.	C&G unit no.
SHC 21	Introduction to communication in health, social care or children's and young people's settings	F/601/5465	1	SHC 21	4222–201
SHC 22	Introduction to personal development in health, social care or children's and young people's settings	L/601/5470	2	SHC 22	4222–202
SHC 23	Introduction to equality and inclusion in health, social care or children's and young people's settings	R/601/5471	3	SHC 23	4222–203
SHC 24	Introduction to duty of care in health, social care or children's and young people's settings	H/601/5474	4	SHC 24	4222–204
HSC 024	Principles of safeguarding and protection in health and social care	A/601/8574	5	HSC 024	4222–205
HSC 025	The role of the health and social care worker	J/601/8576	6	HSC 025	4222–206
HSC 026	Implement person-centred approaches in health and social care	A/601/8140	7	HSC 026	4222–207
HSC 027	Contribute to health and safety in health and social care	R/601/8922	8	HSC 027	4222–208
HSC 028	Handle information in health and social care settings	J/601/8142	9	HSC 028	4222–209
HSC 2002	Provide support for mobility	H/601/9024	46	HSC 2002	4222–211
HSC 2003	Provide support to manage pain and discomfort	K/601/9025	47	HSC 2003	4222–212
HSC 2007	Support independence in the tasks of daily living	T/601/8637	51	HSC 2007	4222–216
HSC 2012	Support individuals who are distressed	L/601/8143	55	HSC 2012	4222–220
HSC 2013	Support care plan activities	R/601/8015	56	HSC 2013	4222–221
HSC 2014	Support individuals to eat and drink	M/601/8054	57	HSC 2014	4222–222
HSC 2015	Support individuals to meet personal care needs	F/601/8060	58	HSC 2015	4222–223
HSC 2028	Move and position individuals in accordance with their plan of care	J/601/8027	68	HSC 2028	4222–232
IC 01	The principles of infection prevention and control	L/501/6737	21	IC 01	4222–264
SS MU 2.1	Introductory awareness of sensory loss	F/601/3442	34	SS MU 2.1	4222–258

= Group M   = Group C   = Group B

Index

Key words are indicated by **bold** page numbers.
CD chapters are indicated after the page number by:

A (HSC 2007)
B (HSC 2012)
C (HSC 2013)
D (HSC 2028)
E (SS MU 2.1)